MW01630042

Mastodons on Parade

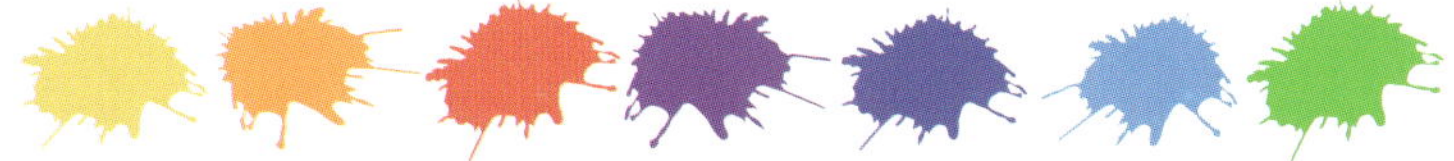

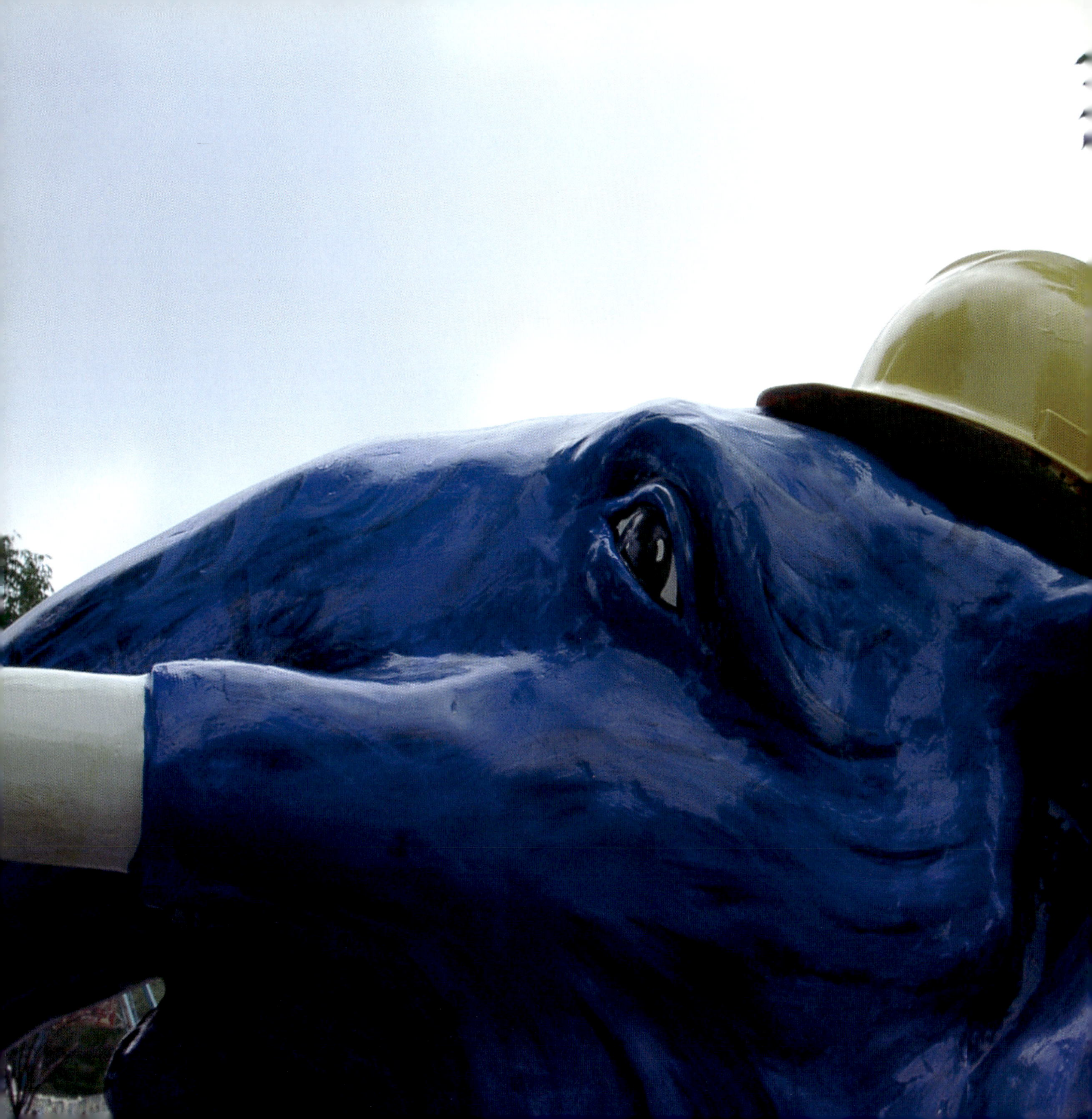

Mastodons on Parade

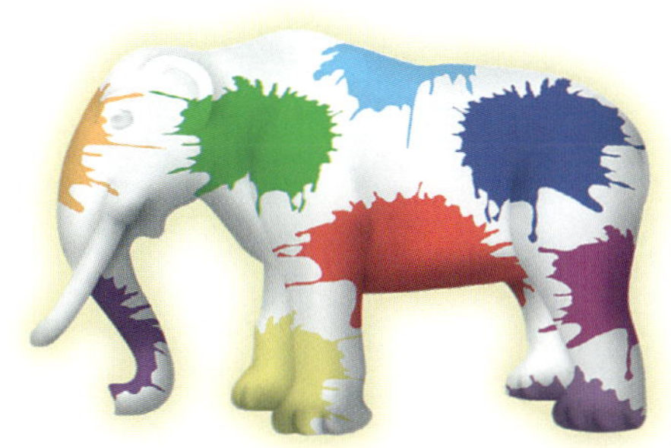

Fort Wayne's community art project 2005

Publication information

Mastodons on Parade

© 2005 by Indiana University–Purdue University Fort Wayne

All Rights Reserved

ISBN 09772363-0-4

This book was created by the IPFW University Relations and Communications and the Publications offices. No part of this book may be reproduced by any means, including but not limited to photocopying, photographing, scanning, or electronic or mechanical means of data storage, reproduction, or retrieval without the prior written permission of the copyright holder.

Printed in USA.

Editor: Dana Wichern

Graphic Designers: Lea Ann Powers Gebhard, John Paxson

Production Assistants: Suzanne Cyrus, Andrew Welch

Contributors: Laurel Alberson, Susan Alderman, Nan Bremer, Deborah Ellsworth, Amy Martone, Patty Martone, Kari Steffen, Louise Teague, Irene Walters

Principal Photographer: Randy Jackson

Contributing Photographers: Elmer Denman, Eugene Harding, *The Journal Gazette,* Richard M. Papazian, Three Rivers Festival, Jim Whitcraft

Indiana University–Purdue University Fort Wayne

2101 E. Coliseum Blvd.

Fort Wayne, IN 46805-1499

260-481-6100

www.mastodons.org

This book is dedicated to:

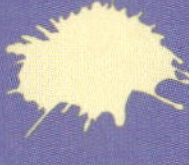 The artists who transformed 102 rough fiberglass forms into fanciful, poignant, and colorful creatures that delighted us all;

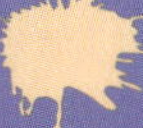 The children who embraced the dons with unbridled glee and enthusiasm;

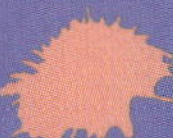 The members of our business community who believed the project had value and worth;

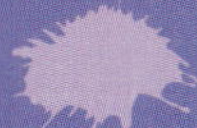 The tourists who came to see what we saw;

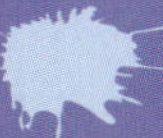 The educators who made the project a learning experience for our youth;

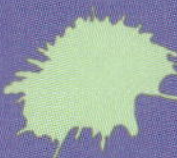 The families who celebrated their birthdays, wedding anniversaries, and other special occasions with pictures beside their favorite dons;

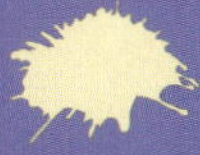 The teams that transported, bandaged, and repaired the dons throughout the summer.

Finally, this book is dedicated to all of you who said to us, "Please don't let this end. Do something to preserve the memories."

That something is this book. Enjoy the spirit.

Acknowledgments

Mastodons on Parade would not have been possible without the assistance, support, and generosity of the communities of both IPFW and Fort Wayne. The following listing is only a brief "thank you" to those who helped make it all happen.

A Party Apart
Advance Sign Co.–Jim Studinski
Bobbi Albert
Audio Visual Integration
Auto Collision Service
Automotive Color &
    Supply–Randy Greenawalt
Jerry Bailey Trucking Inc.
Bishop Dwenger High School
    Football Team
Brooks Construction Co. Inc.
Brotherhood of Maintenance
    of Way Local 1363
Brigitte Brown
Burkhart Advertising Inc.
Mark Carboni
Justin Casiano
Church of Good Shepherd
    MIMEtime
City of Fort Wayne
Ron Clark
Teresa Clark
Concordia High School
    Football Team
Conference & Travel
CRAFTCO LLC–Russ McCormick

Ron Dierkes
Paul Dye
E & B Paving
Edy's Grand Ice Cream
Ehlerding Honda & Kowasaki
    Motorsports
Sharon Eisbart–Corporate Art
Ellison Bakery
Professor Jim Farlow
David Gall
Federated Media
Goldstine Knapke Co.
Got Mail? Volunteers
Grainger
Headwaters Park
Higher Grounds
Holiday Inn Hotel & Suites
    Downtown
Mike Holley
IPFW Dental Laboratory
    Technology Students and
    Albino Perez
IPFW Information Technology
    Services/Applications
    Development
IPFW Learning Resource Center
IPFW Physical Plant
IPFW Stomp Band
Irving Materials
J & S Resource Management Inc.
Randy Jackson
Don Katter
Laborers Local 213
The Honorable Stanley A. Levine
Lincoln Printing Corp.

Lori Lobsiger

MacAllister Machinery Co.

Patty Martone

Tony Martone

Memorial Park Middle School
    Jazz Band

Midwest Technologies

Ron Mitchell

John Motz

National Serv-All

The News-Sentinel

North American Moving
    and Storage

North Side Galleries — Charley
    Shirmeyer

North Side High School
    DanceSkins

Northrop High School
    Football Team

Old Prairie Products Gravel Pit
    of Hanson Aggregates Inc.

Betty Olry

OmniSource Corporation

Paragon FiberGlass Composites LLC

Bill Pickelheimer

Pizza Hut of Fort Wayne

Plumbers and Steamfitters Local 166

Police Athletic League

PUNCH

RECOVERY Technologies

Rogers Co.

The Routsong Family

Sam's Club

Science Central

Scott's Foods

Jeanne Shaheen

Charles Shepard

Shoddy Construction Crew

SMURFIT-STONE Container Corp.

Snider High School Football Team

Steffen Group

Nancy Stewart

Subway — Rick Rutledge

Summit Club

Professor Jack Sunderman

Superior Collision & Paint Inc.

Taylor Rental

WANE

WISE

WPTA

Y.L.N.I.

Y.W.C.A.

Very special thanks go to The Journal Gazette *for its
generous support and enthusiasm for the Mastodons
on Parade project, especially for the multiple times we
were allowed to use the photographs of the mastodons
taken by* The Journal Gazette *photographers Dean
Musser Jr. and Clint Keller.*

*Thanks also go to the IPFW University Relations
and Communications staff (Laurel Alberson, Susan
Alderman, Nan Bremer, Pete Nowak, Louise Teague,
Bart Tyner, Annie Weissner) for their involvement in
Mastodons on Parade.*

Special thanks to Tower Bank

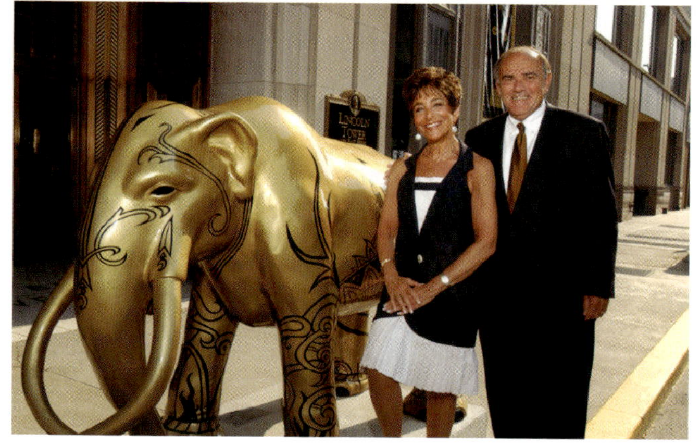

Irene Walters, Executive Director,
IPFW University Relations and
Communications, and Don Schenkel,
President and CEO, Tower Bank

When the idea of a public art project was adopted—an art project that involved placing large fiberglass mastodons throughout the City of Fort Wayne—there was skepticism, raised eyebrows, and an attitude of doubt and incredulity. What would the public think? Was public art an appropriate way to raise public awareness of IPFW's 40th anniversary? And what about those mastodons? Had IPFW administrators lost their sense of judgment?

The one company, however, that enthusiastically embraced the project from its inception was Tower Bank, which ultimately became the official sponsor of the Mastodons on Parade project. Tower Bank provided the funding to sponsor the sculpture and make the initial mold. Its endorsement reinforced and helped champion the project and was the catalyst for garnering other community sponsors.

The initial skepticism was allayed at the May 1 Preview Party when Fort Wayne turned out in huge numbers, nearly 10,000 people, to welcome the mastodons to our city. The Fort Wayne Chamber of Commerce commented that "this project has brought something to the city that we have never felt before." By the culminating and closing event, October 2005, more than 200 local businesses and organizations had provided services, volunteers, and materials to support Mastodons on Parade events and activities.

The setting: the City of Fort Wayne, Ind.; the time: summer of 2005; the atmosphere: surprise, delight, enjoyment, joy, pleasure, amusement, and entertainment! All because of 102 endearing fiberglass mastodons that carried a message of love, hope, and fun; that were created by local artists; and that were made possible by a caring university and a supportive community.

Steering Committee

Chair: Irene Walters

Members: Laurel Alberson, Bobbi Albert, Mark Carboni, Brenda Fishbaugh, David Gall, Lea Ann Powers Gebhard, AnnMarie LeBlanc, Marc Lipman, Patty Martone, Tony Martone, Stephanie McCormick, Dacia Michael, Gail Miller, John Paxson, Dar Richardson, Linda Ruffolo, Jeanne Shaheen, Jenni Showalter, Nancy Stewart, Louise Teague, Dana Wichern, Doris Willis

Contents

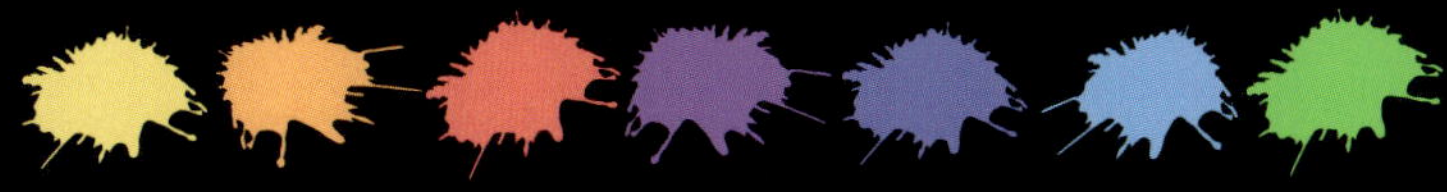

Mayor salutes IPFW

The City of Fort Wayne is a proud supporter of the Mastodons on Parade project. In sponsoring this initiative, IPFW has captured the creative spirit of our community and is to be congratulated for sponsoring the city's first public art project.

Fort Wayne is a diverse community. The Mastodons on Parade activity has brought together its many populations. It has involved the business community with the artistic community. It has given students equal opportunity to work alongside professionals. Our engineers, journalists, mechanics, and bankers have worked with our graphic artists, interior designers, fine artists, and art teachers.

It has been great seeing children learn about the historical significance of mastodons. Parents also are learning with their children about geology and the role mastodons played in northeast Indiana during the Ice Age. It's a pleasure to look out my office each day and see families enjoying the mastodon display at Headwaters Park.

The project has brought increased traffic downtown. It has provided tourists with an additional attraction. It has given our people something in common to talk about and enjoy. In short, it has been good for the city and good for its citizens.

A special benefit of the project is the increased presence of IPFW in the community. The university is to be congratulated for taking a leadership role over the past 40 years. Now, in celebrating its 40th anniversary, IPFW has given Fort Wayne a present.

Graham Richard

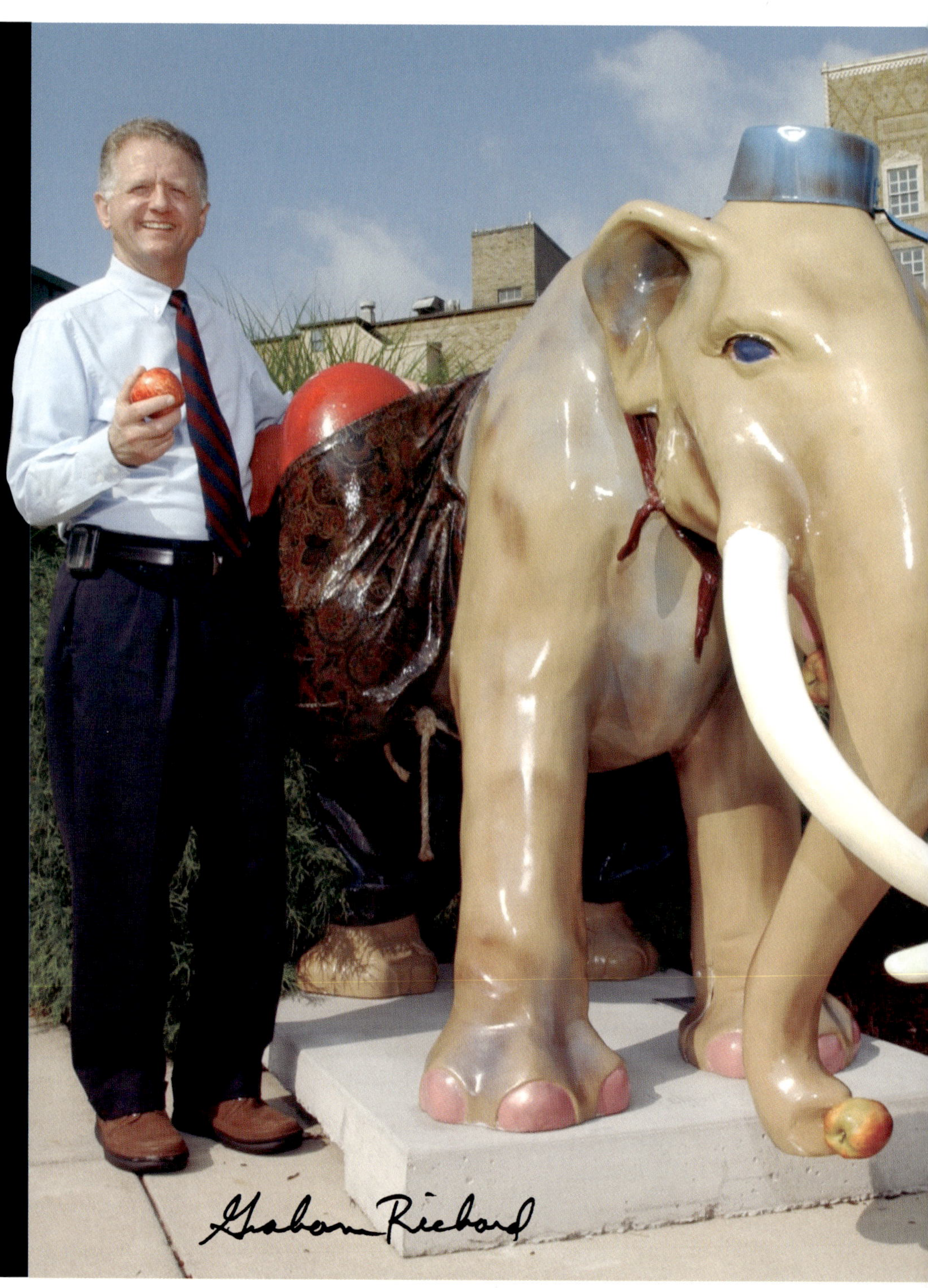

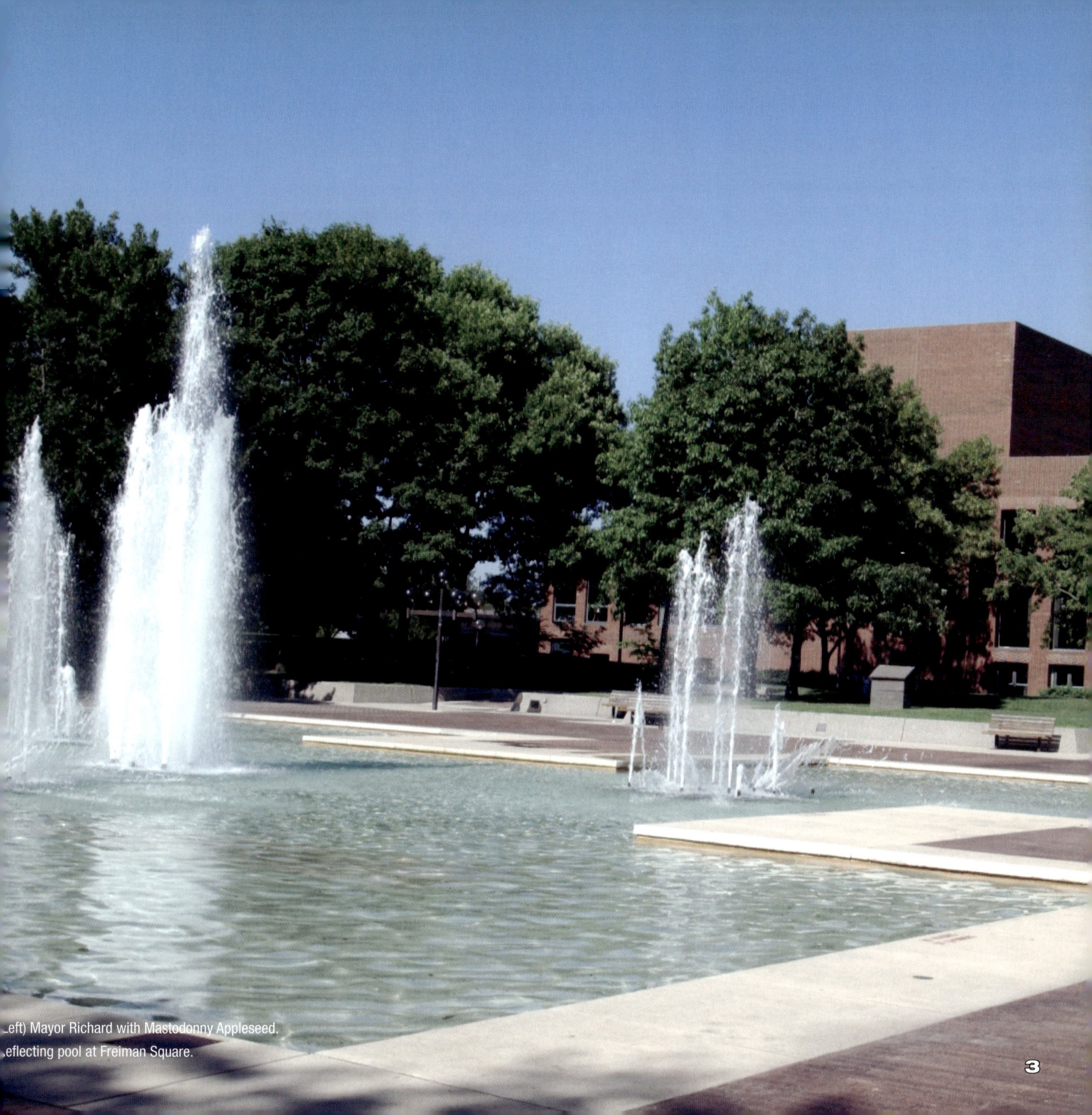

(Left) Mayor Richard with Mastodonny Appleseed.

Reflecting pool at Freiman Square.

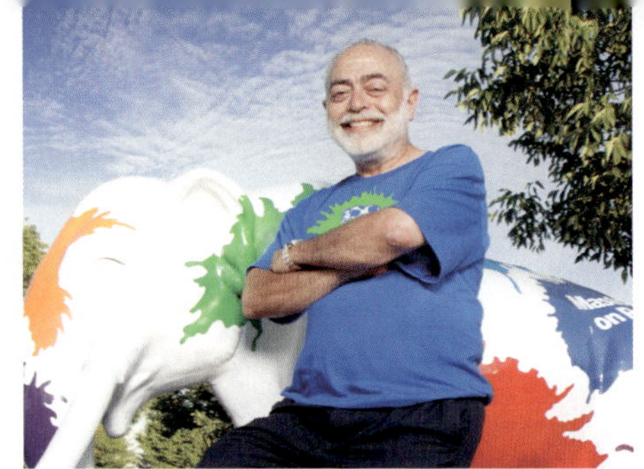

Dear Reader,

It is my pleasure to welcome you to the world of Mastodons on Parade! This project, the first-ever community-wide public art project in Fort Wayne, is IPFW's 40th anniversary gift to the community.

During these past 40 years, IPFW has been honored by this community's generosity. We wanted to give something back, something that would exemplify the diversity and talent of Fort Wayne, something that children from 8 to 80 could enjoy, something that would show the community spirit of Fort Wayne, and quite frankly, something that was just plain fun!

A magnificent herd of 102 mastodons resulted from this project. The wonderful creatures were conceived when partnerships between businesses and artists were formed in late 2004 and early 2005. Some of those partnerships had just a seed of an idea of what the final mastodon would look like; others were much more fully developed.

During the following weeks, and in some cases months, the talented artists and artisans spent countless hours designing, refining, sanding, painting, cutting, gluing, welding, and honing their masterpieces.

When all 102 Mastodons on Parade were introduced to the public at Headwaters Park during the Community Party on May 1, 2005, the most common question heard was, "Are you going to do a book?" And so, in answer to popular demand, and to preserve the images of the mastodons, a number of dedicated wordsmiths and graphic artists combined their talents to put this book together. It tells the story of each mastodon, its artist, and its sponsor.

It is my great pleasure to present to you the official commemorative book of Mastodons on Parade.

Sincerely,

Michael A. Wartell

Chancellor

Indiana University–Purdue University Fort Wayne

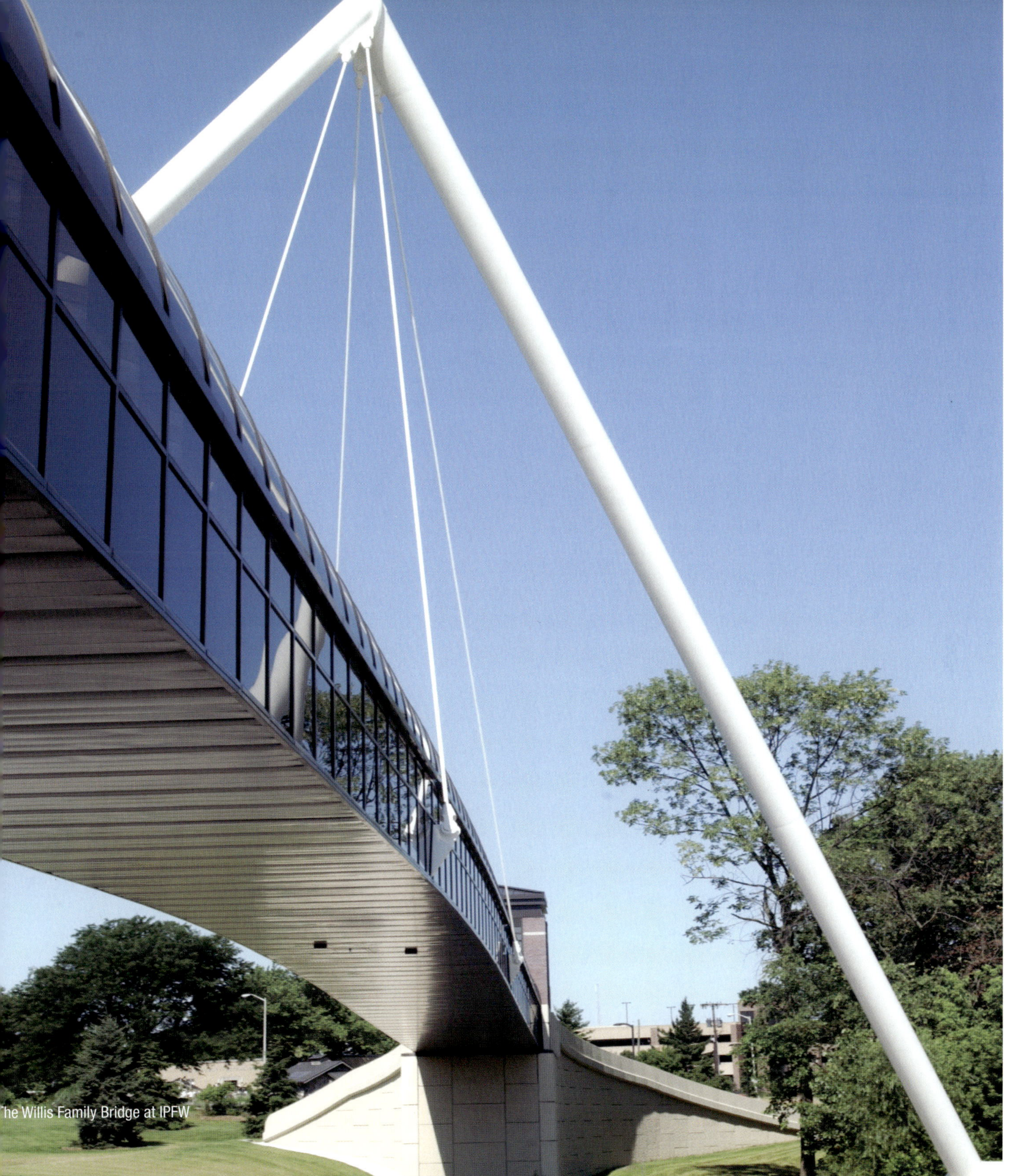

The Willis Family Bridge at IPFW

IPFW contributions to northeast Indiana

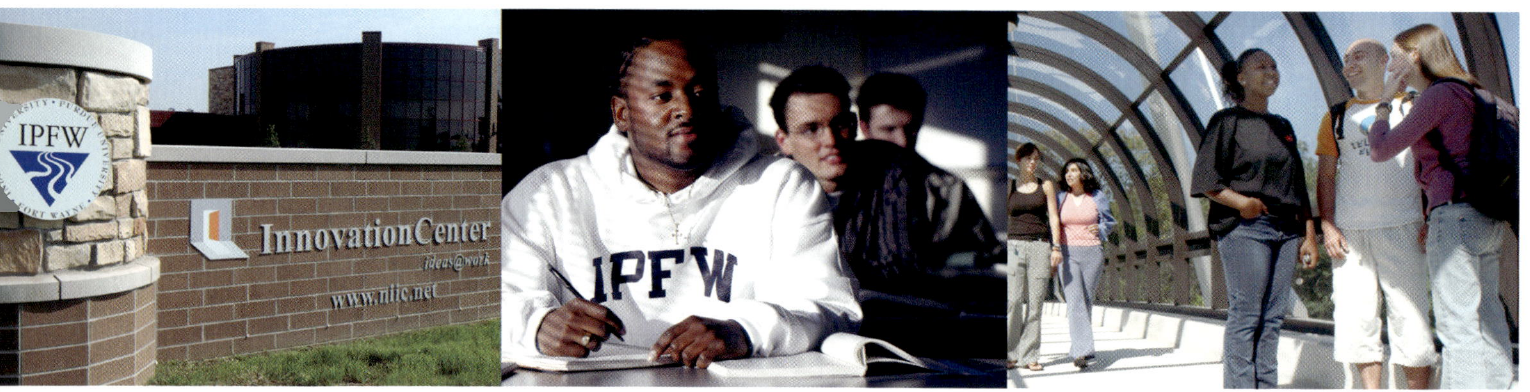

At 40, IPFW is in its prime. Building on the foundation of two internationally renowned universities, Indiana and Purdue, IPFW has grown into a remarkable institution with its own identity. The university has become a premier contributor to the region's academic, cultural, and economic development.

IPFW now offers more than 185 degree options that have helped it reach the milestone of becoming the university of choice for Fort Wayne's top-graduating seniors. In fact, 13 high-school valedictorians and salutatorians from the Class of 2004 chose IPFW over all other higher-education options.

Physically the university has grown from a single building into a multicampus community cornerstone, offering an unparalleled range of educational and cultural opportunities.

With a heady sense of achievement, IPFW is hitting its stride. In the past year, IPFW opened its first Student Housing, promoted a budding Division I basketball team, and planned construction for new facilities for music and health sciences.

In addition, IPFW is involved in hundreds of public- and private-sector endeavors, contributing to the region's health on many levels. IPFW has built a tremendous network of relationships with numerous organizations. Those relationships, and the resources the university can offer, have cemented IPFW's place in the community as a partner, catalyst, advocate, and engine of economic development.

The university interacts with the community in so many ways, it's difficult to catalog them all. Academically, IPFW equips students for a huge range of careers through on-campus, distance learning, and Internet courses as well as outreach classes in surrounding counties and cooperative learning programs with numerous local entities such as hospitals and manufacturers. It also supports businesses, individuals, and families with cultural and enrichment offerings, on-campus clinics providing specialized healthcare services, and expertise and skills in projects and organizations throughout the region.

"IPFW has become a world-class institution," Chancellor Michael Wartell said. "Over four decades, we've remained committed to excellence in teaching research, and learning, and at the same time, responded to the needs of this region. That's been our formula for success, and it's our vision to continue to use it well into the future."

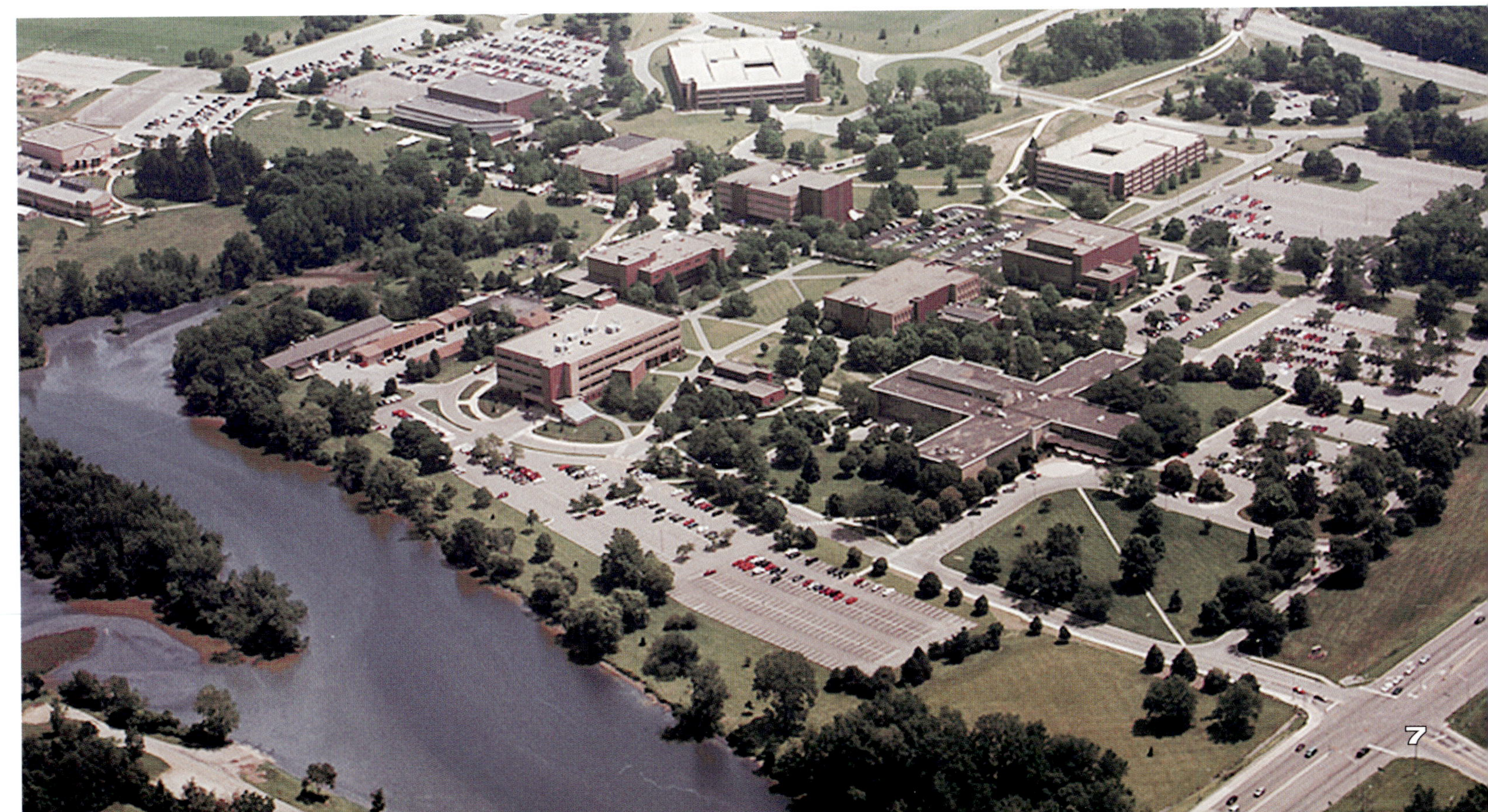

IPFW adopts a mascot

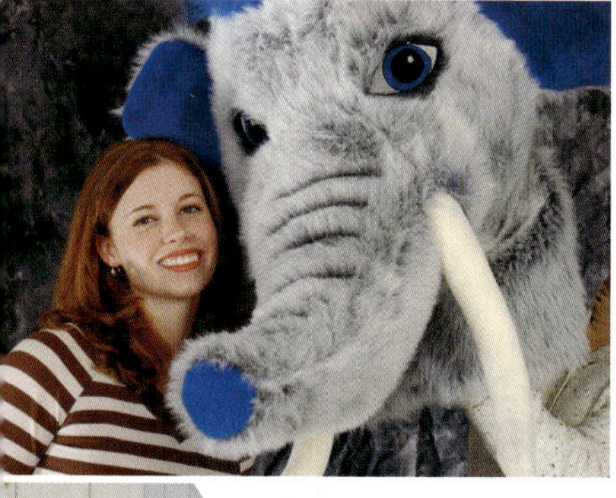

How the mastodon came to IPFW

It all started in the Ice Age more than 10,000 years ago when mastodons roamed the southern Great Lakes region of North America. Now extinct, these stocky mammals stood about 10 feet tall, had long trunks, and weighed about five tons. They were distant cousins of modern elephants.

The Ice Age passed. Landforms changed. Then one day in 1968, Orcie Routsong, a farmer who lived just south of Angola along what is now I-69, decided to dig a pond. The location was a boggy area where nothing much grew and equipment got stuck. Pond excavators unearthed a large bone.

Realizing it could not have belonged to a horse or cow, Routsong contacted a number of people to see if anyone was interested. Nobody was. Then he reached Jack Sunderman, chair of the IPFW geosciences department, who asked, "How big is it?"

When told it was about four feet long and six to eight inches across, Sunderman said, "I'll be right there."

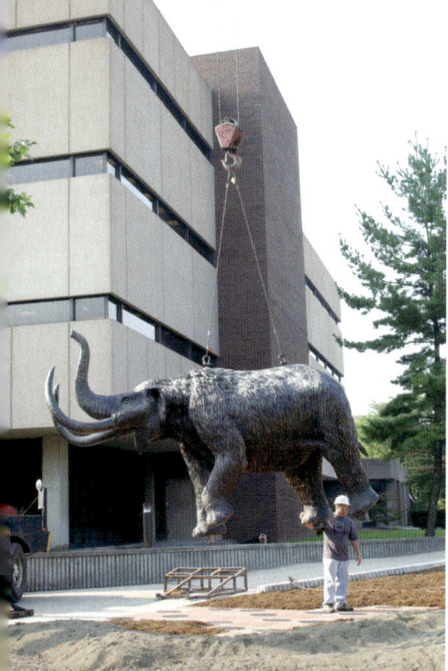

The IPFW Department of Geosciences took on the excavation. Using metal rods as probes, geology students along with faculty members Geoffrey Matthews and Bernd Erdtmann joined Sunderman. They were able to locate about two-thirds of the skeleton as well as the skull of a baby mastodon nearby. The Indiana-Purdue Student Government Association provided funds for additional machine excavation in hopes of finding more bones, but nothing major surfaced.

Routsong graciously agreed to place the adult mastodon skeleton on permanent display at IPFW. It is still in the lobby of Kettler Hall. The baby mastodon skull was placed on loan to Science Central, a Fort Wayne hands-on, student-oriented science activity center, where it remains today.

Getting courage to be different

In spring 1970, the IPFW student newspaper *The Communicator* began a drive for students to name a mascot for the university. Suggestions included the Boiler-Hoosiers, Warhawks, Marauders, Hobbits, and Frontiersmen.

Steve Pettyjohn, IPFW student body president for 1968–69, wrote a letter to the editor, extolling the virtues of the mastodon as a mascot. "Let's have the courage to be a little different," he wrote. The next year, the Geology Club lobbied then-student-body-president Mark Souder (now an Indiana Congressman) to support the choice of a mastodon. Souder appointed a committee, they took a vote, and the mastodon became the IPFW mascot.

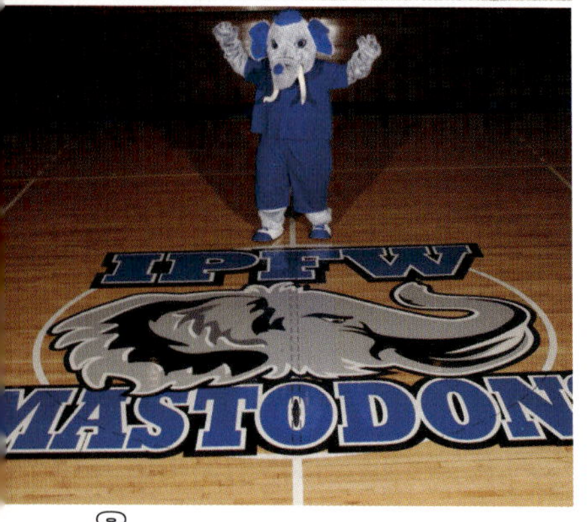

After more than five years of planning and with thanks to the generosity of STAR Financial Bank, a full-sized, bronze, scientifically accurate replica of a mastodon was dedicated at IPFW's 40th birthday party Sept. 14, 2004. A number of the Mastodons on Parade beasts will also find a permanent home on the IPFW campus. The new mastodon playground, expected to be completed in spring 2006, will give children a place to romp with some of the herd.

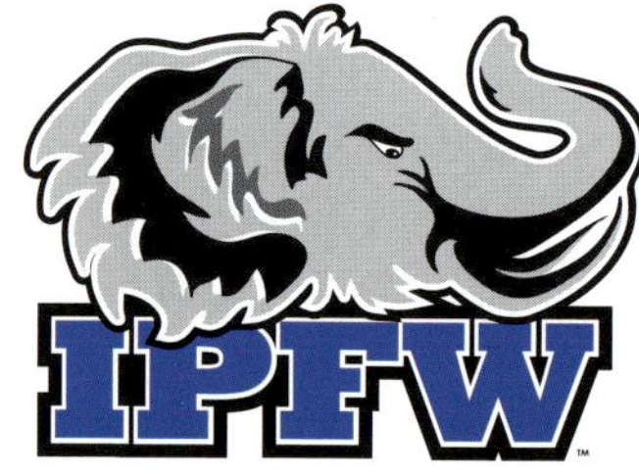

Finding the unexpected:
An interview with the Routsong family

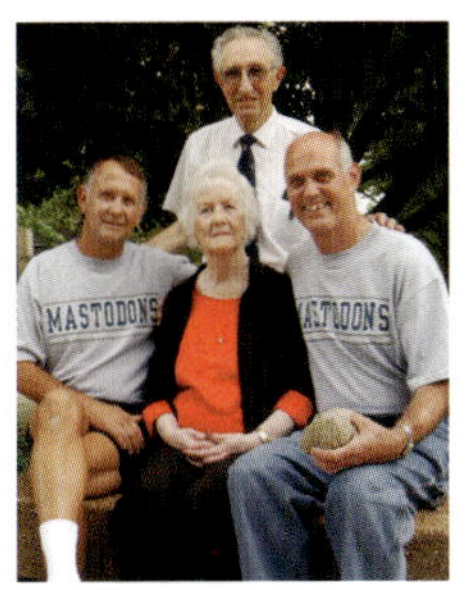

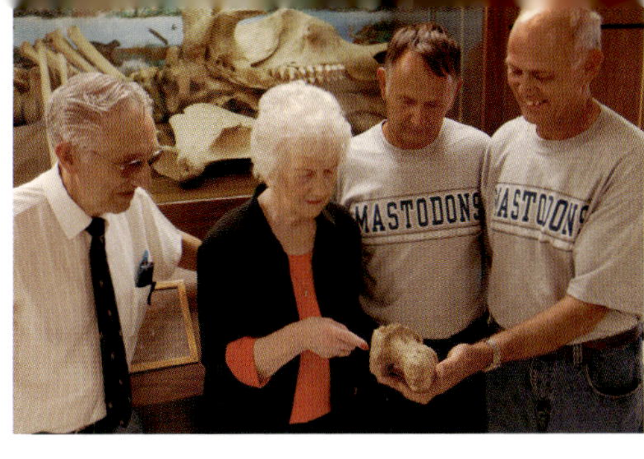

Jack Sunderman, Virginia Routsong, Lynn, Orcie Jr.

Standing near the mastodon bones, now glass encased in Kettler Hall, the Routsongs reminisced on their discovery so many years ago.

It was 1968. Orcie Routsong Jr. was a teen who enjoyed hunting for the arrowheads his dad's cultivator turned up. He found a number of them, especially in the boggy areas of the farm just south of Angola. Brother Lynn was serving in the U.S. Army, stationed in Michigan. Orcie Sr. and Virginia Routsong ran the farm.

Asked how they felt at the time about finding such large bones, Lynn said, "We were just very curious. It was exciting."

Orcie Jr. agreed: "Well, we knew they weren't ordinary. Dad just wanted to dig a pond to begin with. You couldn't grow anything on that bog because you'd just sink in. The excavator piled up the dirt from his digging alongside the pond. Then when the rain washed the dirt off that big bone, we thought we had something."

Once Orcie Sr. made contact with Professor Jack Sunderman, IPFW geosciences department head, faculty and students began excavating with purpose. Most of the bones found were between five and six feet below ground level.

"The student body gave $1,000 to expand the size of the pond in hopes of finding more bones," Sunderman said. "When the money ran out, the excavator continued working on his own time for awhile, but nothing much turned up."

Virginia Routsong, widow of Orcie Sr. who died in 1975, has vivid memories of the IPFW students who excavated the farm. "I remember the only girl working on the project," she said. "She got dirtier and dirtier until she was covered in mud. At the end of the day, she jumped in the pond to get cleaned up."

The Routsongs gave the skeleton to the campus for permanent display. "It's especially nice having him (the mastodon skeleton) so close," Orcie Jr. said. "Our children like to visit him every time they come down here. My daughter even brought her prospective husband over to look at the bones. It was her way of seeing if he would fit in the family."

The family is thrilled that IPFW students selected the mastodon to be the university mascot. "It makes us proud that we had a hand in naming the (IPFW) teams," Lynn said. "It was fun. We shared that story with everyone."

There are a number of other bogs on the Routsong farm. When asked if they had plans to dig in those areas, Lynn said, "We'd get the tractor stuck trying to get in."

But Orcie Jr. added, "I now subscribe to an archeology magazine and have been reading about ground-penetrating radar. We would be interested if anybody wanted to check that out."

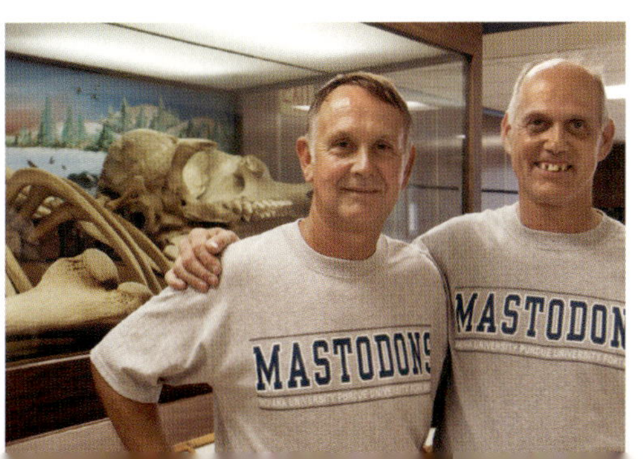

Lynn Routsong, Orcie Routsong Jr.

IPFW celebrates 40 years!

In 2004-05, IPFW proudly celebrated 40 years of academic excellence in northeast Indiana. As part of the yearlong observance, the university planned a range of special events involving the public and presented a number of lasting legacies to commemorate its four-decade milestone. Legacies included a trail enumerating the native trees of Indiana on campus, a new scholarship fund for returning students, a self-guided walking tour of the campus, and a public art project.

Mastodons on Parade, the city's first public art project, focused on the unique IPFW mascot. University officials sought sponsors and artists for 40 fiberglass beasts—one for each year of IPFW's 40 years, but the project far exceeded expectations. In all, 102 mastodon sculptures found their way into the heart of the community.

The project showcased local talent and gave recognition to area sponsors. It gave joy to the people. Benefits of the Mastodons on Parade project included:

- A rejuvenated community spirit with a coming together of culturally diverse populations

- An increased presence of IPFW in the community

- Additional tax dollars to the city and county

- Increased foot traffic in downtown Fort Wayne

- Charitable contributions to the United Way of Allen County

Sponsors purchased fiberglass mastodons at one of several sponsorship levels and worked with artists to deck out their beasts in whatever styles they saw fit—from grand funk to fine art, from the philosophical to the whimsical.

Mastodons spent summer 2005 on public display. The project officially ended with an auction at the Grand Wayne Center on Oct. 21, 2005. Auction proceeds went to the United Way of Allen County.

A birthday bash kicked off the yearlong celebration. IPFW unveiled its newest landmark, an 11' x 18' bronze mastodon donated by STAR Financial Bank. Local American Idol winners and Spike and the Bulldogs kept the party going. The event ended with the first Omnibus lecture of the season featuring The Capitol Steps, a political sketch comedy group.

IPFW athletics showed its 40th anniversary spirit by focusing the theme of the 2004 homecoming celebration on the 40 years. In April, the university sponsored a Kids Fest at Walb Student Union which featured 40 family fun events and involved an estimated 1,500 people. Another activity for the big 40th centered on geocaching, a new sport which involves use of a GPS (Global Positioning System) unit to search out caches (in this case, mastodon caches).

And a good time was had by all!

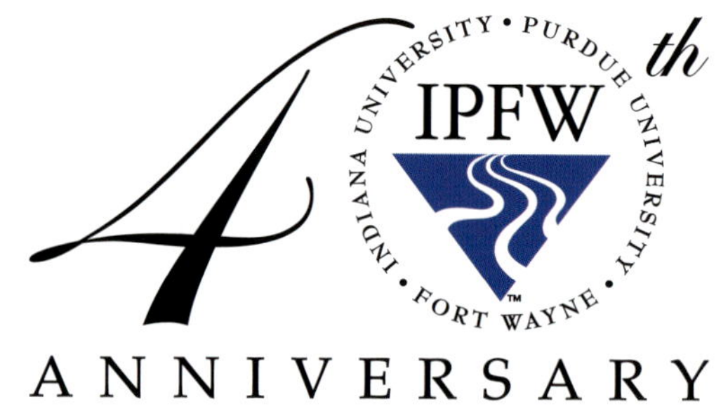

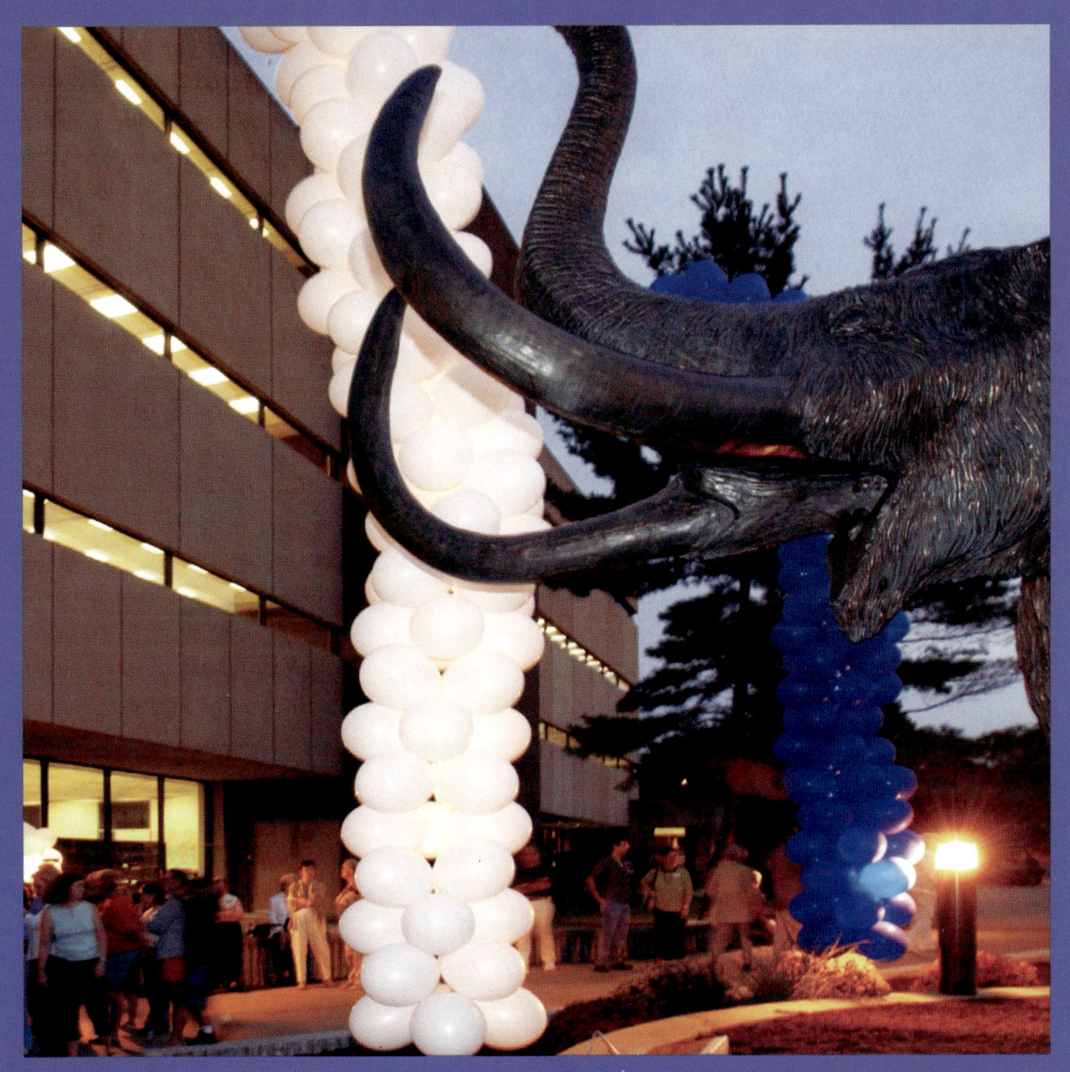

From prototype to models

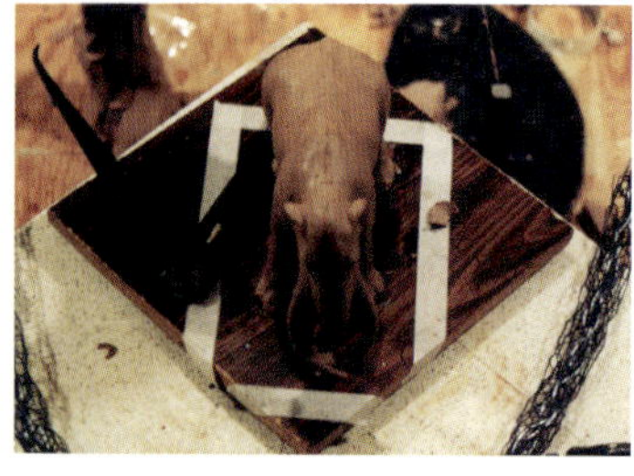

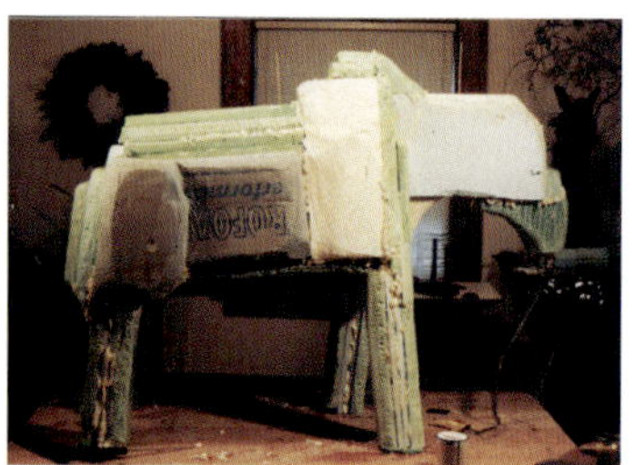

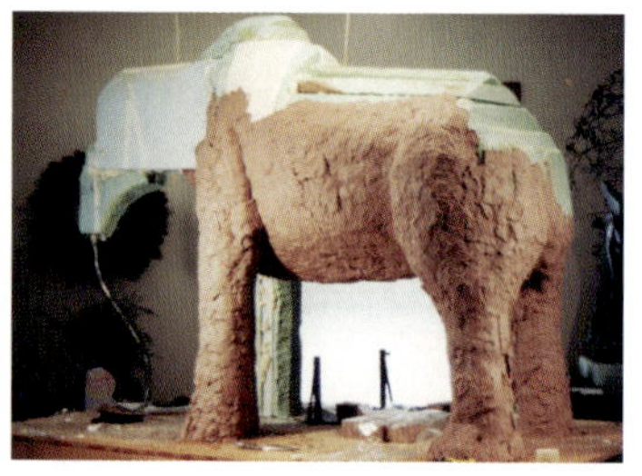

Making the prototype

Teresa Clark, sculptor and IPFW alumna, took on the task of creating a mastodon clay model. Using her dining room as a studio, she installed additional support in the basement to hold the 900 pounds of clay it took for the prototype. The model was half the size (about four by six feet) of a real mastodon.

The tusks took some special attention. As a safety precaution to keep viewers from an accidental goring, Clark rounded the tips and crossed the tusks.

Paragon Fiberglass in Garrett, Ind., produced the first fiberglass mastodon. Delivered in late August to Tower Bank artists, the first casting weighed 180 pounds. Following a problem with the original mold, Midwest Technologies in Battle Creek, Mich., made a second tooling and trimmed 15 pounds off the original model's weight. As Midwest Technologies created the statues, Paragon transported them to Garrett. From there, North American Moving and Storage delivered them to artists in the Fort Wayne area between December and March. There were 102 mastodons in all.

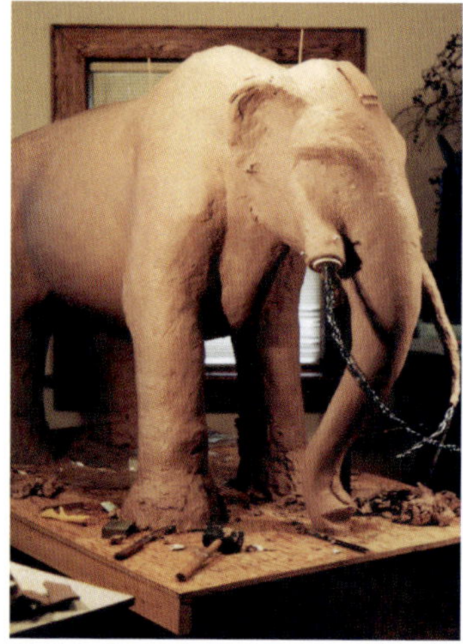

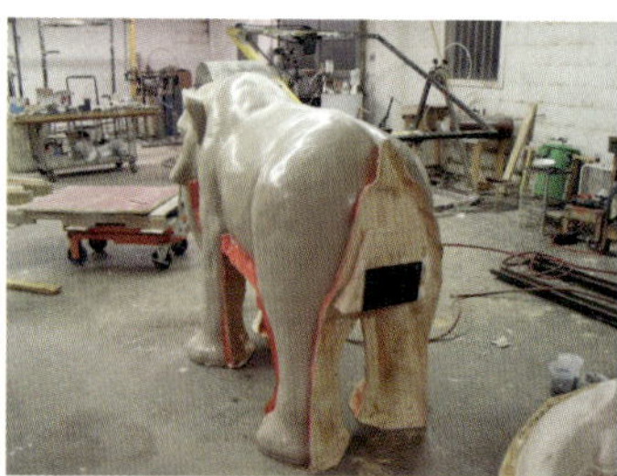

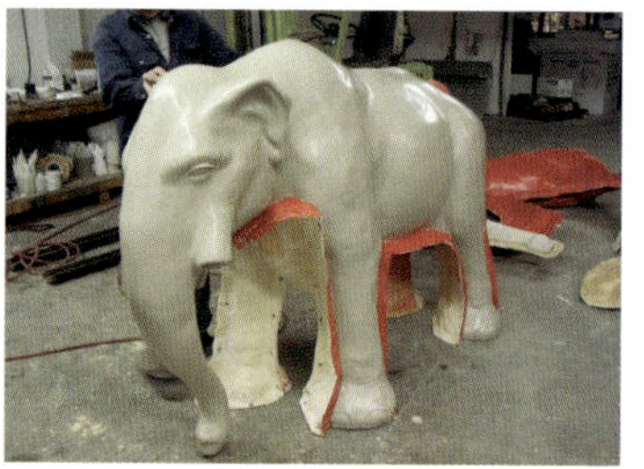

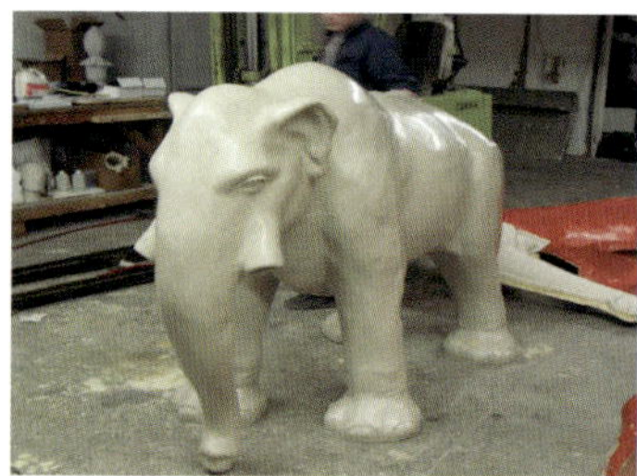

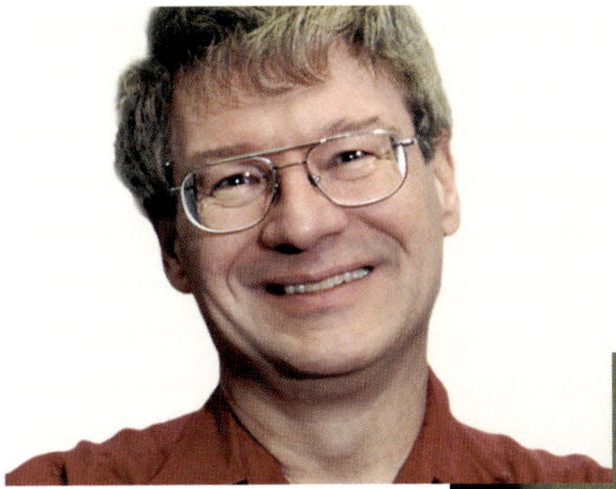

Jim Farlow, professor,
Department of Geosciences,
critiqued the mastodon model
for form, size, and proportion.

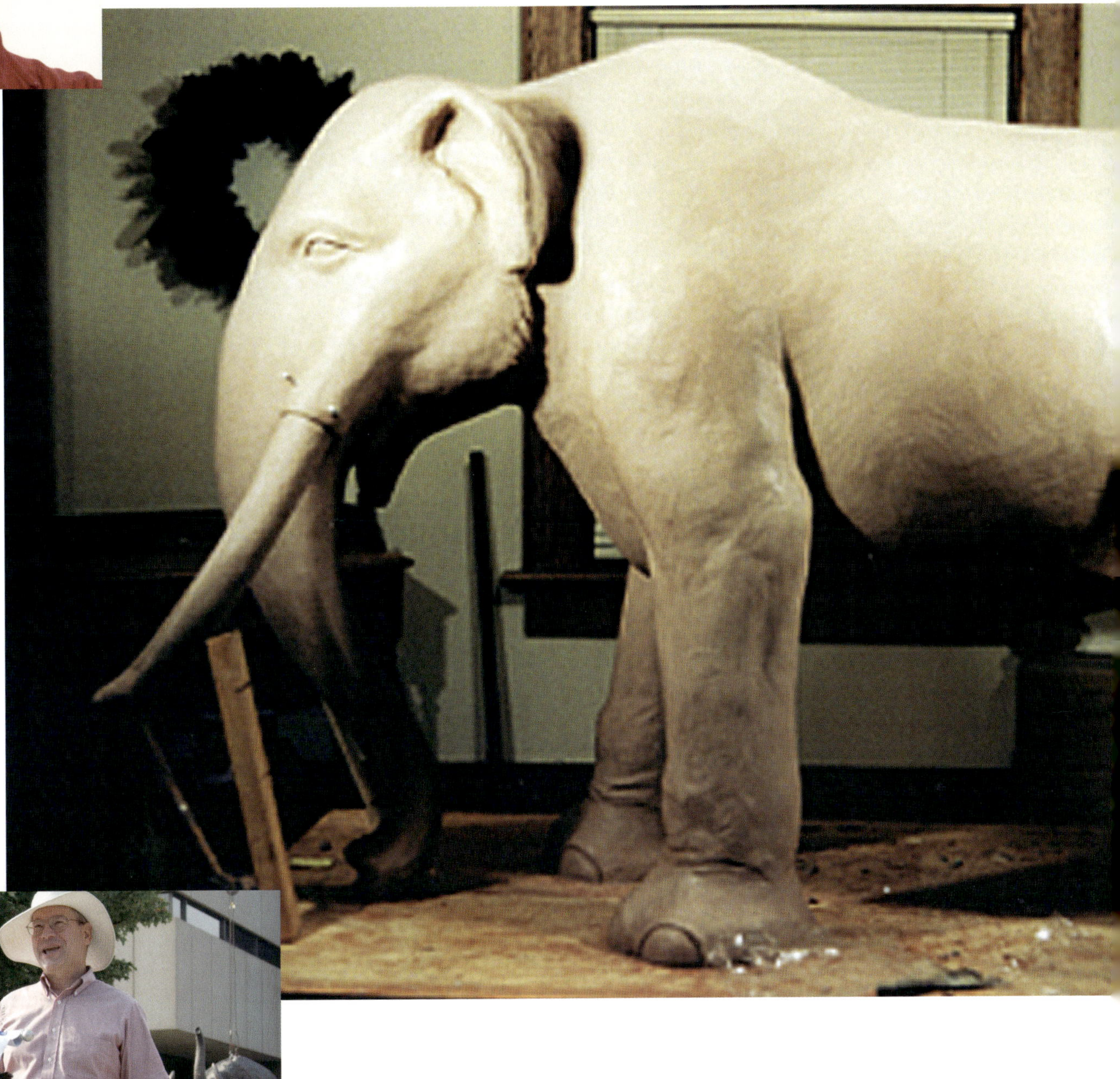

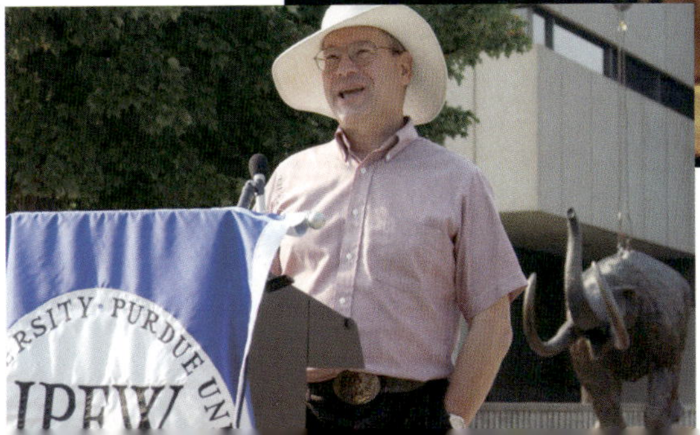

From models to artwork

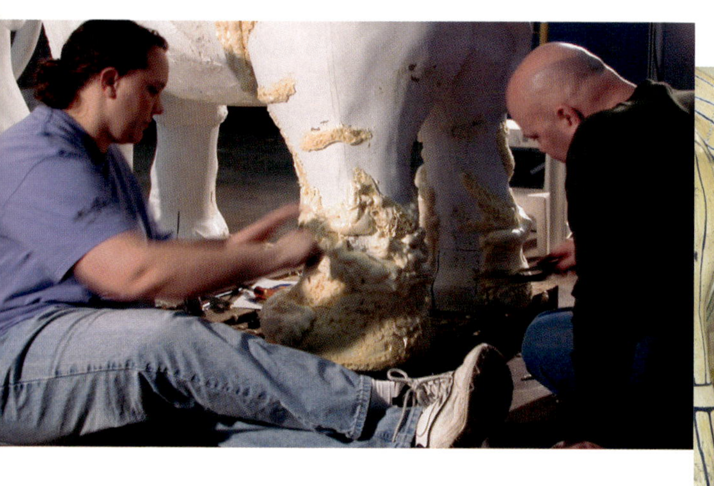

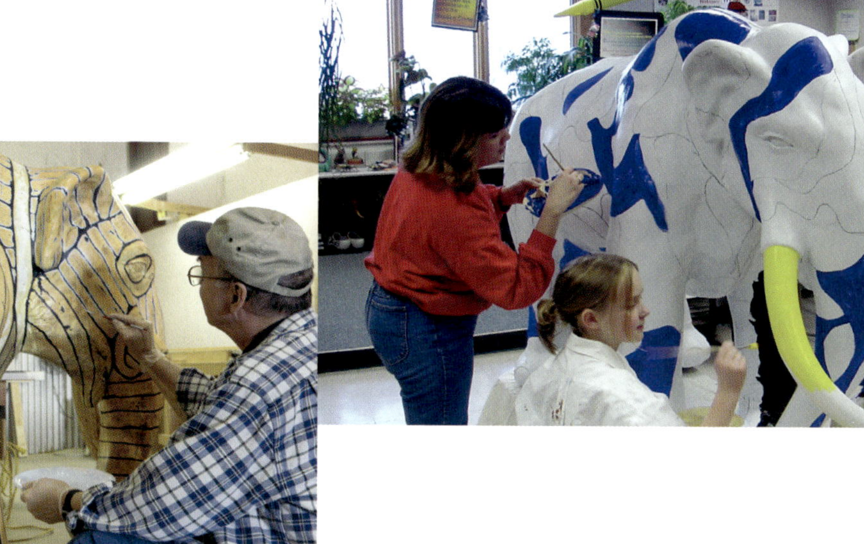

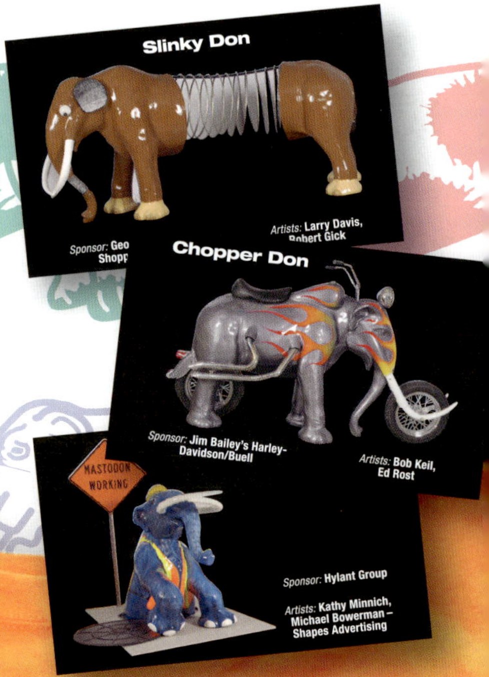

...and to merchandise

Merchandise included T-shirts, trading cards, posters, and stuffed animals.

www.mastodons.org

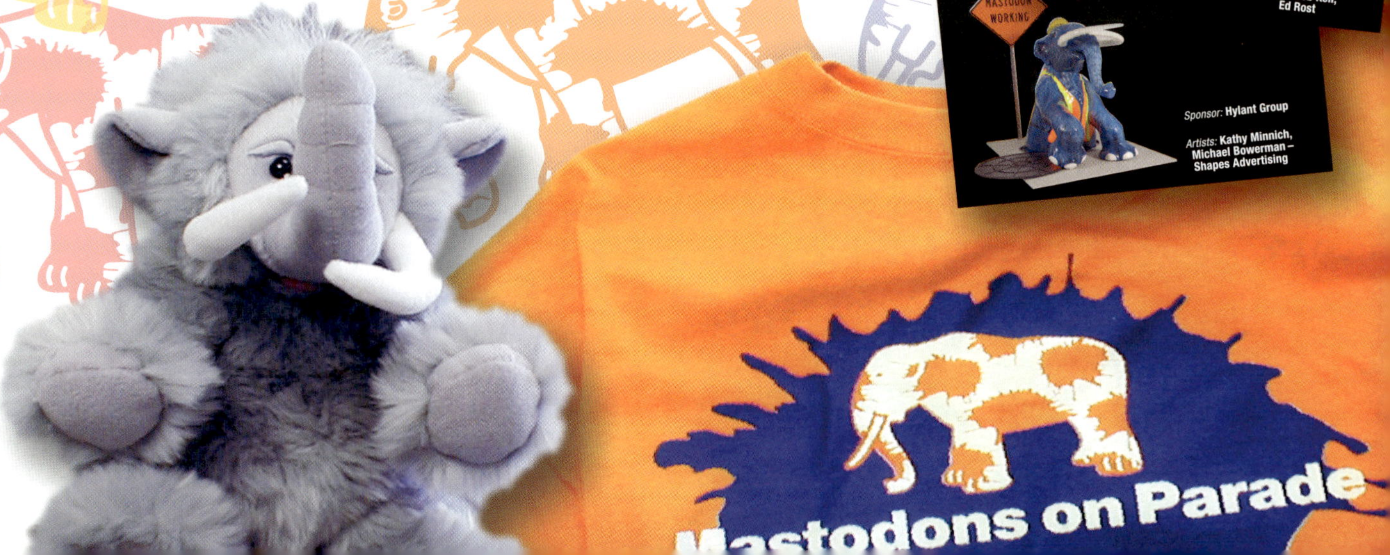

Look who's talking

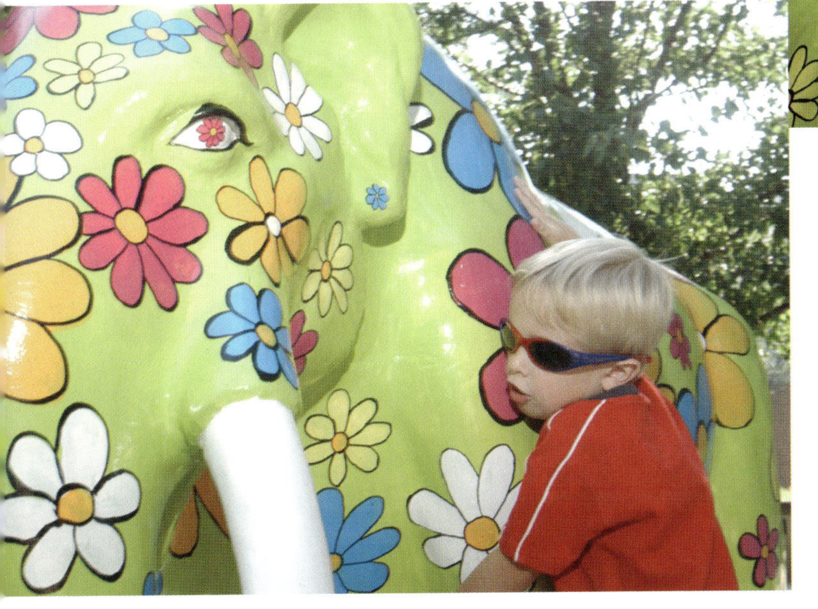

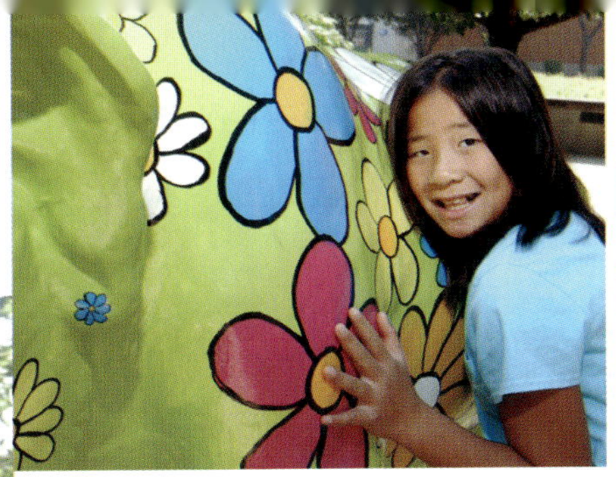

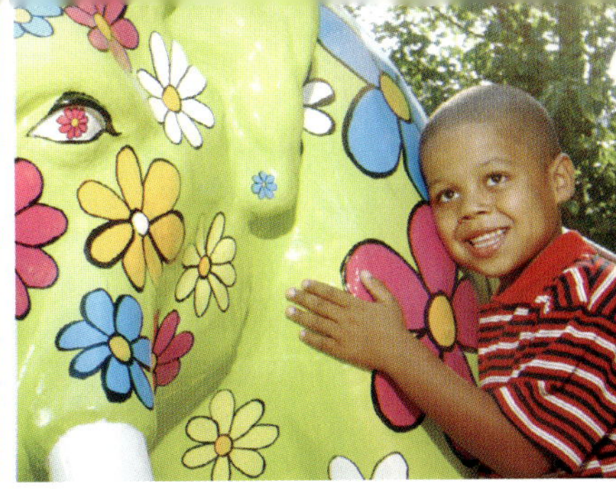

One of the distinguishing features of Fort Wayne's Mastodons on Parade, as compared to the art projects of other cities, is the addition of sound. Yes, 22 of those mastodons talk.

Stephen Zavodny, owner of J&S Resource Management, Inc., installed a sound device through the access panel in the foot of the mastodon, which allows each mastodon to speak. Pushing the blue button on the don's shoulder activates the sound.

Several of the upbeat musical selections are original songs sung by the school children. Community Action of Northeast Indiana, an organization providing a variety of child services, features preschool children singing "Happy Birthday" in its Party Animal. The World Wide Alumni Don sings IPFW's fight song, the Mini Don has drum music, and Leo roars like a mastodon-lion.

Some of the mastodons speak in the first person. AeroDONamic talks about his dream of flying, and Walkodon reminisces about the forests, lakes, rivers, and vegetation 10,000 years ago. He also gives his impressions of Fort Wayne in 2005. Mast-o-mind talks about the fun of learning, and Miguel the Mastodon speaks in Spanish.

Children love to push the sound buttons. They put their ears right on the mastodon to hear the message.

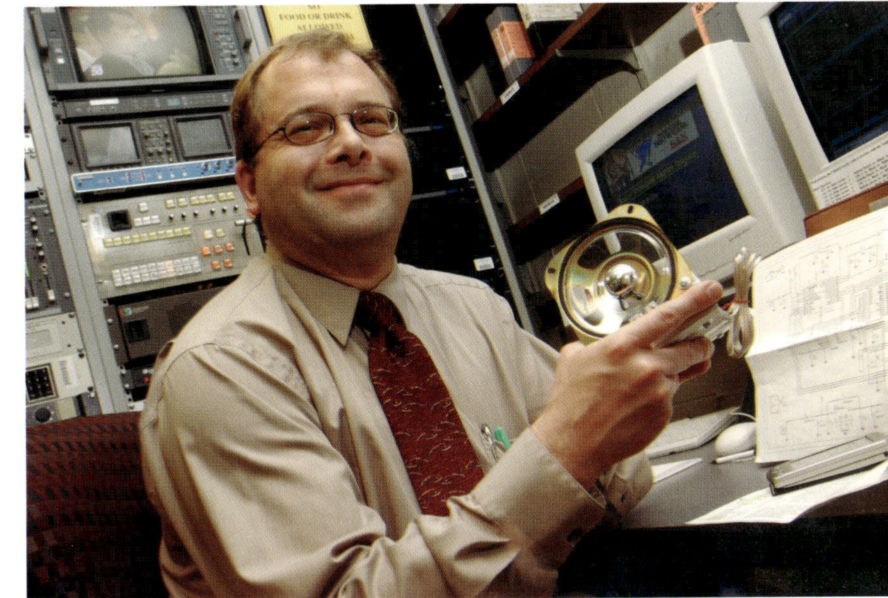

Stephen Zavodny, owner of J&S Resource Management Inc.

Development of the curriculum

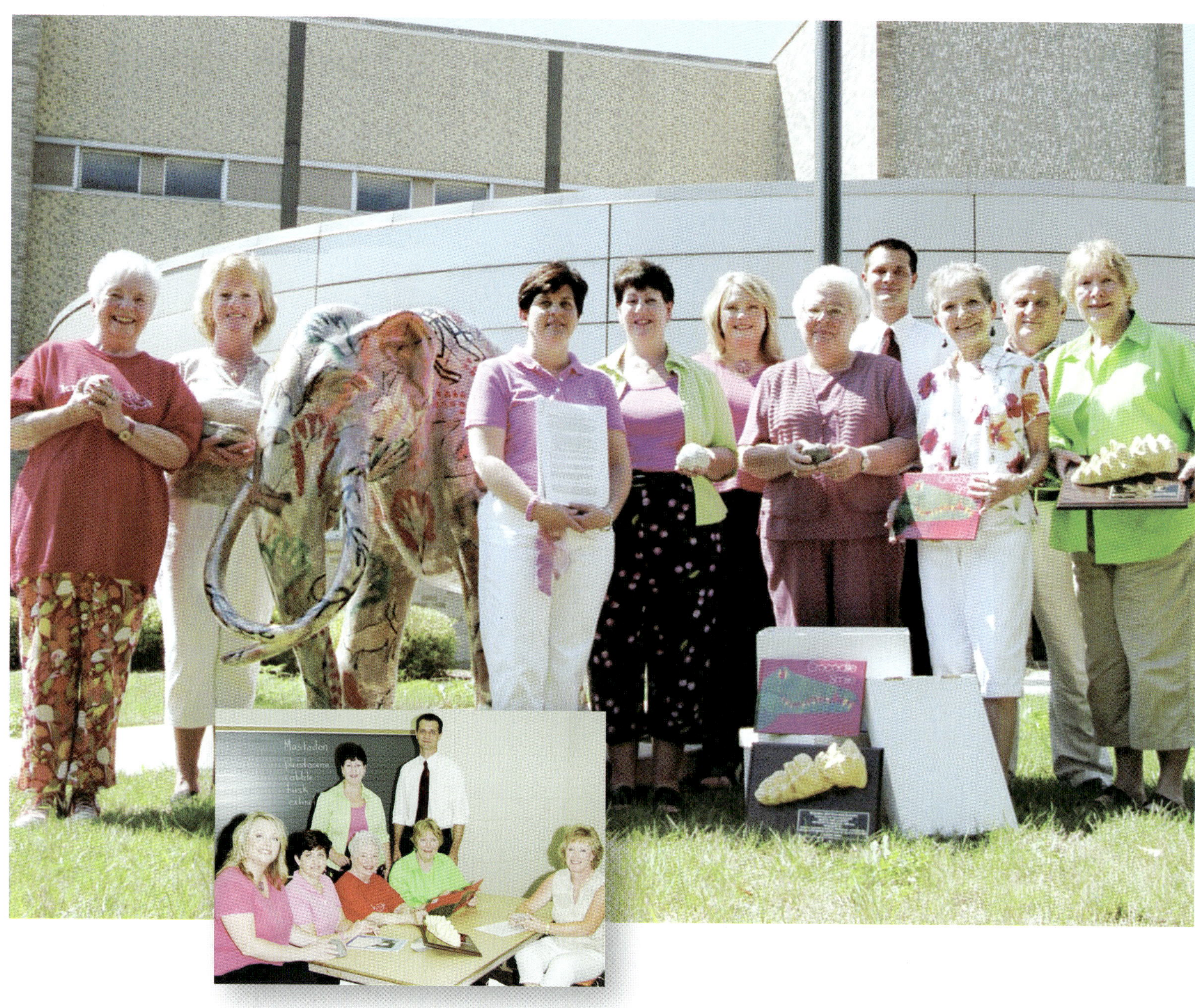

Educators involved in delivering curriculum, from left: Patty Martone, Louise Swihart, Cave O Don, Amy Martone, Sara Quigley, Valeri Hurst, Leanne Mensing, Todd Pelfrey, Bonnie Stuelpe, Dave Platt, Dana Wichern. **Curriculum developers, seated from left:** Valeri Hurst, Amy Martone, Patty Martone, Dana Wichern, Louise Swihart; **standing from left:** Sara Quigley, Todd Pelfrey

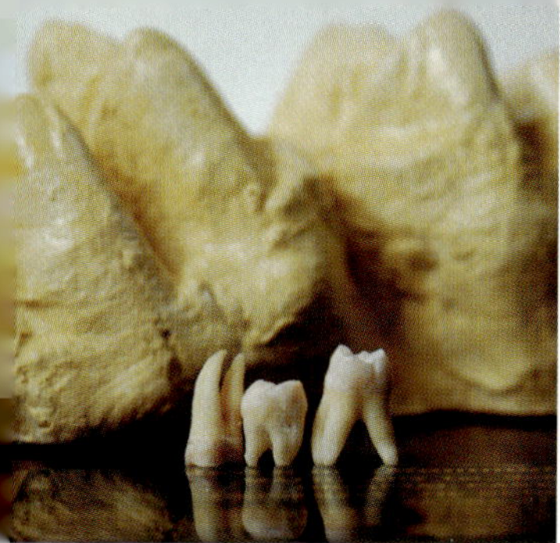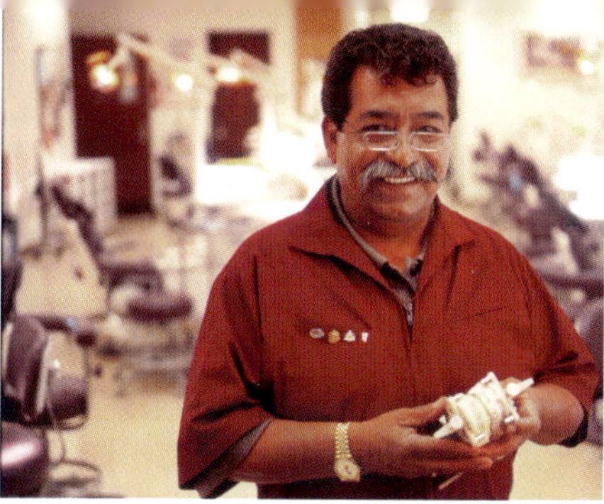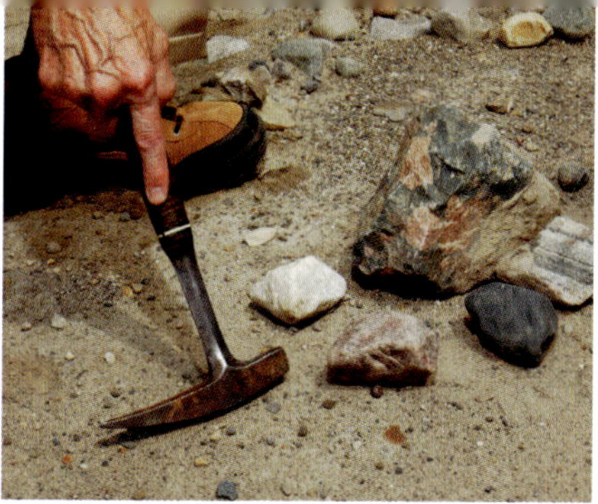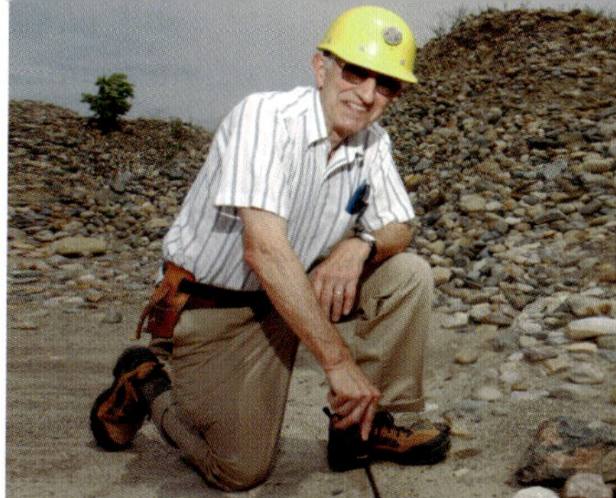

Above, from left: Human and mastodon teeth, Associate Professor Albino Perez, cobbles, Professor Emeritus Jack Sunderman

Adhering to the university's mission to educate, the Mastodons on Parade education committee developed kindergarten through 12th grade curricular materials about the mastodon and the Ice Age. Materials were in compliance with Indiana standards for mathematics and language arts for kindergarten through fifth grade. The curriculum also included enrichment materials and a teacher's packet of background information. Selected sections were created for students able to handle more complex concepts.

A unique aspect of the curriculum was its dissemination entirely through Internet sites, making it available to parents, youth-serving agencies, and public libraries. Each of the major school corporations in the county included a link to the curriculum on its Web site. IPFW carries the complete curriculum at www.mastodons.org/curriculum.

To give students a better feel for the Ice Age, a display box of real materials was circulated among schools. It included an exemplary collection of five cobbles (rocks brought to the area during the Ice Age), a book with a CD addressing the concept of extinction and changing environments, and a casting of the three teeth from a mastodon upper jaw along with three human teeth for comparative purposes.

Under the direction of Associate Professor Albino Perez, students in the dental laboratory technology program cast the mastodon teeth. Jack Sunderman, professor emeritus, dug the cobbles at Old Prairie Products Gravel, and the United Way of Allen County funded the books and CDs in the display box.

Mainly, the educators wanted the learning to be meaningful and fun. Students got involved in predicting how many mastodons would fit in their kitchen, writing about The Three Little Vores (omnivores, herbivores, and carnivores), and creating bar graphs of various animal attributes (toes, legs, teeth).

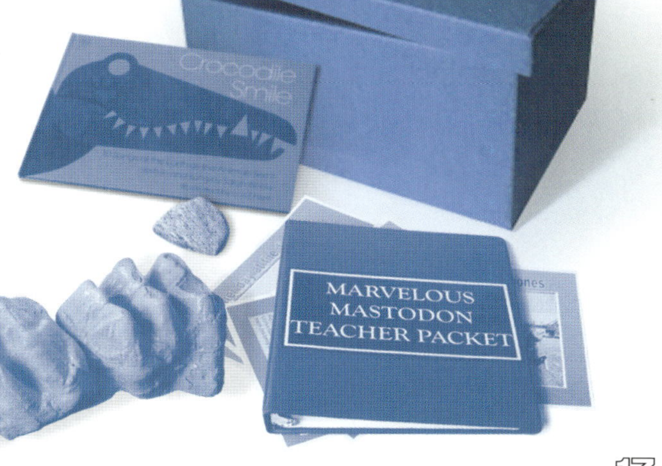

The adoption party: Sponsors sign on

Mastodons on Parade was strictly a family affair. On Oct. 7, 2004, IPFW hosted an adoption party for sponsors to adopt their mastodons officially. The Honorable Stanley A. Levine, judge, Allen County Superior Court, signed the Decree of Adoption for each of the sponsor-petitioners.

In the decree, the court found that "the Petitioners are of sufficient ability to rear the mastodon and to furnish sustainable support and education for the mastodon, ultimately at IPFW."

Decree of Adoption

MASTODONS ON PARADE

Allen Superior Court
38th Judicial District
Allen County - Indiana

IN RE:	The ADOPTION	)	
of	Mastodon Replica	)	**CAUSE NO:**
	MINOR	)	02D07-0409-AD-IPFW- 0064
and	Professional Federal Credit Union	)	
	SPONSOR PETITIONER	)	

Comes now the Petitioner, having been first duly sworn, and appearing before this court.

The court finds that:

The mastodon who is the subject of this adoption was born in Garrett, Indiana.

The Court further finds that the allegations of the Petitioners are true; that all necessary consents have been given and that the petition is in the proper form.

The Court further finds that all reports and recommendations have been filed; and that the mastodon has been for a suitable time, under the supervision of an approved agency, namely IPFW.

The Court further finds that the Petitioners are of sufficient ability to rear the mastodon and to furnish suitable support and education for the mastodon, ultimately at IPFW.

The Court finds that all notices required to be made upon sponsors, putative and legal, have been made in compliance with the statutes and laws.

IT IS THEREFORE ORDERED, ADJUDGED AND DECREED THAT THE ABOVE ENTITLED Petition for Adoption is granted.

The Court further Orders that the mastodon's birth certificate be amended in accordance with the judgment herein.

The Court further Orders and Decrees that a Certificate of this Order of Adoption, signed and sealed, be delivered to the proper Board, Commission or Office having charge of the permanent records of birth in the state in which the mastodon was born.

DATED: October 7, 2004

Stanley A. Levine
Judge, Allen Superior Court

Consent to Adoption

IPFW being the organization having lawful custody of mastodon, whose adoption is being sought, hereby consents to the adoption of # 0063 mastodon.

DATED: October 7, 2004

Michael Wartell
Chancellor, IPFW

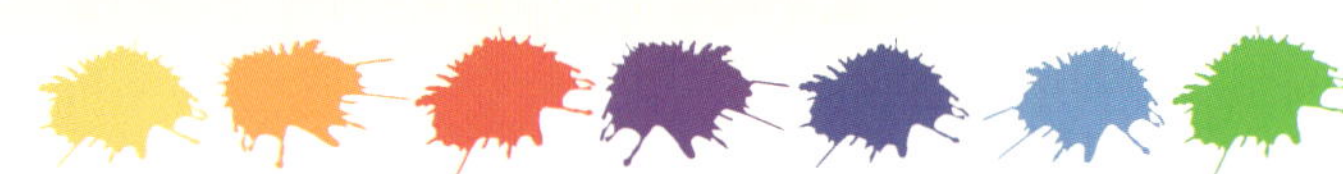

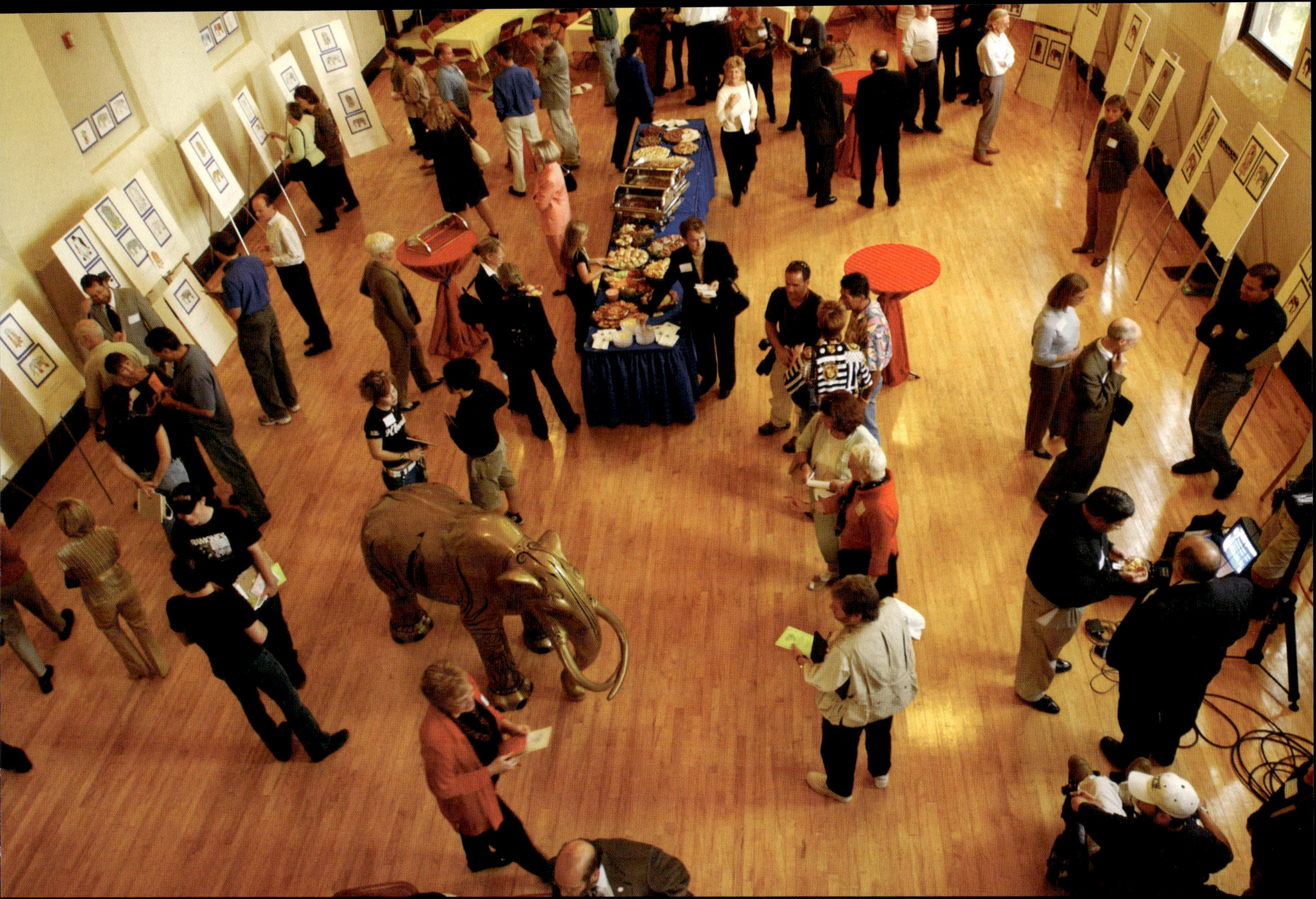

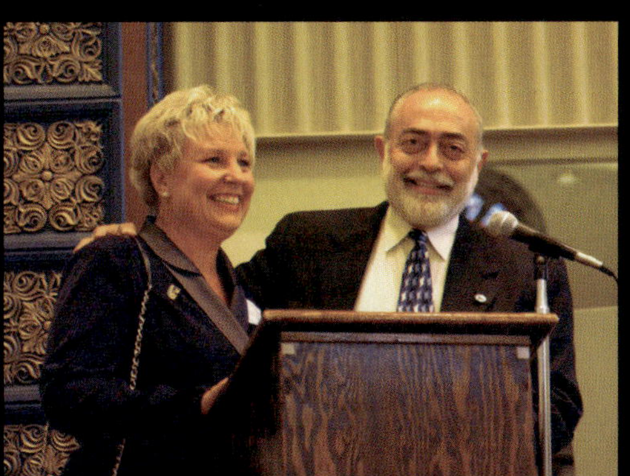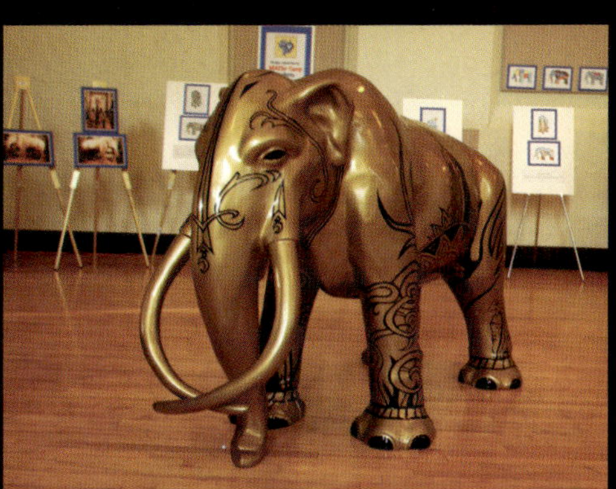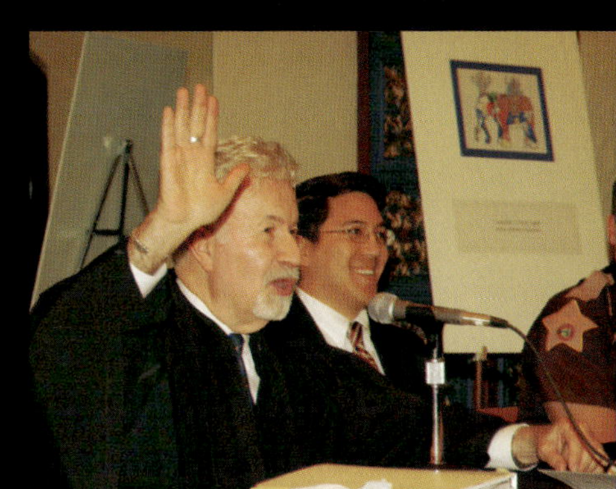

Photos, from left: Stephanie McCormick, President and CEO of the United Way of Allen County, and IPFW Chancellor Michael Wartell; DecoDon sponsored by Tower Bank (the first completed mastodon); and The Honorable Stanley A. Levine

The preview party: Meet the herd

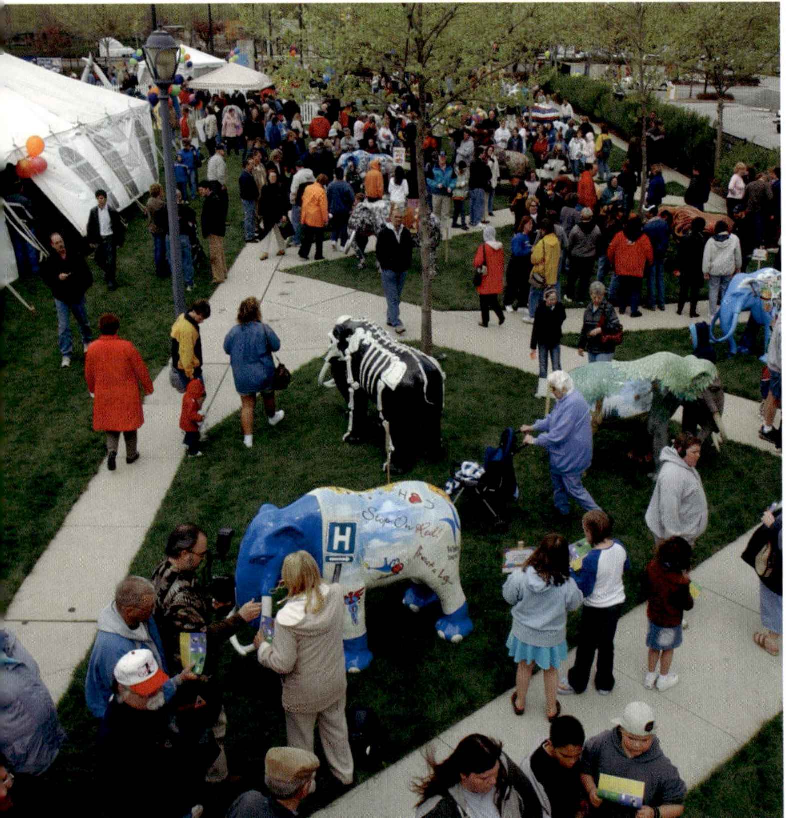

About 10,000 eager spectators met the mastodons at Headwaters Park for a community party. Participants were treated to slices of a 500-pound cake in the shape of a mastodon standing on four legs. They also enjoyed entertainment and games. Youngsters dug for cobbles and fossils in the sand pit, and more than 1,600 party goers voted for their favorite dons.

Winners of the People's Choice Awards were:

> Don at Work
>
> Chopper Don
>
> Dona in the Box
>
> AeroDONamic
>
> Do it Yourself Don
>
> MAST "er" Builder
>
> Slinky Don
>
> Paths-odon: Crossroads of America
>
> Trojan Don
>
> Mastodonny Appleseed

Following the event, the dons were delivered to their summer locations and bolted onto concrete pads. High school athletes shouldered much of the lifting and worked with the transportation team in waning light.

May 2, 2005: Early-morning commuters who drove south on Clinton Street discovered a herd of 49 colorful mastodons lining both sides of the street at Headwaters Park. Driving around town, people found other mastodons stationed in front of offices, banks, the Grand Wayne Center…in short, they were everywhere. They were in shopping malls, they were at schools. One was next to a hitching post in an Amish area.

Everybody was talking. Everybody was going downtown to see the mastodons. It was love at first sight. Students dressed for the prom chose the mastodons over their living room fireplaces for photos. Calvin, a two year old, astonished visitors as he called out the names of the dons one by one. An accident left the tusk of Justice Don broken, but the community responded with bandages, a crutch, flowers, and a signed get-well card. Grocery store cashiers in nearby towns were overheard talking about the mastodons. Grandparents brought their grandkids. Fort Wayne's diverse populations were all there…at all hours. They were all smiling.

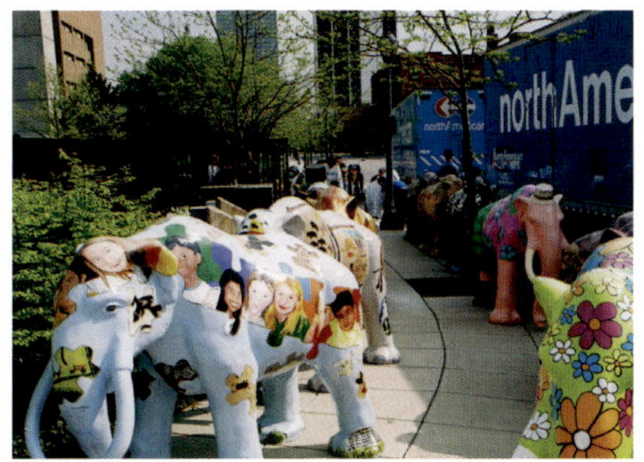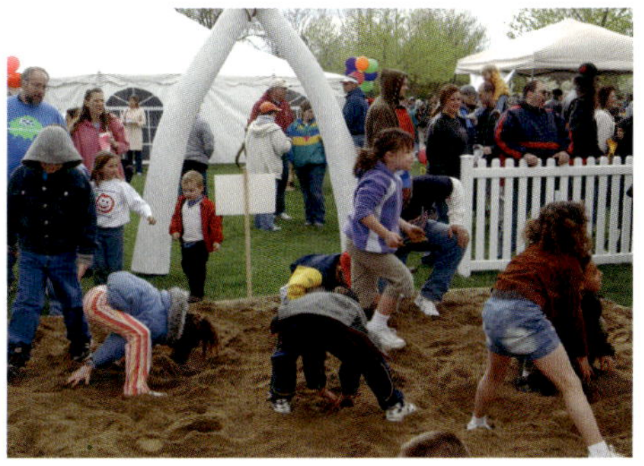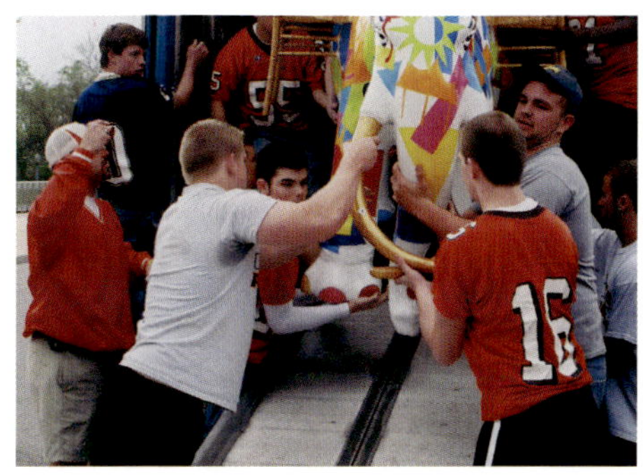

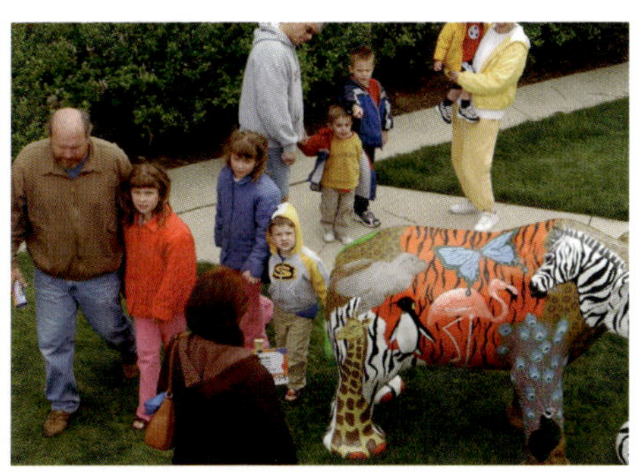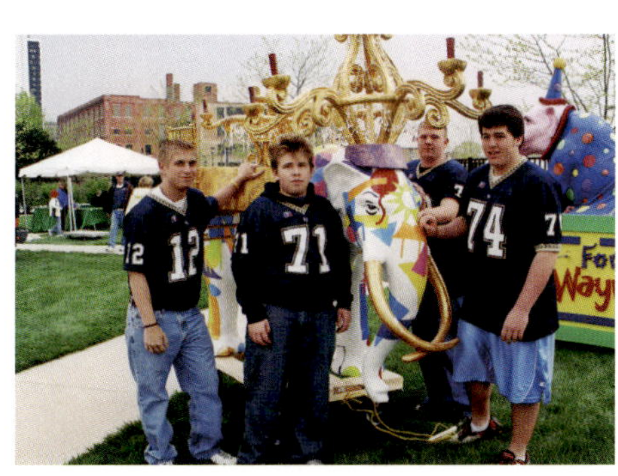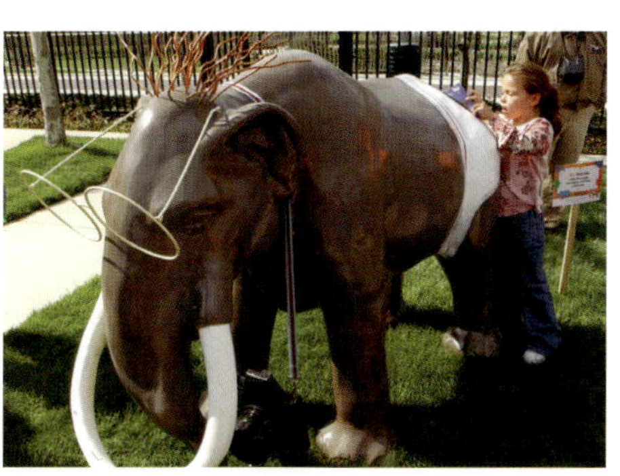

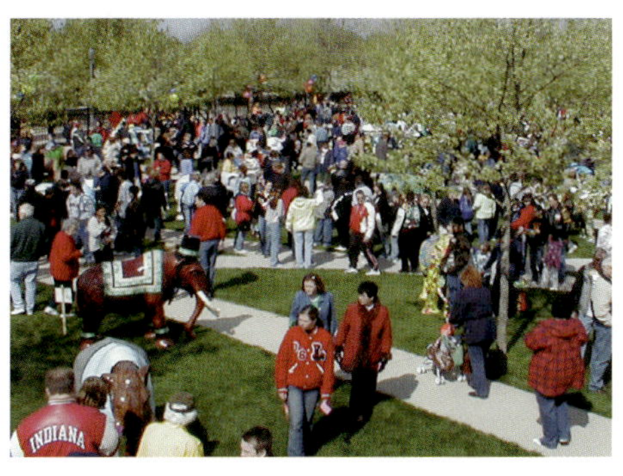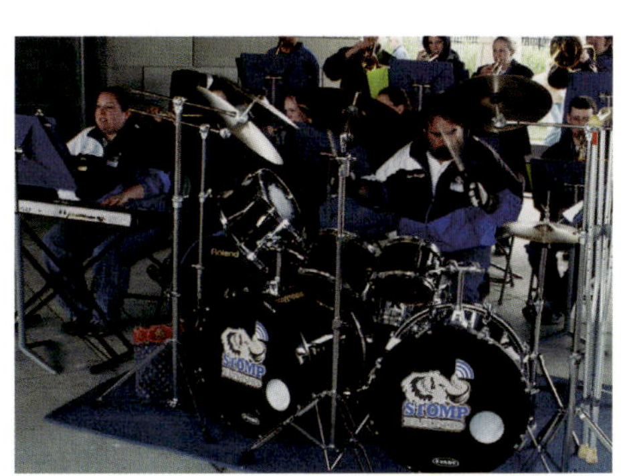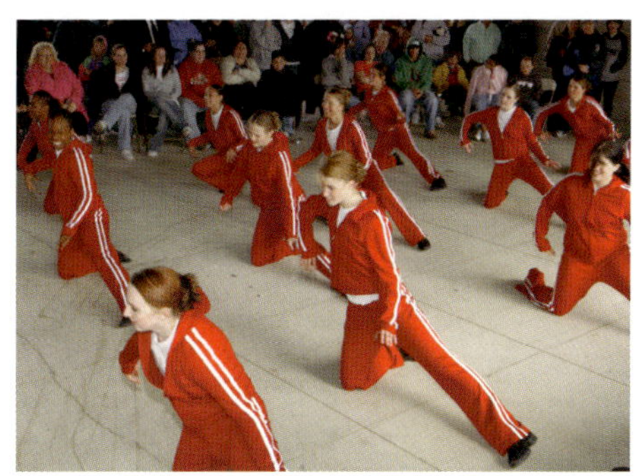

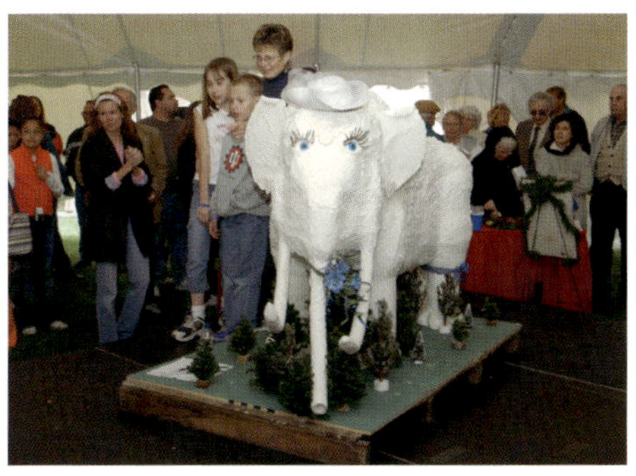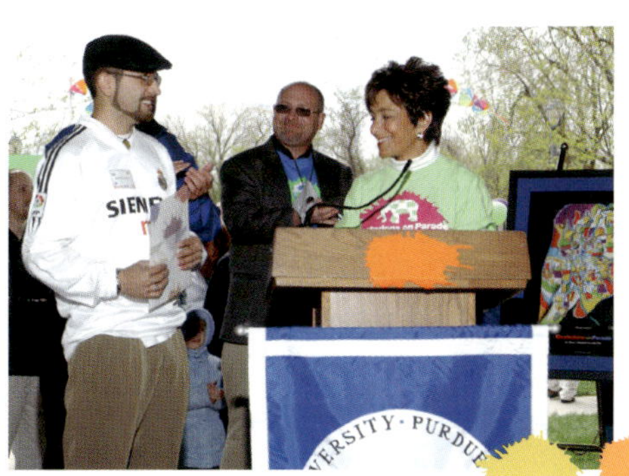

Photos, top to bottom, left to right: The herd lined up; digging for rocks; high school moving crew; meeting the dons; high school moving crew; glasses and all; the preview at Headwaters Park; the IPFW Stomp Band; North Side DanceSkins; a mastodon-sized cake by Betty Olry; Justin Casiano, Mark Evans, and Irene Walters

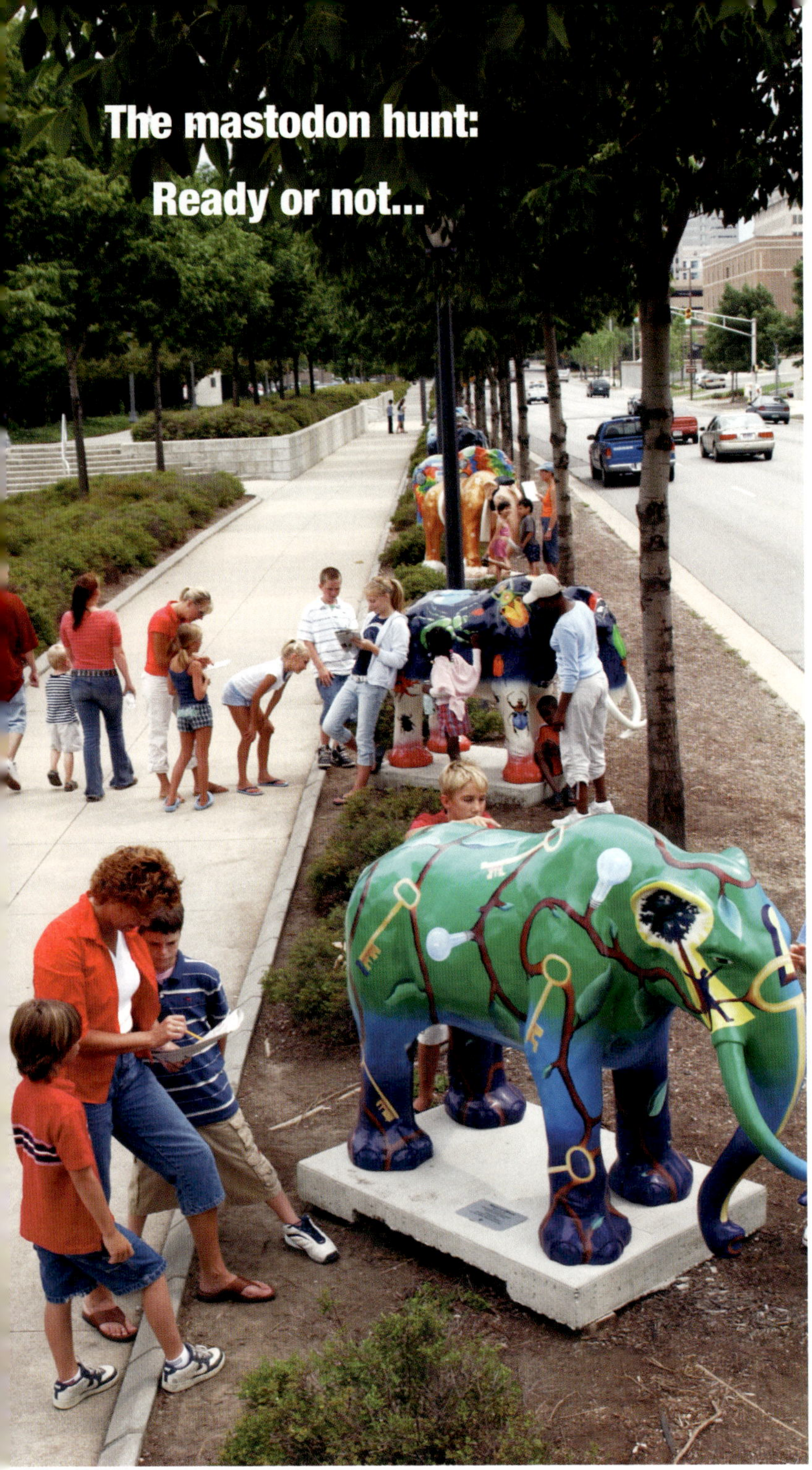

The mastodon hunt:
Ready or not...

Once the mastodons were on display, IPFW and Fort Wayne Newspapers challenged the community to match each mastodon to its location. The prize for the competition was a four-day, three-night package for four people to Disney World. Round-trip airfare was provided by Conference and Travel from Fort Wayne, Ind., to Orlando, Fla.

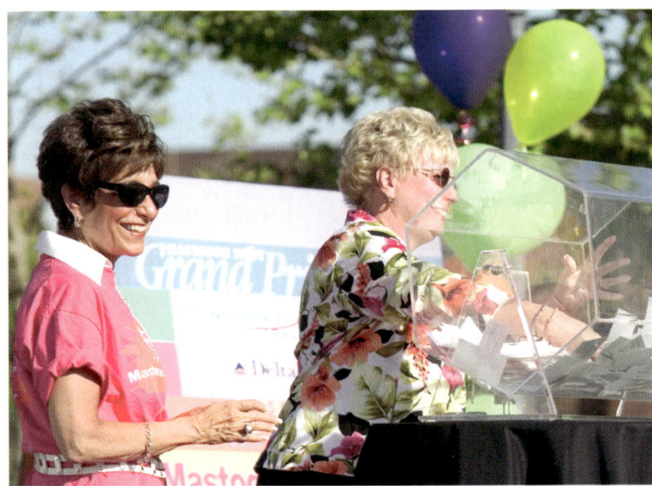

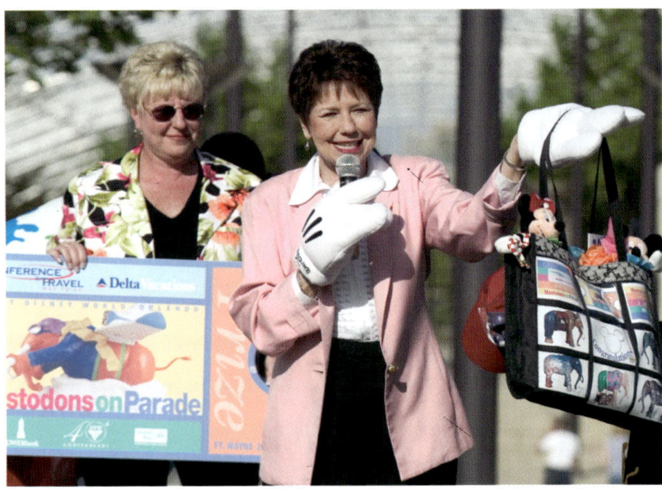

I'm going to Disney World!

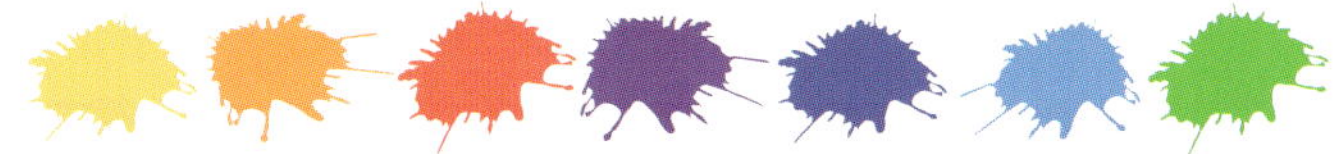

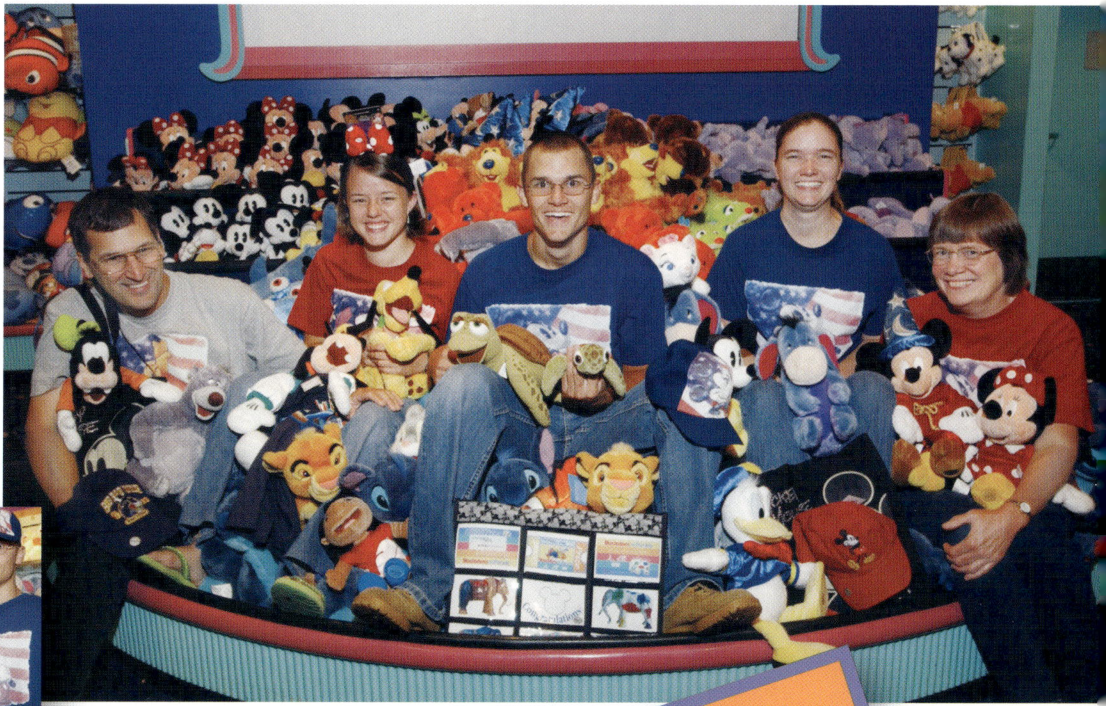

Andrew Spooner, a 17 year old from Fort Wayne, won the Mastodon Hunt prize. The total number of entries for the contest was 2,316. Spooner's name was randomly chosen from more than 1,200 correct entries.

The Spooner family shopped at The Disney Store in Glenbrook Mall before the trip.

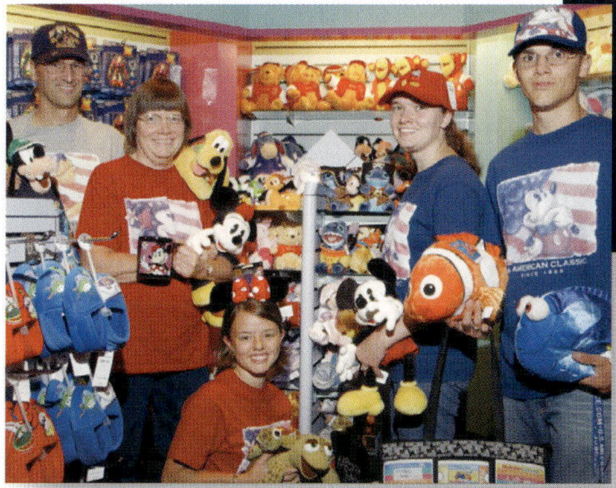

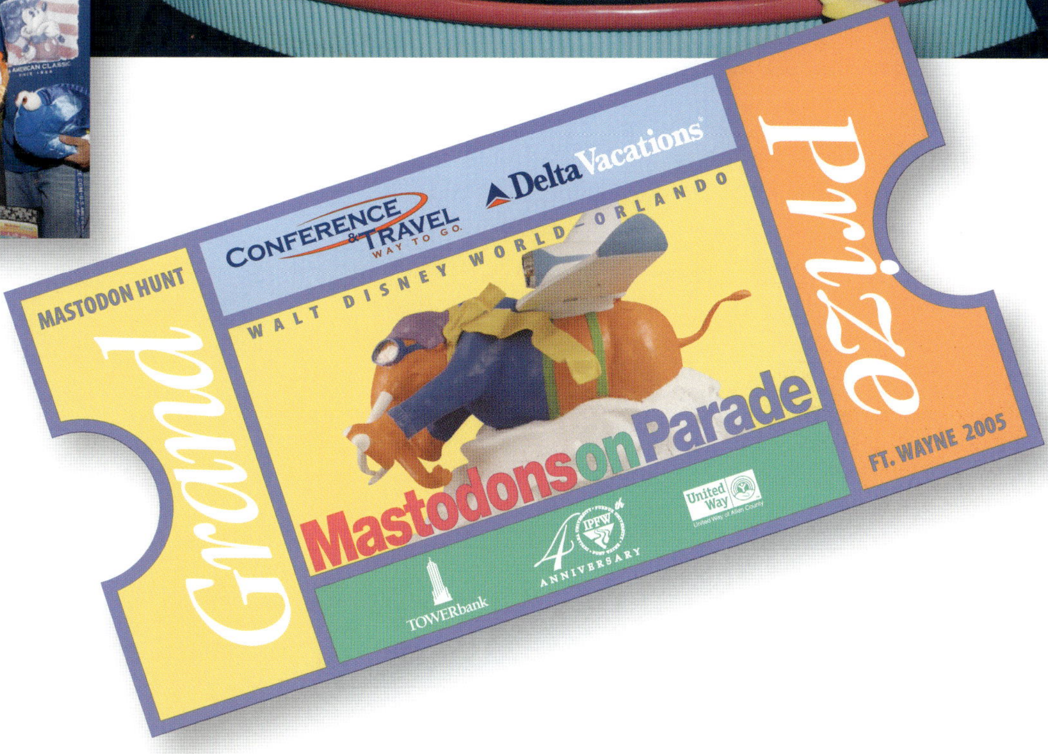

The artists' party

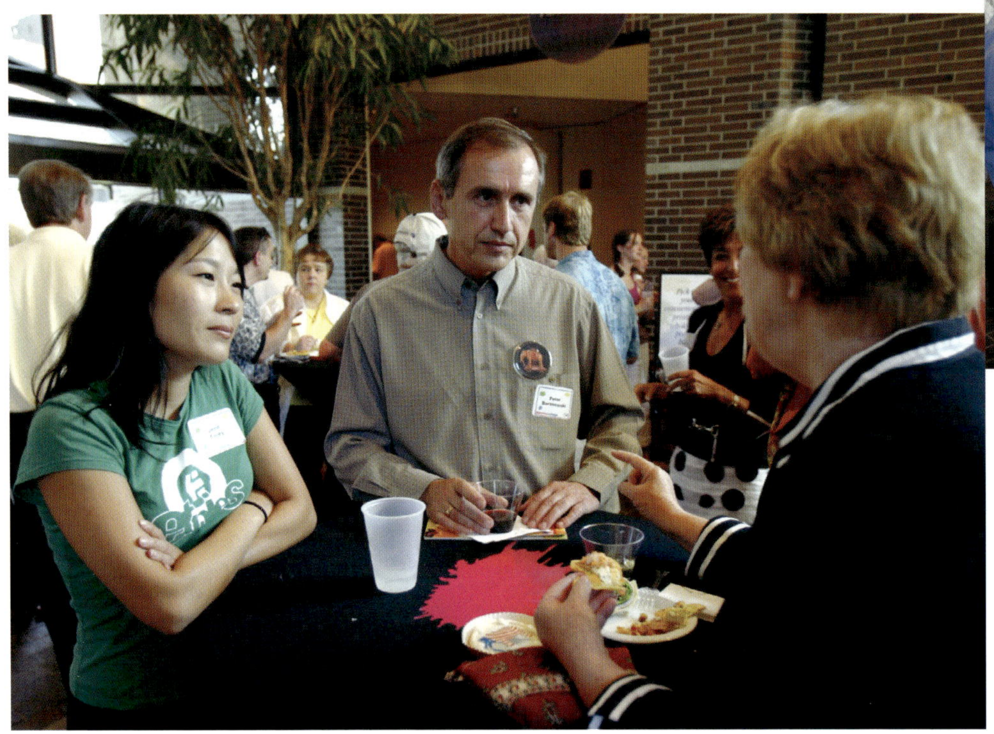

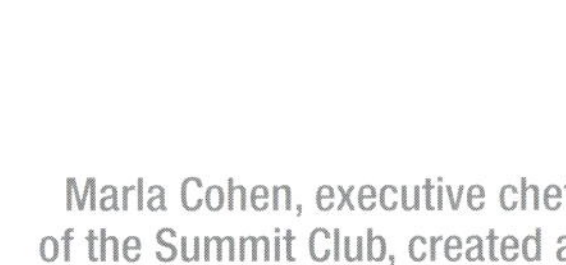

Marla Cohen, executive chef
of the Summit Club, created a
mastodonic feast.

Feasting on look-alike mastodon bones and decorated
cookies, don artists were thanked for their community
contributions and hard work at a reception at the Fort Wayne
Museum of Art on June 22, 2005. Entertainment included
special awards, some unusual don stories, and a visual review
of the Mastodons on Parade project. It was an event honoring
those whose brushes, jewels, creativity, and paint produced a
herd of charming creatures.

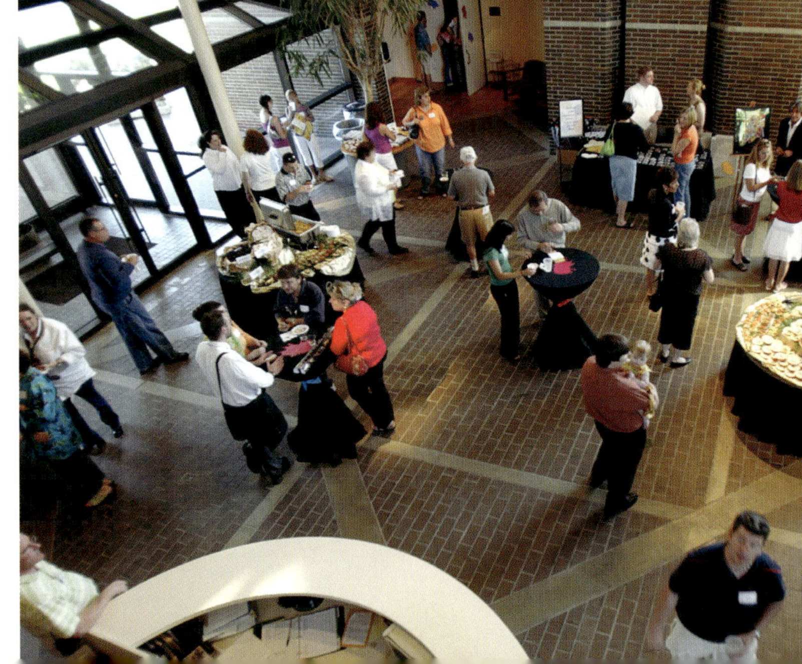

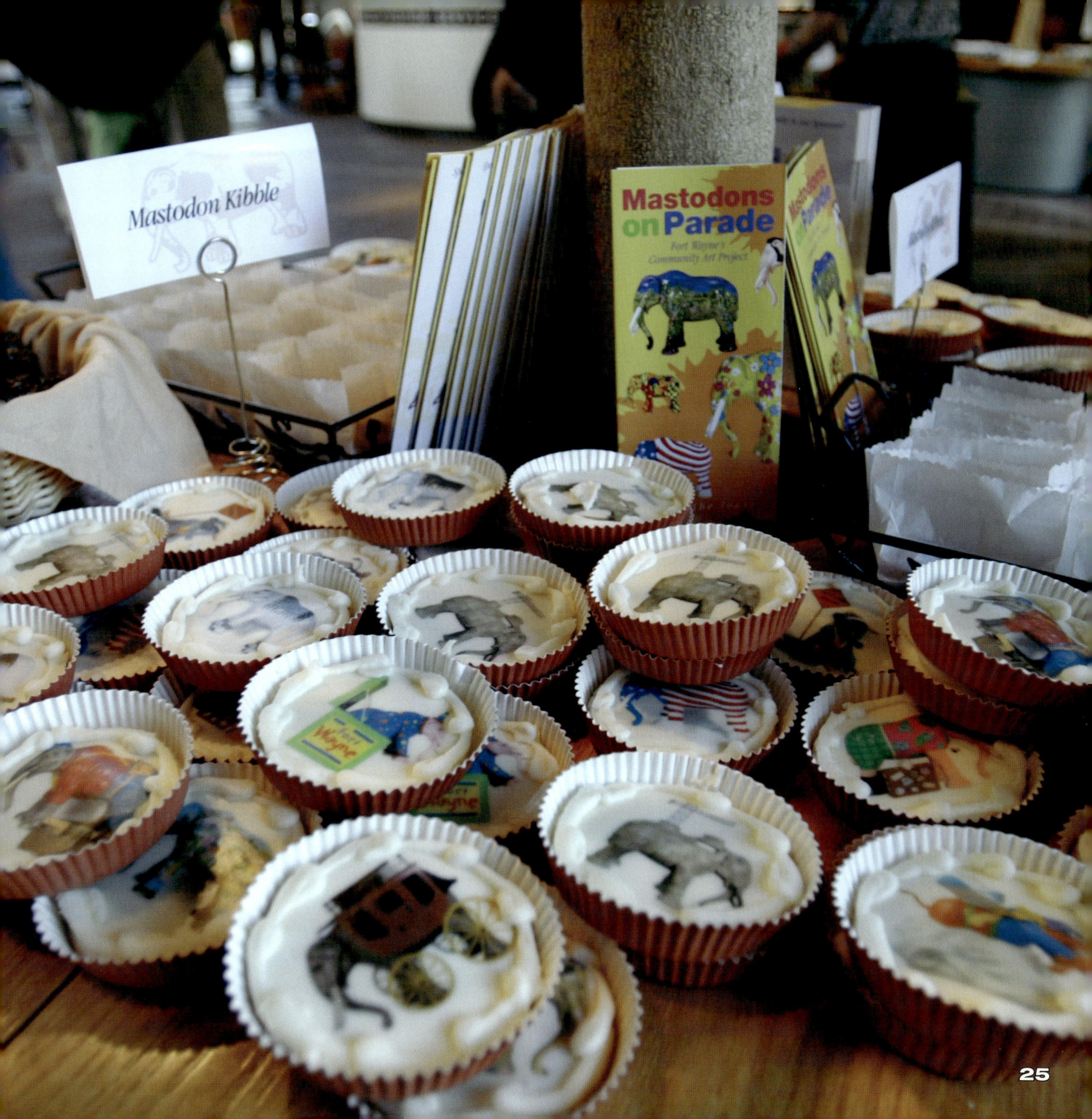

Mastodon Kibble
Mastodons on Parade
Fort Wayne's Community Art Project

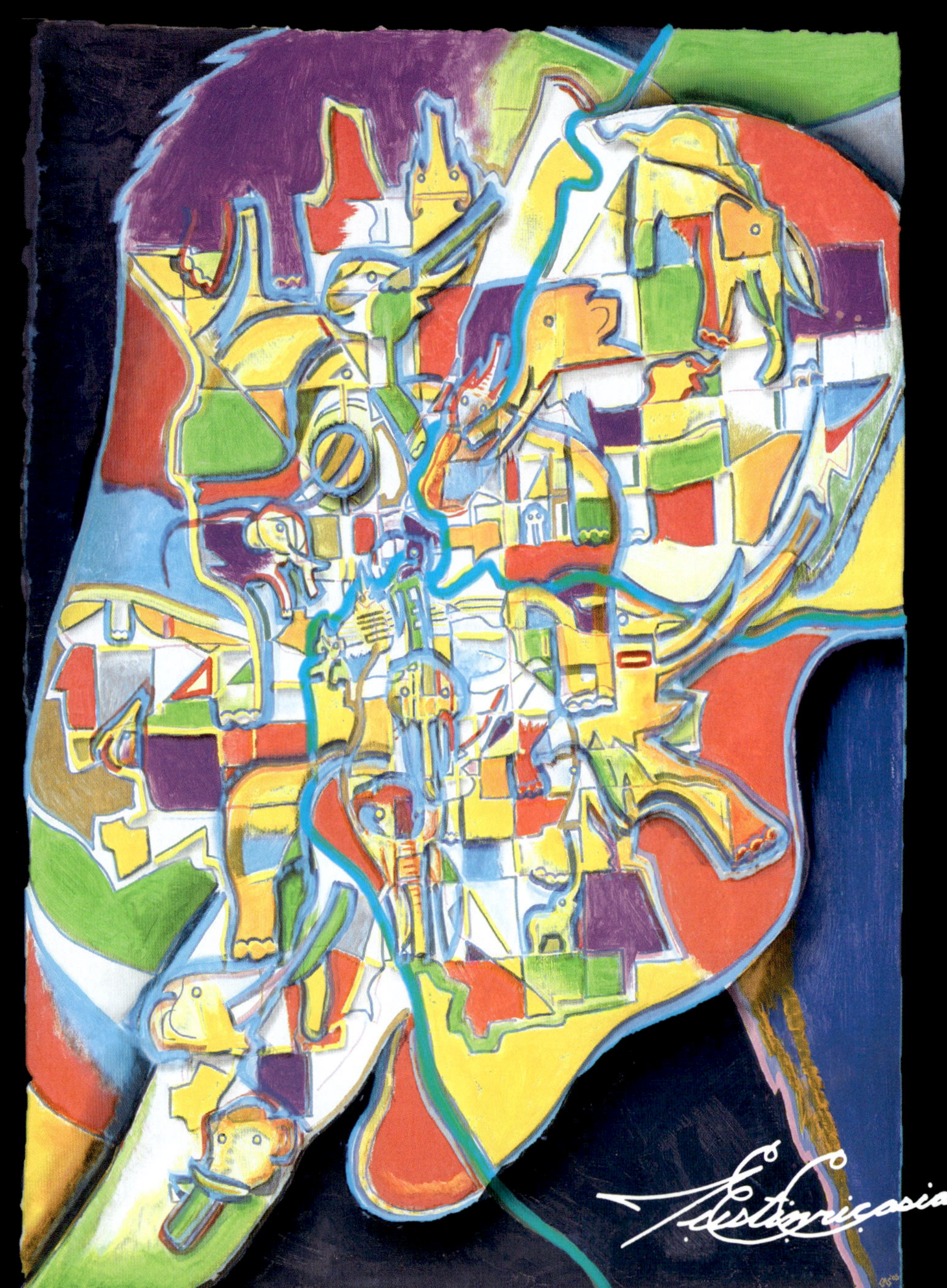

Commemorative art: Mastodon City Limits

Finding a way to thank the sponsors and salute the artists who created the mastodons generated a lot of discussion. Ultimately, the steering committee agreed that a unique keepsake was needed.

The IPFW Department of Visual Arts sponsored and juried a contest for the creation of a commemorative lithograph. Justin Casiano, an IPFW art student, created a design that superimposed city icons, the three rivers, and stylized mastodon forms in the outline of a mastodon's profile. Filled with brightly colored geometric graphics, Casiano's work captures the spirit and joy of the Mastodons on Parade project. A signed and numbered limited-edition print, entitled "Mastodon City Limits," was awarded to each artist and sponsor who participated in the creation of a mastodon.

Mastodon City Limits
Justin Casiano, 2005
Mixed media on art board

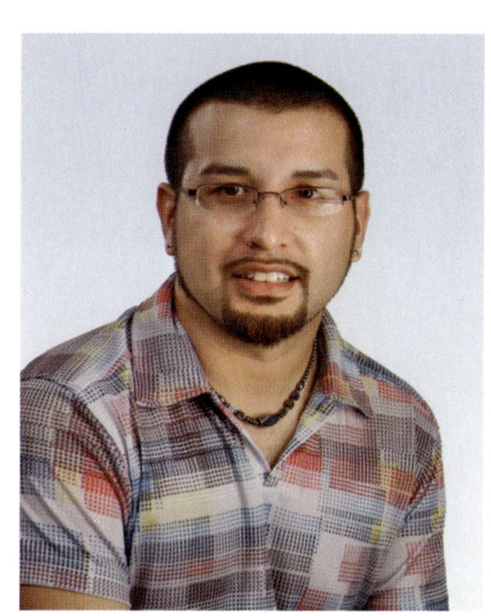

The Three Rivers Parade: Art on the loose

With their tusks gleaming and their bodies awash in color, 11 of the Mastodons on Parade greeted thousands of people lining the streets for the July 9, 2005, Three Rivers Festival parade. It was a steamy, sweltering Saturday morning for the 71 volunteers who pushed and pulled the 10 People's Choice dons and SplatoDon, IPFW's mastodon, as the drum major.

The university's Stomp Band entertained along the route as artists and IPFW representatives waved to the community. The crowd reacted with shouts of appreciation and rousing cheers for their favorites.

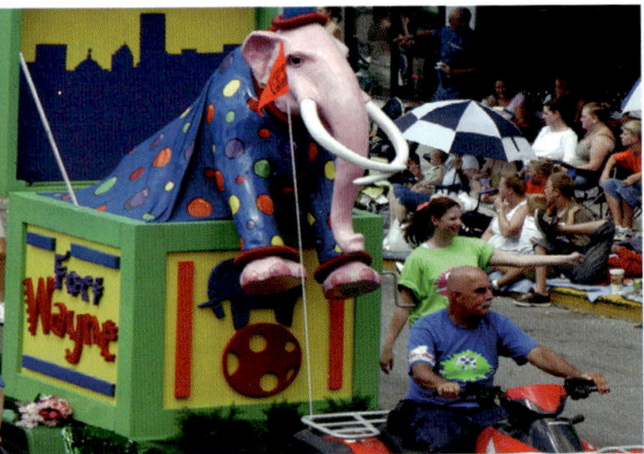
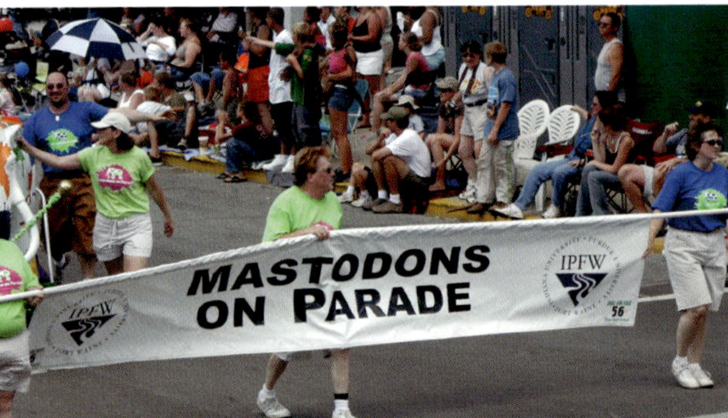

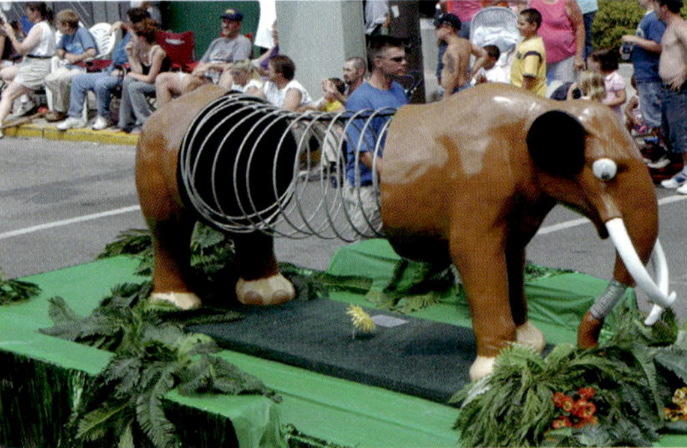

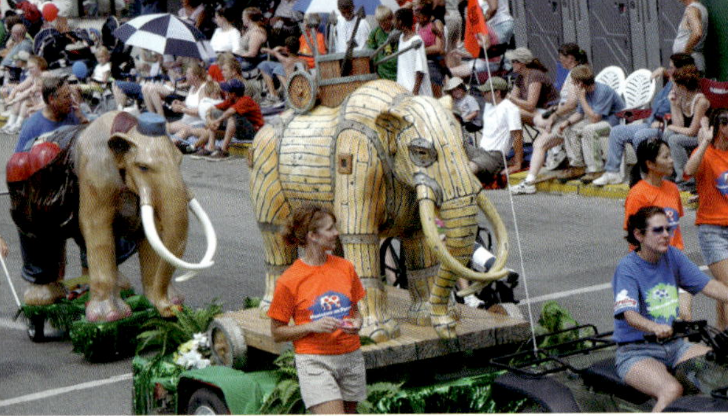
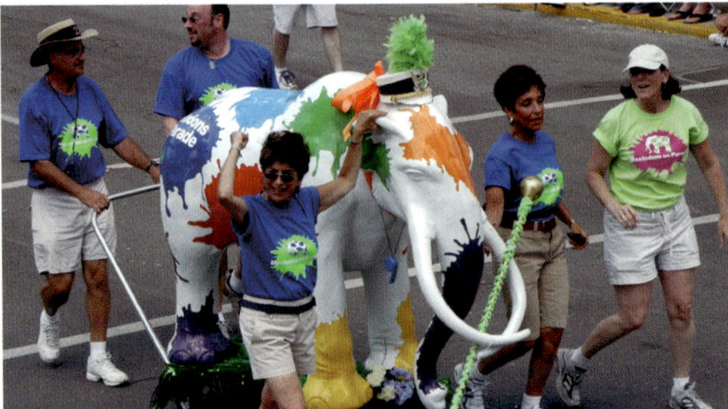
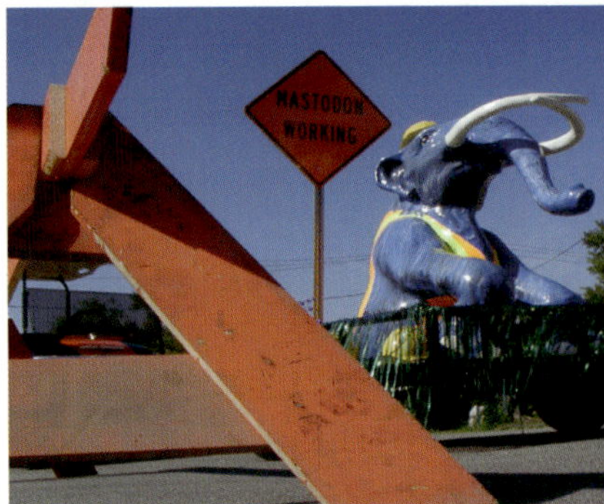

IPFW won the "Noncommercial Sweepstakes Best Overall" award for the Mastodons on Parade entry.

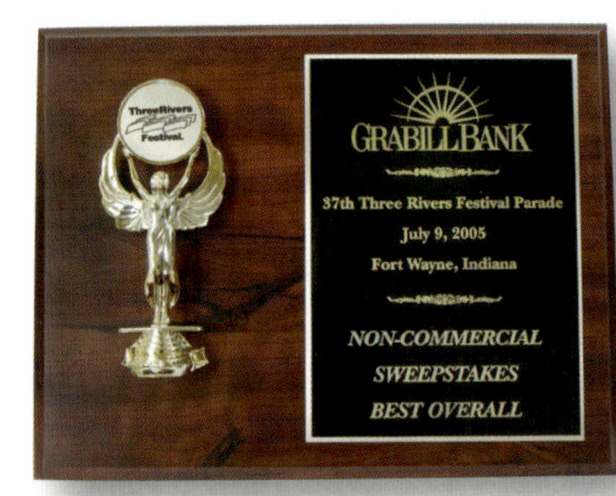

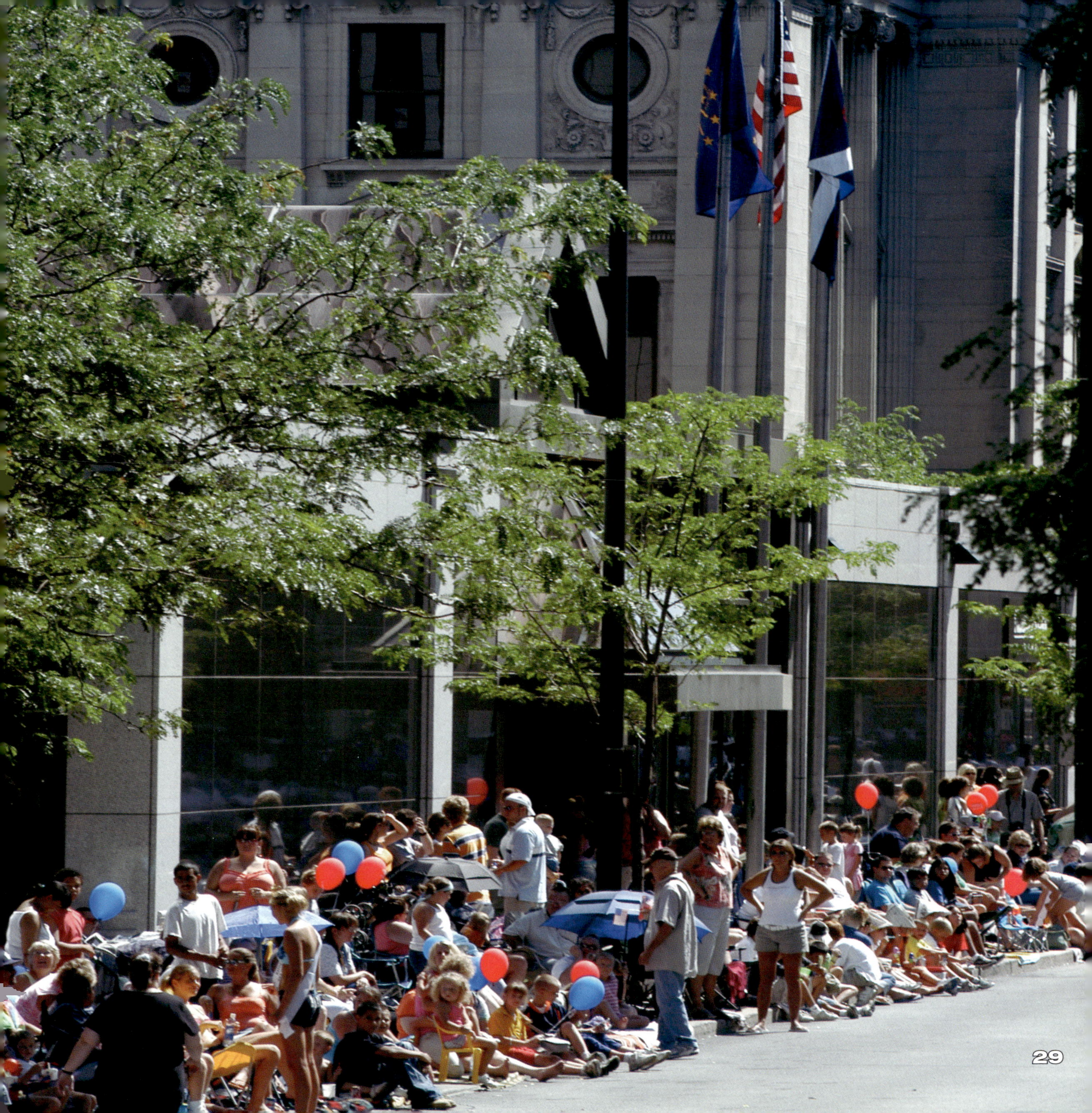

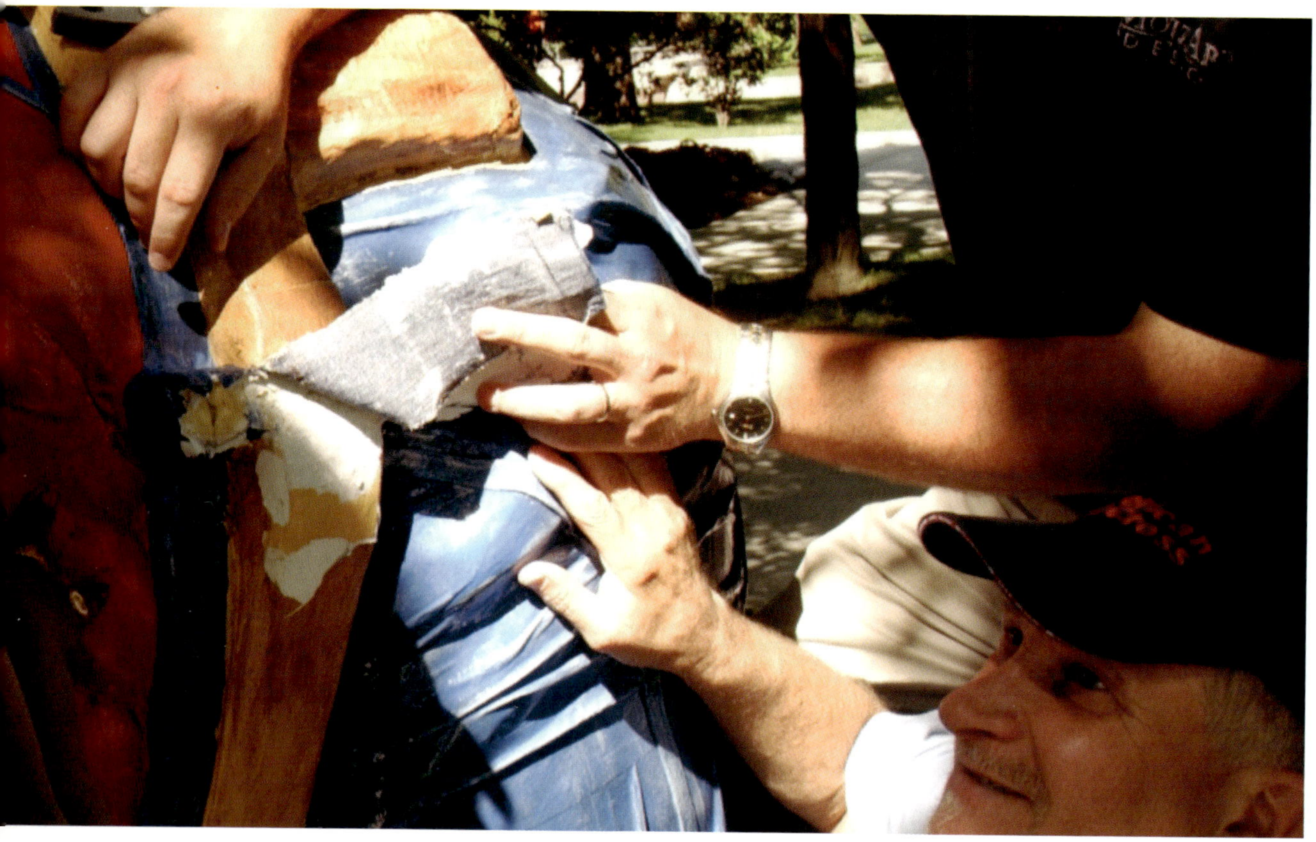

Mastodon Monitors and Menders: **(from left)** Bill Pickelheimer, Tony Martone, Don Katter, John Motz, Brigitte Brown, Randy Jackson

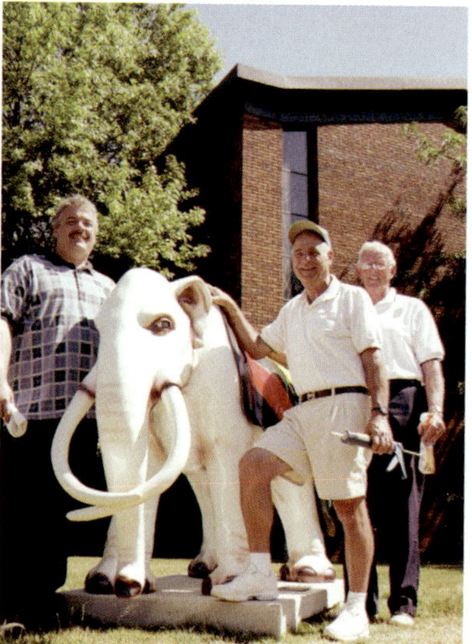

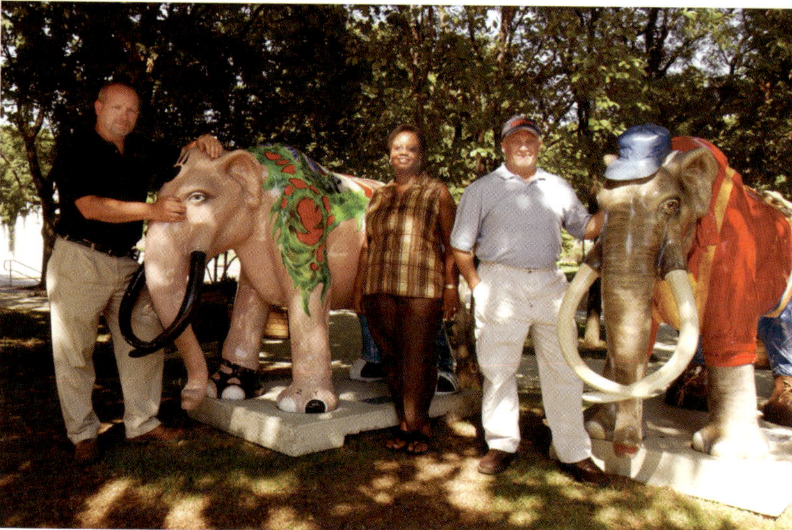

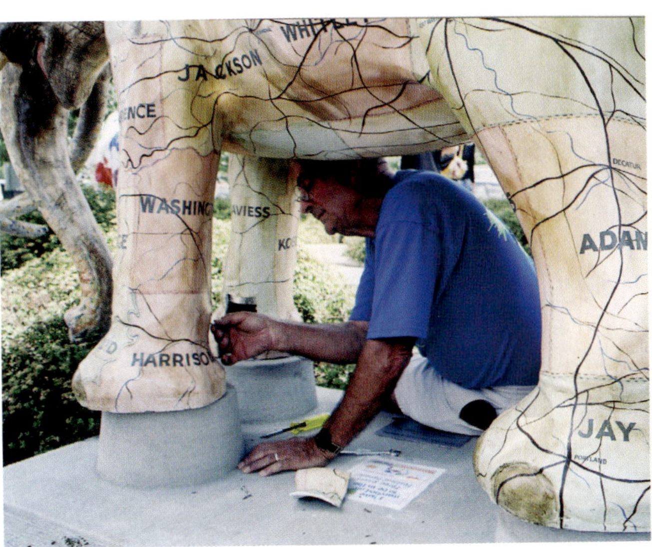

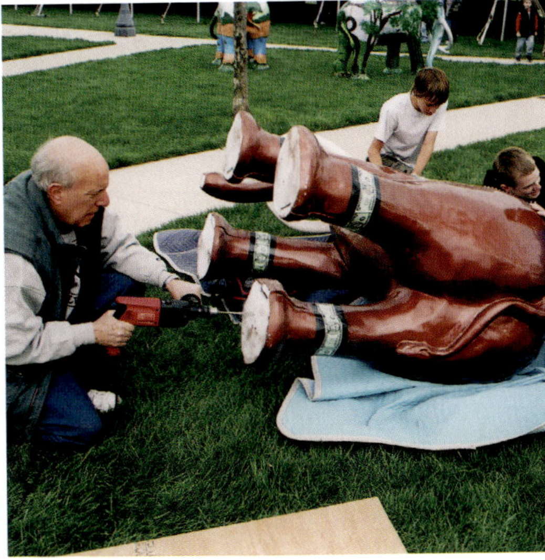

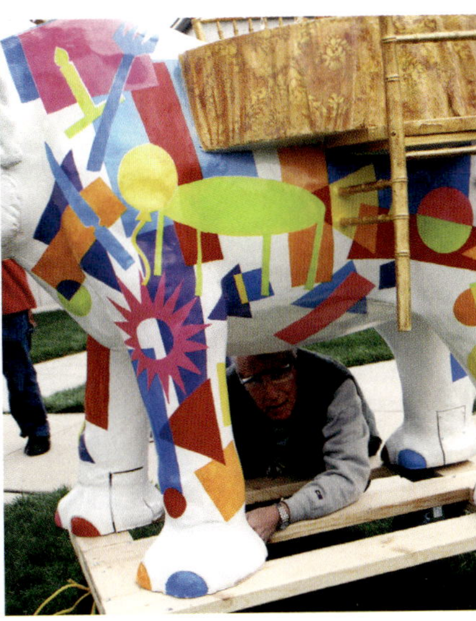

Call them marshals, monitors, or the EMS team—a group of community volunteers gave hours of service to the dons. Once on display, the mastodons were subjected to Mother Nature's wrath. Although they were prepared for inclement weather, some mastodons needed special attention. This dedicated team of workers patched, painted, and pasted the tusked beasts. They were on call for everything from moving a mastodon from its base to hoisting one onto a parade float to answering an unexpected mastodon need.

With tools in hand, the marshals were on the march, ready to meet whatever needs arose. This unit provided dedicated and ongoing service throughout the Mastodons on Parade project.

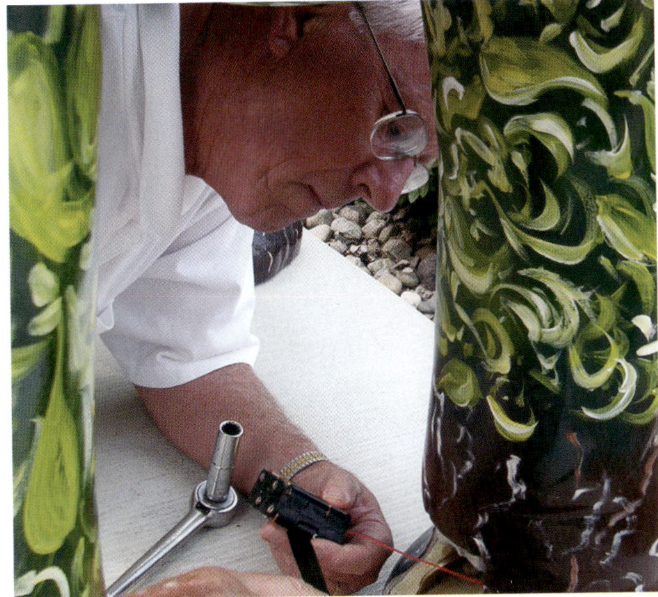

Top left: Tony Martone
Top middle, right: Bob Walters
Left: Don Katter

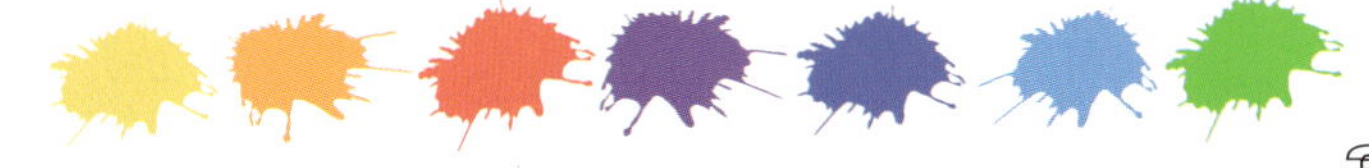

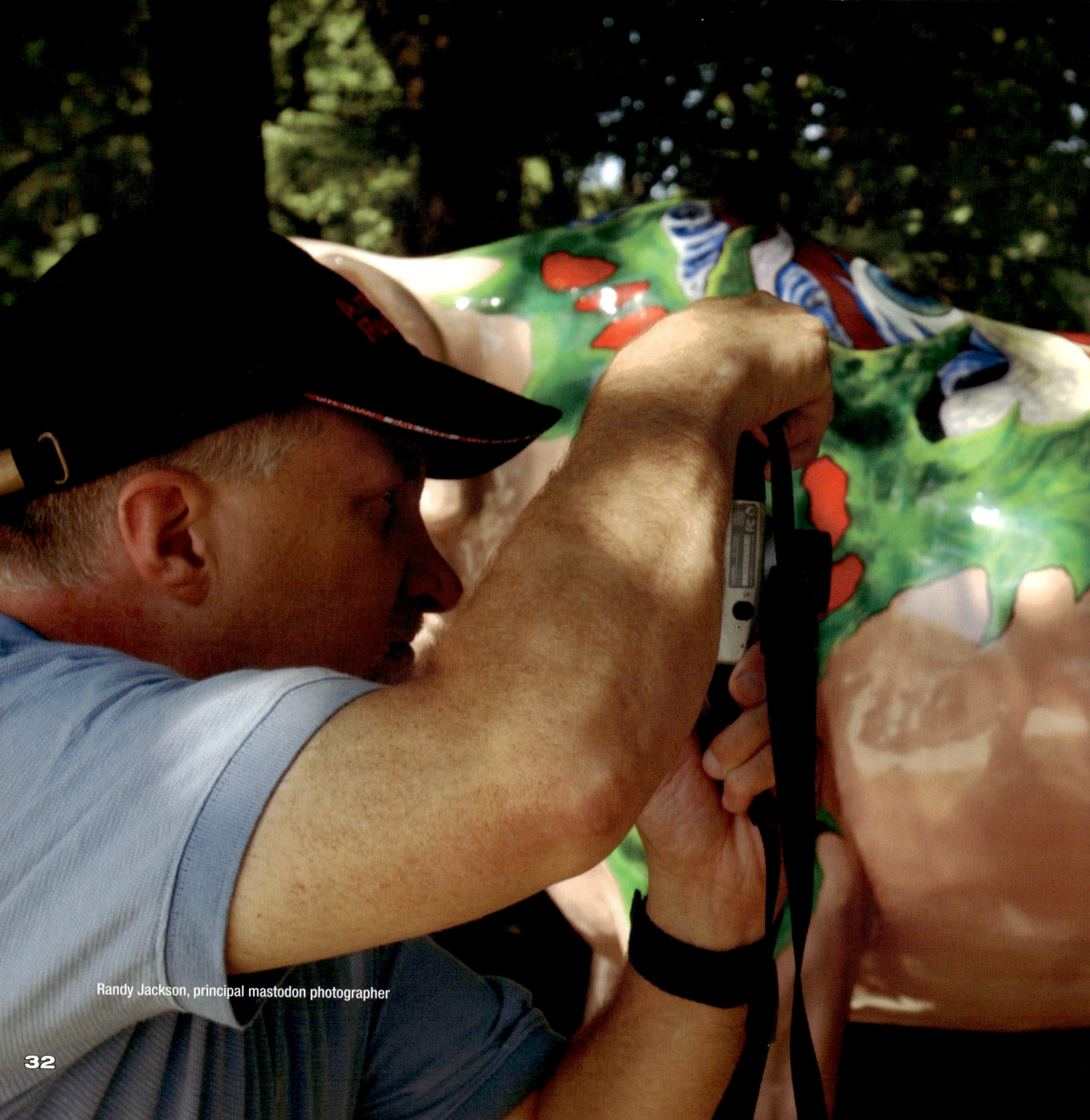

Randy Jackson, principal mastodon photographer

Mastodons on Parade

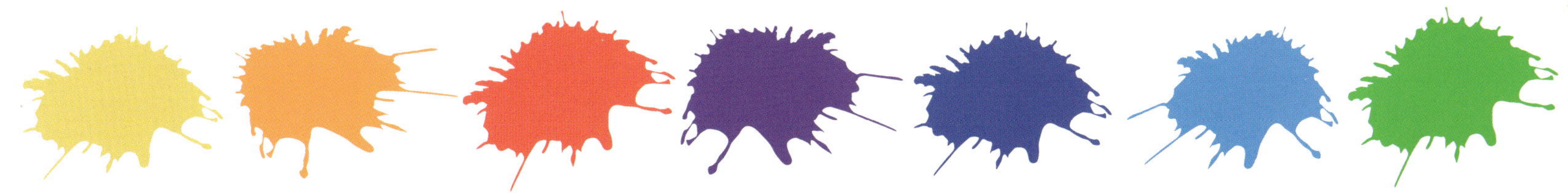

Dons of Distinction

Dons of Distinction

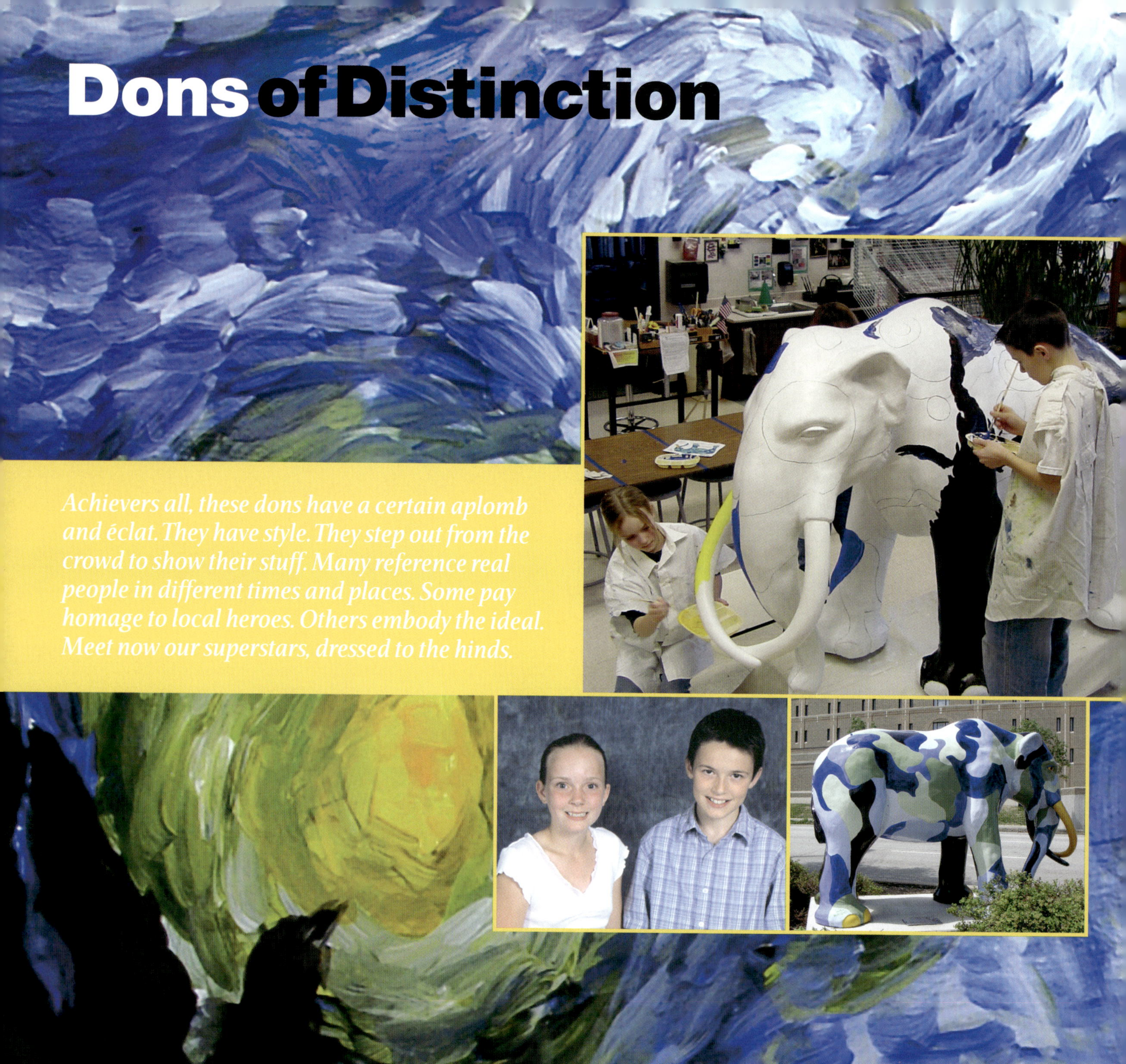

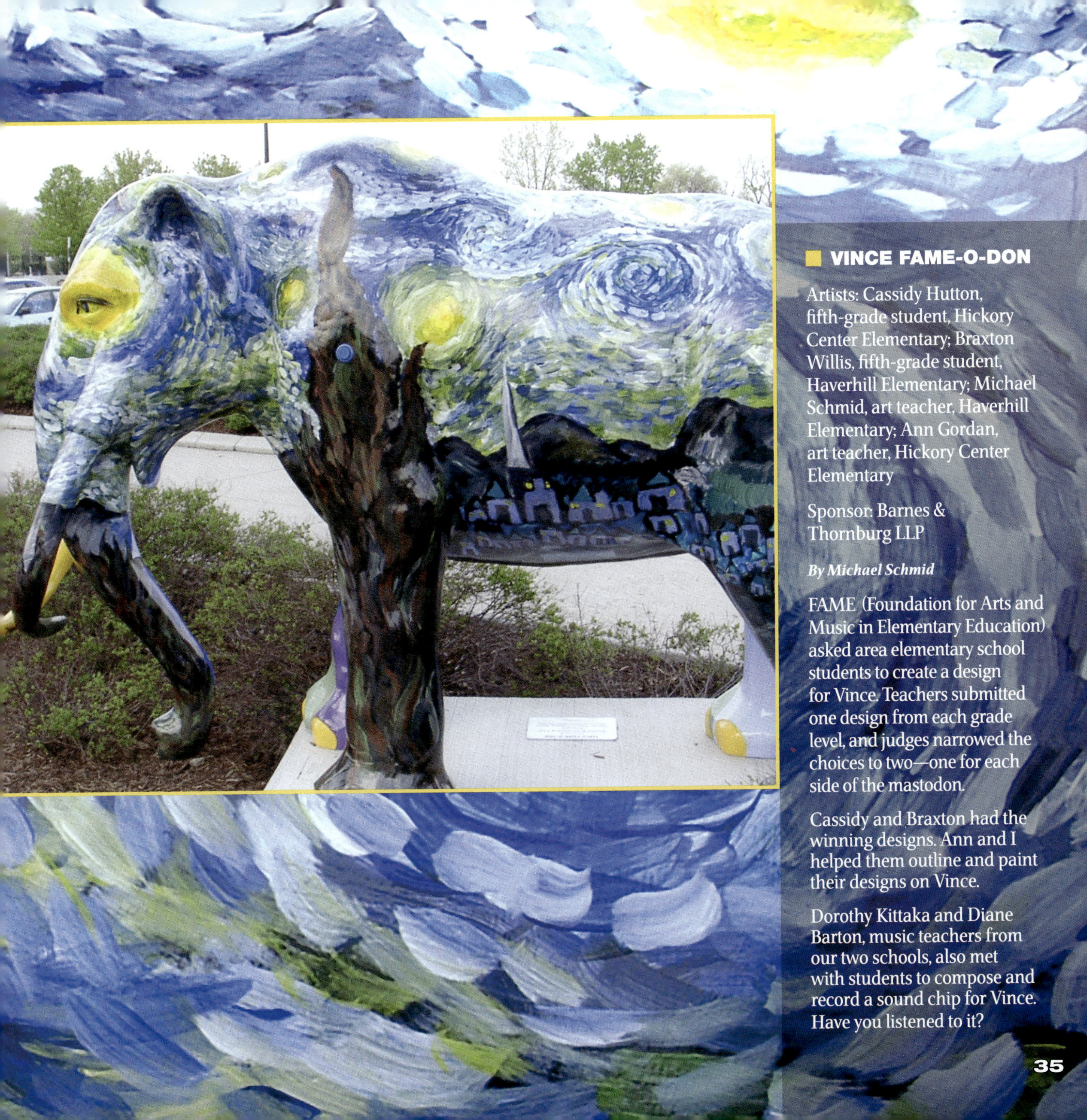

VINCE FAME-O-DON

Artists: Cassidy Hutton, fifth-grade student, Hickory Center Elementary; Braxton Willis, fifth-grade student, Haverhill Elementary; Michael Schmid, art teacher, Haverhill Elementary; Ann Gordan, art teacher, Hickory Center Elementary

Sponsor: Barnes & Thornburg LLP

By Michael Schmid

FAME (Foundation for Arts and Music in Elementary Education) asked area elementary school students to create a design for Vince. Teachers submitted one design from each grade level, and judges narrowed the choices to two—one for each side of the mastodon.

Cassidy and Braxton had the winning designs. Ann and I helped them outline and paint their designs on Vince.

Dorothy Kittaka and Diane Barton, music teachers from our two schools, also met with students to compose and record a sound chip for Vince. Have you listened to it?

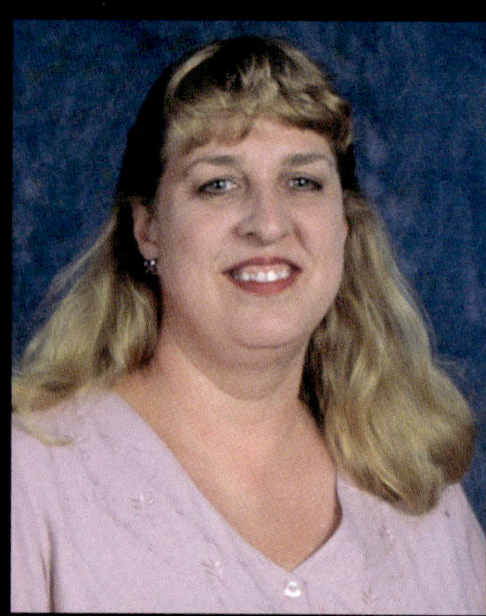

■ FINANCIAL DON

Artist: Valerie McBride, professional artist

Sponsor: Lincoln Financial Group Foundation

The first time my Labrador walked into the garage and saw me working on Financial Don, she stopped in her tracks and then ran for the door. Later, she was able to be a constant companion to us.

My goal was to create an Abraham Lincoln mastodon and cover him with imitation Lincoln pennies, $5 bills, and jeweling.

For his top hat, I used a bucket. His bow tie is fleece, coated with fiberglass resin and bolted on. Metallic copper paint creates that "new penny" look in the sun.

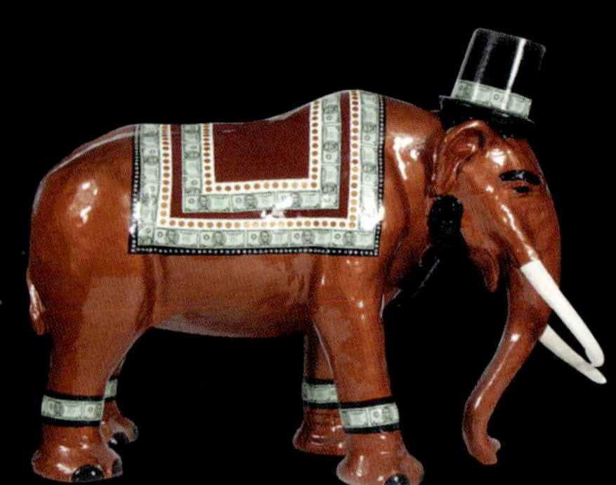

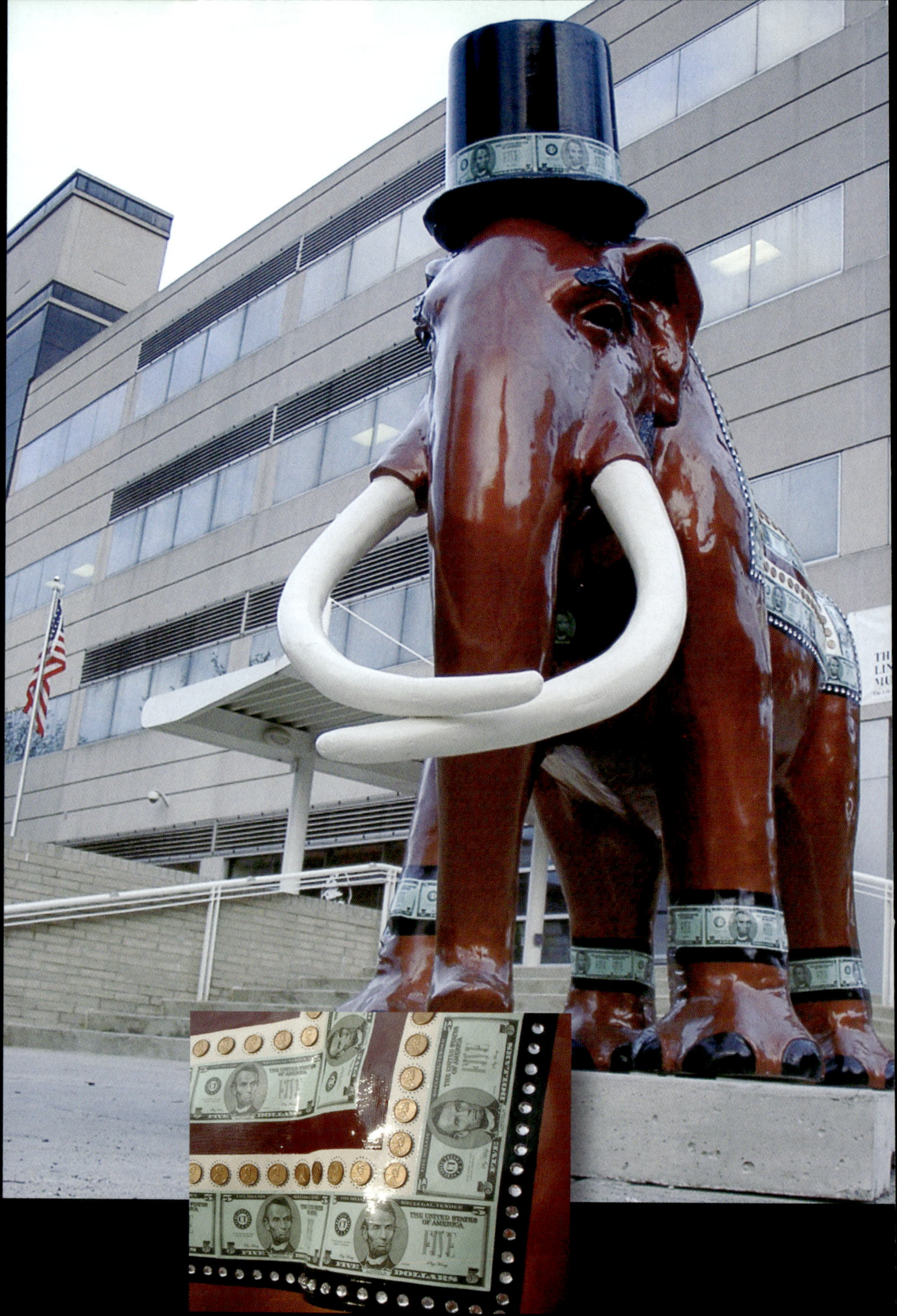

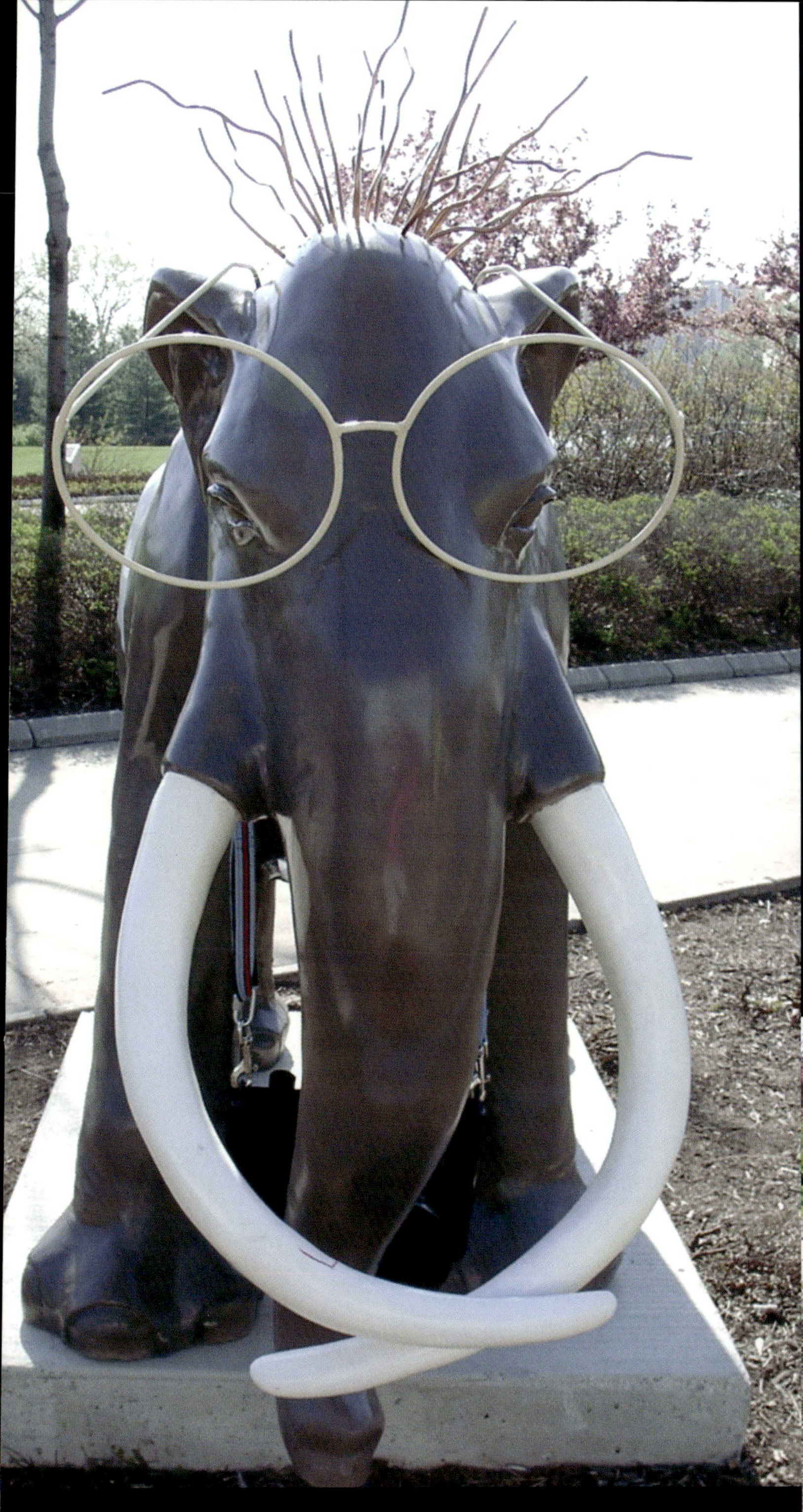

Artists: Jason Roemer,
Lodge Design

Jarrett Hagy, Lodge Design
(*pictured, right*)

Sponsor: Galliher Photography

By Jason Roemer

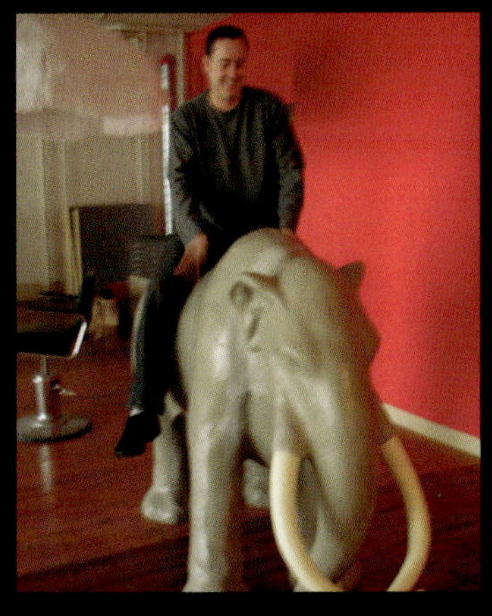

Tom Galliher, one of Fort Wayne's most beloved photographers, asked us to participate in this event. We decided to turn our mastodon into a likeness of Tom himself.

For help, we asked Greg Hull, professor at the Herron School of Art (Indianapolis), to fabricate a pair of James Joyce-style eyeglasses and an old Kodak camera. Greg and his art students delivered. With the addition of copper wire for a shock of wavy hair, we almost had it down.

There was just one thing missing—some comic relief. Thank goodness for tighty-whities!

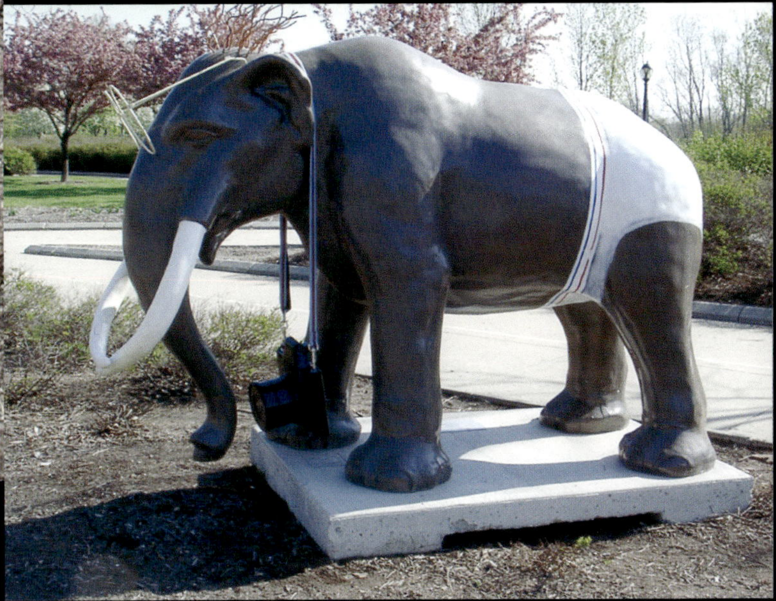

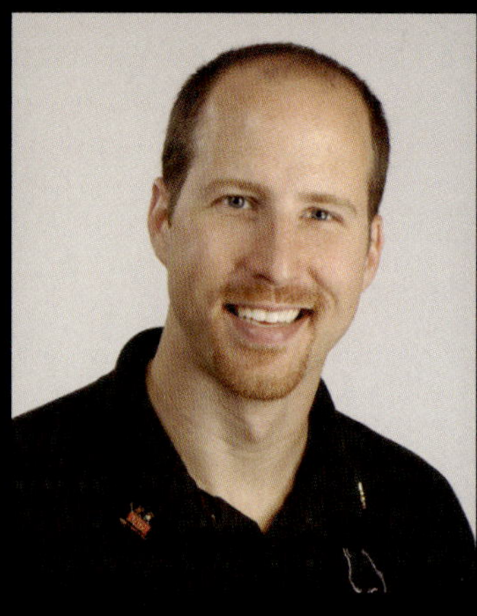

MASTODONNY HAWKS

Artist: Troy Ganser, director
The T.A.G. Art Company

Sponsor: Equity Investment Group

The trickiest part of building Mastodonny Hawks was designing the skateboard and the special base for mounting it because the skateboard had to be proportionate to Mastodonny and modified for mastodon use. Hawks is equipped with safety gear to ensure he doesn't scrape a knee—or a trunk. He also sports a designer outfit. It's handcrafted and made of fiberglass.

Don't expect any great tricks. This hawk is too heavy to fly.

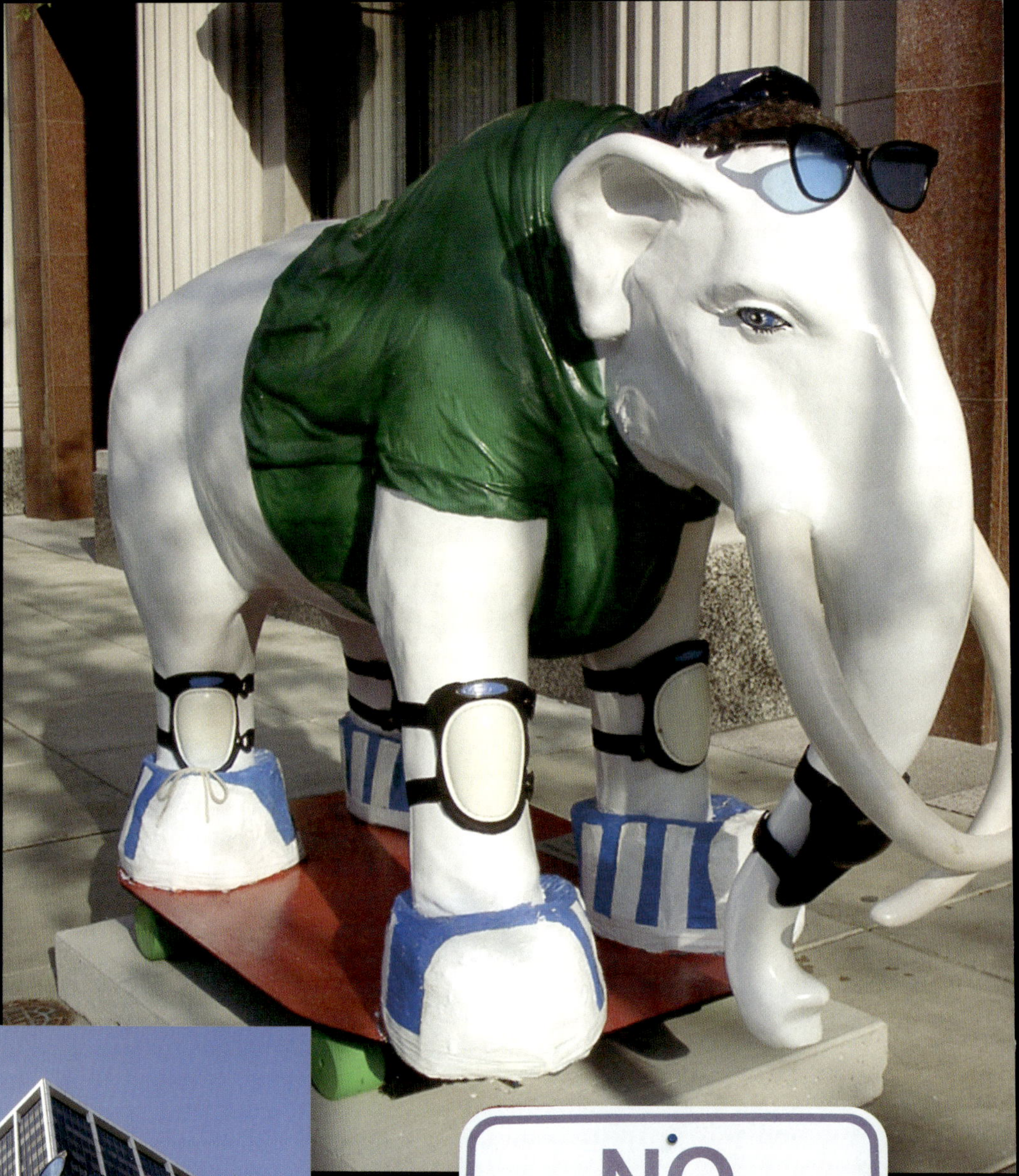

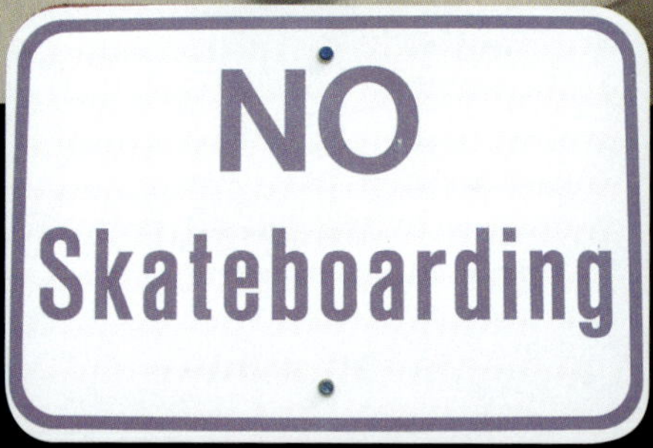

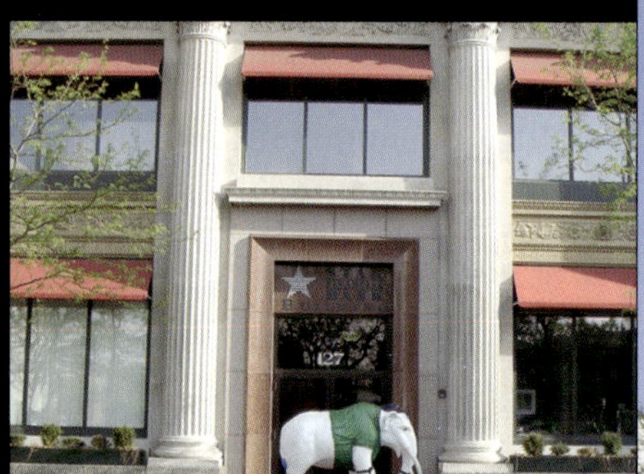

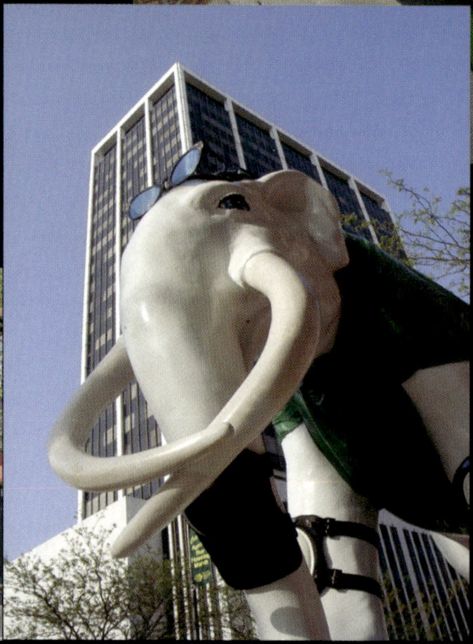

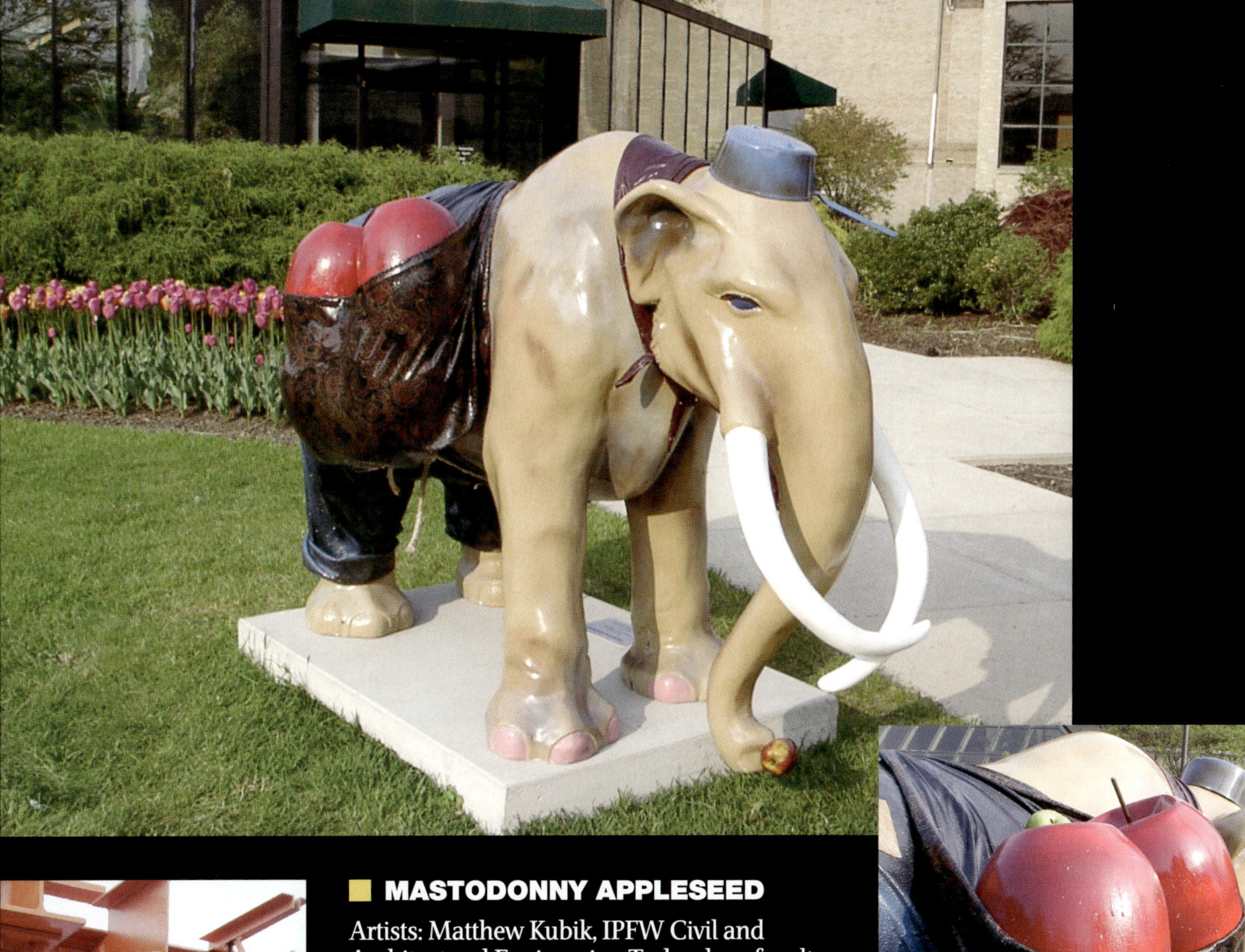

■ MASTODONNY APPLESEED

Artists: Matthew Kubik, IPFW Civil and Architectural Engineering Technology faculty (*pictured, left*); Sharon Kubik (*not pictured*)

Sponsor: City of Fort Wayne

By Sharon Kubik

When Matt saw the designs that two other IPFW department members had come up with, he thought we should follow their lead with a design high in artistic content. I said, "Let's just do it for fun. Let's do Johnny Appleseed!"

I was responsible for tailoring all of Donny's clothing, including his jeans with the 62-inch waist. We also wanted Donny to have a sack of big apples, but we couldn't find any really big craft ones anywhere—not even online.

Just two days after Easter, however, we happened on some huge plastic Easter eggs at a local craft store and thought they might work. I put them in the oven to soften and then reshaped the tops to look like apples. Yep, those apples in Donny's knapsack are baked.

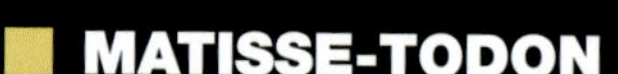

■ MATISSE-TODON

Artists: Concordia Lutheran Grade School

Angie Owen, Concordia art instructor

Sponsor: Phillips Financial Services

By Angie Owen

About 400 students at Concordia Lutheran School (grades kindergarten through 8) created Matisse-todon. First, they learned about Henri Matisse in art class. They also learned a song about him in music class.

Using the gloves and masks donated by parents, everybody helped with the sanding. The seventh graders painted on the primer and the eighth graders, who had researched Matisse's paintings, drew the designs on our mastodon.

Then something horrible happened! Matisse-todon was stolen! The fifth graders conducted an investigation to find the culprits. We learned that our cooks had stolen him in hopes of making minced mastodon meat pie for our school lunches!

Safely returned to us, Matisse-todon was ready for painting. We used nine rolls of painter's tape and lots of bright colors. Everyone got a chance to paint. In fact, you can ask any of us, and we'll point out to you the section we painted.

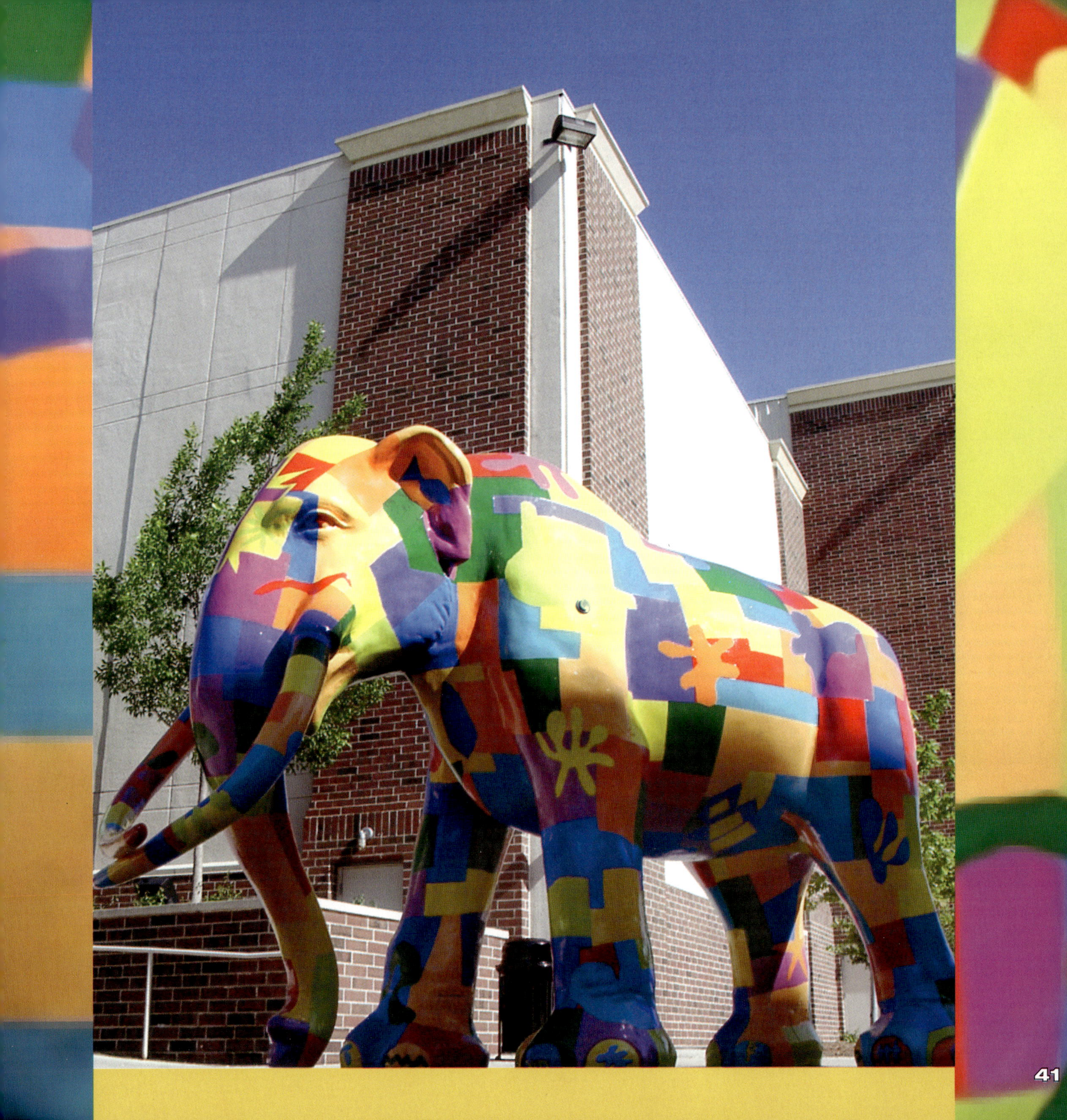

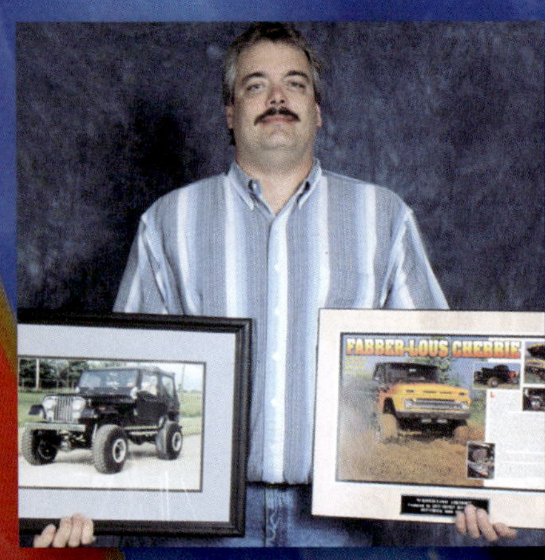

MASTODON JOE

Artist: Bill Pickelheimer, owner of Auto Art

Sponsor: Saint Joseph United Methodist Church

Pastor Sid Gauby at Saint Joe Methodist Church asked me to work on the mastodon project. His was the only church to sponsor one, and I was honored to be chosen.

Janet Corah, a church member, came up with the concept of Mastodon Joe and the Coat of Many Colors. I designed a fiberglass robe to fit Joe. Then I sprayed the coat with multiple colors and hand pinstriped it in gold.

The outpouring of support during Joe's progress was overwhelming. The greatest thing to me was bringing the dreams of the whole church to life.

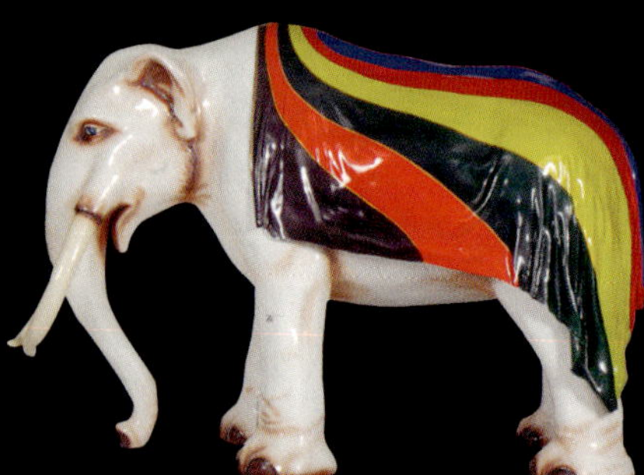

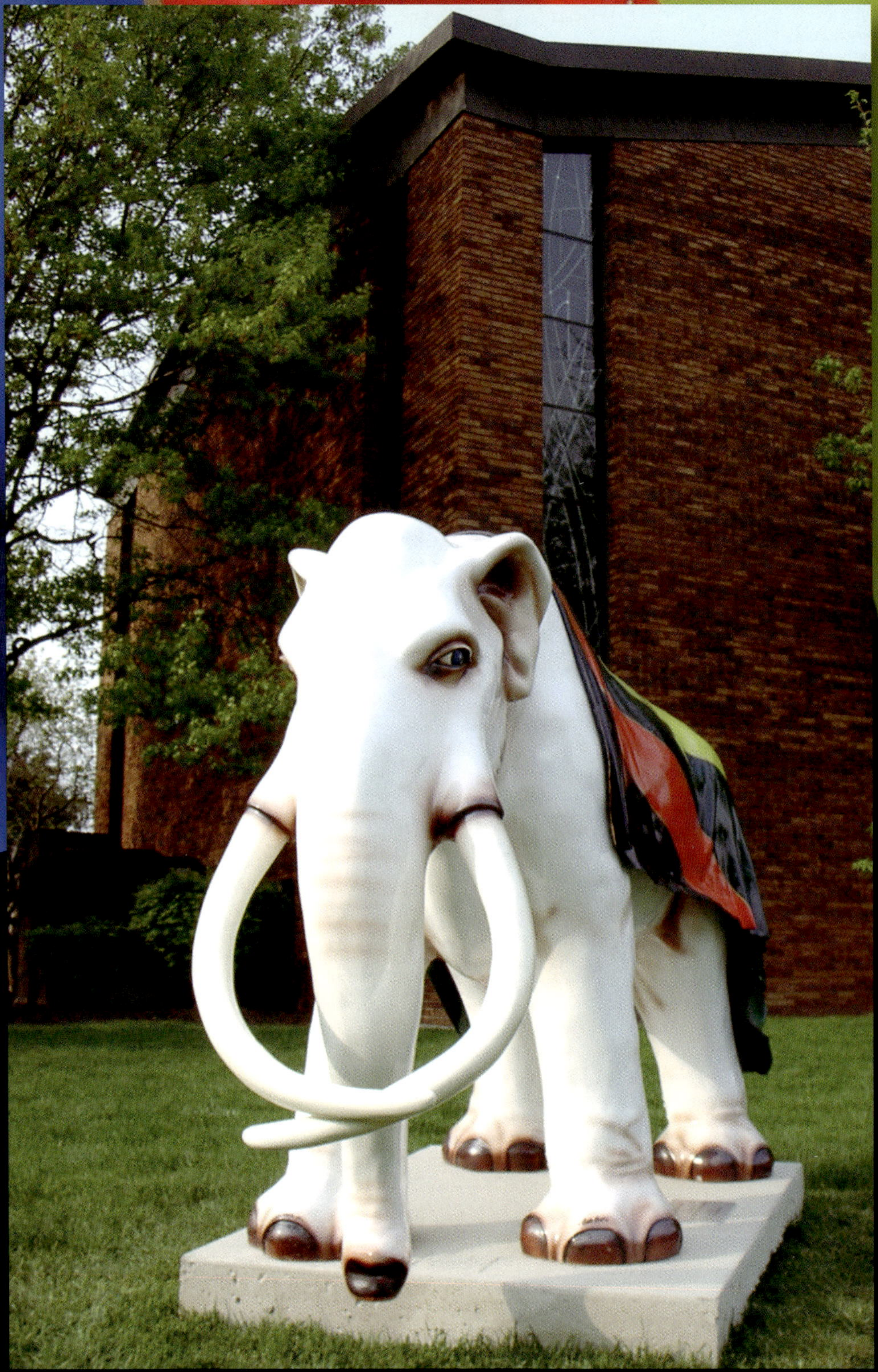

■ DON D. TOURIST

Artist: Sue Perl, fine artist, graphic artist

Sponsor: Convention and Visitors Bureau

The hat Don D. Tourist wears belonged to my husband's uncle. When the sponsor requested a tourist mastodon, I pictured him as a mismatched wanderer with plaid shorts, flowered shirt, black socks, and sandals.

I figured he needed a hat of some kind and remembered the old hat my husband "inherited" from his uncle. It fit perfectly on Don D.'s head. Voila!

Don D. says, "Welcome to Fort Wayne," and "Don't forget the sunscreen!"

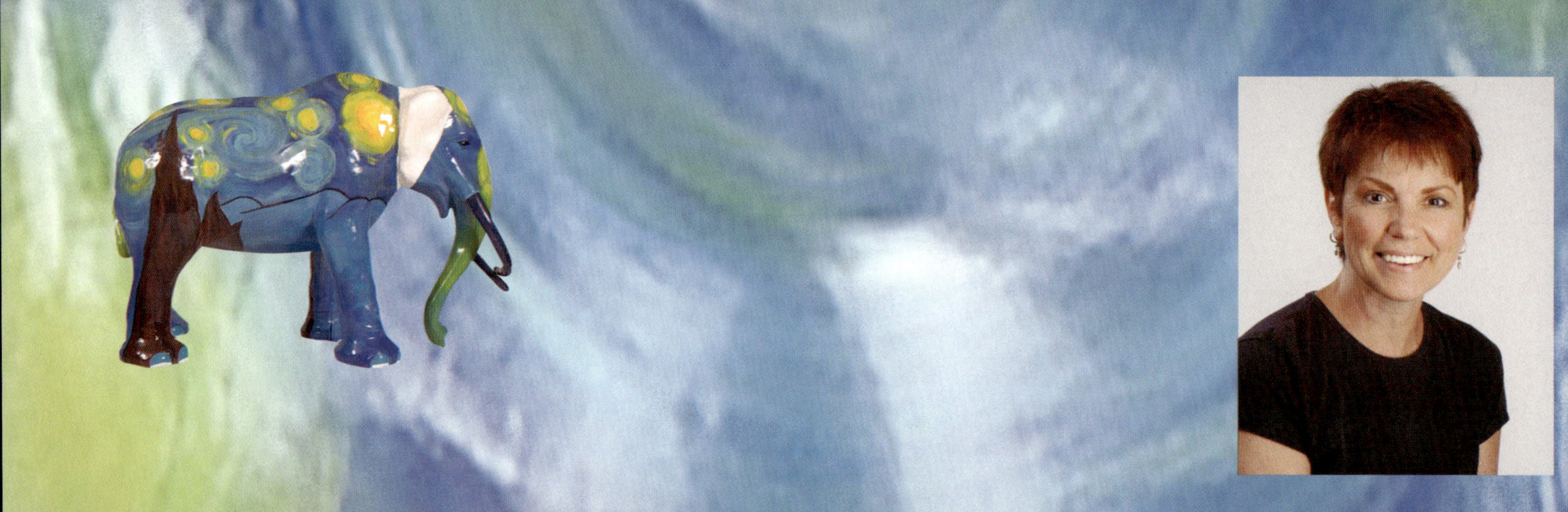

■ VINCENT VAN MASTODON

Artist: Teri Marquart, professional artist

Sponsor: Briljent LLC

My chosen medium is a cross between decorative arts and fine crafts. Frequently termed functional art, it is full of bold colors, patterns, textures, and shapes. I've painted everything from chairs to floor cloths, from lamps to boxes, from tables to ceilings, and now even a mastodon.

Thrilled to be part of the mastodon project, I am even more pleased that it has been so well received by the community.

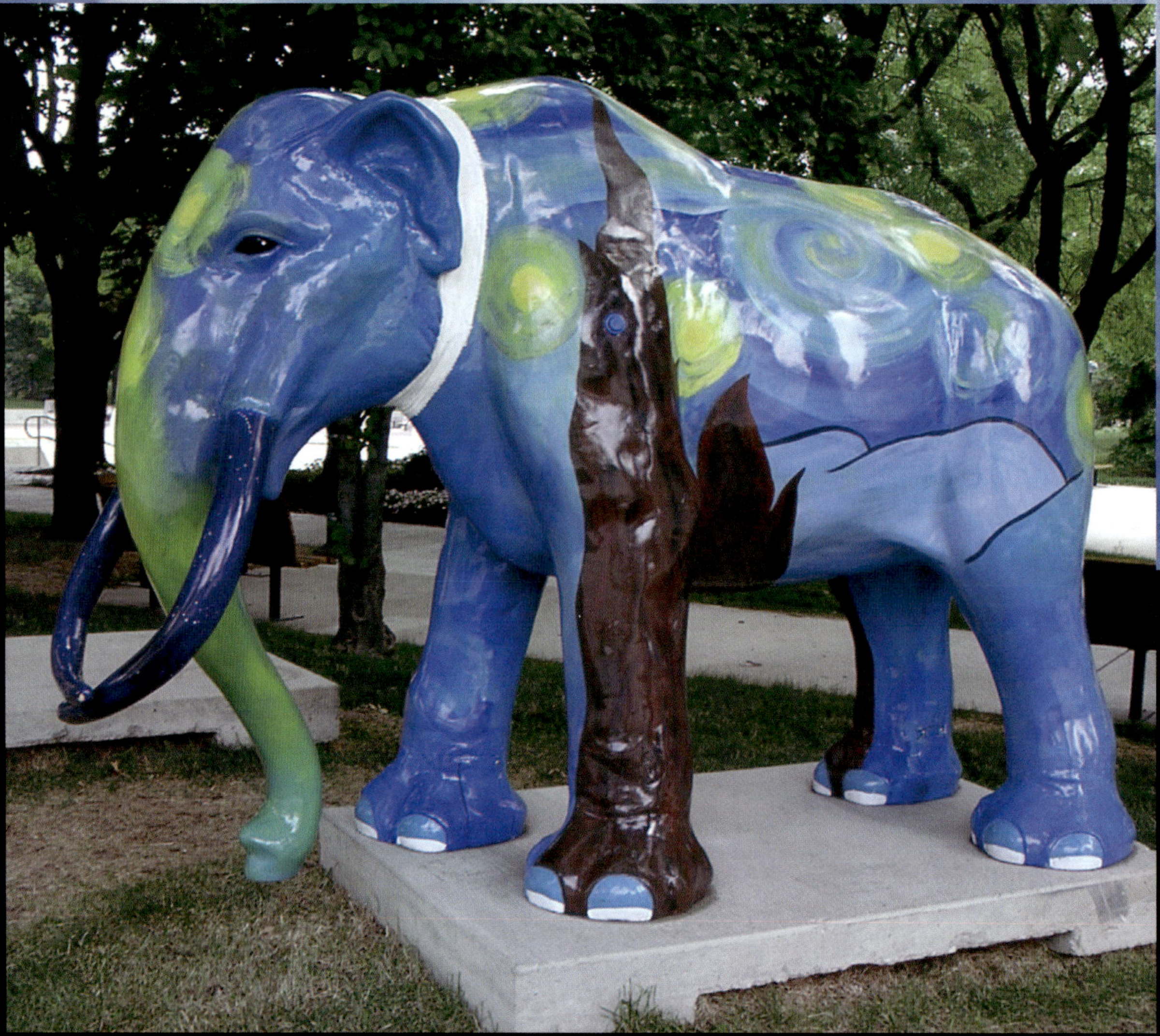

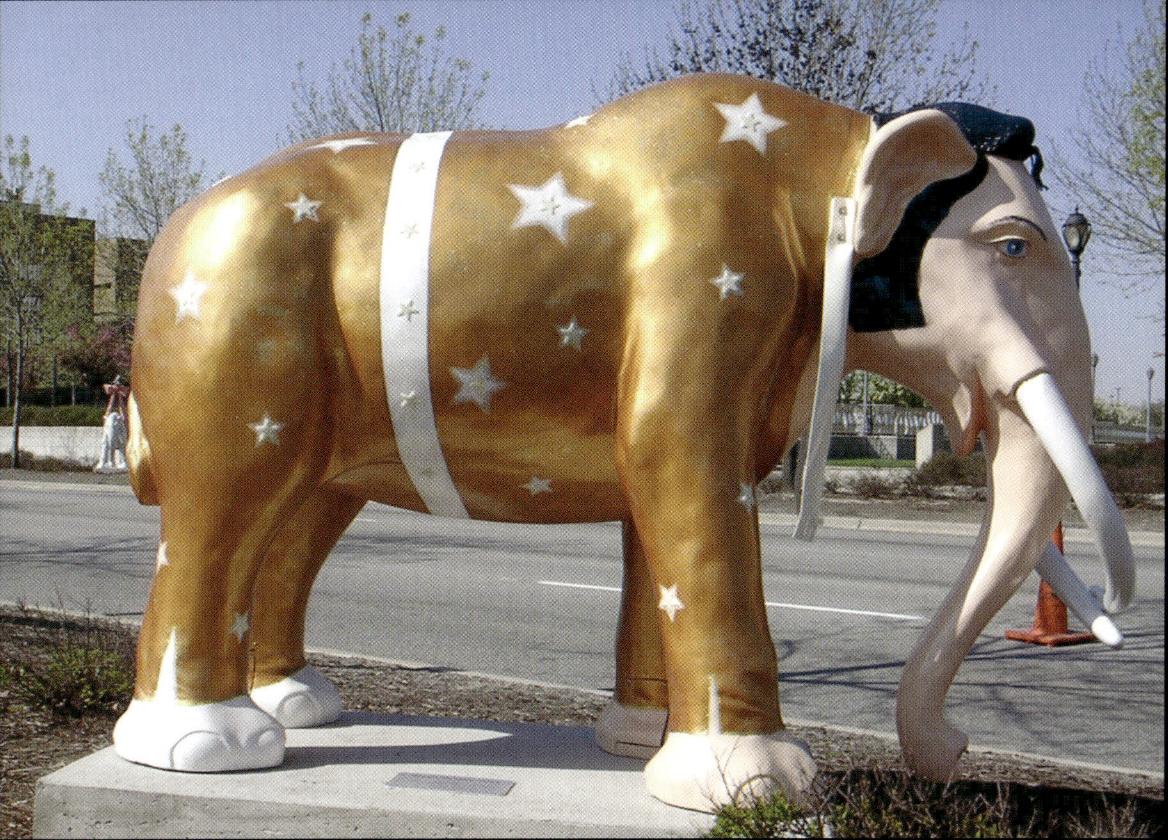

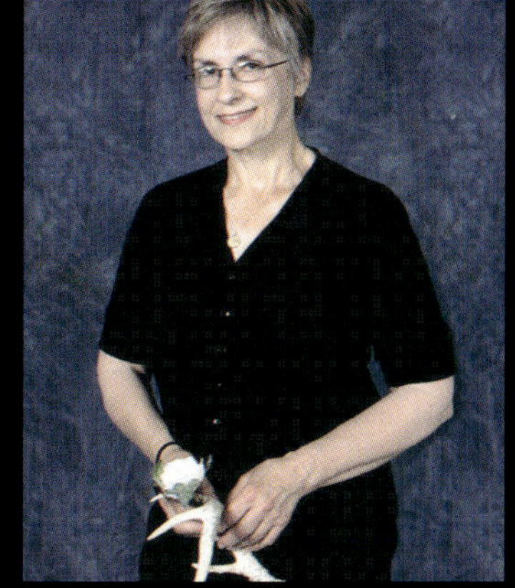

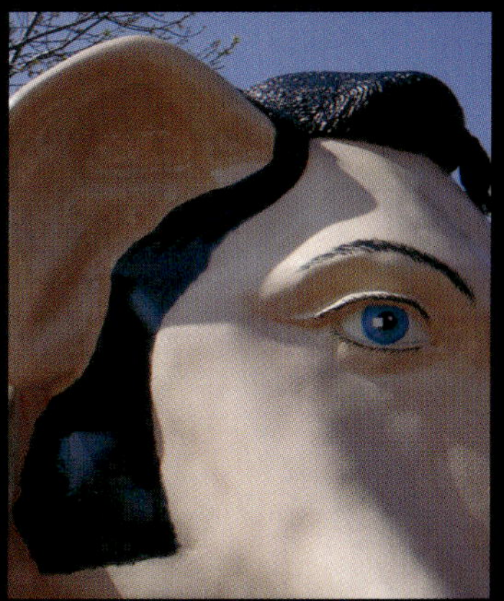

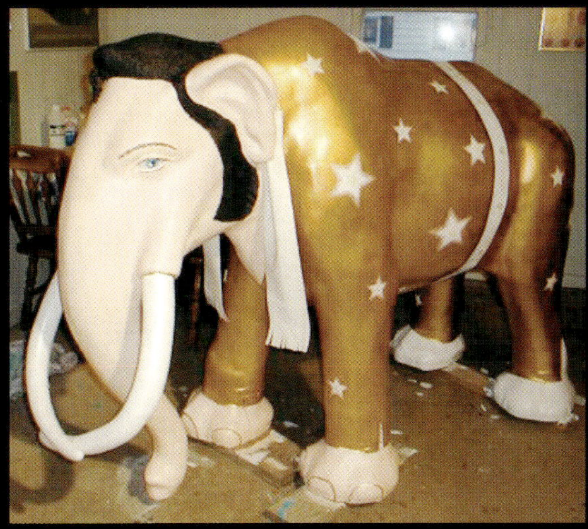

■ BIGGA HUNKA LOVE

Artist: Sue Perl, fine artist, graphic artist

Sponsor: Sweetwater Sound Inc.

When I read the request for artists to participate in Mastodons on Parade, the first thing I thought of was Elvis. Yes, I am an Elvis Presley fan. I'm not a "Visit-Graceland-Annually" fan but enough of one to have some old 45s still in their dust jackets that I used for inspiration.

Look at Elvis' pompadour. It's self-hardening clay with strands of yarn painted black. The stars on his metallic gold jumpsuit glow at night.

After finishing Elvis and another mastodon, I still think this project is a great way to get Fort Wayne to look at art and a way to bring people downtown.

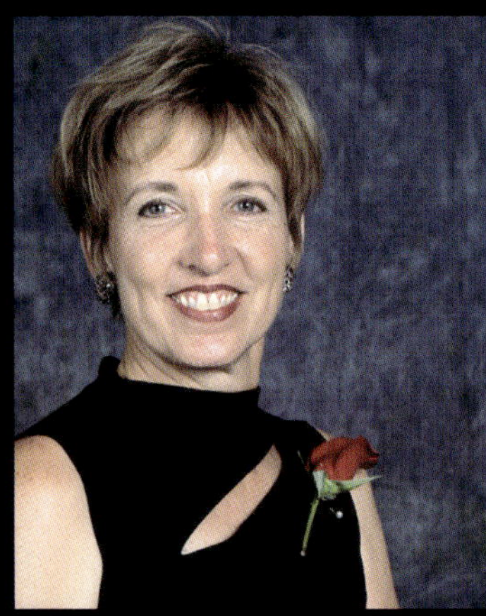

■ ROSE

Artist: Gwen Gutwein, professional artist

Sponsor: *Health Cares Magazine*

Rose reflects a woman in today's world. She totes a purse with a cell phone on her shoulder. She has an iPod strapped to her gold trunk. Her toenails are freshly polished!

The roses covering her trunk represent the beauty, fragility, and determination of women. Puzzle shapes on her body represent the aspects of work, home, and family that women fit together in daily life.

Silhouettes depicting women involved in meditation, yoga, and jogging show other aspects of a woman's life. The butterflies pulling a pink fabric over her body symbolize both beauty and diversity.

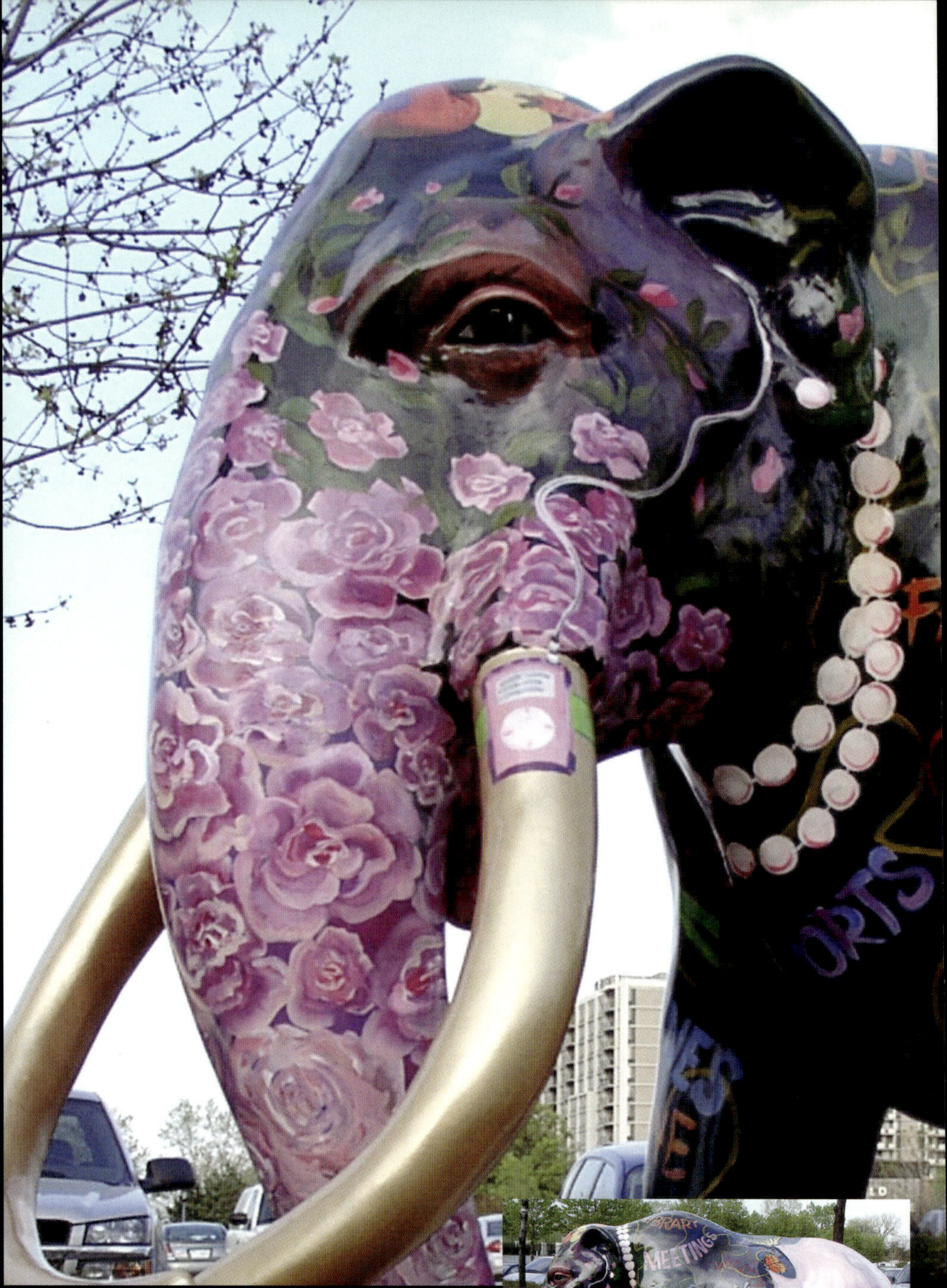

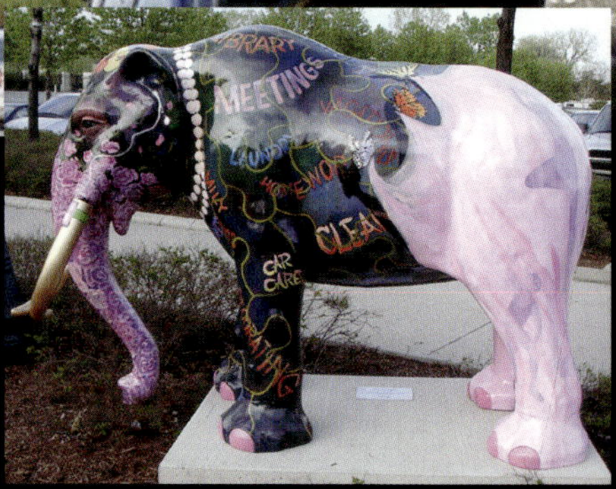

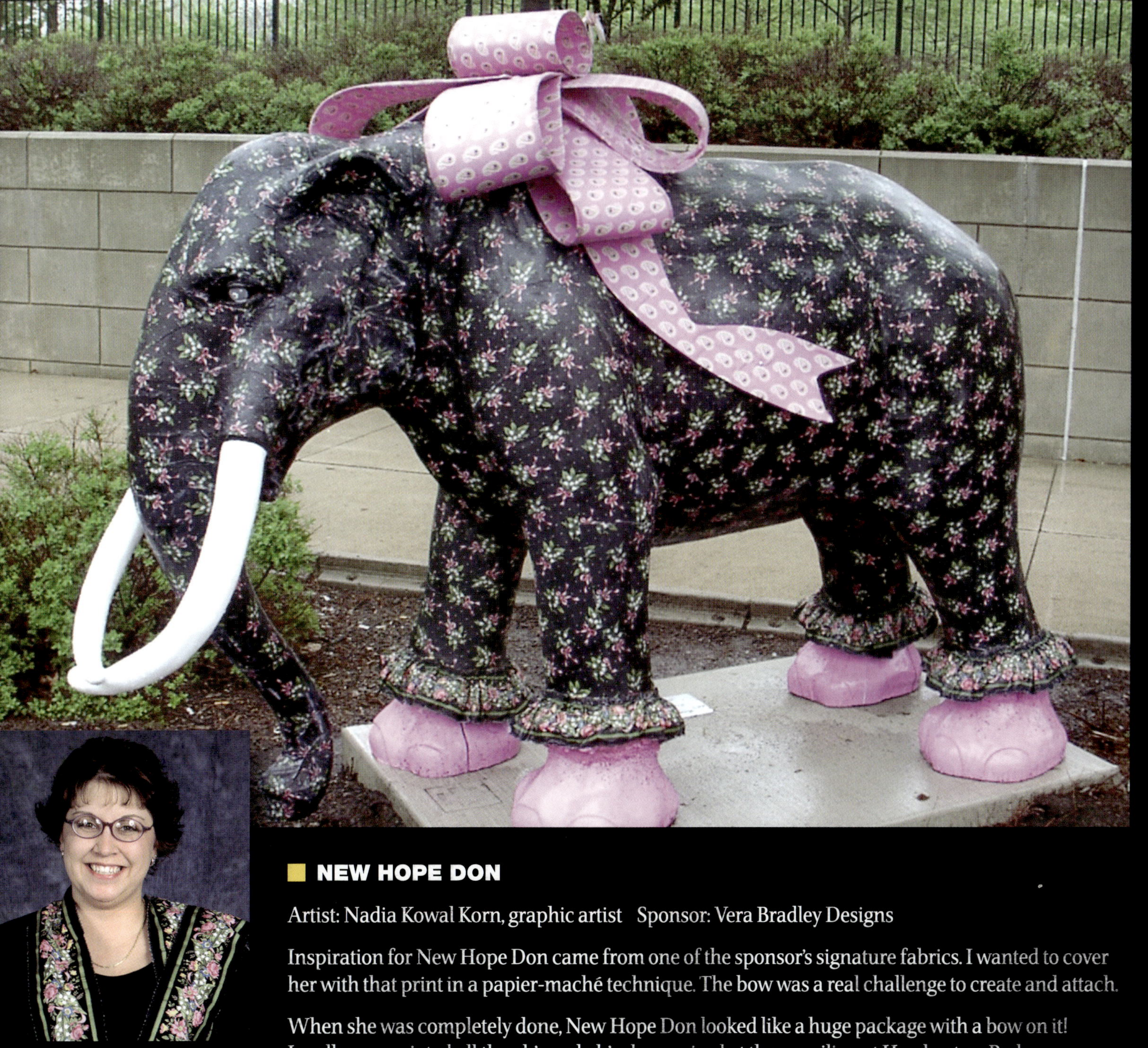

NEW HOPE DON

Artist: Nadia Kowal Korn, graphic artist   Sponsor: Vera Bradley Designs

Inspiration for New Hope Don came from one of the sponsor's signature fabrics. I wanted to cover her with that print in a papier-maché technique. The bow was a real challenge to create and attach.

When she was completely done, New Hope Don looked like a huge package with a bow on it! I really appreciated all the oh's and ah's she received at the unveiling at Headwaters Park.

I am thankful to IPFW for choosing such a grand event for its 40th birthday celebration and to the community for allowing us to be so expressive.

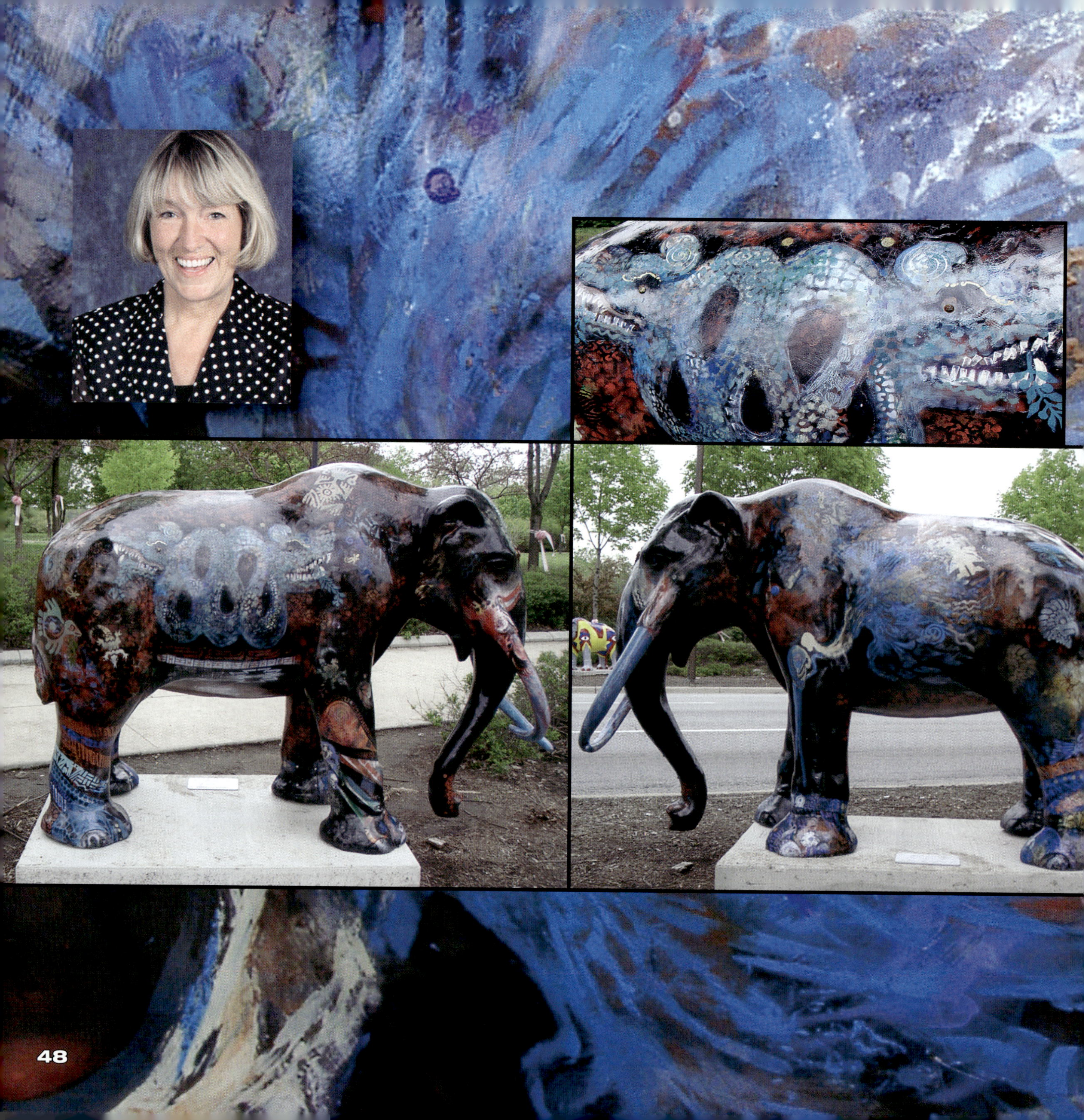

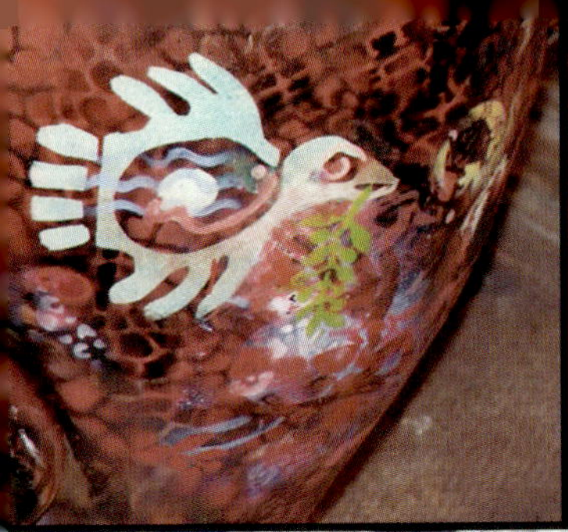

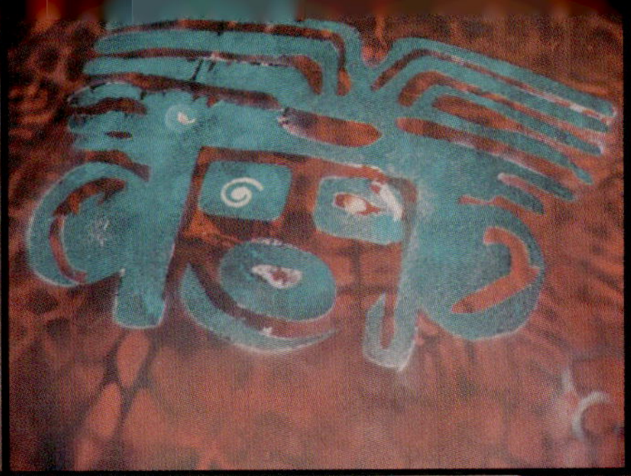

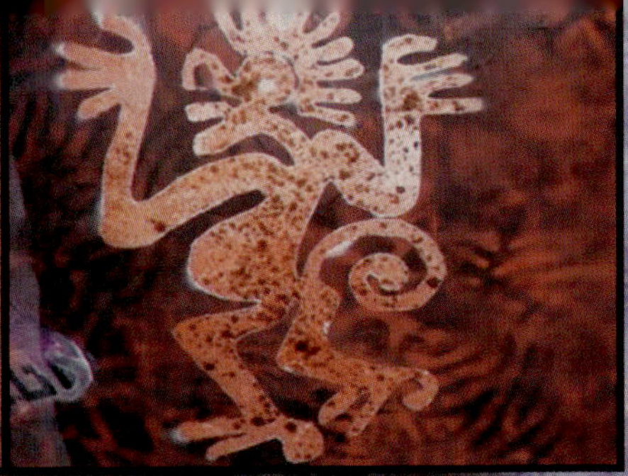

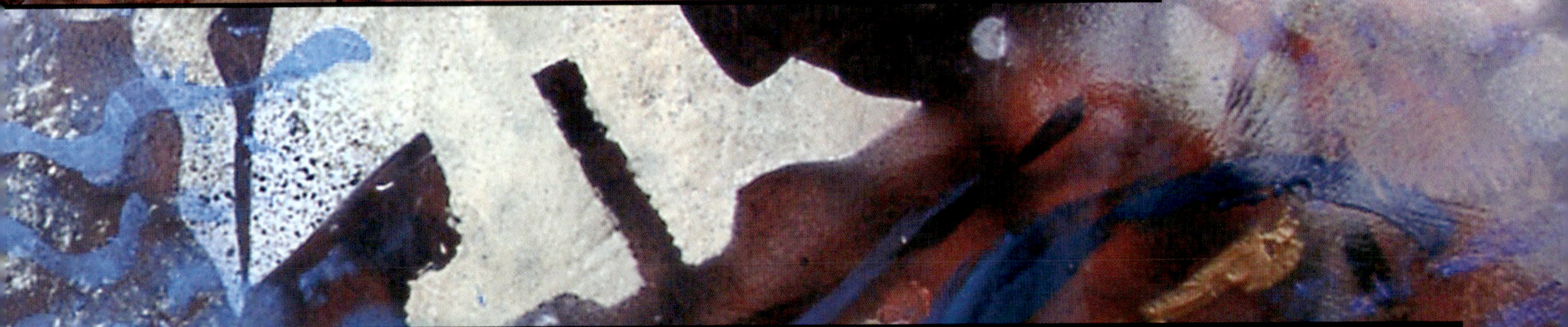

■ MASTER-DON-PABLO

Artist: Jody Hemphill Smith, professional artist, Castle Gallery

Sponsor: Brenda Fishbaugh, former student of the late Professor Paul Provost

The real-life namesake of my mastodon is Paul Provost, an IPFW professor and anthropologist who conducted extensive field work with the Shipibo people in the Peruvian Amazon, the Tibetans in exile in northern India, the Aborigines of the Australian Outback, and the Nahua people in Mexico.

When Master-Don-Pablo arrived at Castle Gallery, my husband, Mark, and I primed him with black paint, dressed him in a black beret and large, red rose, and put him outside the gallery for the Fort Wayne Museum of Art Trolley Tour. With his long trunk, guests thought he signified that the gallery was a Republican institution. Not so. He's strictly independent.

By the time Christmas rolled around, Don-Pablo looked adorable with his candy cane tusks, Santa hat, and necklace of lights. Even so, he yearned to become what he always knew would be his destiny—a multicultural symbol of world harmony.

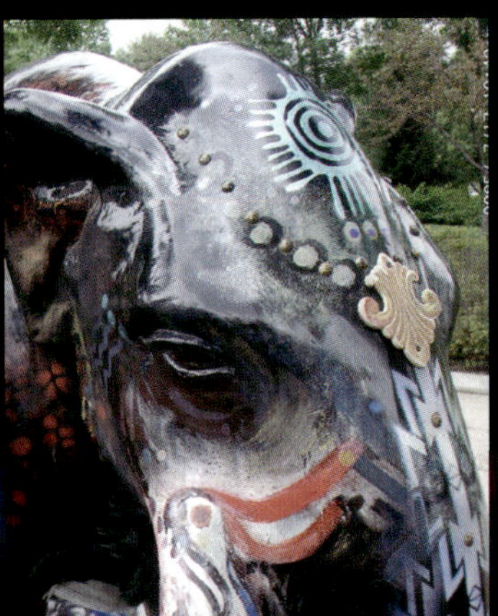

I incorporated images and symbols from each of these cultures into a multilayered color treatment. The variety of images demonstrates how many different world views can peacefully coexist.

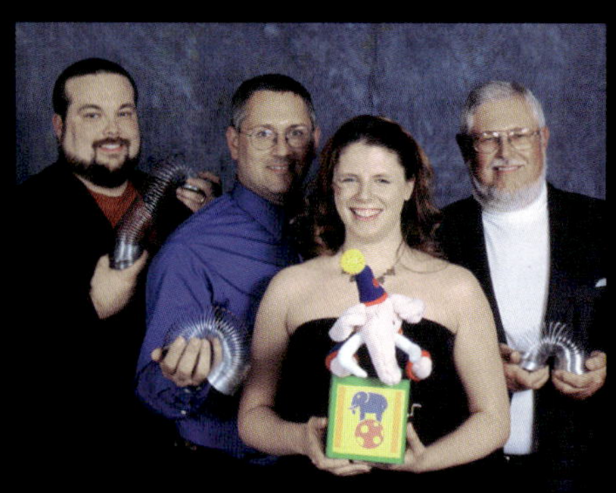

Artist: Larry Davis, graphic artist
(*pictured far left with family members*)

Sponsors: The Zacher Company and
Dupont OBGYN

As a former prop master for Disney on
Ice, I've worked with all sorts of artistic
materials. I've never had the chance,
though, to create a prop from design
to finished piece.

For a graphic artist, the artwork came
easy, but the fabrication was another story.
Luckily I had a retired tool & die maker
(pictured far right: Richard Gick, my father-
in-law) and his nephew Robert Gick (an
applications engineer, pictured second from
left). And I had my own pièce de résistance
who is my wife and the greatest artist
I know, Tammy Davis.

We all questioned the feasibility of
getting Dona done on time, but we never
questioned if she would work. At the big
unveiling in Headwaters Park, she met the
mayor and about 10,000 people. She even
played "Pop Goes the Weasel" when people
turned her crank.

Dona, I am in awe of you.

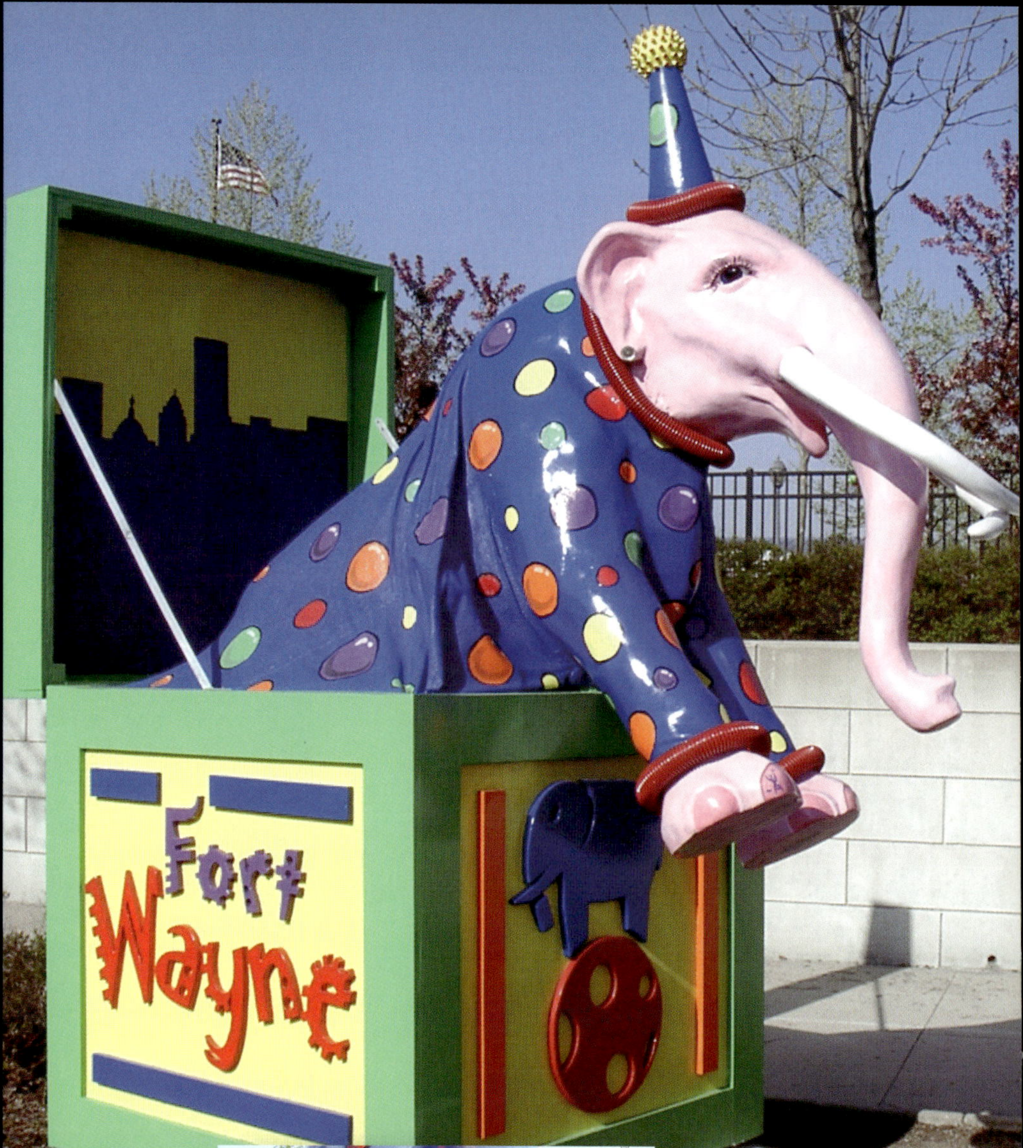

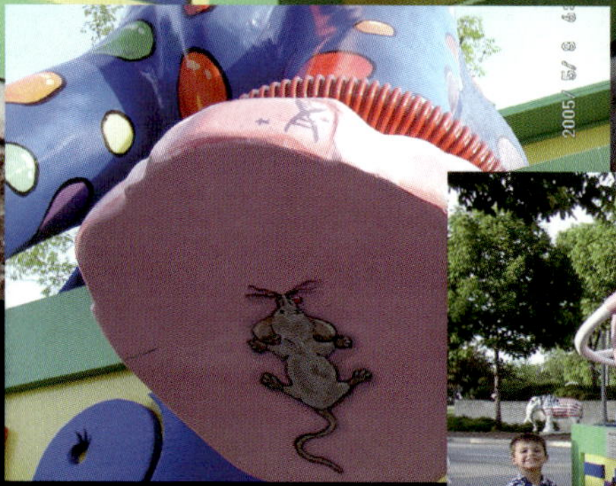

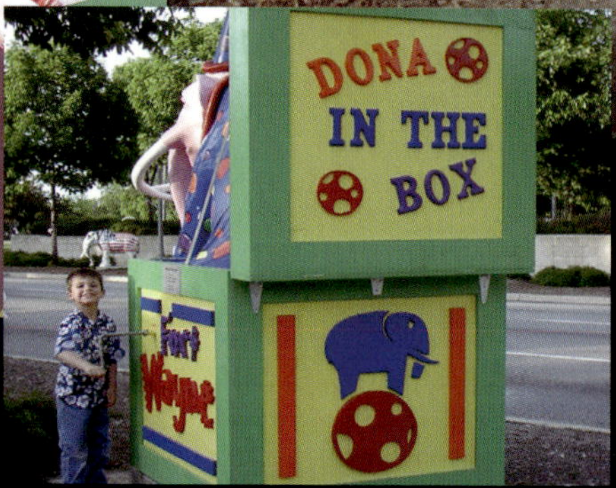

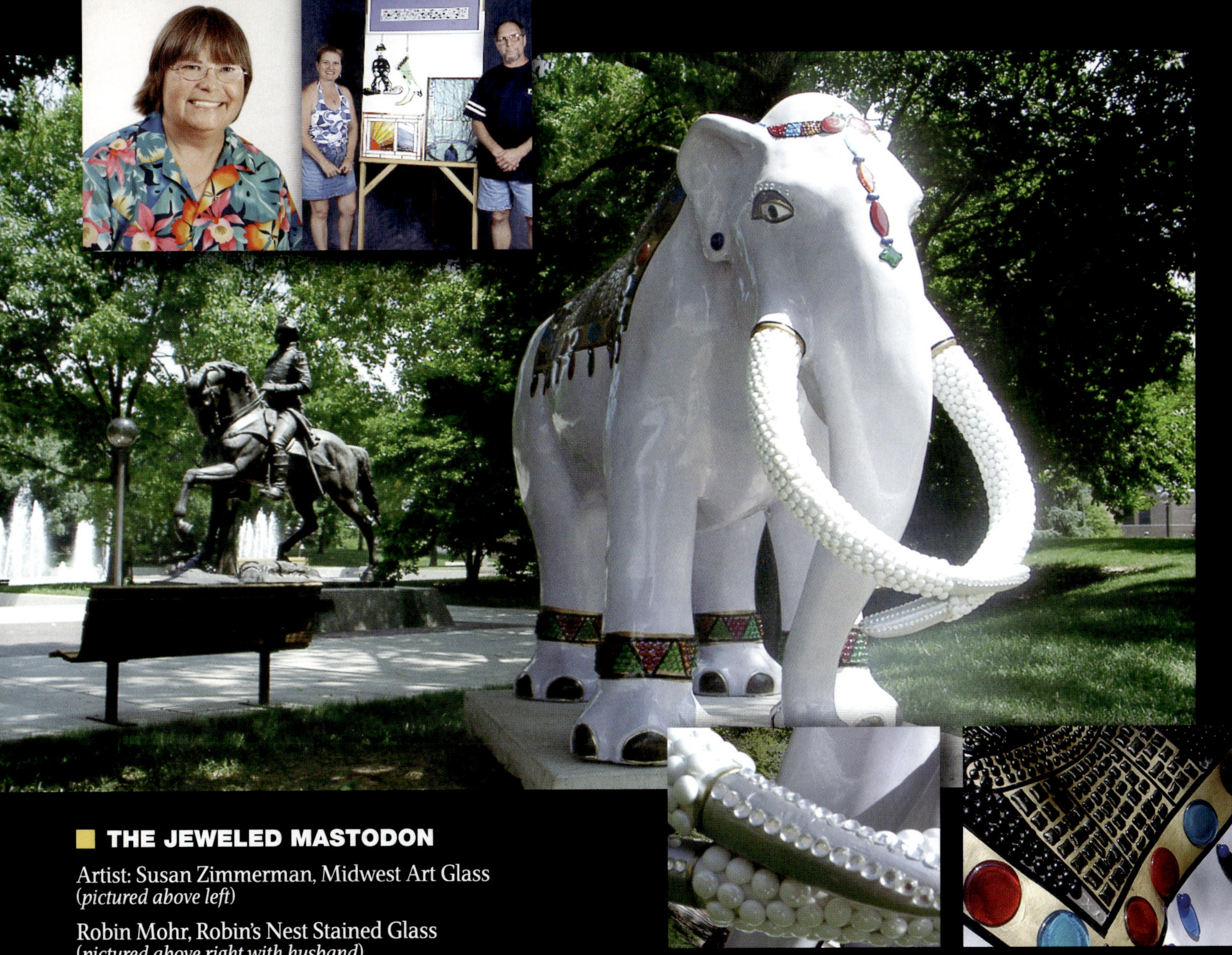

◼ THE JEWELED MASTODON

Artist: Susan Zimmerman, Midwest Art Glass
(*pictured above left*)

Robin Mohr, Robin's Nest Stained Glass
(*pictured above right with husband*)

Sponsor: Will Jewelers

By Robin Mohr

When I first heard of the mastodons, I thought, "Wow, if I weren't so busy, I'd love to do a jeweled don." Weeks passed. I just couldn't get him out of my head. Too busy or not, I just needed to bring him to life.

Once we established the design, Susan and I set about making the glass jewels. We cut the glass, ground the edges, and placed double layers of each jewel in the kiln. It took a full firing just for the larger pieces.

Then we placed each piece on our don by hand. We did not think our fingertips could be so incredibly bruised as we glued, positioned, and then pressed really hard to make sure the bond was strong.

I truly miss greeting him every day but can honestly say I am glad he is done.

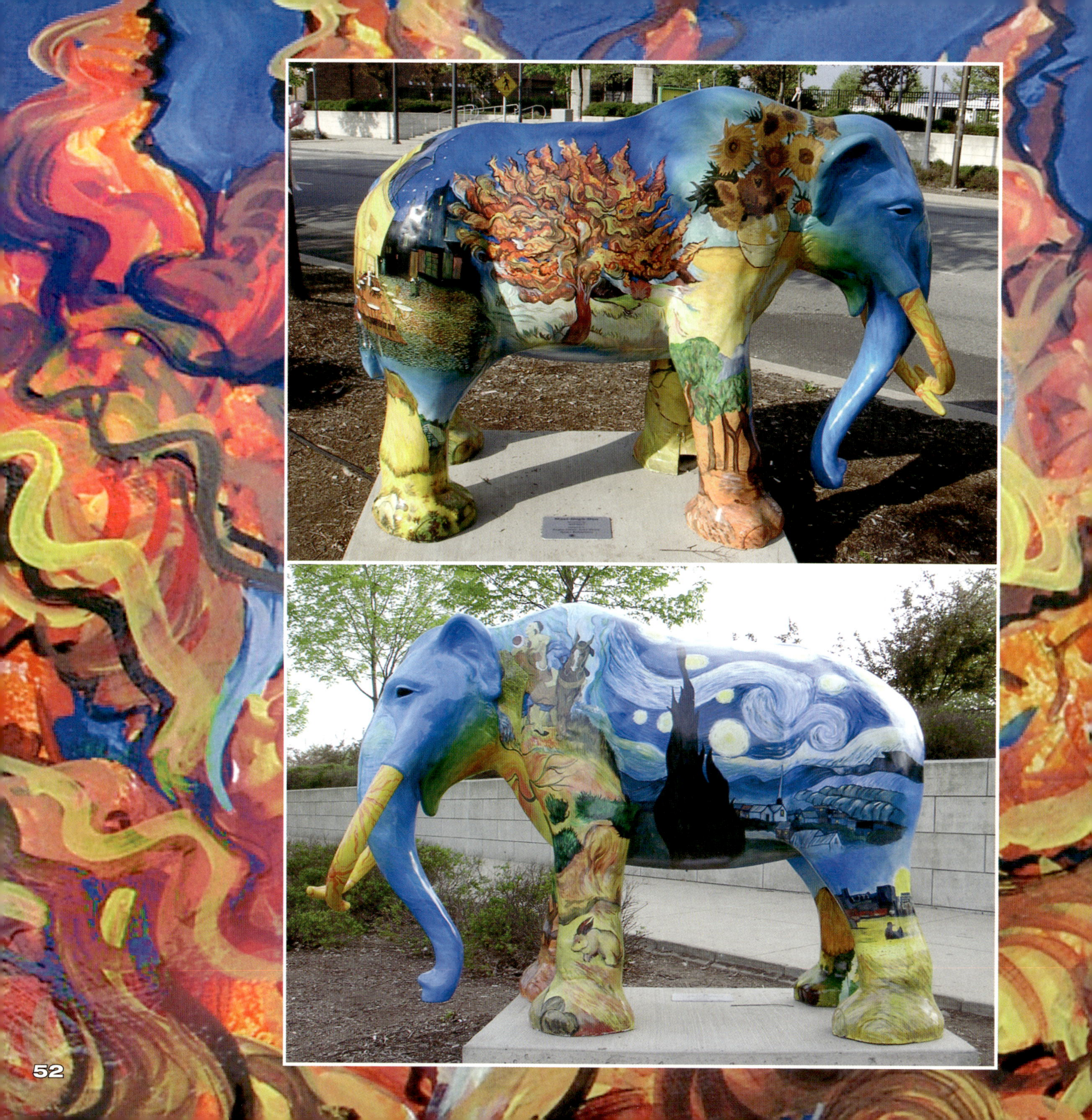

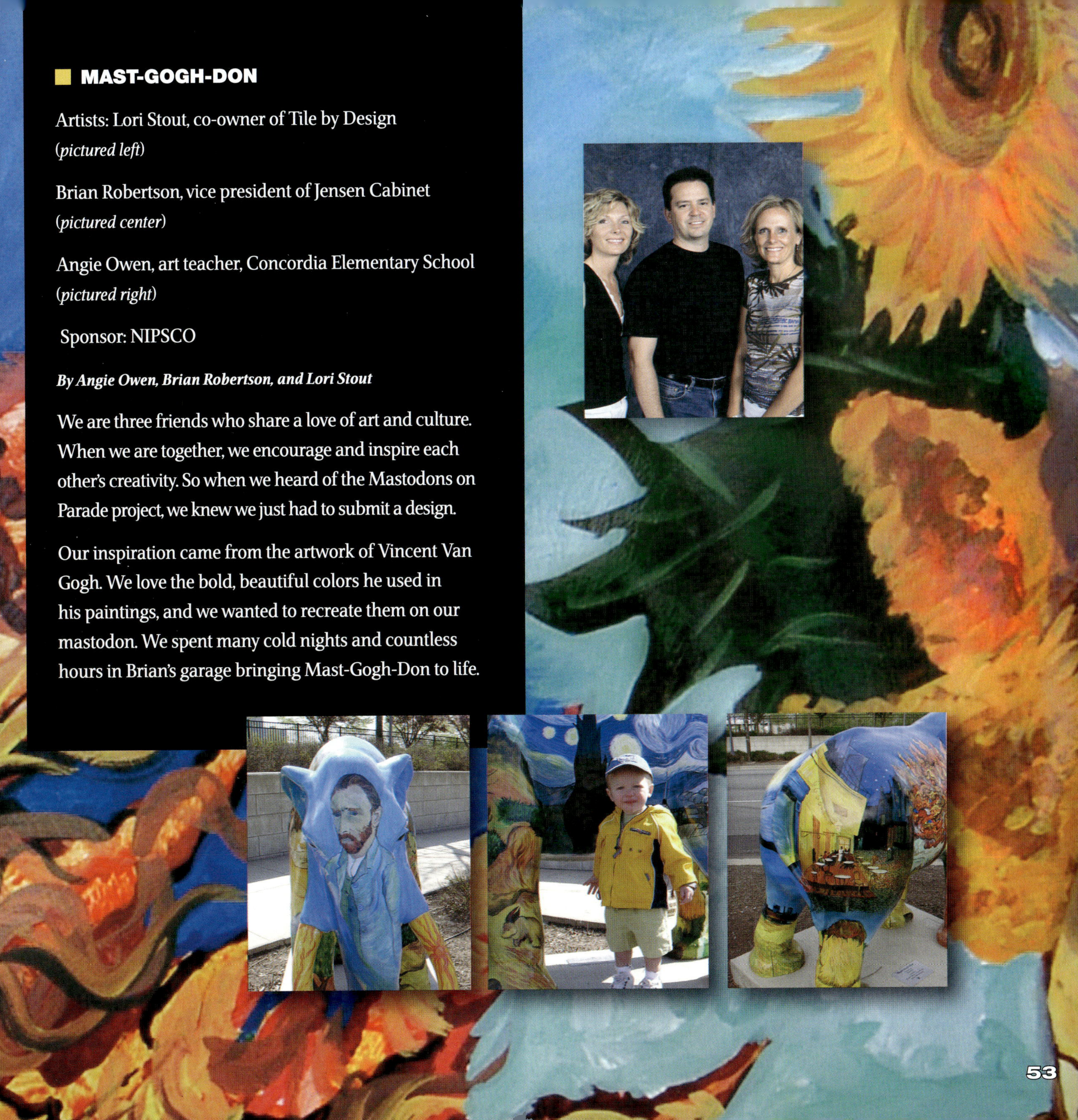

■ MAST-GOGH-DON

Artists: Lori Stout, co-owner of Tile by Design
(*pictured left*)

Brian Robertson, vice president of Jensen Cabinet
(*pictured center*)

Angie Owen, art teacher, Concordia Elementary School
(*pictured right*)

 Sponsor: NIPSCO

By Angie Owen, Brian Robertson, and Lori Stout

We are three friends who share a love of art and culture. When we are together, we encourage and inspire each other's creativity. So when we heard of the Mastodons on Parade project, we knew we just had to submit a design.

Our inspiration came from the artwork of Vincent Van Gogh. We love the bold, beautiful colors he used in his paintings, and we wanted to recreate them on our mastodon. We spent many cold nights and countless hours in Brian's garage bringing Mast-Gogh-Don to life.

Artist: Rhonda Bennett

Sponsor: Jefferson Pointe Shopping Center

The final design is a combination of mixed media including a collage of photos, word art, fabric, glass beads, and acrylics. Each picture/photo was copied to special paper, hand trimmed, and carefully arranged to make a statement within the style theme. The quilt was handmade by local quilter Jenny Plassman and then hand trimmed with beading. The final result is collage of style with an Indian-inspired flair.

The Don of Style took over 100 hours (we stopped counting after that) to complete. The final design was a collaborative effort with special thanks to the following people for their donations and assistance: Naked Clay Café staff; David, Taylor, Zach, and Jacob Bennett; Darla Eigenschink; Molly Jordan; Glass Link; Klopfenstein Furniture; copy crew at Office Depot Northcrest; and Jefferson Pointe maintenance staff.

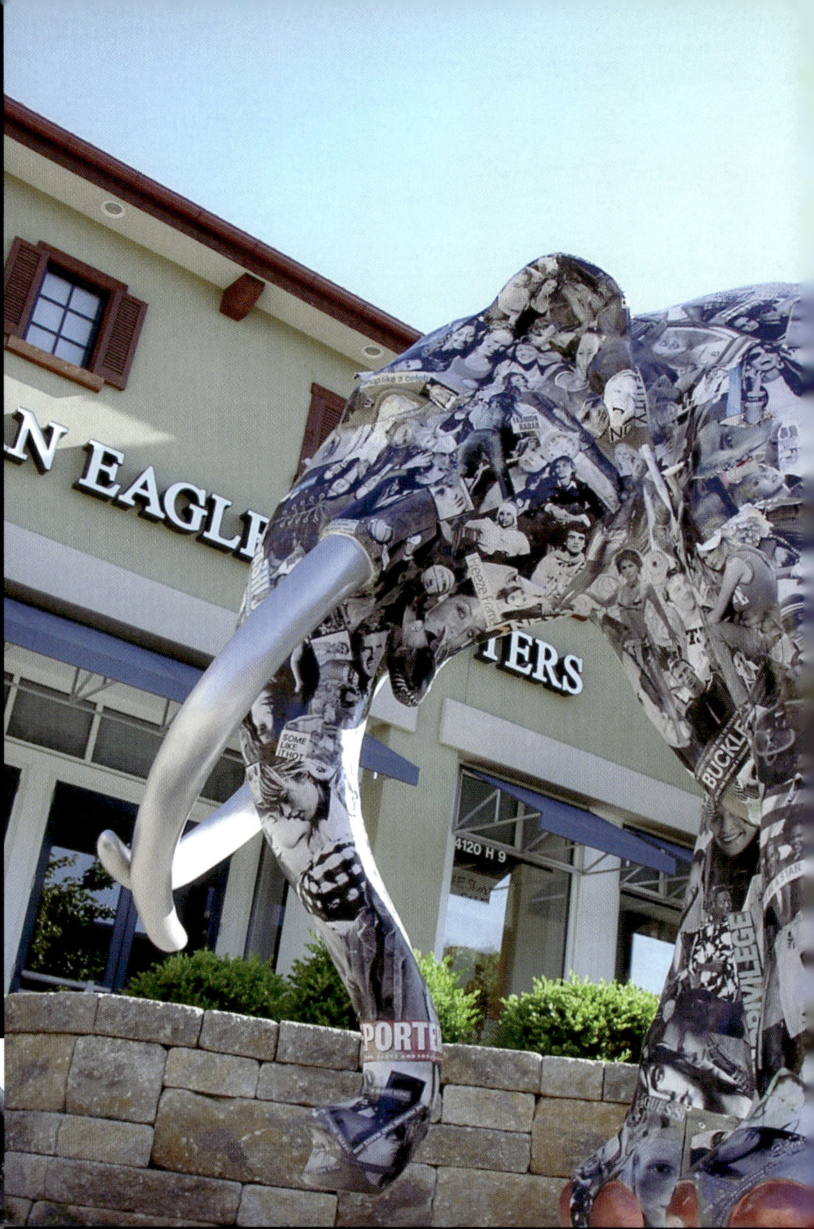

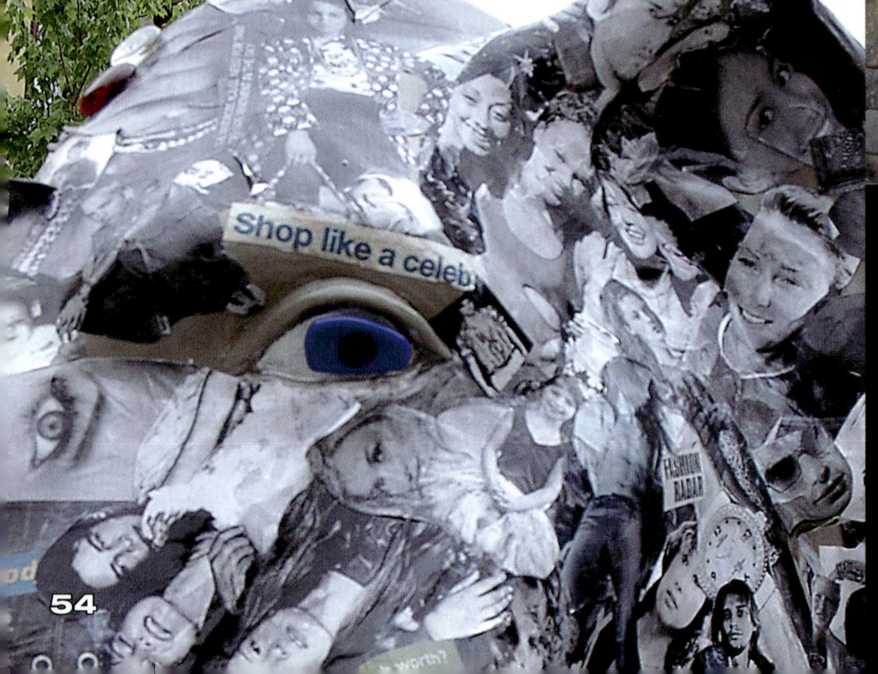

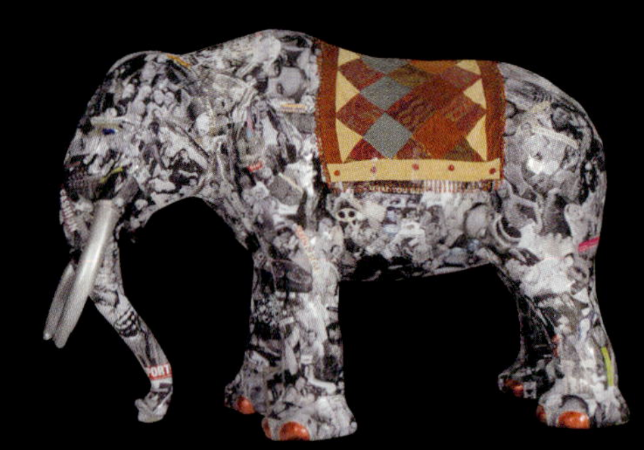

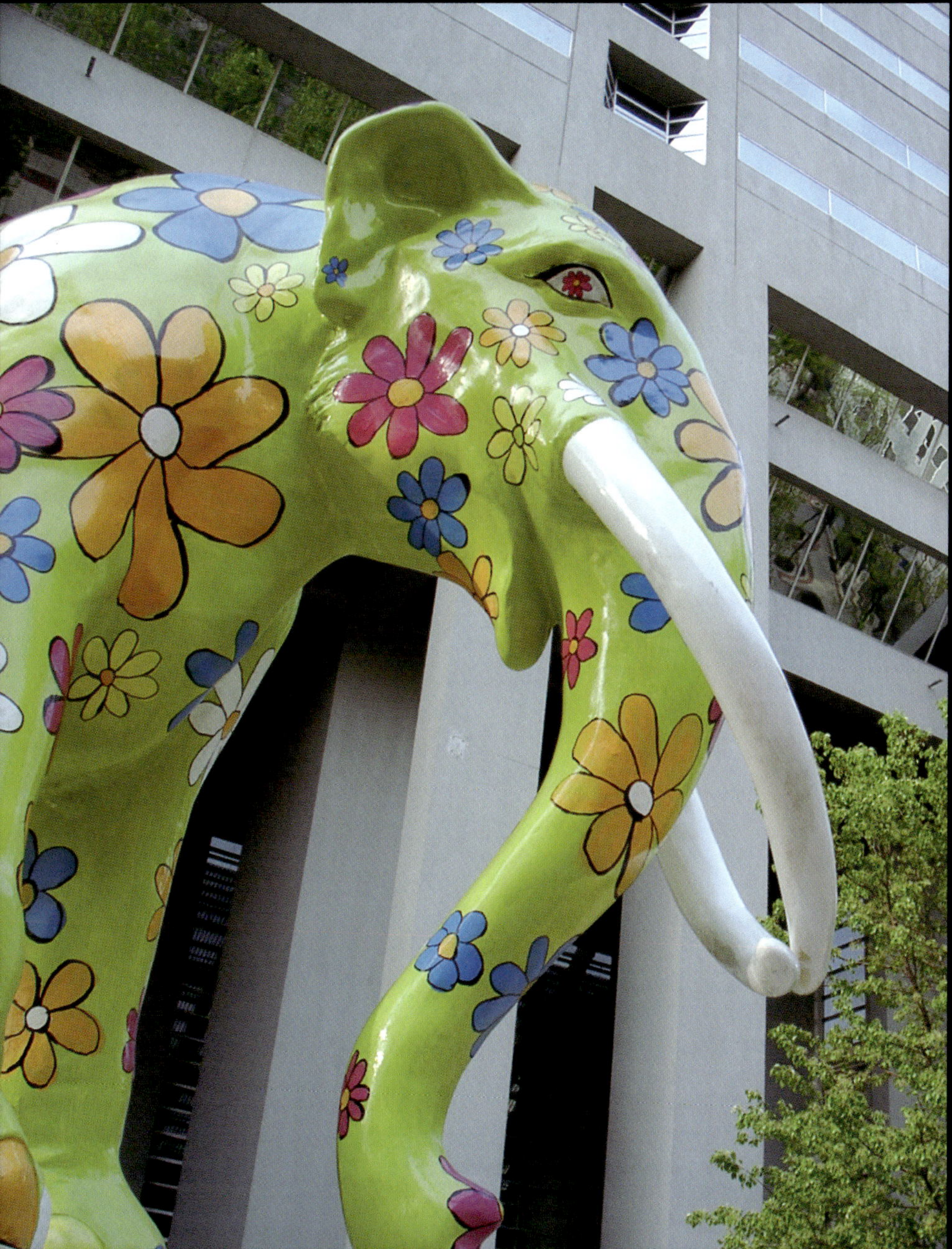

Make everyone smile—that was the inspiration for my mastodon. I wanted my design to be simple but also vibrant. I knew I needed loud colors.

During the unveiling, I stood back, watched, and listened to people's reactions. They smiled and laughed. Children thought she was beautiful.

All my life I have been drawing, painting, and creating, but this was the first time I truly felt like an artist.

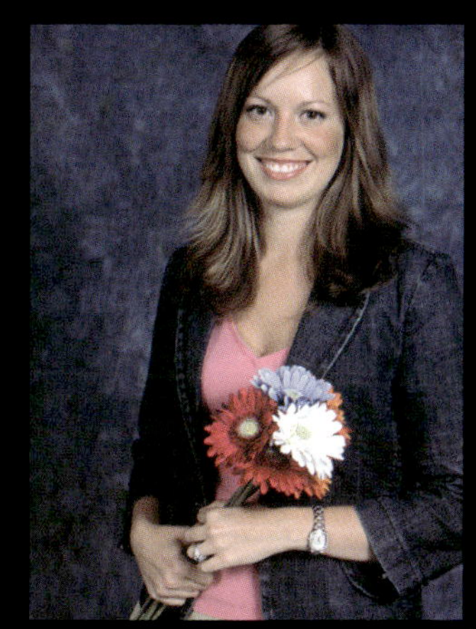

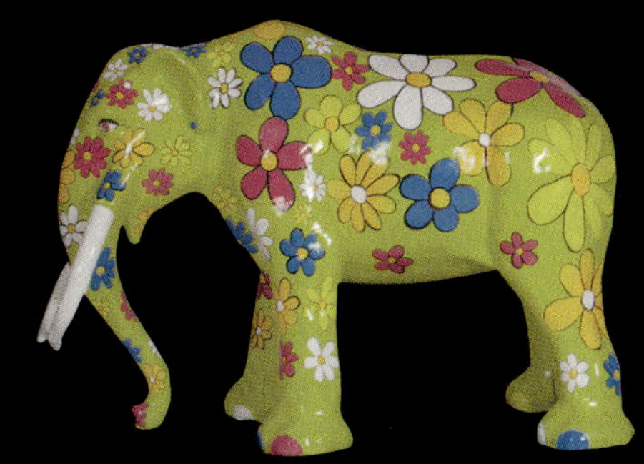

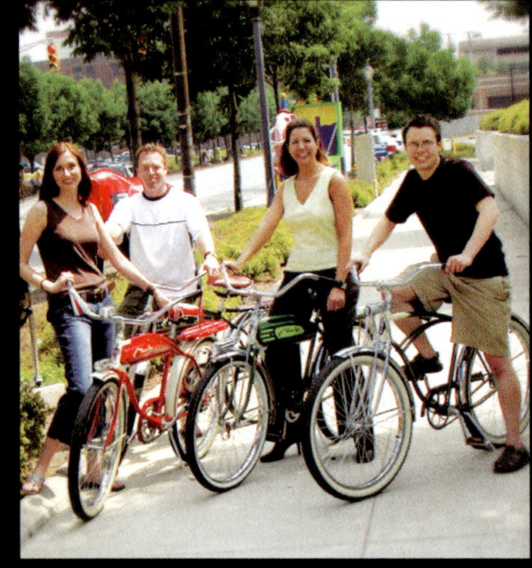

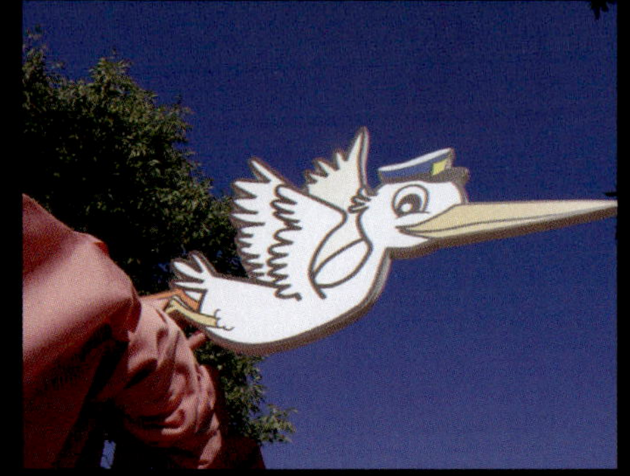

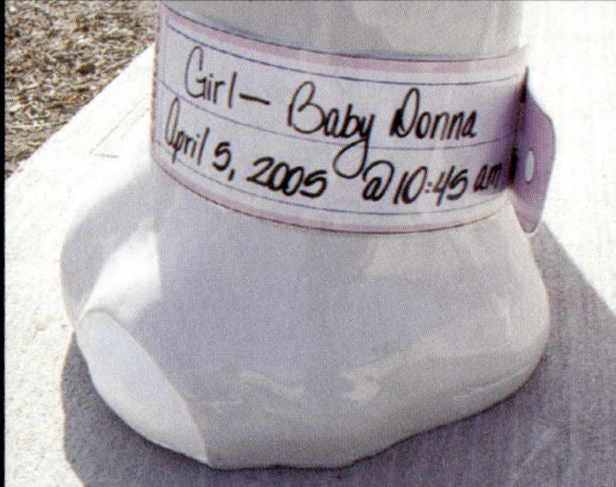

Artists: Boyden & Youngblutt, agency artists (*pictured above*)

Sponsor: Dupont Hospital

By Andy Boyden, agency principal and creative director

Yes, Baby Don is definitely the LARGEST baby born at Dupont Hospital!

Of course, the creative concept for him was a birth in its own right. It came out of wanting to celebrate babies and wanting to salute the hospital's caring staff.

Most people ask, "How does that stork stay up there?" We created a structural illusion for the mastodon with that stork.

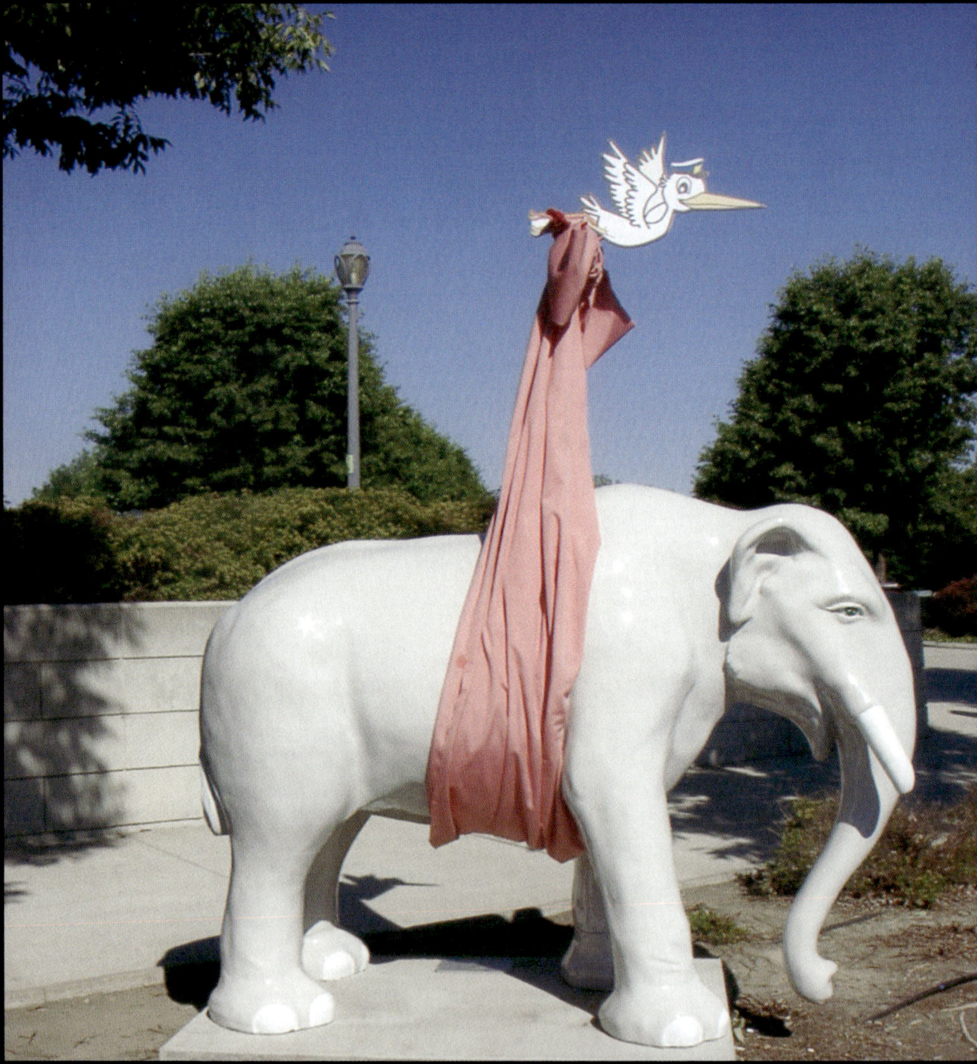

Mastodons on Parade

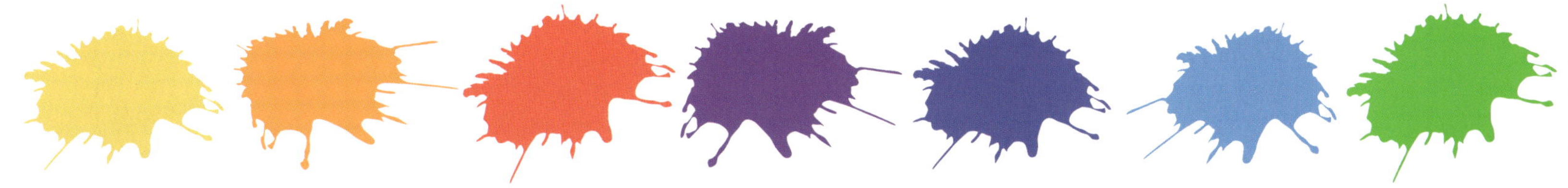

Dons at Work

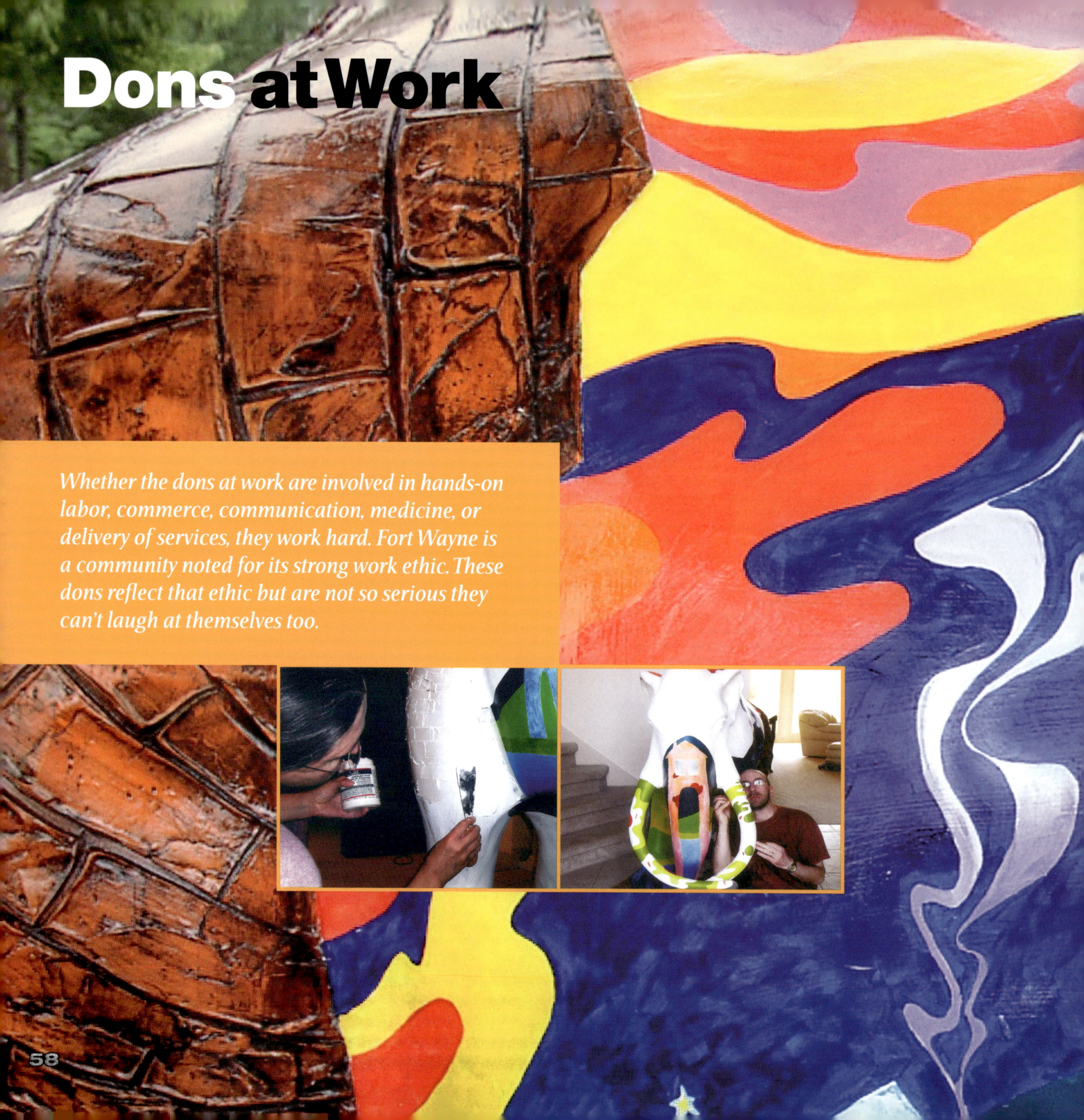

Dons at Work

Whether the dons at work are involved in hands-on labor, commerce, communication, medicine, or delivery of services, they work hard. Fort Wayne is a community noted for its strong work ethic. These dons reflect that ethic but are not so serious they can't laugh at themselves too.

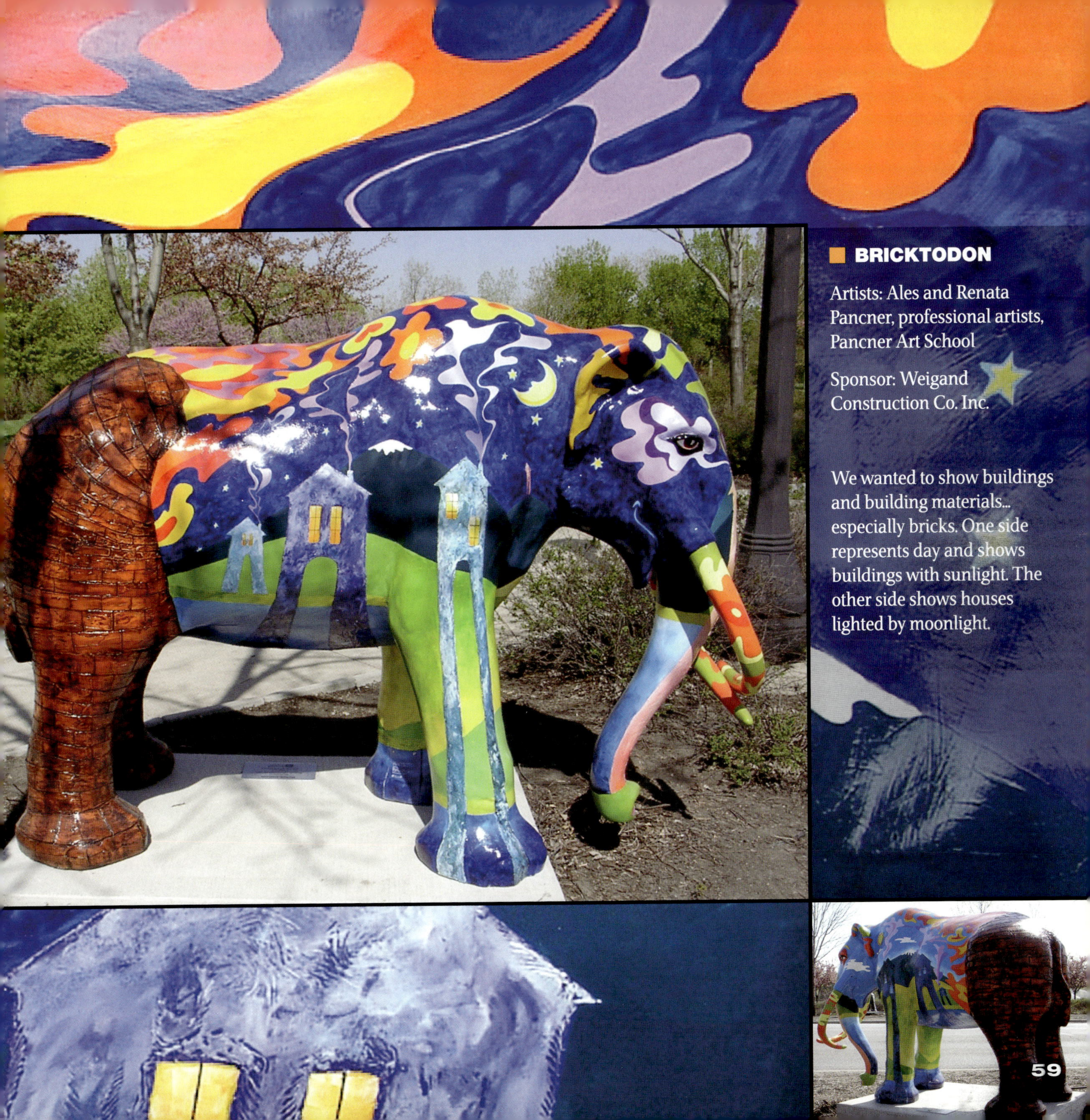

BRICKTODON

Artists: Ales and Renata
Pancner, professional artists,
Pancner Art School

Sponsor: Weigand
Construction Co. Inc.

We wanted to show buildings
and building materials...
especially bricks. One side
represents day and shows
buildings with sunlight. The
other side shows houses
lighted by moonlight.

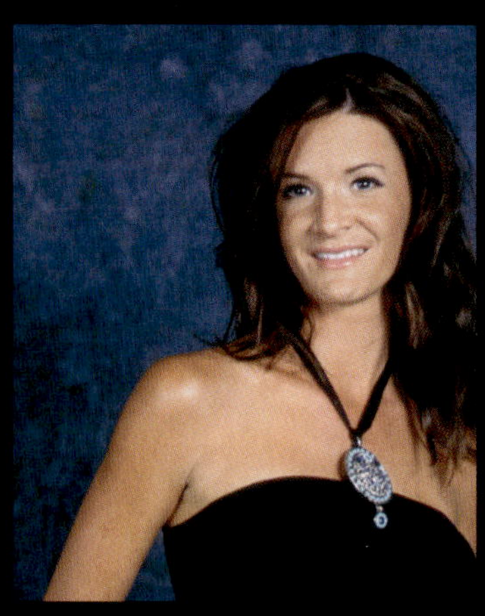

■ DOLLAR DON

Artist: Vanessa Shaver, mural artist, graphic designer

Sponsor: National City

What an honor to be involved in such an undertaking! Mike Eikenberry and I collaborated on a design. We wanted to stick with a banking theme and decided that dollars would be the best way to portray that.

So Dollar Don was born! We had to move him from one house to another because he was too large to get down the stairs into the basement. We did the final work on him in a cold garage.

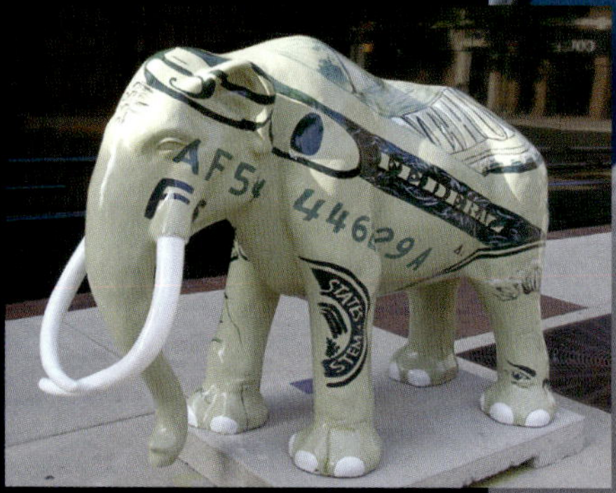

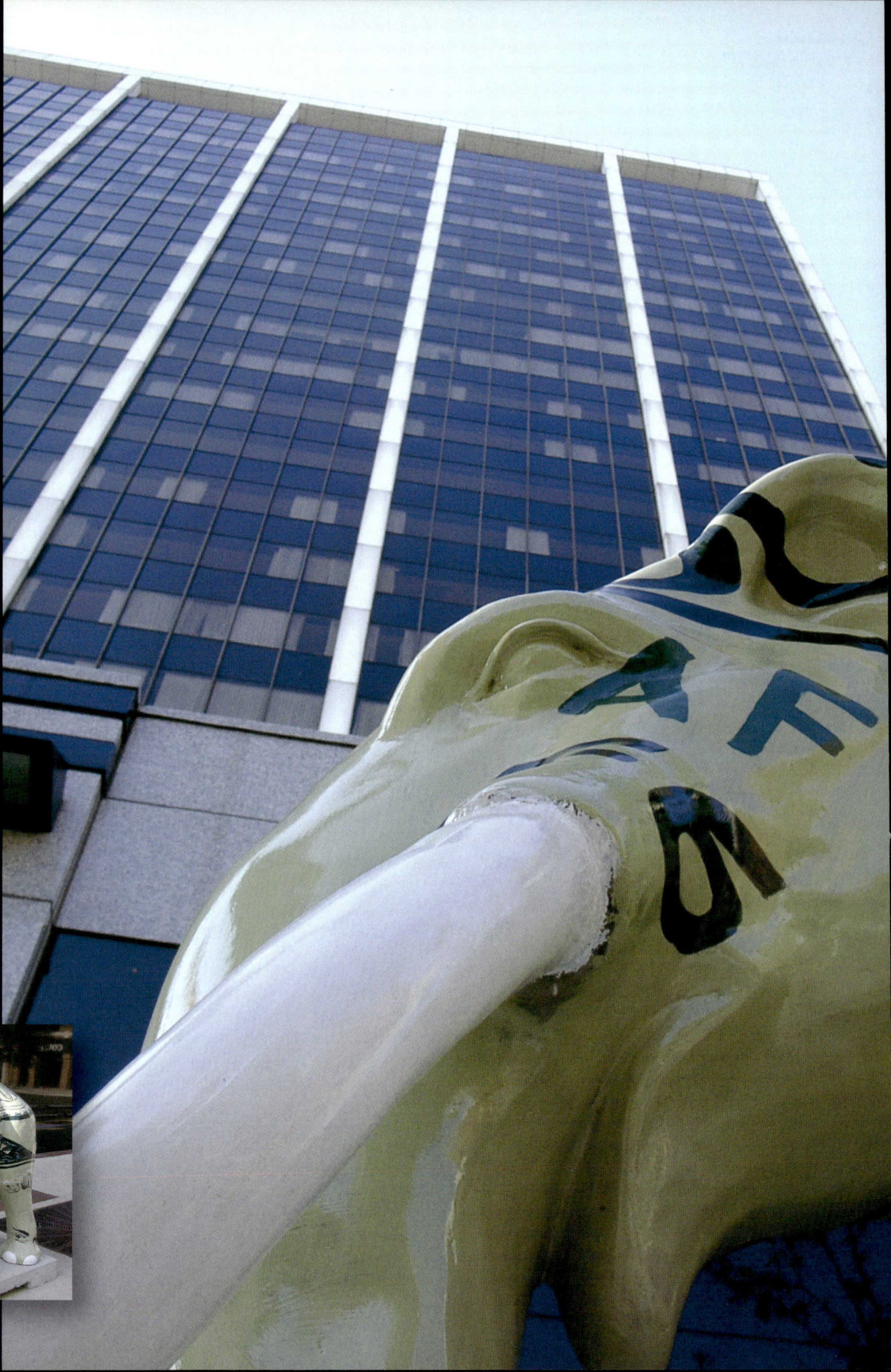

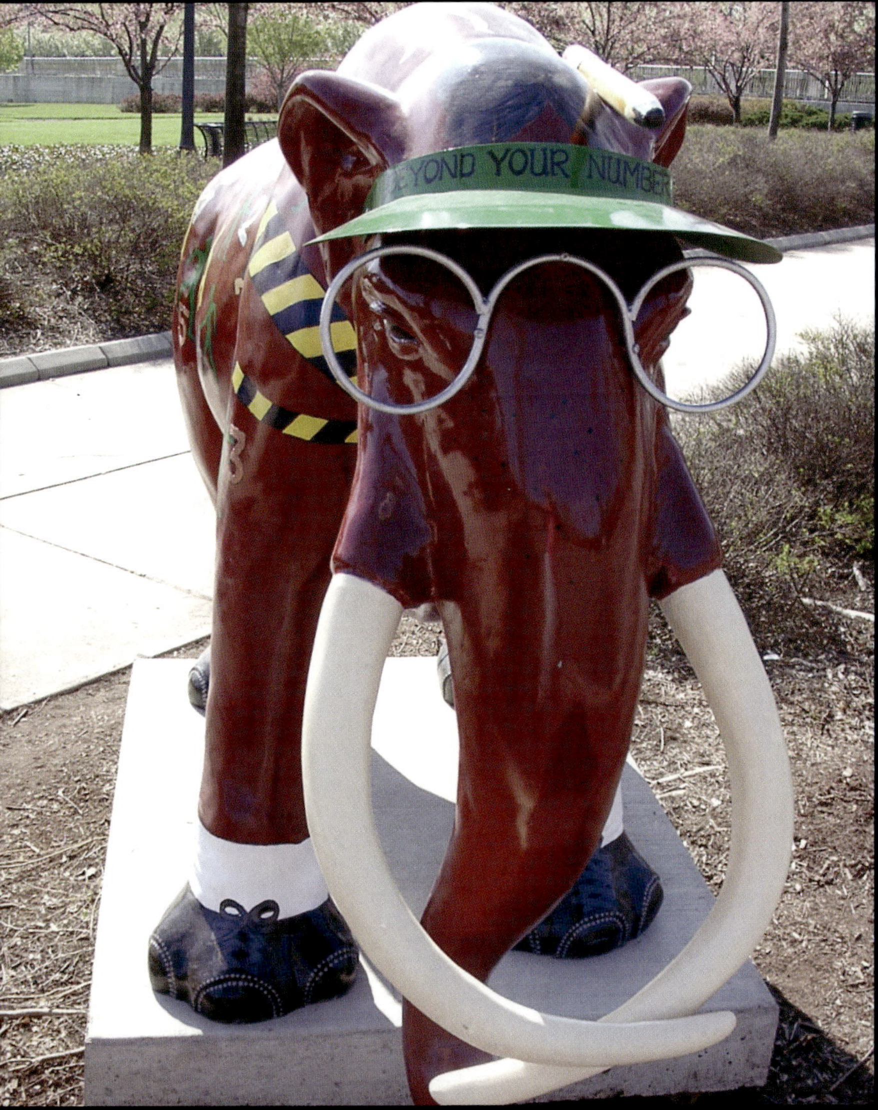

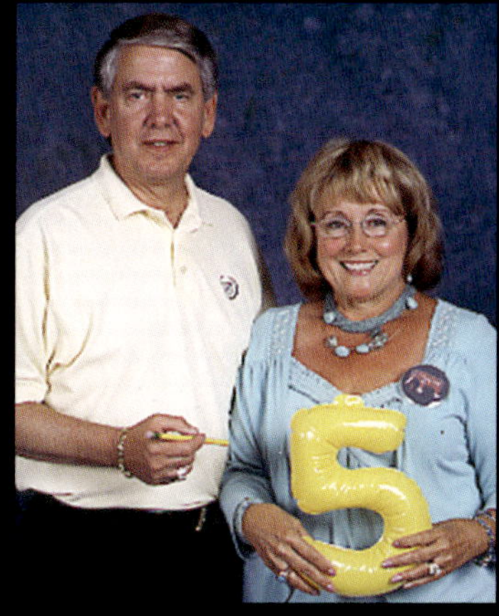

■ ACCOUNTODON

Artists: Barbara Sather/art teacher
(*pictured with husband*)

Students, Bishop Luers High School

Sponsor: BKD

By Barbara J. Sather

Everyone knows that if you want to do good work on math problems, you need a #2 pencil over your ear. That's exactly where Sparky (our nickname for AccountoDon) keeps his spare!

Figures of people all over his back depict accountants balancing numbers. Sparky also has an interactive button which tells listeners that he is trying to get "beyond your numbers."

Everyone got involved, including our head custodian, Mark Jones. The students were eager to put their mark on a public piece of art. Getting people to participate in and appreciate art is what I am all about.

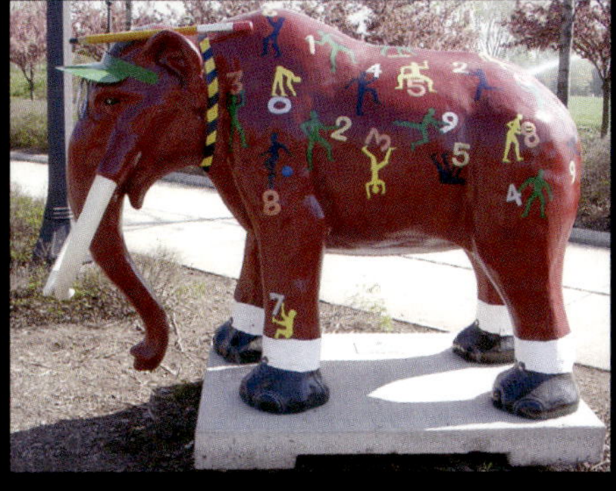

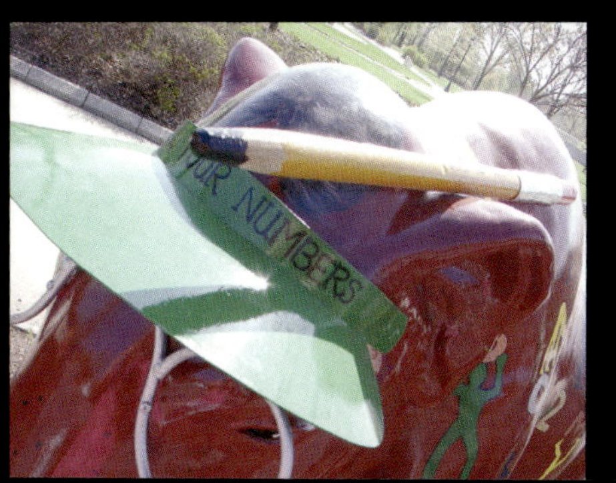

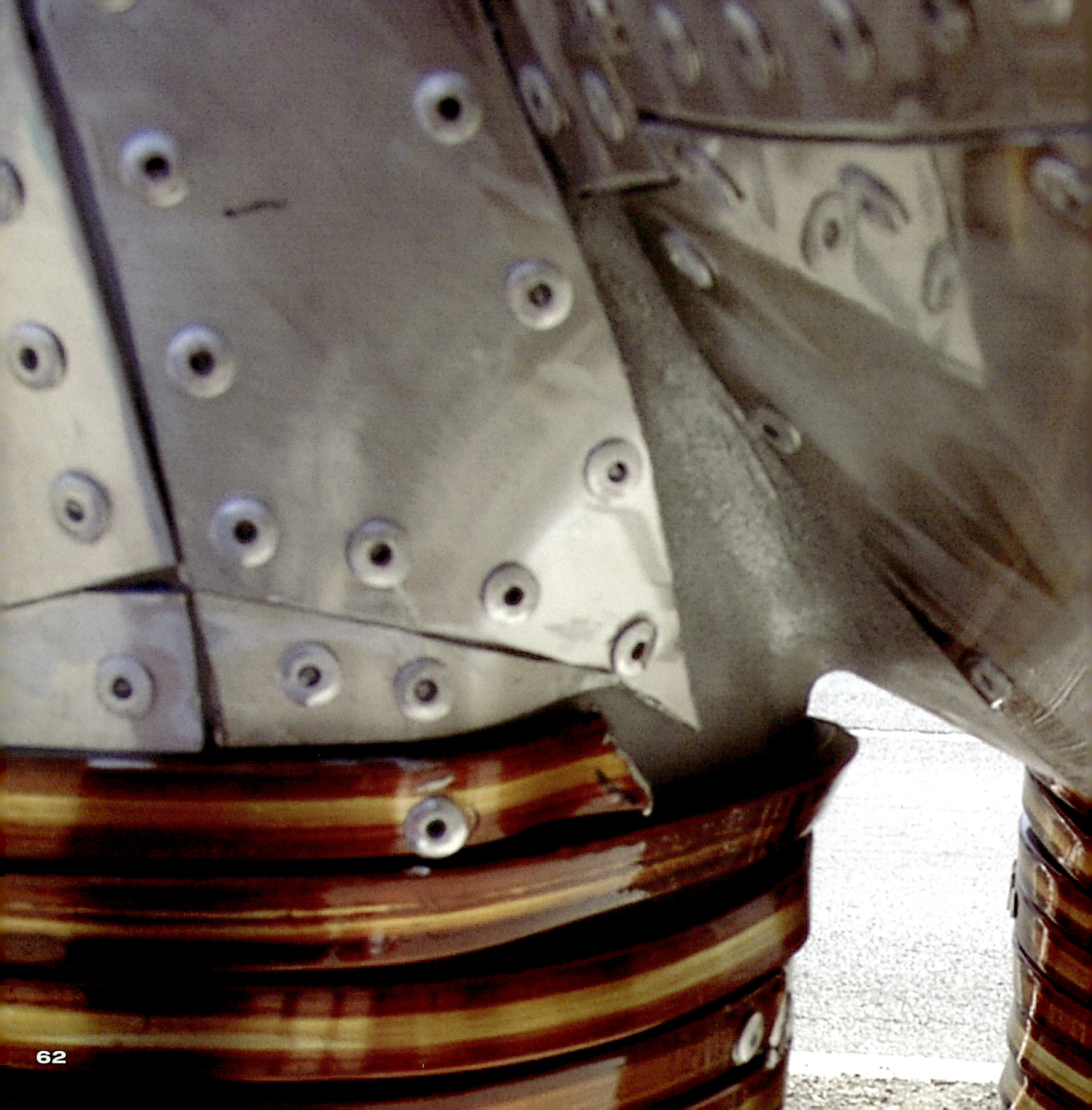

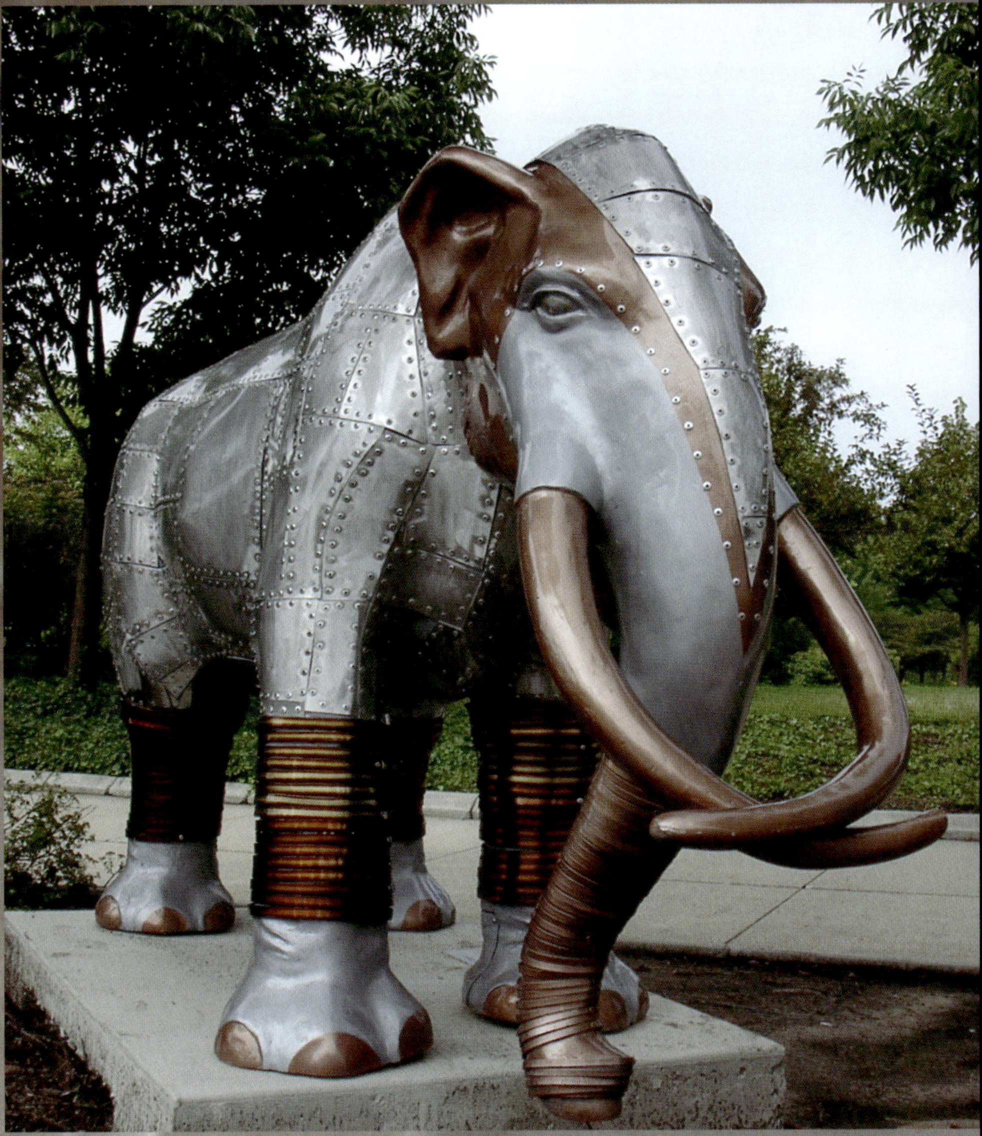

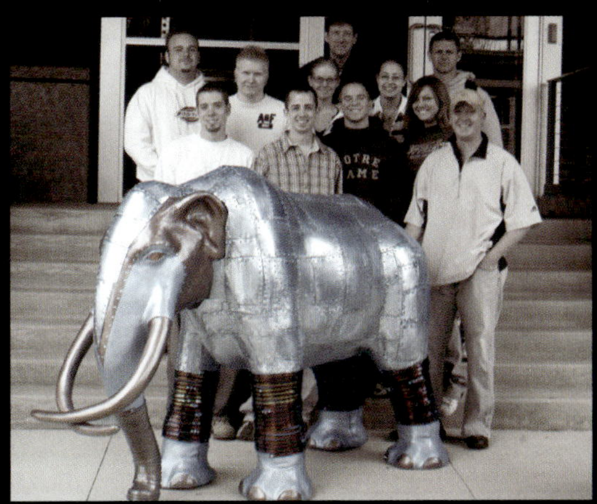

■ OMNI DON

Artist: University of Saint Francis, American Advertising Federation College Chapter

Sponsor: OmniSource Corporation

By Alan Nauts, Program Director for Communication Arts and Graphic Design, University of Saint Francis, Faculty Advisor AAF Student Chapter

Jeremy Heinhold, one of the members of the Advertising Federation chapter, developed the design. It is a visual representation of the sponsor's product and relies on use of various metals to encase the mastodon in armor.

Upperclass chapter members visited the scrap yard to choose materials for Omni Don. They acquired sheets of thick aluminum and large copper wire. In making the aluminum pieces fit, they needed more rivets than anticipated and ended up using thousands of rivets, two rivet guns, and hundreds of work hours to complete the job.

Omni Don ended up a shining success.

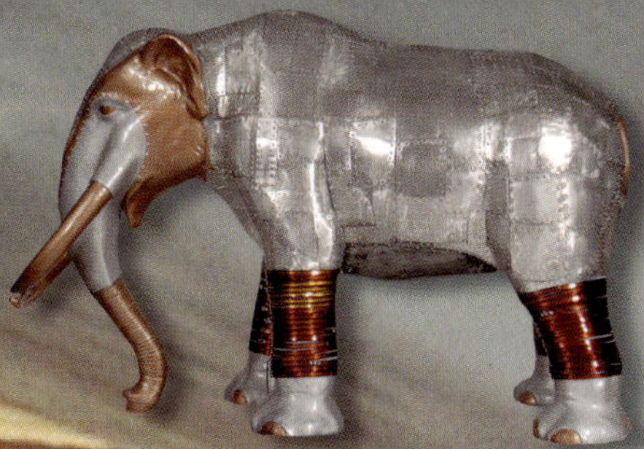

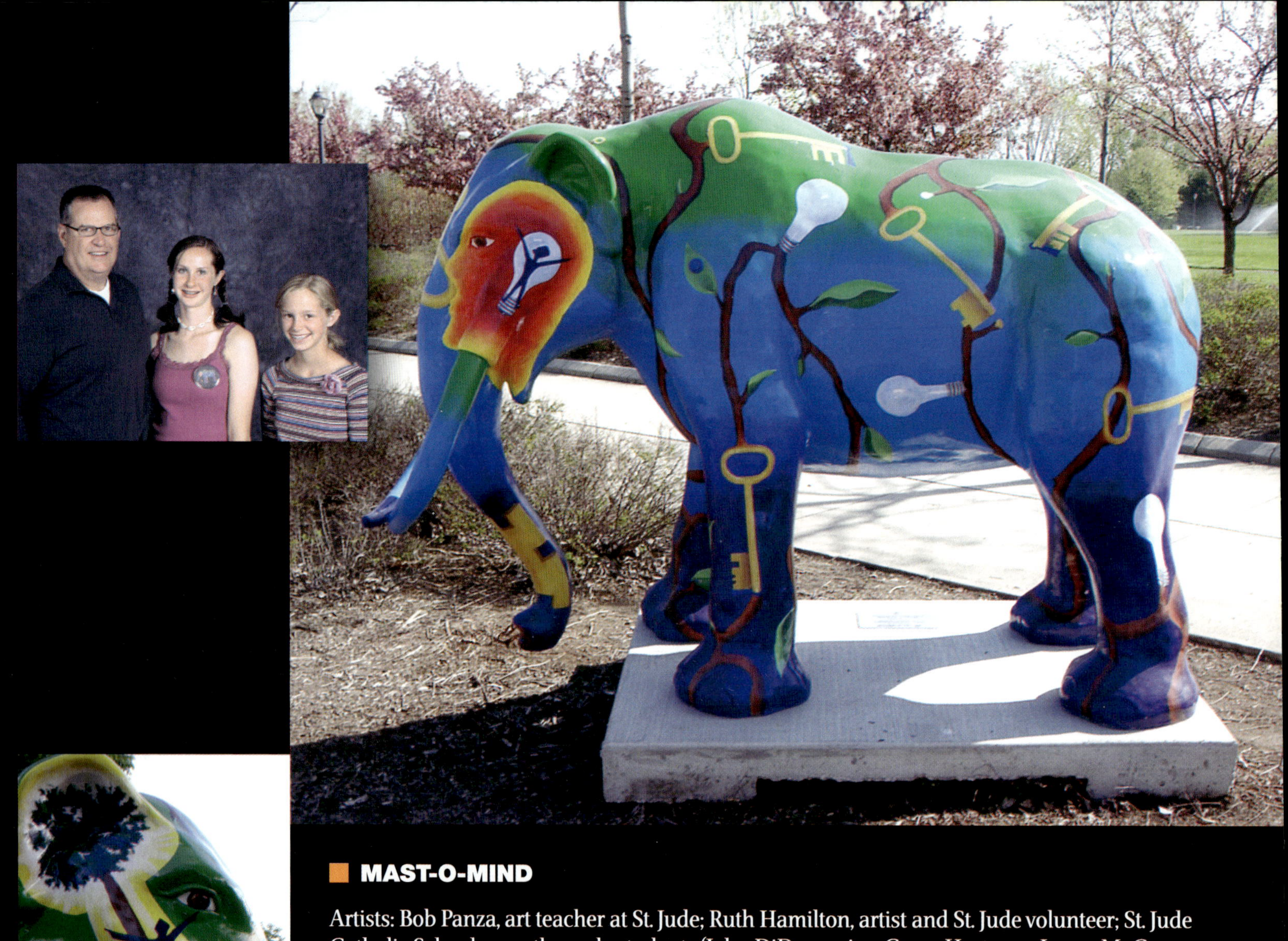

◼ MAST-O-MIND

Artists: Bob Panza, art teacher at St. Jude; Ruth Hamilton, artist and St. Jude volunteer; St. Jude Catholic School seventh-grade students (John DiDomenico, Grace Hartman, Lucas McGowan, Luke Momper, Lauren Palmer, Molly Richardson) (*Pictured are Bob Panza with Lauren Palmer and Grace Hartman*)

Sponsor: IPFW Division of Continuing Studies

By Bob Panza

Our students said painting a five-foot, 175-pound fiberglass replica of a mastodon was challenging, fun, and awesome. For me, it was a unique opportunity to teach about the process of creating art on a mammoth (or mastodon) scale.

Mast-o-mind communicates the benefits of lifelong learning. The design depicts the tree of knowledge as the source of open minds and new ideas. An overall vine pattern rooted in the feet of the mastodon sprouts light bulbs and golden keys.

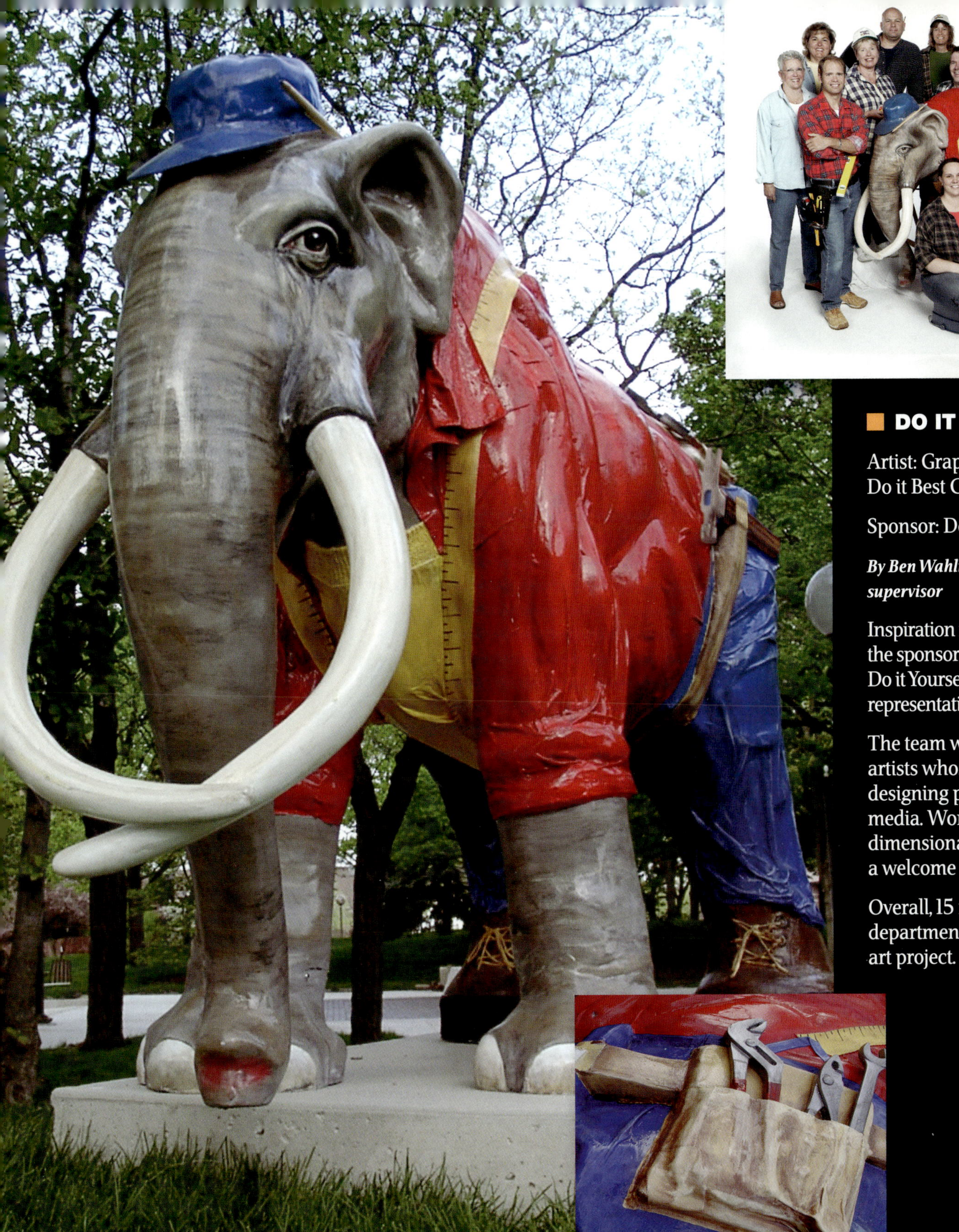

◼ DO IT YOURSELF DON

Artist: Graphics Department,
Do it Best Corp. (*pictured above*)

Sponsor: Do it Best Corp.

By Ben Wahli, advertising graphics supervisor

Inspiration for the design came from the sponsor's employees, who felt the Do it Yourself persona was the ultimate representation for their company.

The team was comprised of creative artists whose typical day involves designing print and interactive media. Working on a three-dimensional mastodon form was a welcome challenge.

Overall, 15 members of the graphics department worked on the public art project.

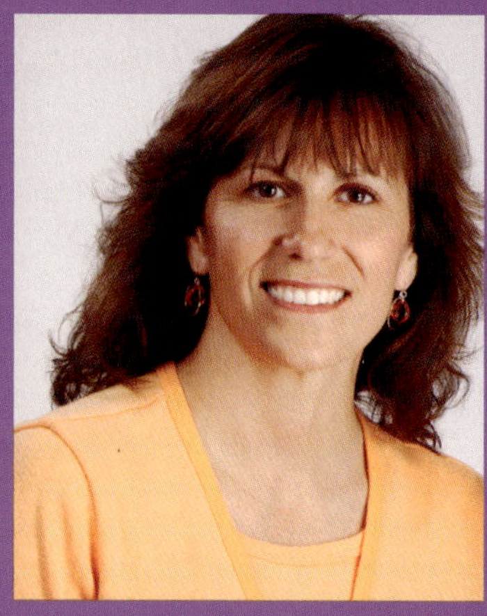

■ RADESCENT DON

Artist: Christy Weber, commercial
art director

Sponsor: Fort Wayne Radiology

My friend Karen Rothermund, marketing
director at Fort Wayne Radiology, asked if
I would be interested in this unique project.
Working together, we created the design for
RADescent Don. He is modeled after the
figure in the sponsor's logo and is fondly
known as The Radman.

We wanted a holographic look but had
to settle for chrome and a color-changing
paint. My daughter Kelsey and I completed
the project in three weeks.

It was great to be part of such a fun
community project. I was very impressed
with all the talent and creativity that was
shown by all the people involved.

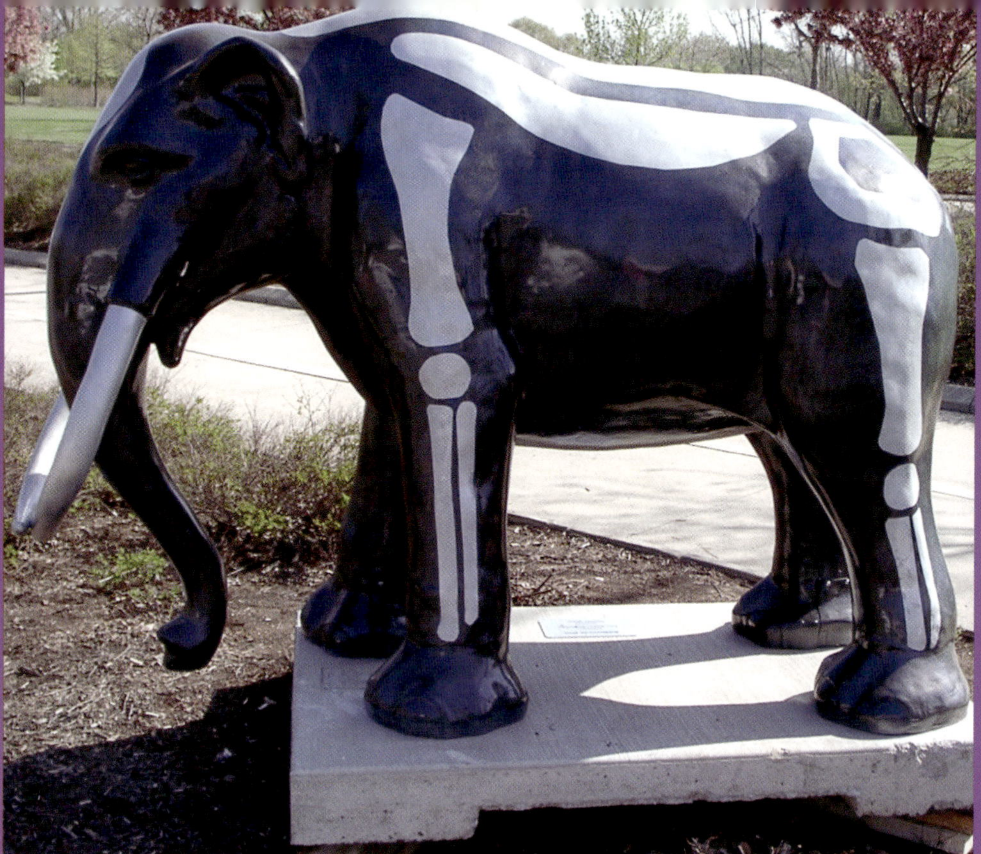

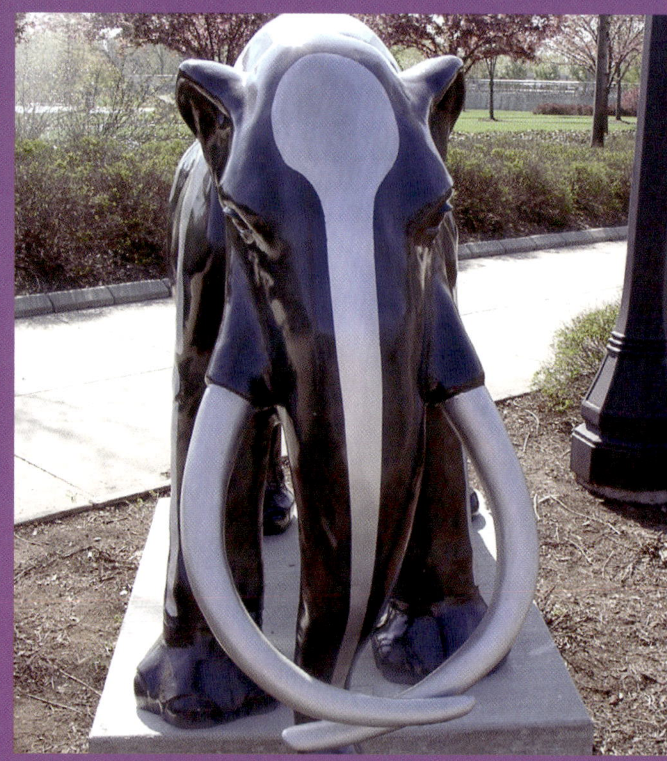

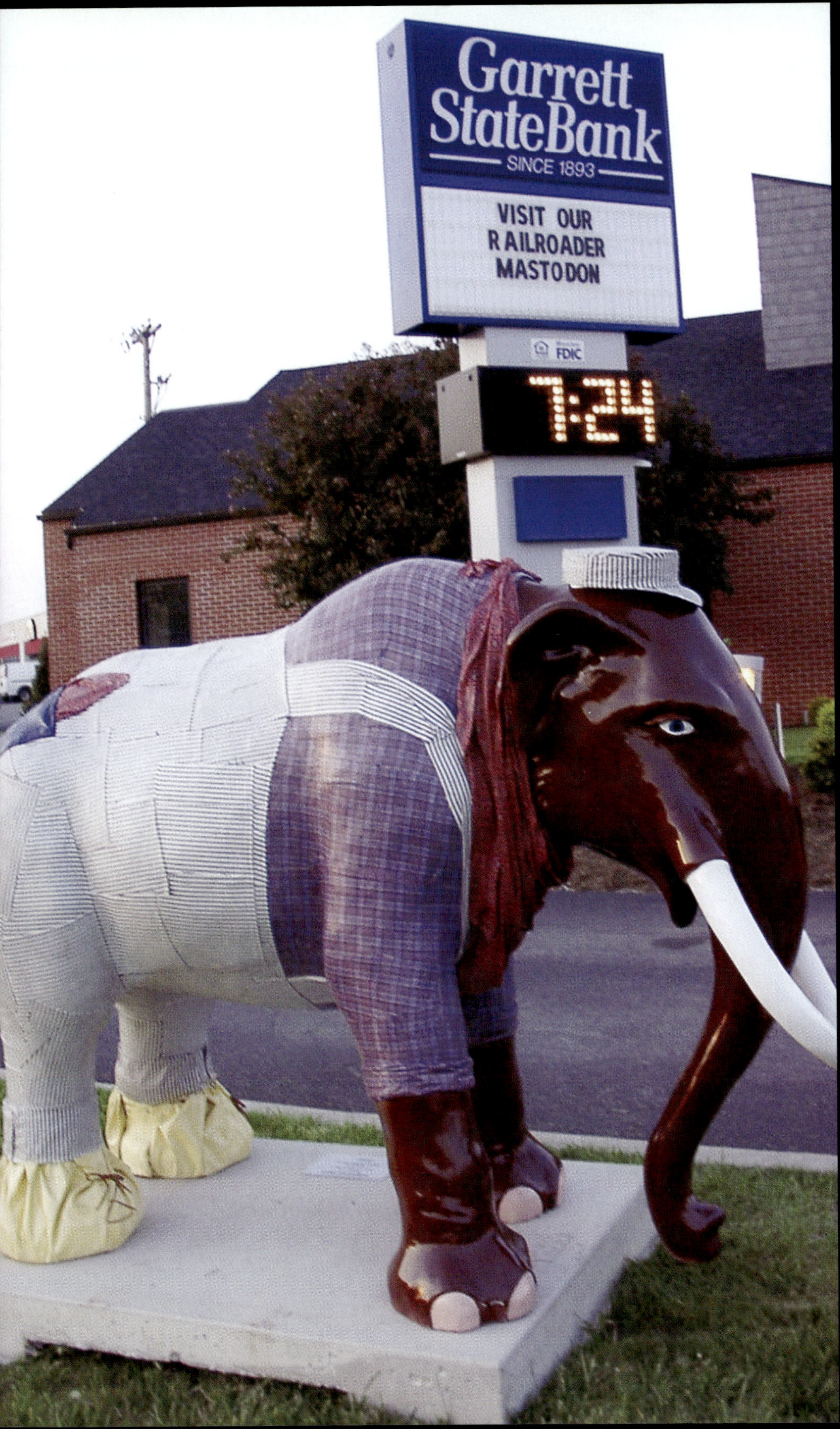

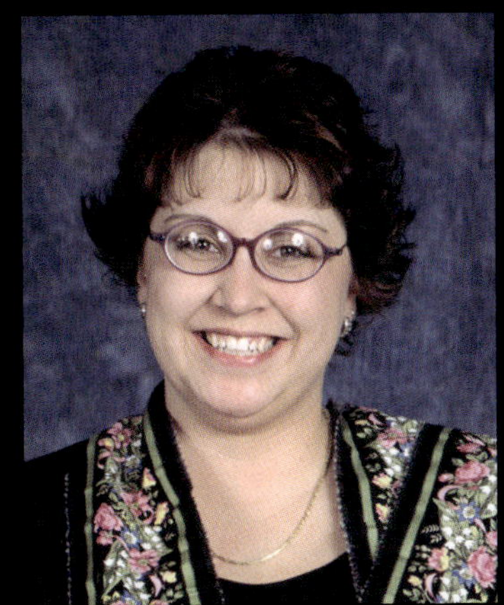

◼ ENGINEER DON

Artist: Nadia Kowal Korn, graphic artist

Sponsor: Garrett State Bank

I welcomed the chance to work on the fiberglass mastodons so much that I took on two of the creatures. Engineer Don was my second project.

The sponsor wanted something that represented its history. Since the railroad founded the bank and tracks go right through the town, I made my mastodon into a train engineer. Engineer Don was created with paints and fabric maché techniques. He has his hat and his overalls on, along with a flannel shirt and work boots.

It was a challenge, but I tried very hard to make the two dons look very different while using the same medium and techniques.

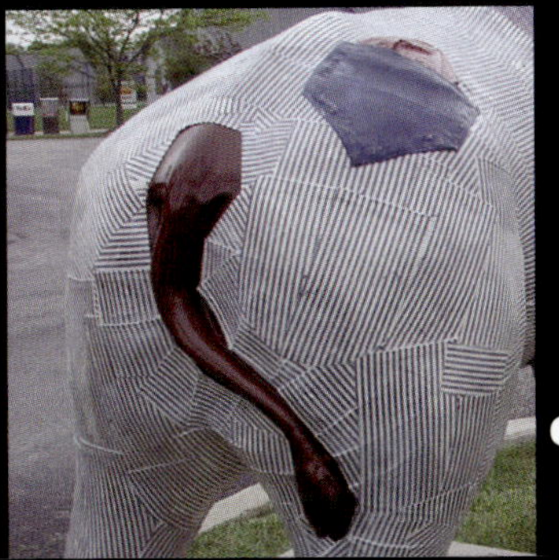

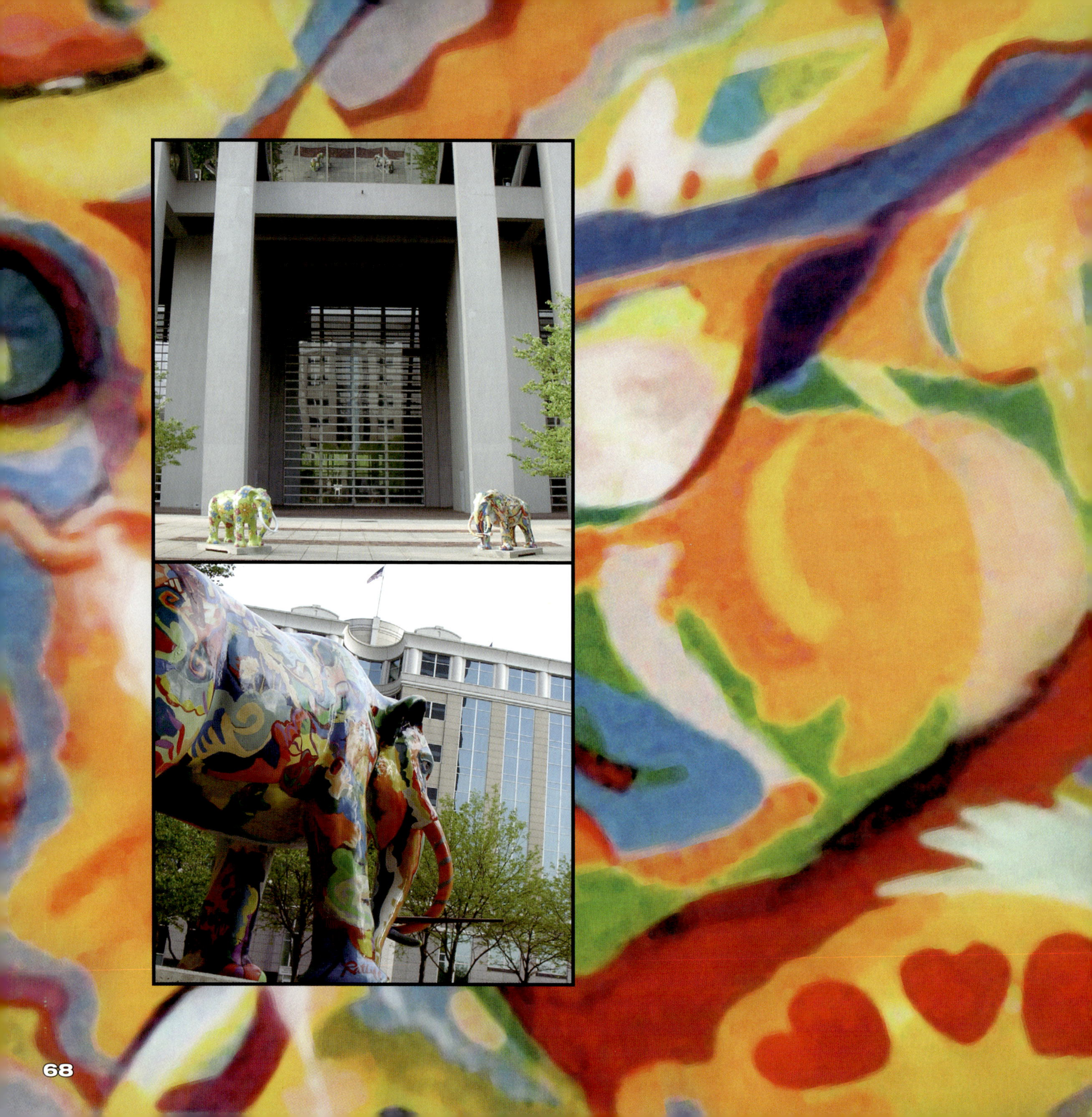

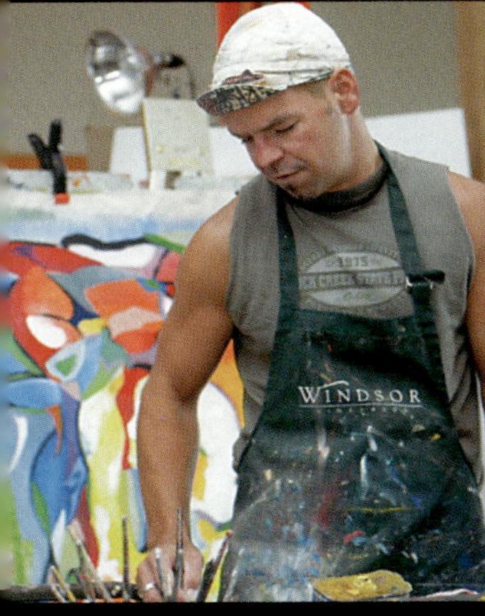

PEOPLE AT WORK DON

Artist: Terry Ratliff, professional artist

Sponsor: Indiana Michigan Power

Portrayed in a colorful camouflage of sorts, People at Work Don is a tribute to the working people in our community.

Overall, there are displays of vibrant color and beautiful patterns. Hidden within the camouflage are hammers, a saw, a wrench, a chemist, a nurse, and a farmer along with other workplace tools and career types.

Look at it twice, and you will see something new, guaranteed!

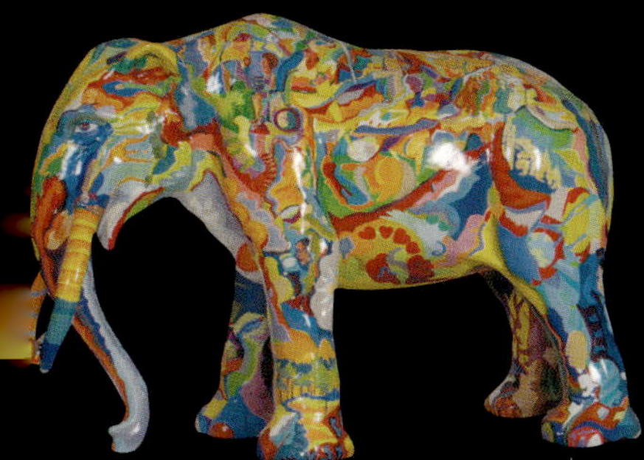

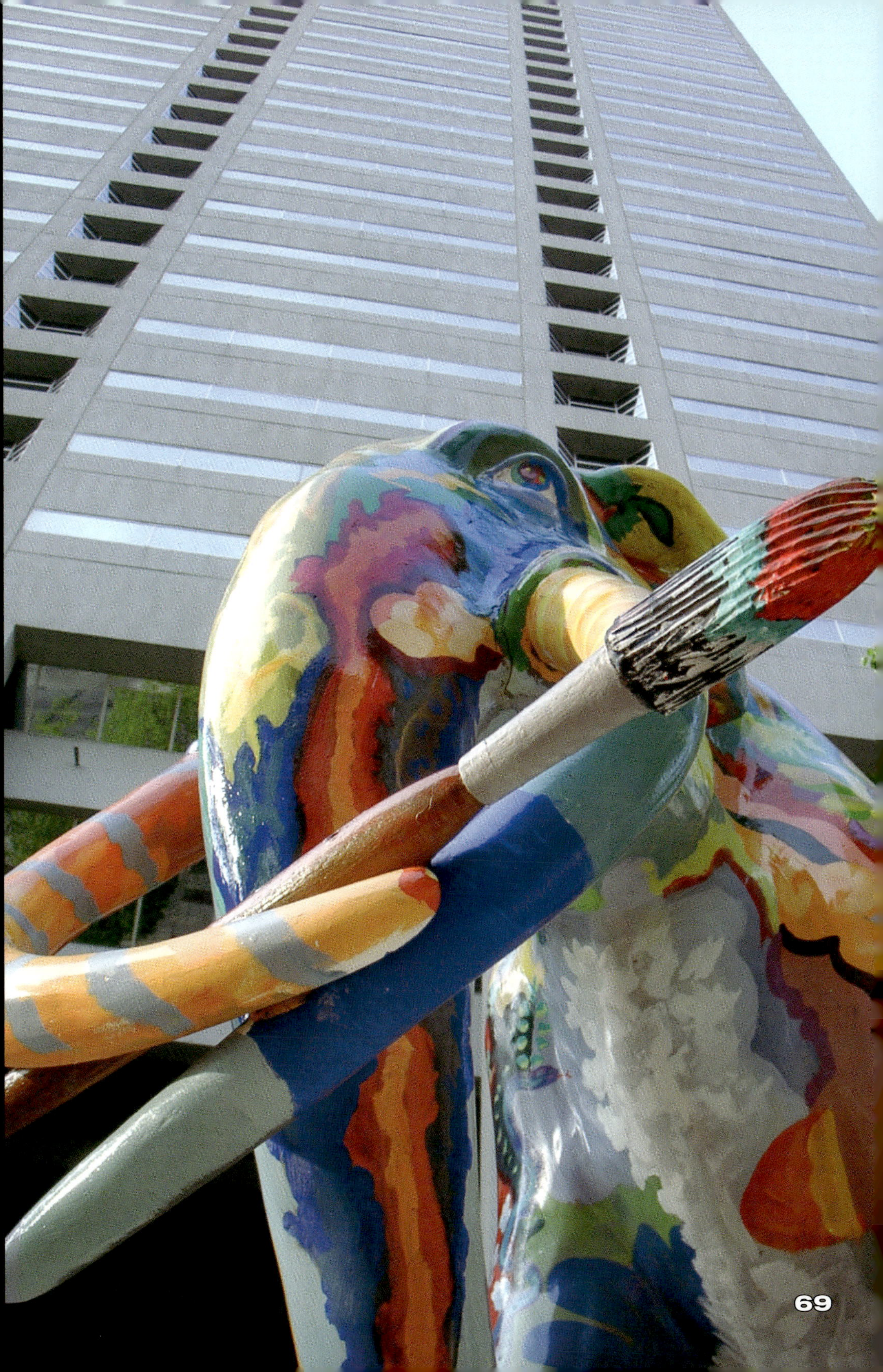

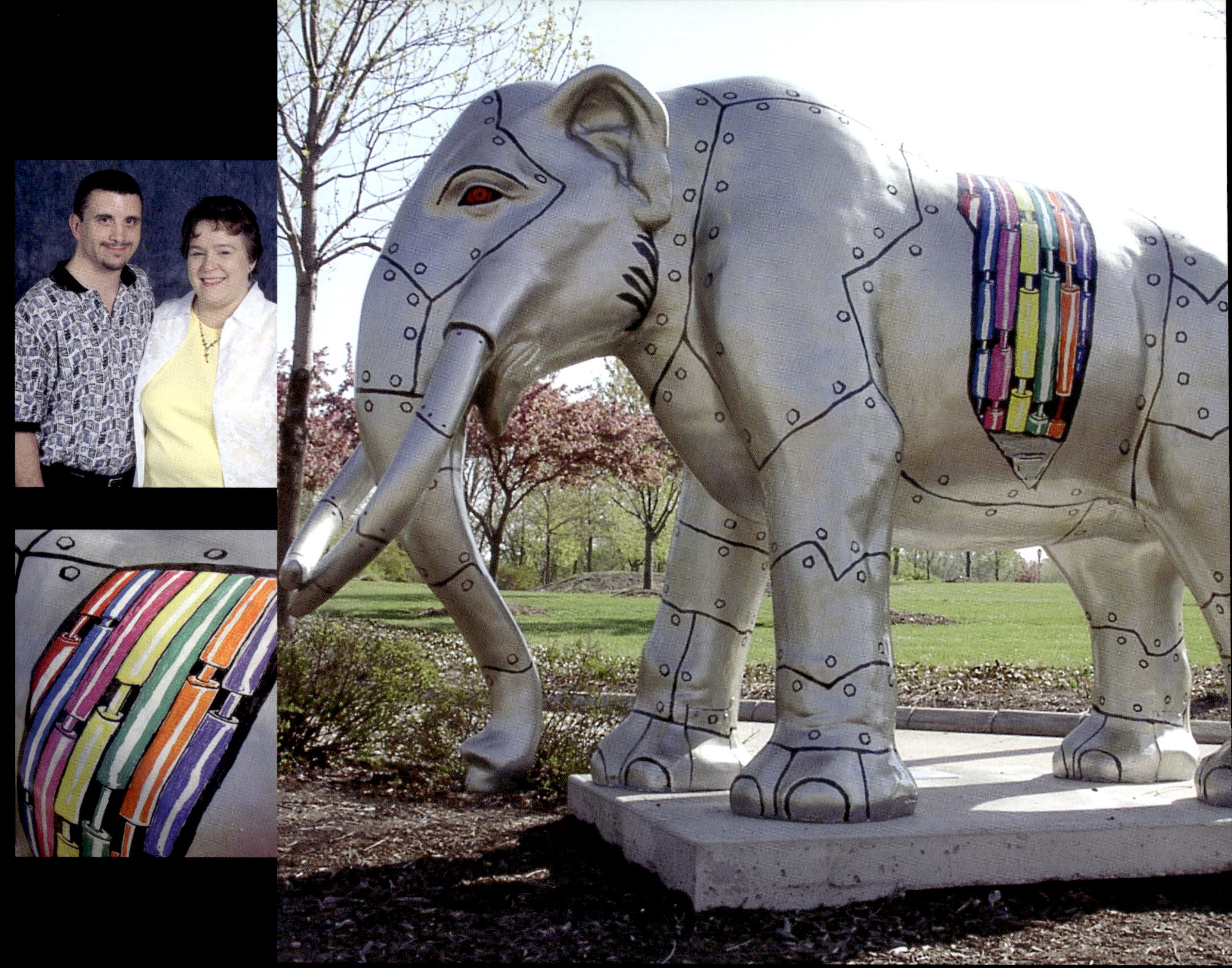

◼ ROBOTODON

Artist: Michael Hassig, freelance artist (*pictured above with girlfriend*)

Sponsor: Audio Visual Integration

My girlfriend, Holly Tustuson, showed me the information about the art project in her IPFW Alumni newsletter. Robbie, the nickname for our mastodon, was my first art project and at first seemed a little overwhelming.

While I worked on him, he just became like a part of the family. When he started to take shape and become a life-sized vision of my drawing, it was a thrill to know I could be a part of something so great.

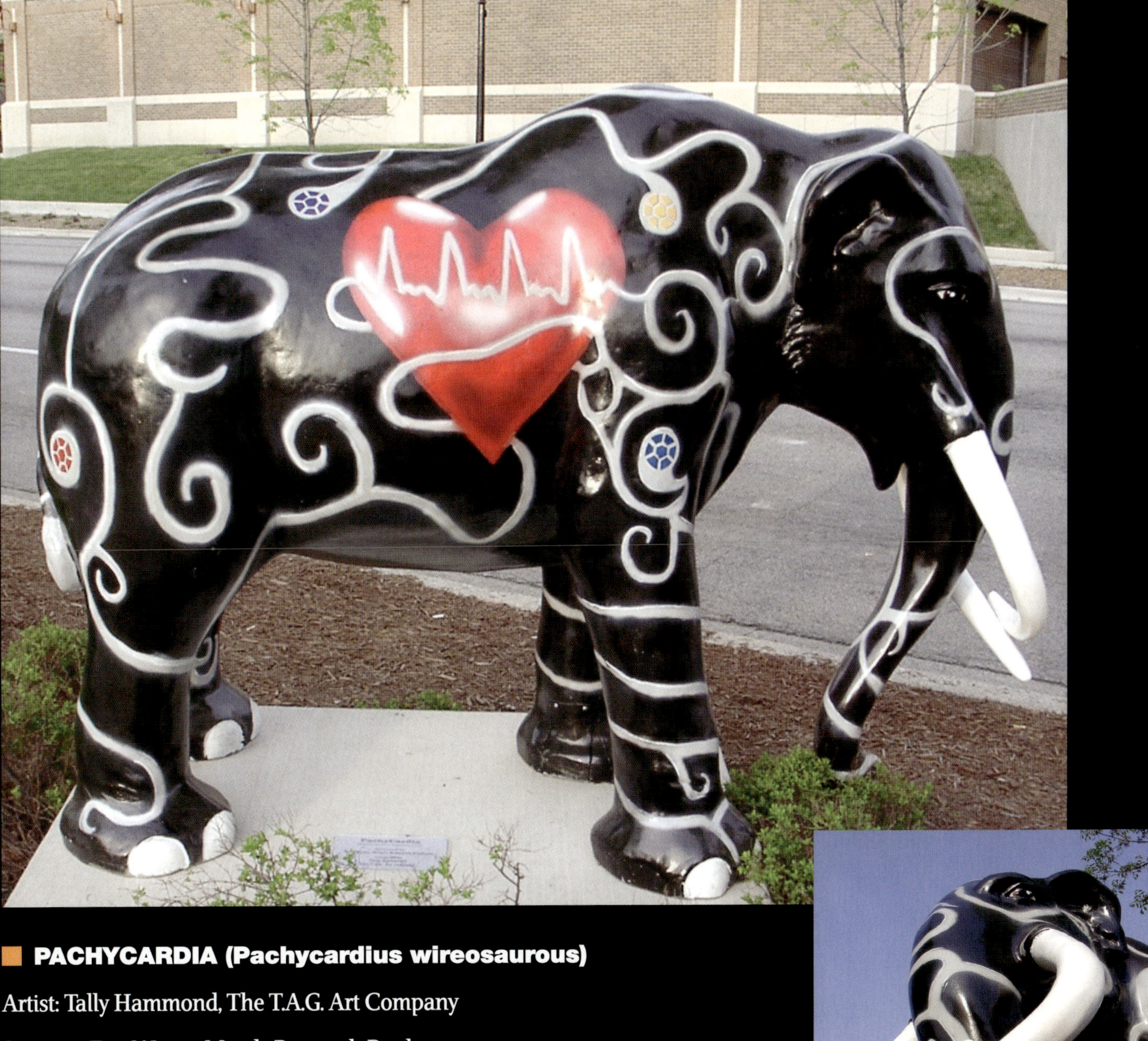

▌ PACHYCARDIA (Pachycardius wireosaurous)

Artist: Tally Hammond, The T.A.G. Art Company

Sponsor: Fort Wayne Metals Research Products

By Troy Ganser

PachyCardia was the first of the dons our team completed (The T.A.G. Art Company created six dons for Mastodons on Parade). The design includes the various products the sponsor creates for all forms of medical and industrial applications. The art is a combination of airbrush techniques and hand painting.

Our team spent well over 1,700 hours, all volunteer, over a four-month period to create a mini herd of six mastodons.

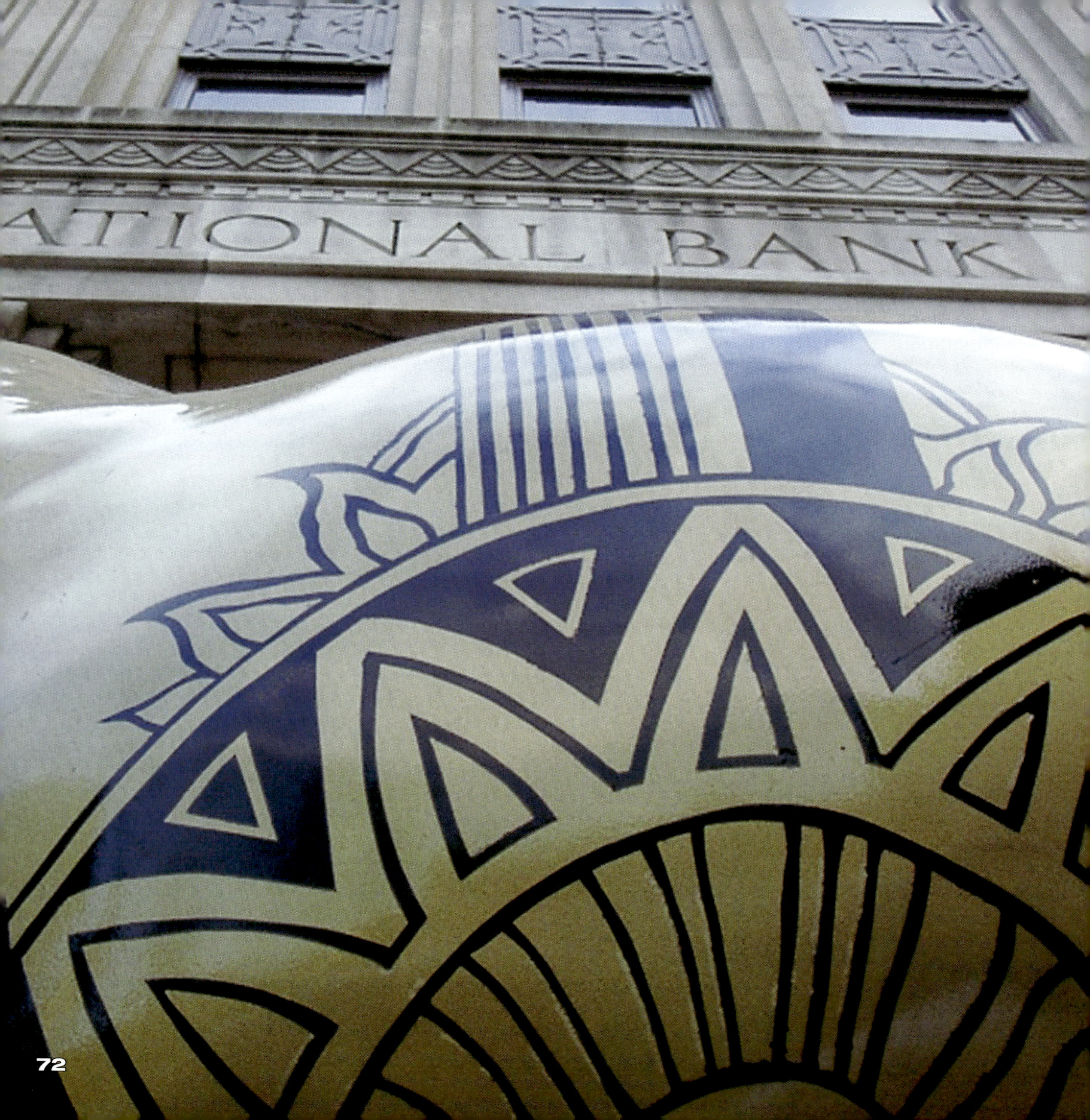

ATIONAL BANK

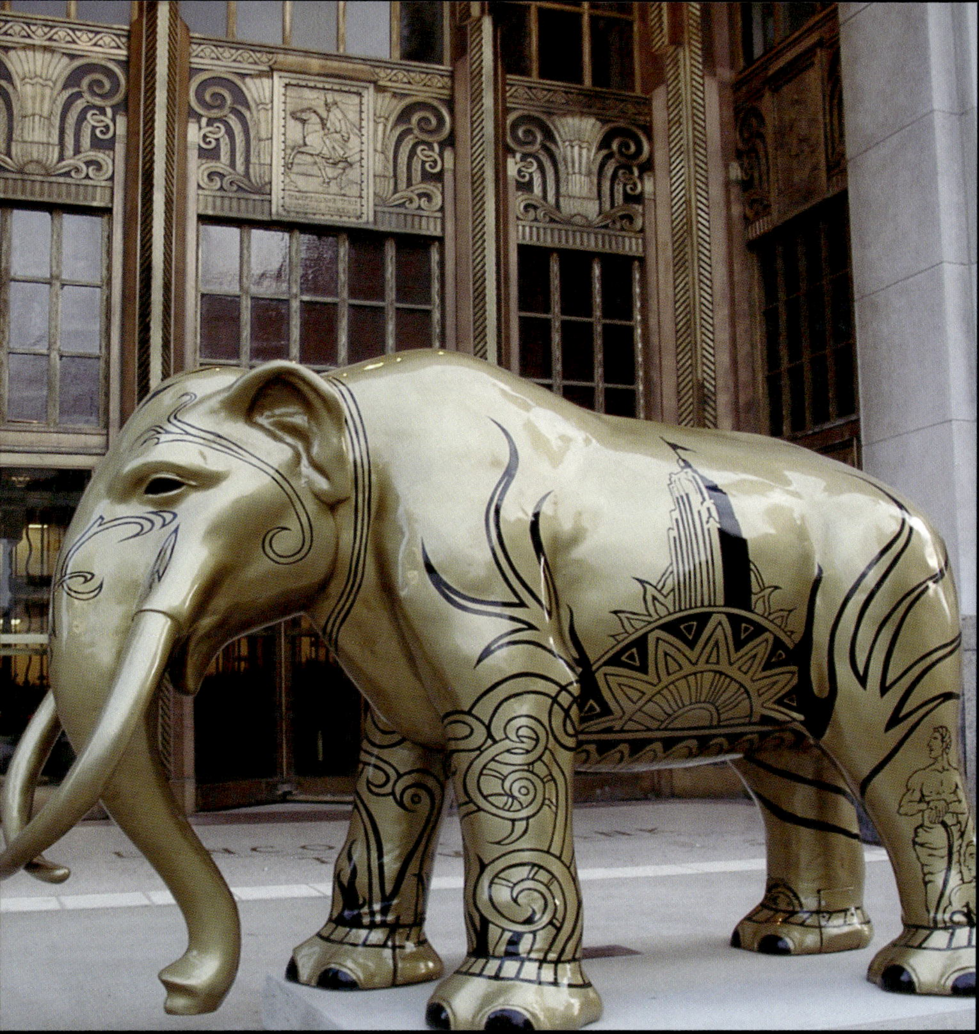

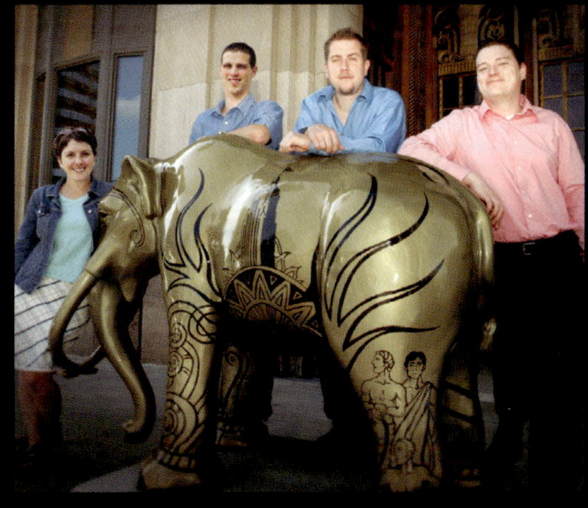

■ DECODON

Artists: Julie Farison, Jeremy Jones, Jeff Dollens, Andy Holbrook
(*pictured above, left to right*)

Sponsor: Tower Bank

Since Tower Bank was the major sponsor of the event, our mastodon was needed several months ahead of the rest of the herd. DecoDon was on display and served as a hands-on example to potential designers.

The art deco style was inspired by the interior and exterior of the historic Tower Bank building—one of the most dramatic buildings in Fort Wayne's skyline. The gold and black color scheme was the unifying element of the design.

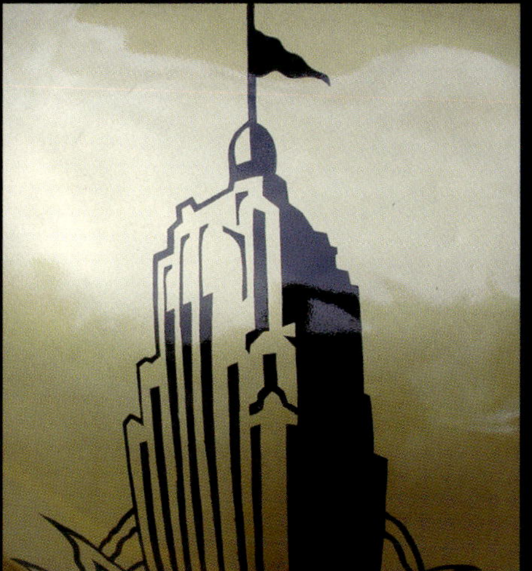

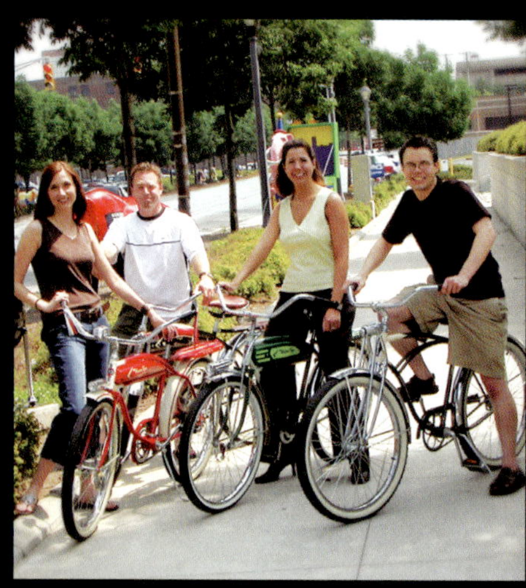

CAST-O-DON

Artist: Boyden & Youngblutt, agency artists
(*pictured above*)

Sponsor: Lutheran Hospital

By Andy Boyden, agency principal and creative director

Our sponsor wanted a mastodon that would be fun to look at again and again. We came up with the idea of wrapping him in a cast which folks at Fort Wayne Orthopedics actually applied.

Signatures on the cast represent Lutheran's extensive care for the community. It would have been great if patients, staff, volunteers, nurses, and doctors had all signed the cast, but there just wasn't enough "don" to go around!

We intentionally left Cast-O-Don's trunk unwrapped so he could wave, "Hello."

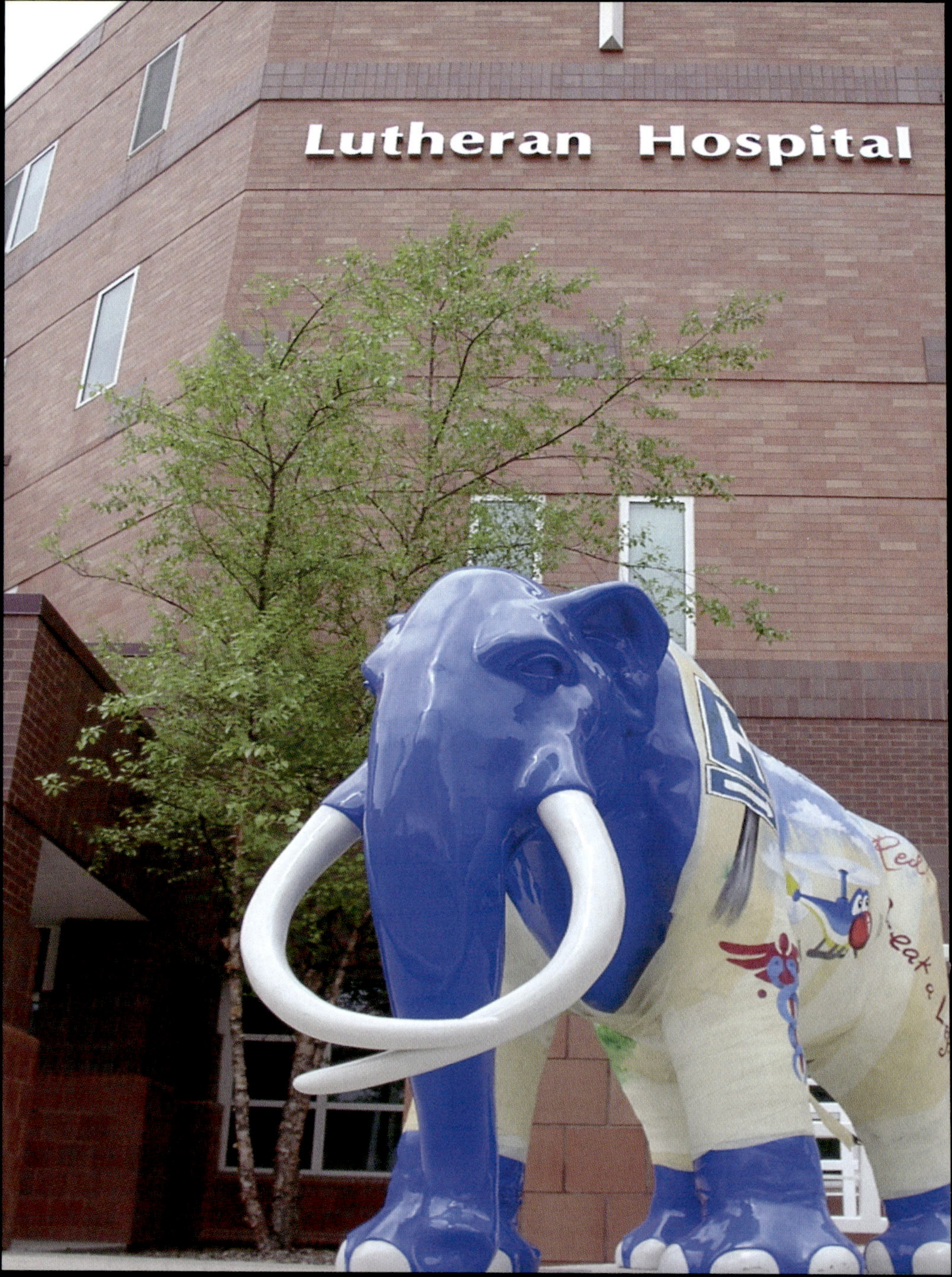

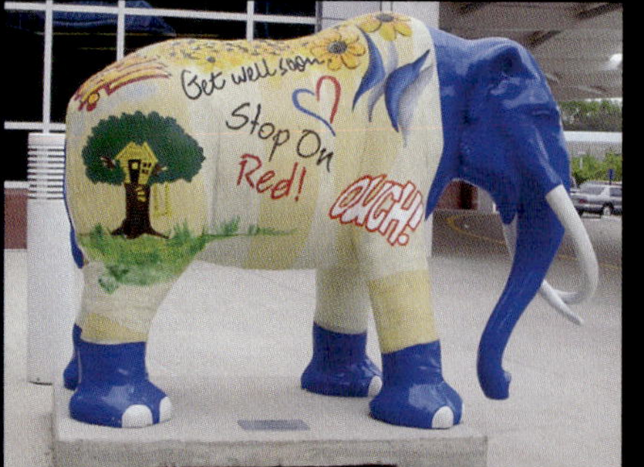

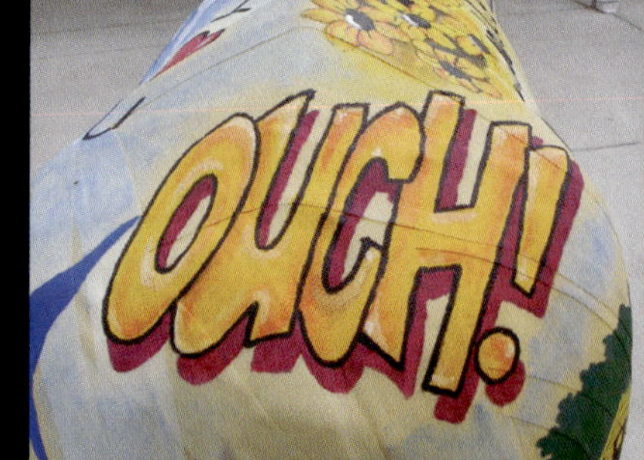

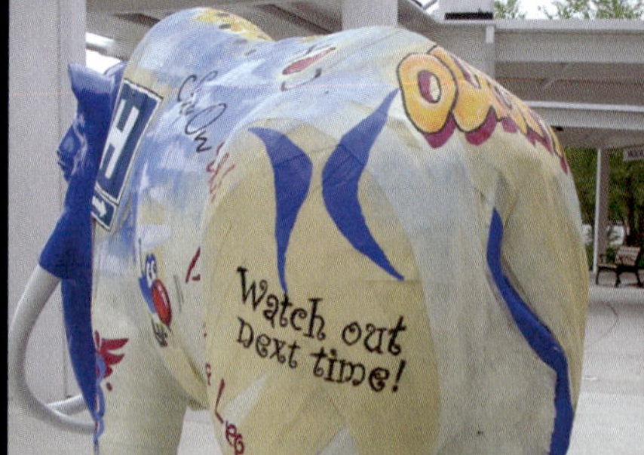

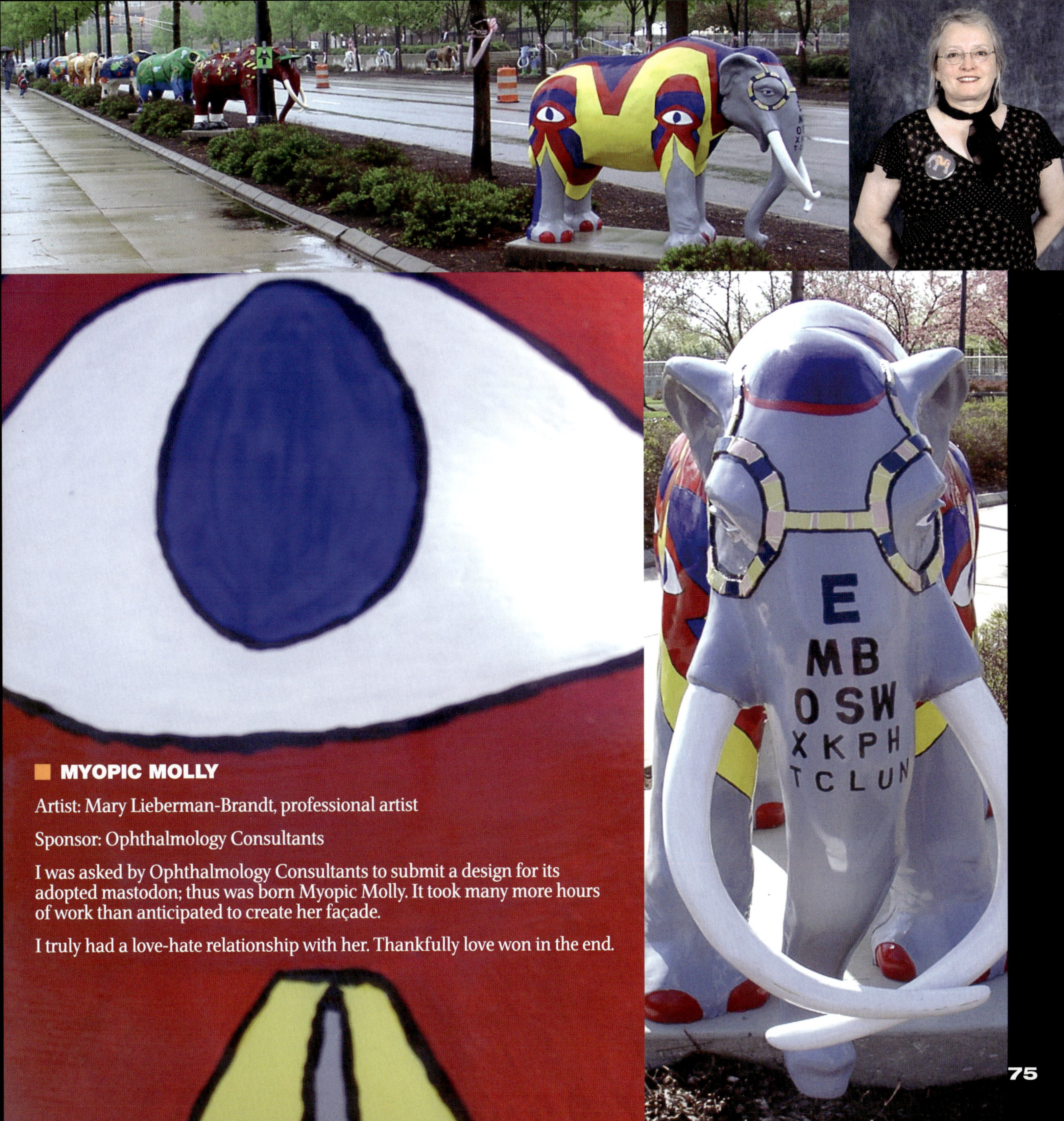

MYOPIC MOLLY

Artist: Mary Lieberman-Brandt, professional artist

Sponsor: Ophthalmology Consultants

I was asked by Ophthalmology Consultants to submit a design for its adopted mastodon; thus was born Myopic Molly. It took many more hours of work than anticipated to create her façade.

I truly had a love-hate relationship with her. Thankfully love won in the end.

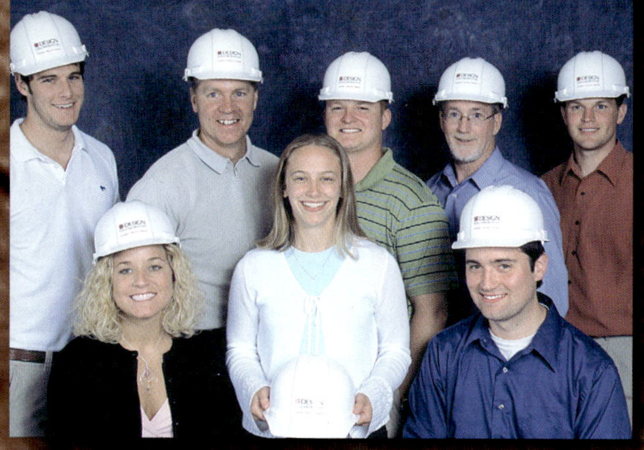

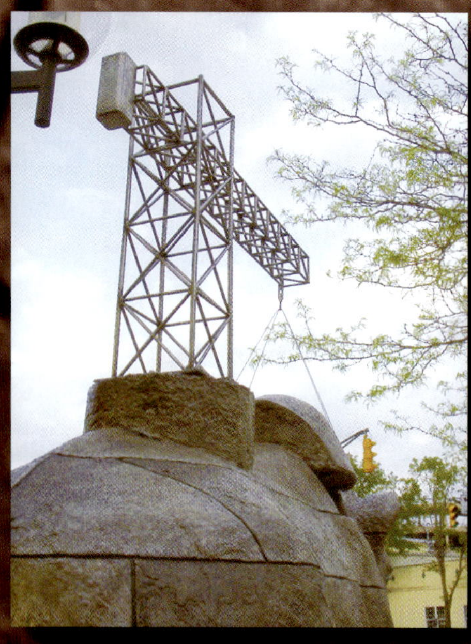

■ MAST"ER" BUILDER

Artists: Design Collaborative, Engineering Resources,
C. Miller & Sons (*pictured above*)

Sponsors: Design Collaborative and Engineering Resources

Form, function, and fun all come together in the MAST"er"
Builder. The design shows our passion for the building process,
and the project itself gives us a way to connect with the
IPFW celebration.

There is a miniature bridge crane dropping the very last building
block into place on our mastodon. Whew! Almost done.

The textured surface on MAST"er" Builder is really a coating of
bondo, a material normally used in car repairs. After it set up,
we used hand-held tools to create the grout lines. Finally, several
layers of paint gave the appearance of a textured brick surface.

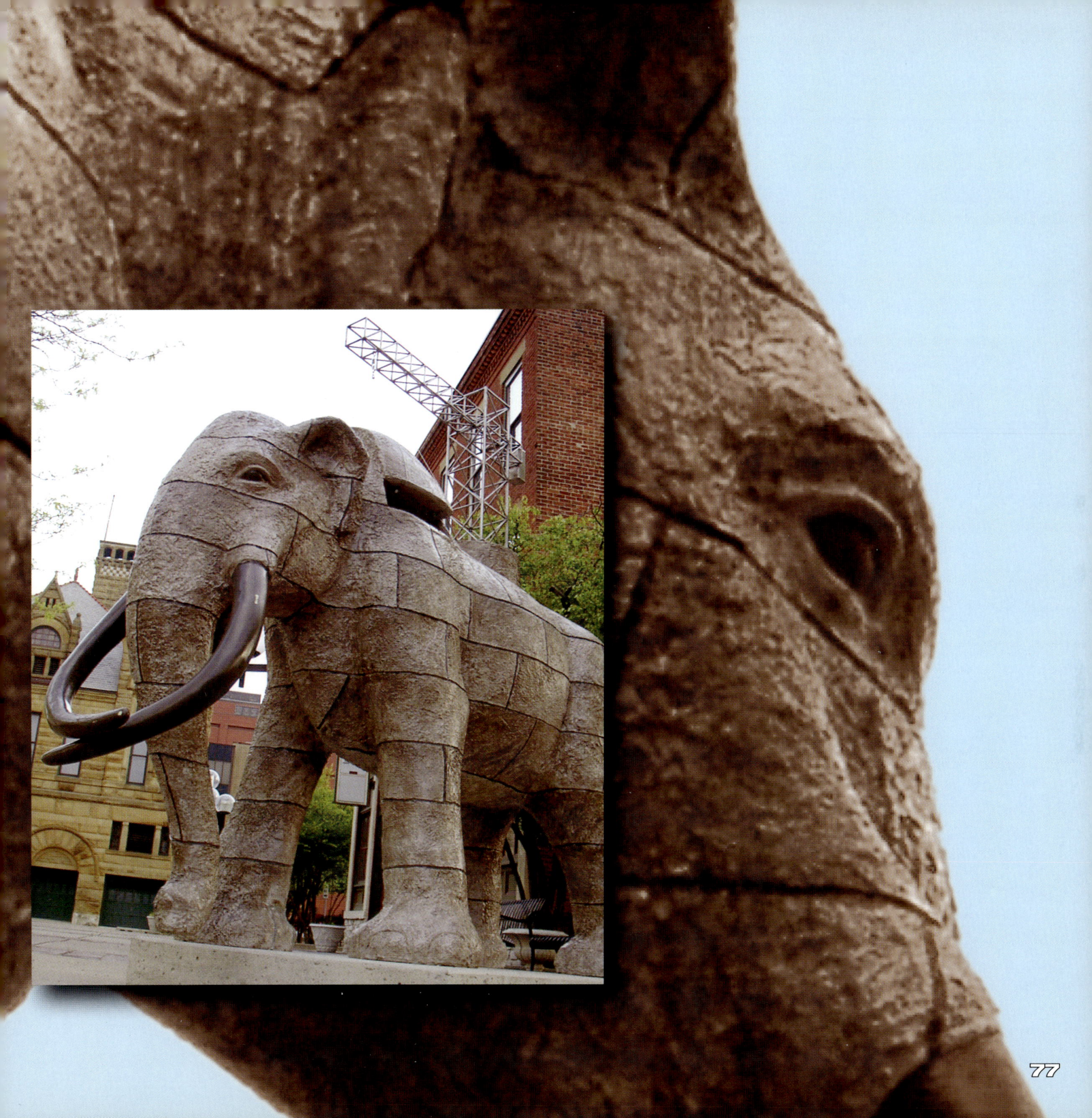

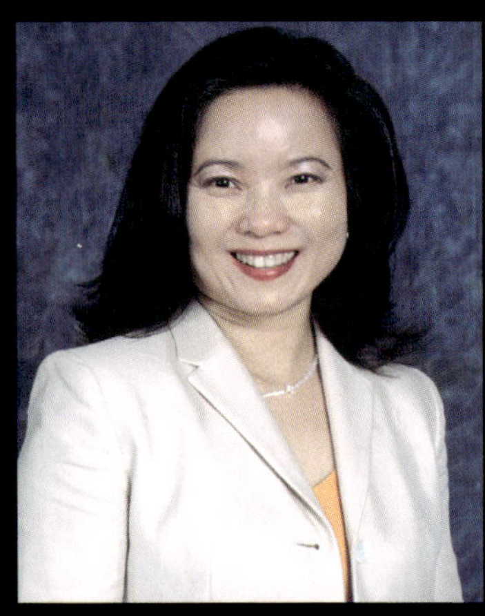

ARCHITECTURE DON

Artist: Suining Ding, IPFW Interior Design faculty

Sponsor: SchenkelShultz

The idea was to create an architectural-looking mastodon with a simple and classical design. The original concept came from ancient Roman architecture—the Pantheon.

Architecture Don's legs were painted with Ionic columns to represent the strength of architecture. His body was painted with a coffered ceiling and an oculus which emphasize the architectural character.

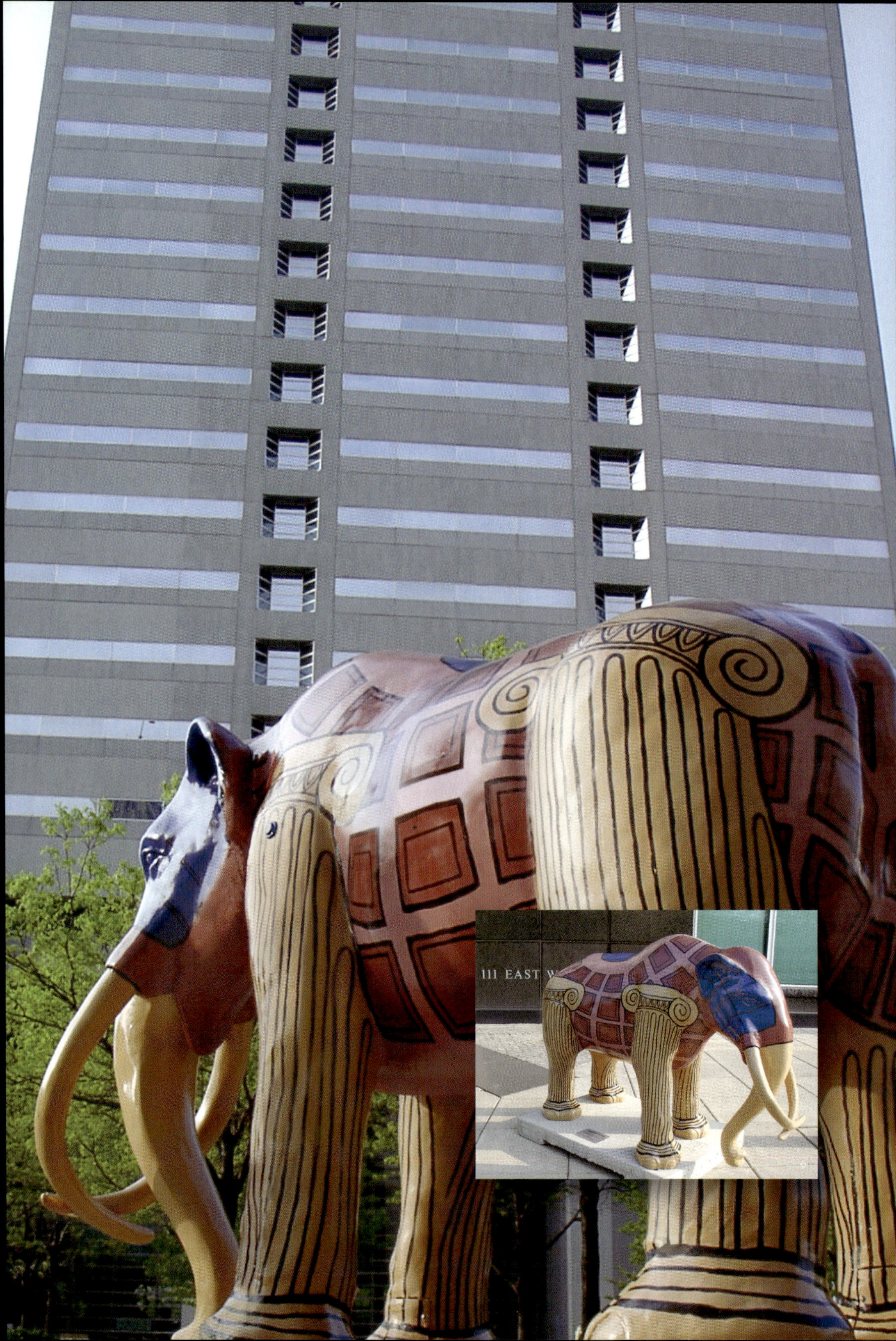

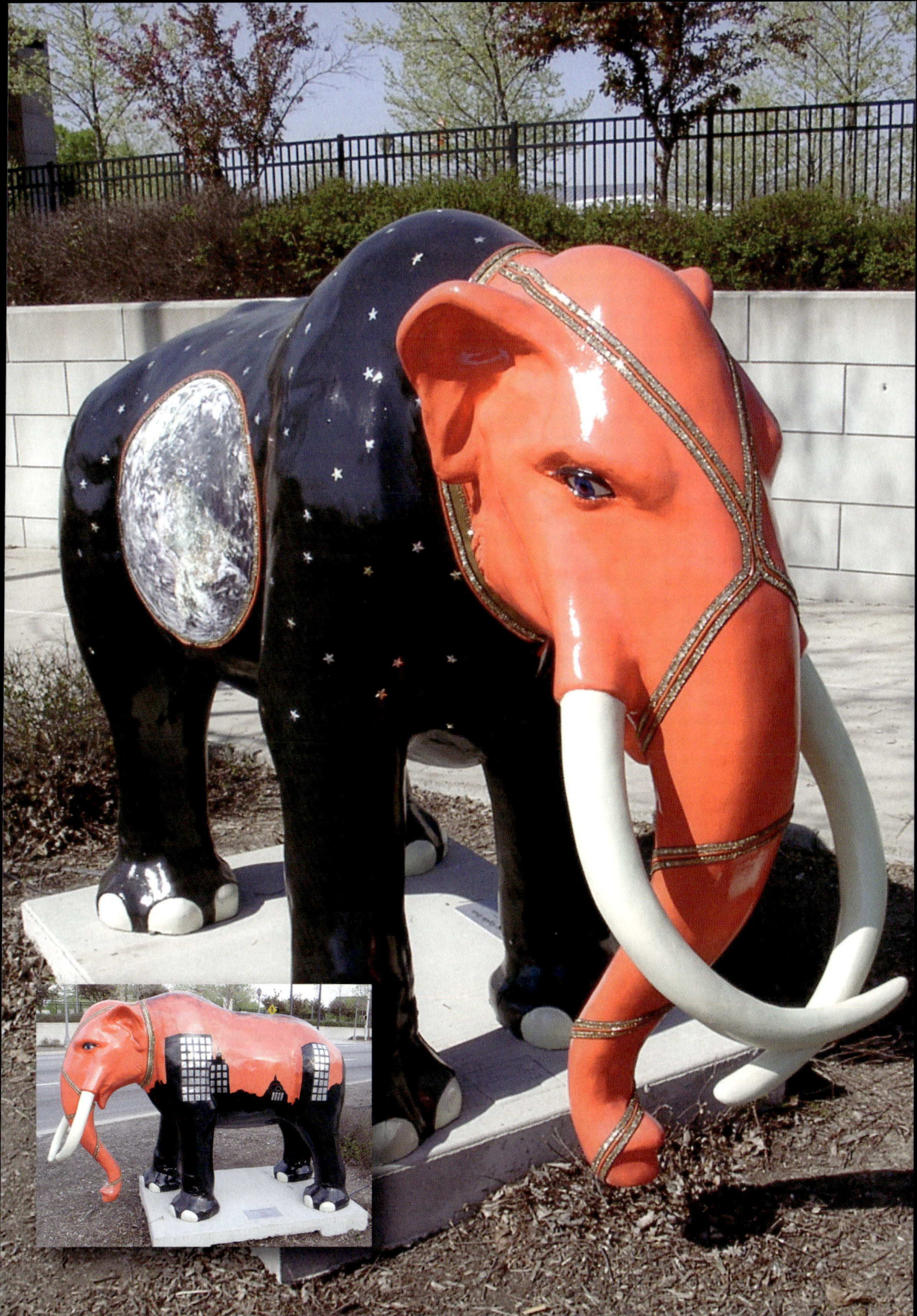

FIBER OPTIC DON

Artists: Don Hoekema, artist,
Adam Martin, artist

Sponsor: Verizon

By Don Hoekema

Fiber Optic Don is a down-to-earth tribute to IPFW and the high-tech world of telecommunications. The project gave us an opportunity to work on a truly unique canvas.

One side of our don depicts earth floating in fiber optic, lighted space. The other side shows the Fort Wayne skyline, also lighted by fiber optics. We even used fiber optic rope to thread around don's trunk.

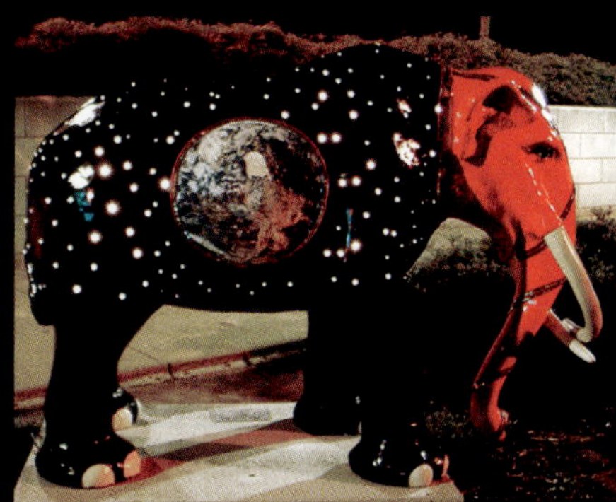

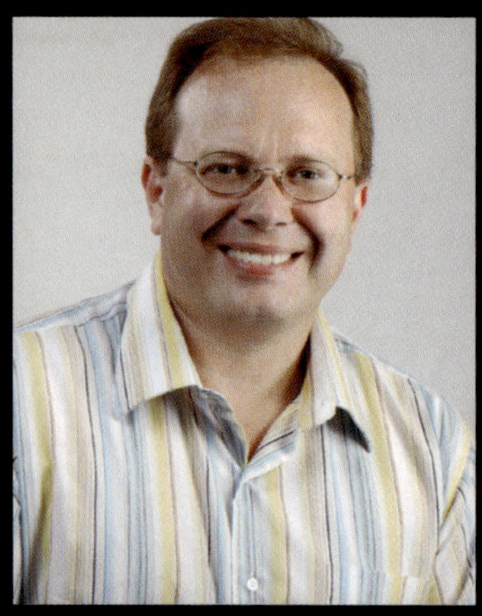

■ BROADCASTODON

Artist: Gregg Tarr

Sponsor: WANE–TV 15

As the art director at WANE-TV 15, I was approached about creating the station's mastodon. Both the project size and working with paints I'm not accustomed to gave me some concern. Still, I come from an artistic family, was born and raised in Fort Wayne, and thought it fitting to be part of this fun and challenging project.

I hoped my involvement would please my coworkers, friends, and others in the community, but most of all, I hoped to please my two young sons.

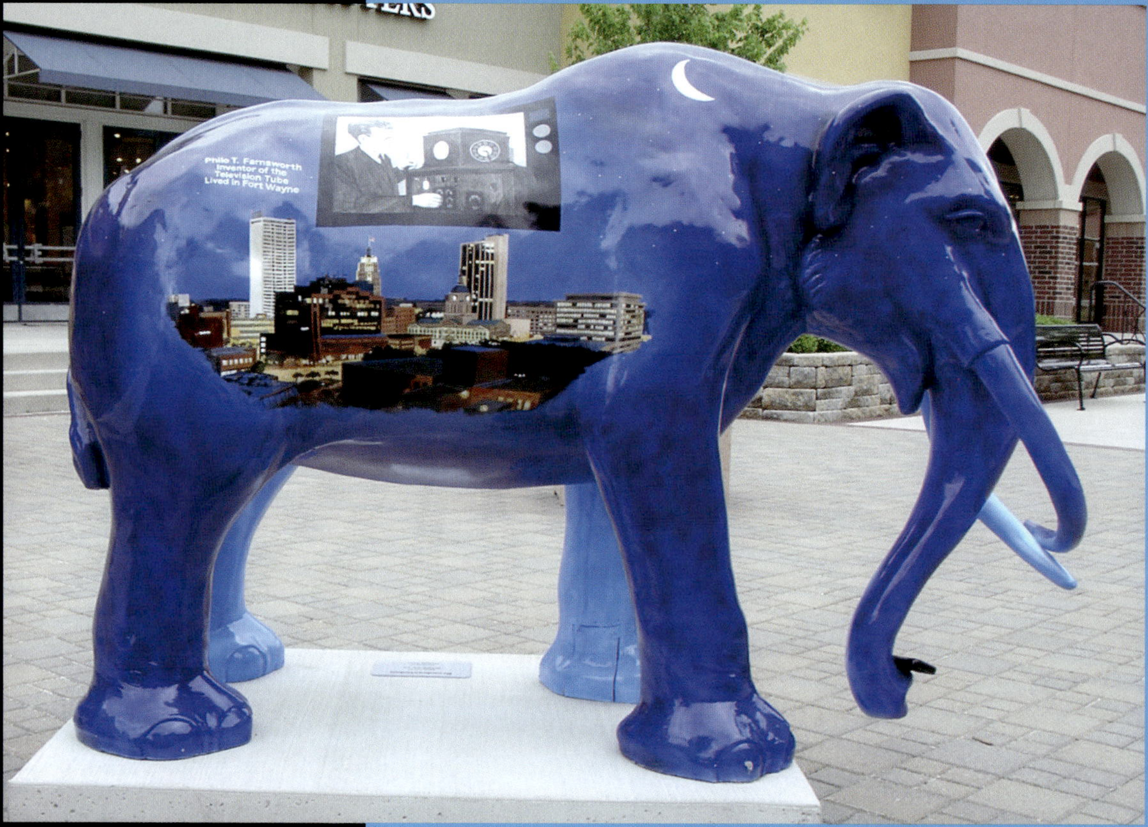

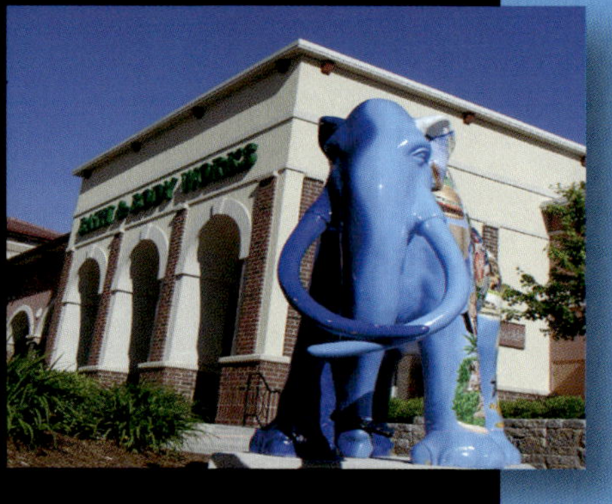

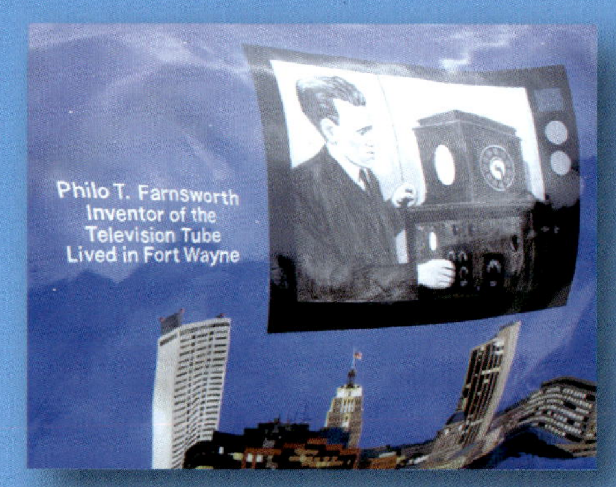

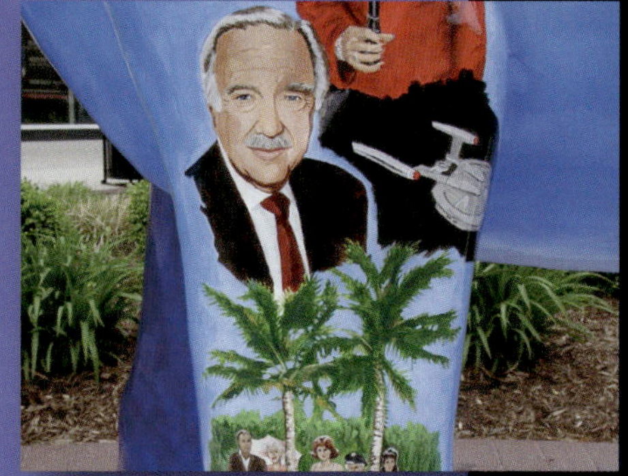

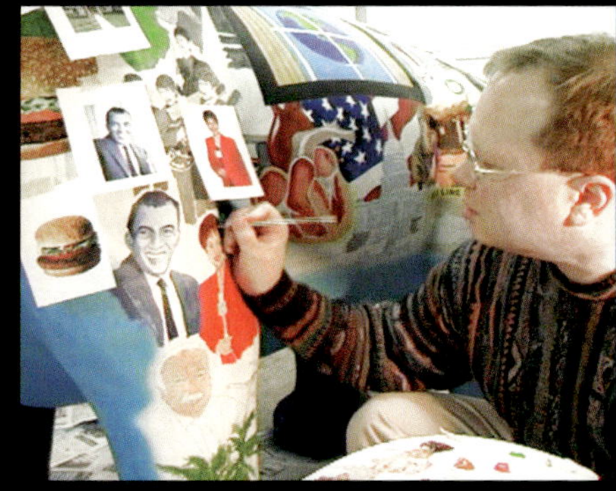

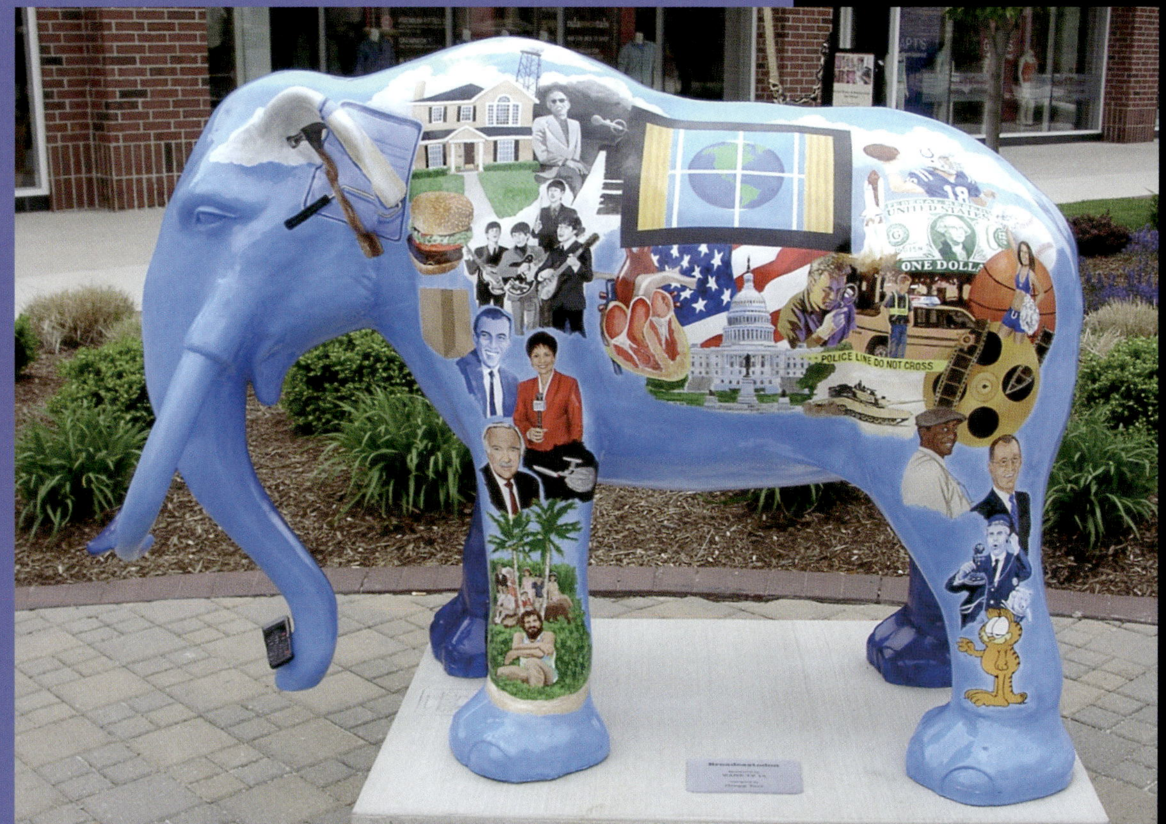

Using realistic images, my design concept is based on the connection between television and Fort Wayne through Philo T. Farnsworth, a Fort Wayne resident who invented the television tube. I wanted to give tribute to Farnsworth and show how television has become a window to the world.

Since programs are broadcast 24 hours a day, I divided Broadcastodon into day and night sides. Finally, attached a remote control to his trunk. I thought it would be fun if the mastodon were in control of his own viewing habits—just like the rest of us.

■ BUSINESTODON

Artists: Andrew Sprague, senior art director, *Business People Magazine* (*pictured left*)

Thomas Schriner, art director, *Business People Magazine* (*pictured right*)

Sponsor: *Business People Magazine*

By Andrew Sprague

We jumped at the opportunity to work on a mastodon. We certainly were not going to let our vast inexperience with painting mastodons get in the way.

Once the idea of a don in a business suit was put out there, we knew we had the concept. We didn't have the resource of time to do this project twice, so it had to work and look right from the get-go.

Once we figured that repeated masking off of areas, painting, and then pulling off the masks would get us in the ballpark of what we wanted, we began. Four weeks later we gave birth to a 165-pound BusinestoDon.

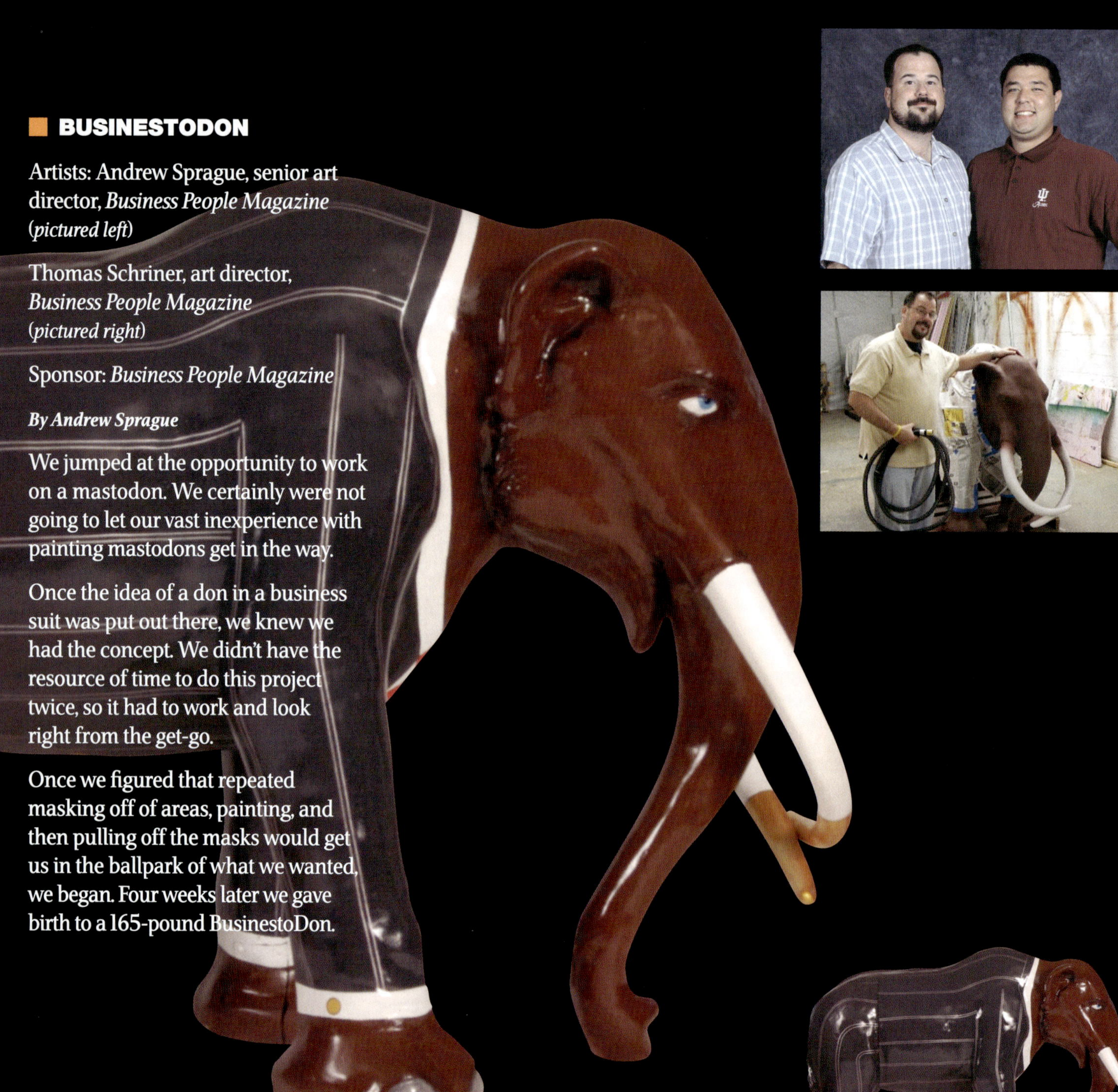

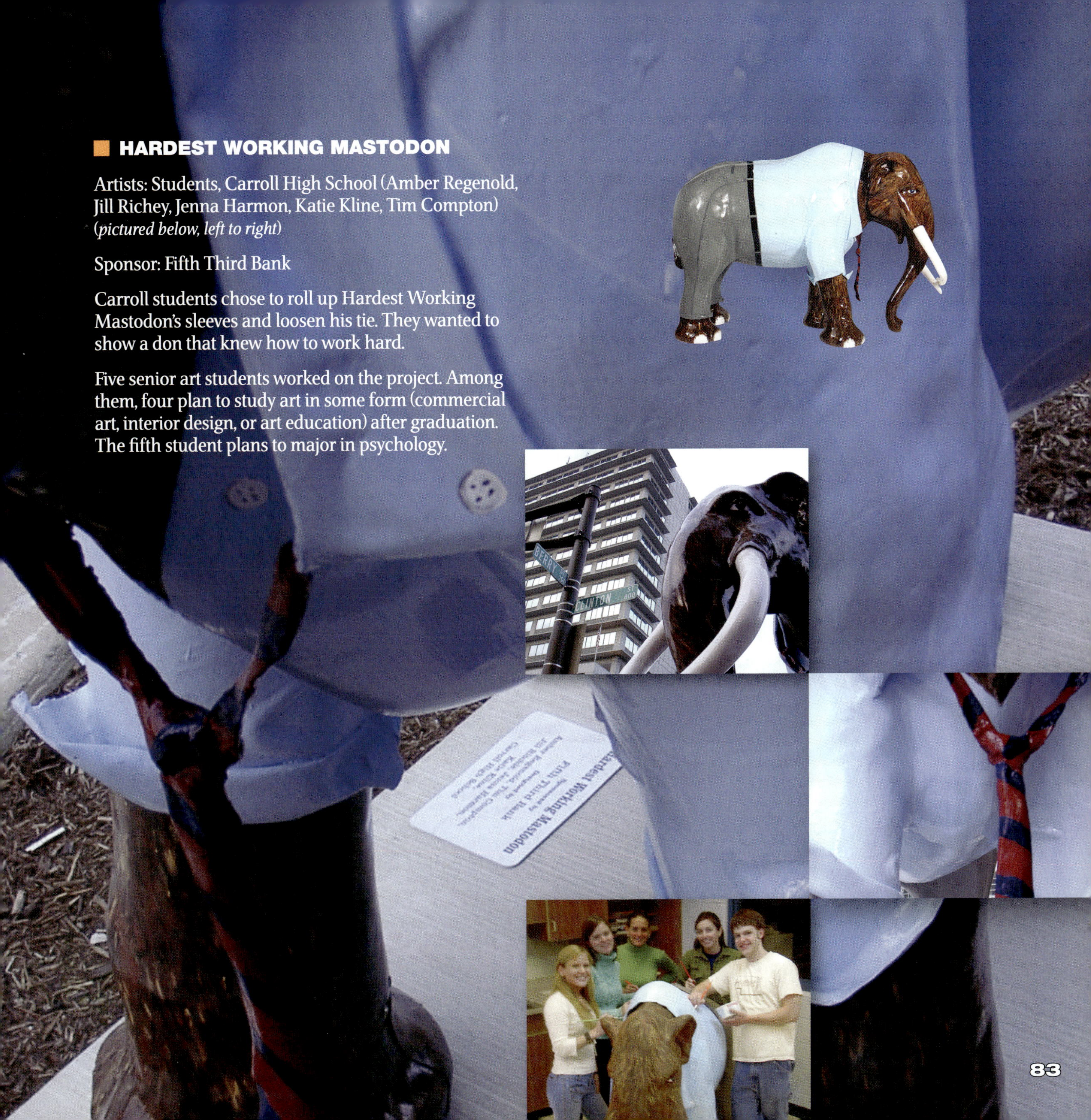

■ HARDEST WORKING MASTODON

Artists: Students, Carroll High School (Amber Regenold, Jill Richey, Jenna Harmon, Katie Kline, Tim Compton) (*pictured below, left to right*)

Sponsor: Fifth Third Bank

Carroll students chose to roll up Hardest Working Mastodon's sleeves and loosen his tie. They wanted to show a don that knew how to work hard.

Five senior art students worked on the project. Among them, four plan to study art in some form (commercial art, interior design, or art education) after graduation. The fifth student plans to major in psychology.

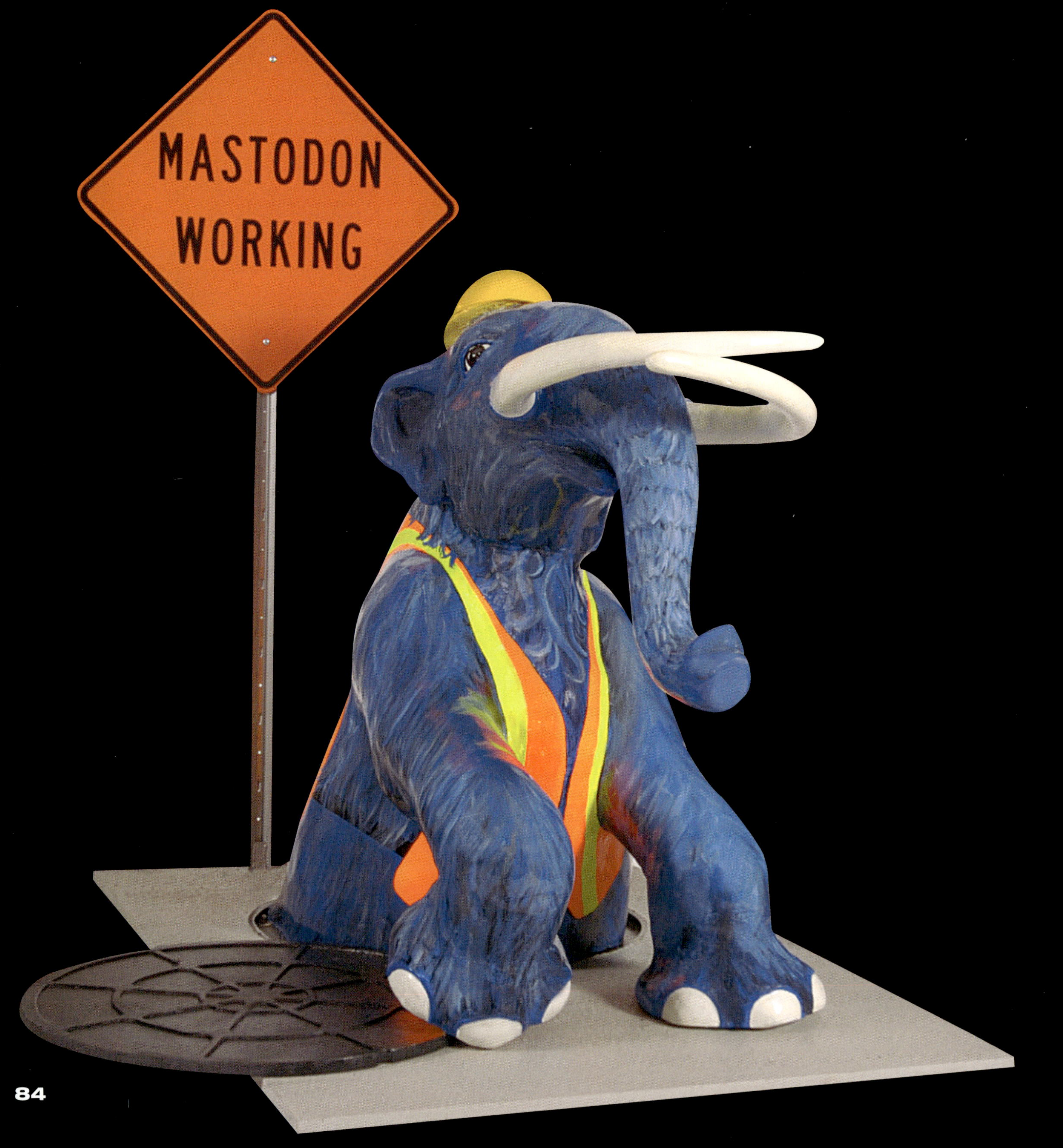

MASTODON
WORKING

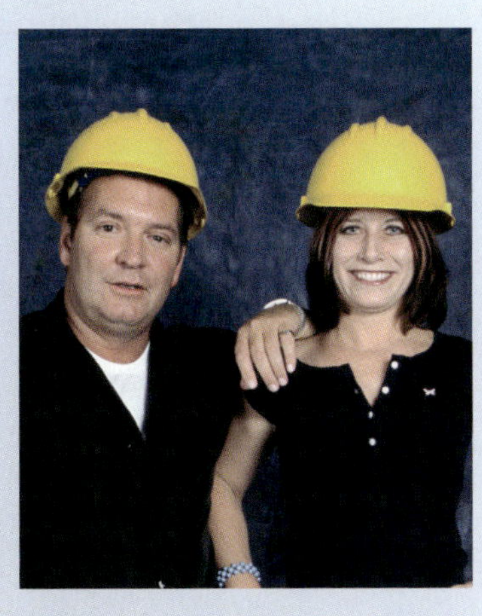

■ DON AT WORK

Artists: Michael Bowerman, Shapes Advertising (*pictured above, left*)

Kathy Minnich, Shapes Advertising (*pictured above, right*)

Sponsor: Hylant Group

By Michael Bowerman

While brainstorming ideas for our mastodon, Kathy and I did a lot of complaining about having two of the main routes to our office closed at the same time due to construction. You just couldn't get here easily from anywhere, so the construction theme was born!

We set up an area in Kathy's garage and worked on weekends over the winter to get Don at Work done. We planned on cutting him apart and repositioning his front legs with fiberglass but weren't quite sure how to do it. Kathy just happened to run into Deb Decker, an old friend who works with fiberglass. Deb and Lesley Koenemann, a coworker, spent an hour constructing new knees for him after we prepped him for surgery.

If you're wondering why Don at Work is blue, well, we just naturally chose blue to go along with the IPFW color.

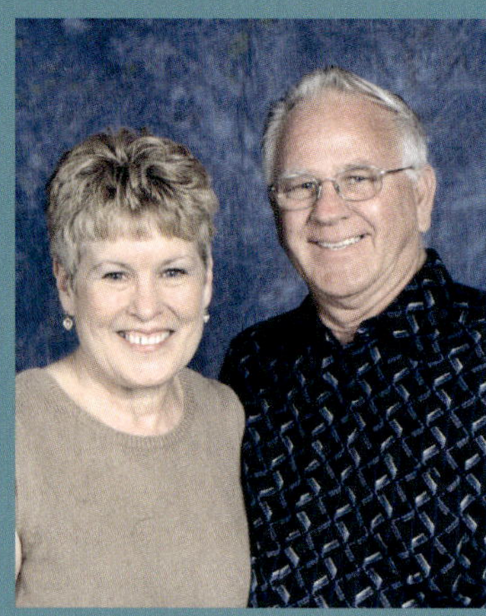

DR. DENNIS TREE

Artist: Karen Starn, graphic artist and illustrator (*pictured with husband*)

Sponsor: Alliance of the Isaac Knapp District Dental Society

Dr. Dennis Tree was created in my studio at Fort Wayne ArtSource and not in my home studio for obvious reasons...he's too big for the house.

After talking to Ellen Tom, a member of the Alliance, I knew what to do. The project took about 60 hours to complete. Marge Shomo and Diane McIntosh, two other artists from ArtSource, helped with painting the topcoat colors of his scrubs and the lettering on his name label.

Dr. Tree is very much a professional and reminds us that flossing is important.

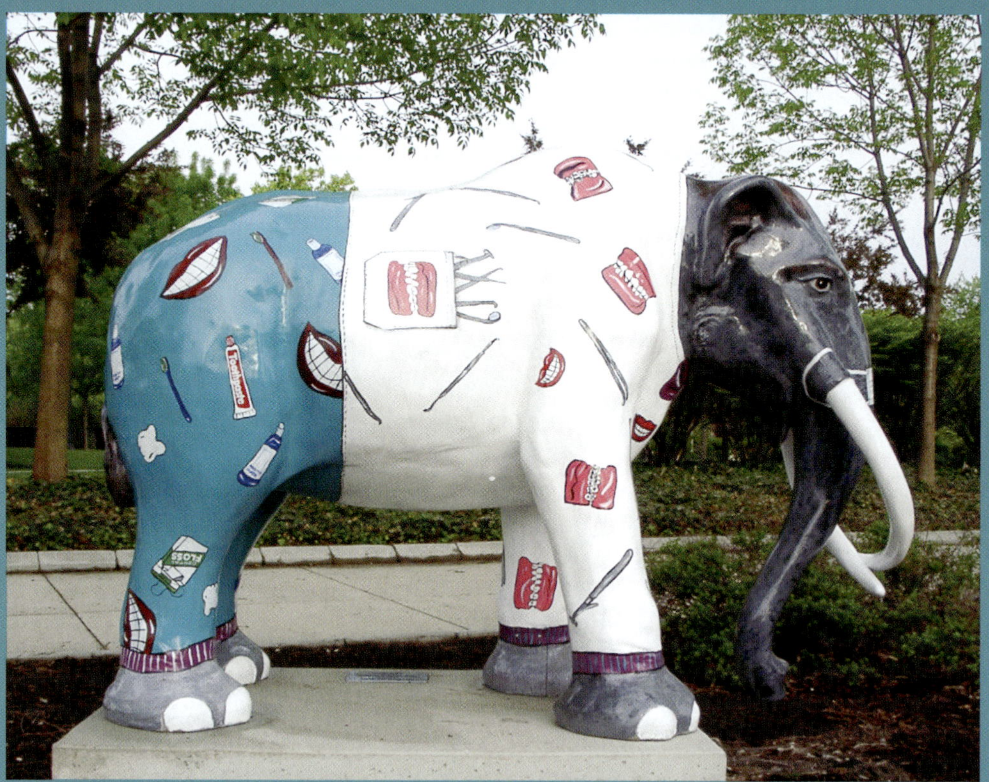

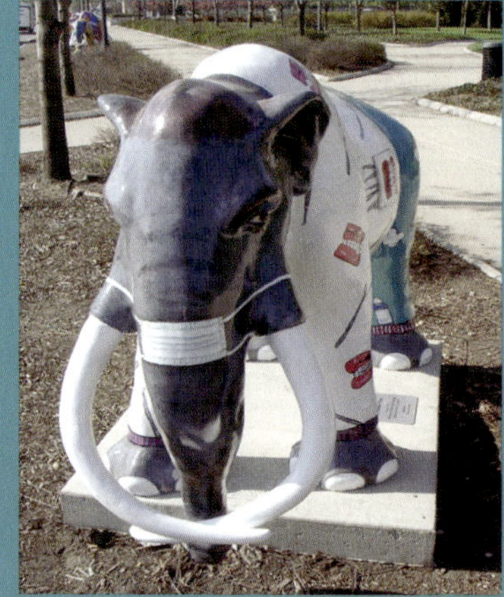

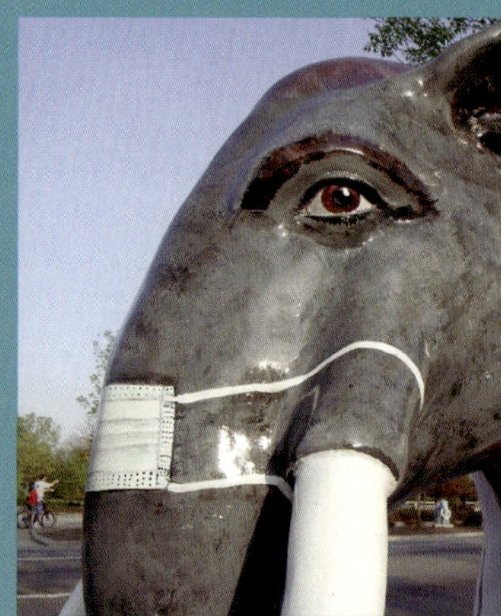

Mastodons on Parade

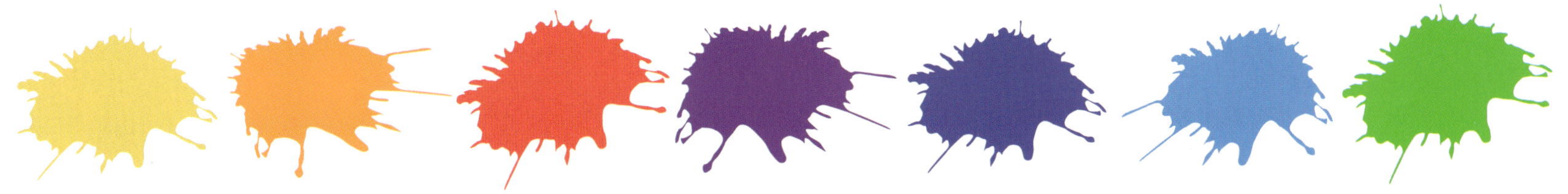

Dons at Play

Dons at Play

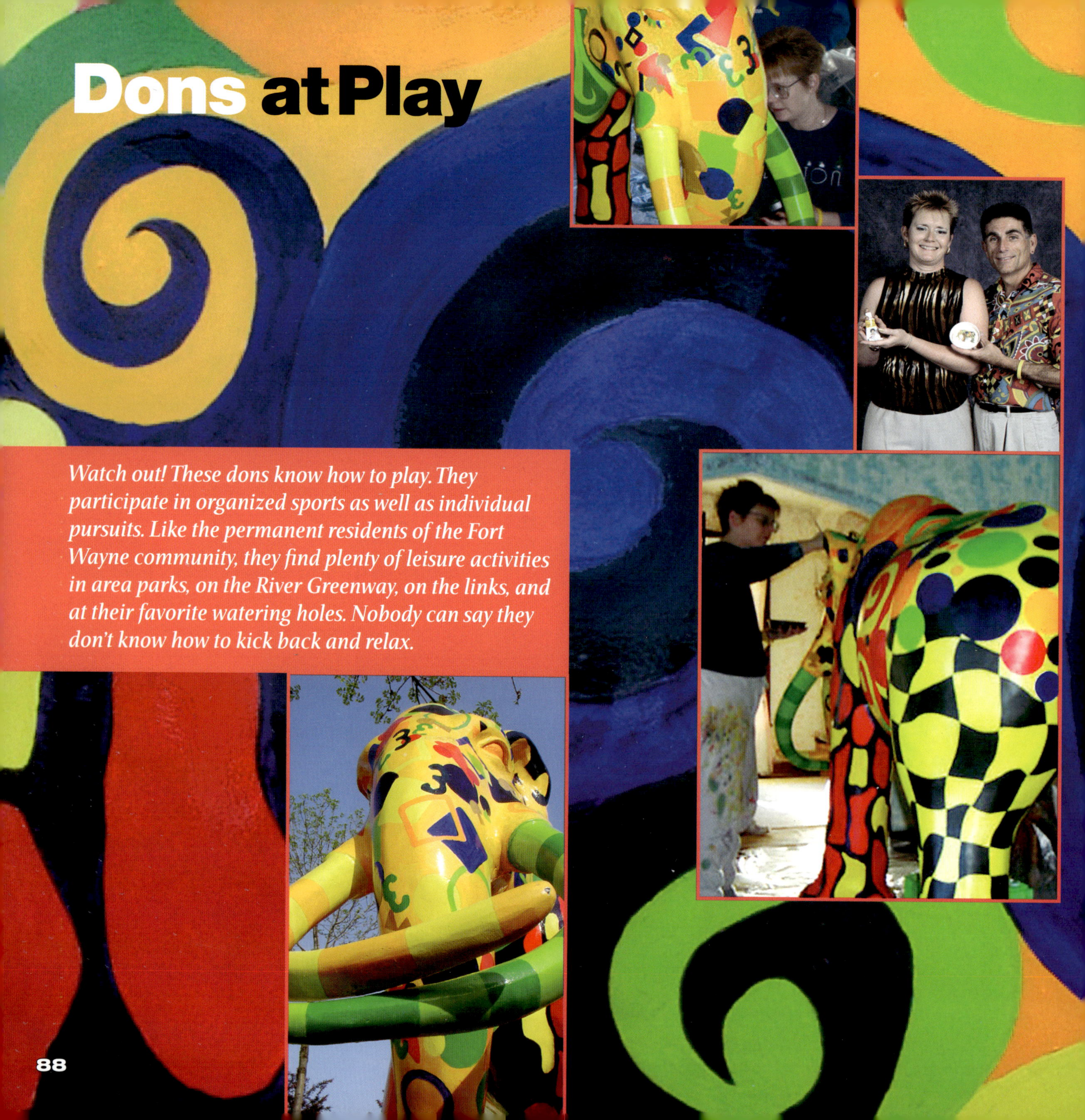

Watch out! These dons know how to play. They participate in organized sports as well as individual pursuits. Like the permanent residents of the Fort Wayne community, they find plenty of leisure activities in area parks, on the River Greenway, on the links, and at their favorite watering holes. Nobody can say they don't know how to kick back and relax.

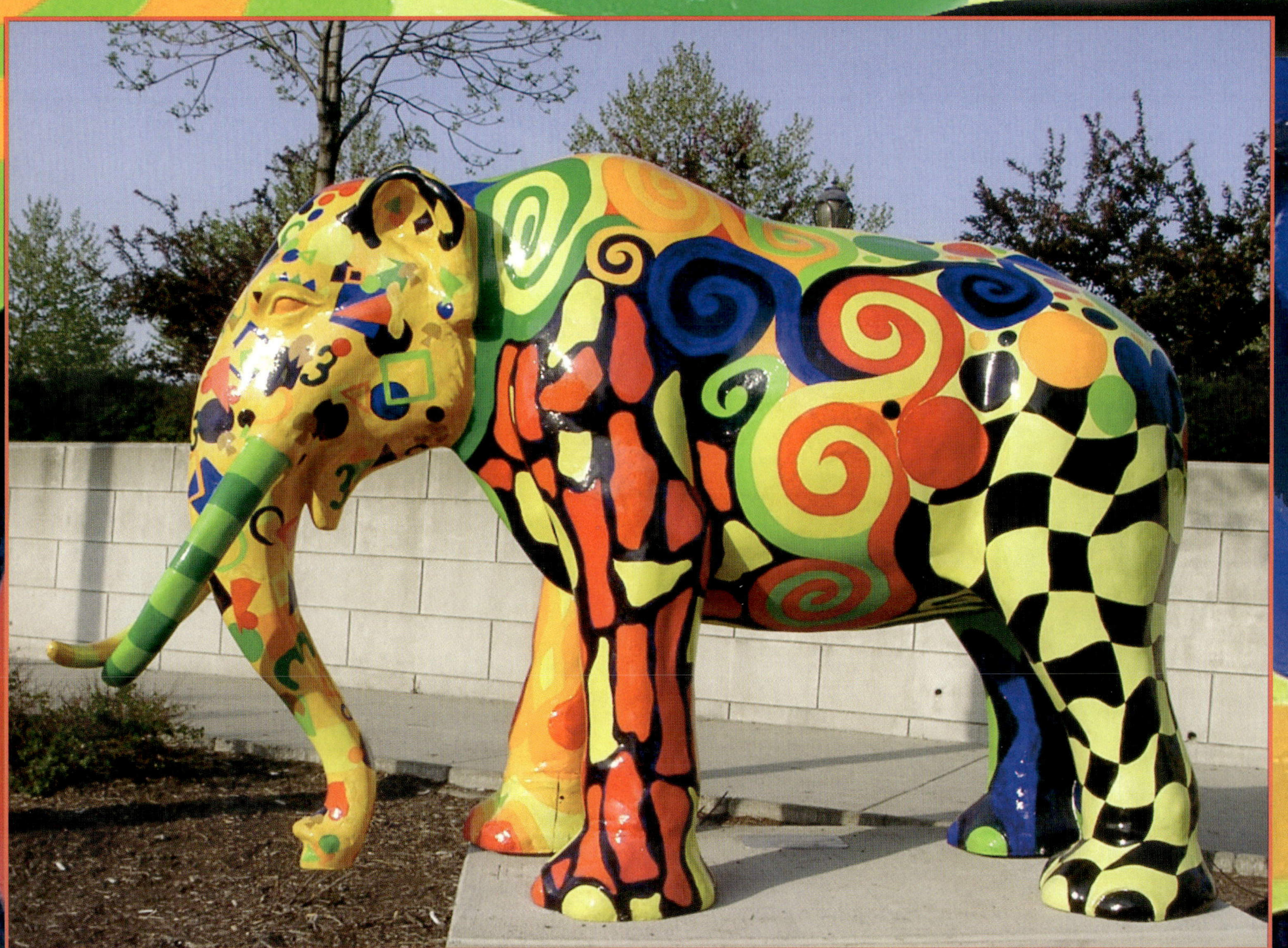

◼ BISTRO DON

Artist: Rhonda Andrews Woodruff, professional artist (*pictured with husband*)

Sponsor: Pizza Hut

A news blurb on WBNI said IPFW was up to something. I thought it would be something different and something big, and I wanted to be part of it.

My favorite part of the whole project was seeing everyone's face when I told them my studio was my dining room. My original inspiration came from the psychedelic '60s with its bright colors and wild designs.

It took an immense amount of support to complete this project. My husband was responsible for my care and feeding. Fox & Fox provided technical support and put up with me, a sometimes grumpy and tired employee.

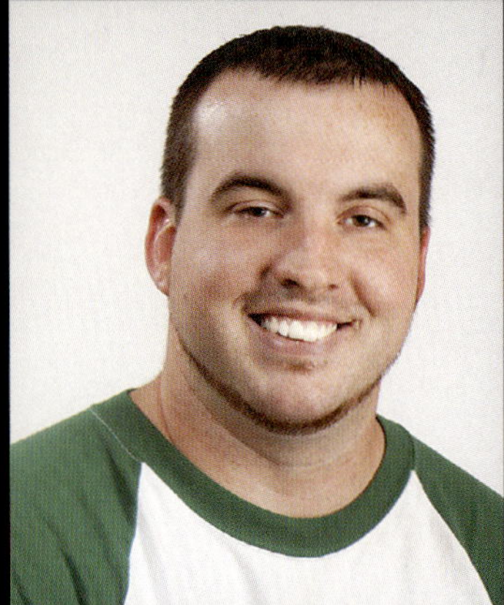

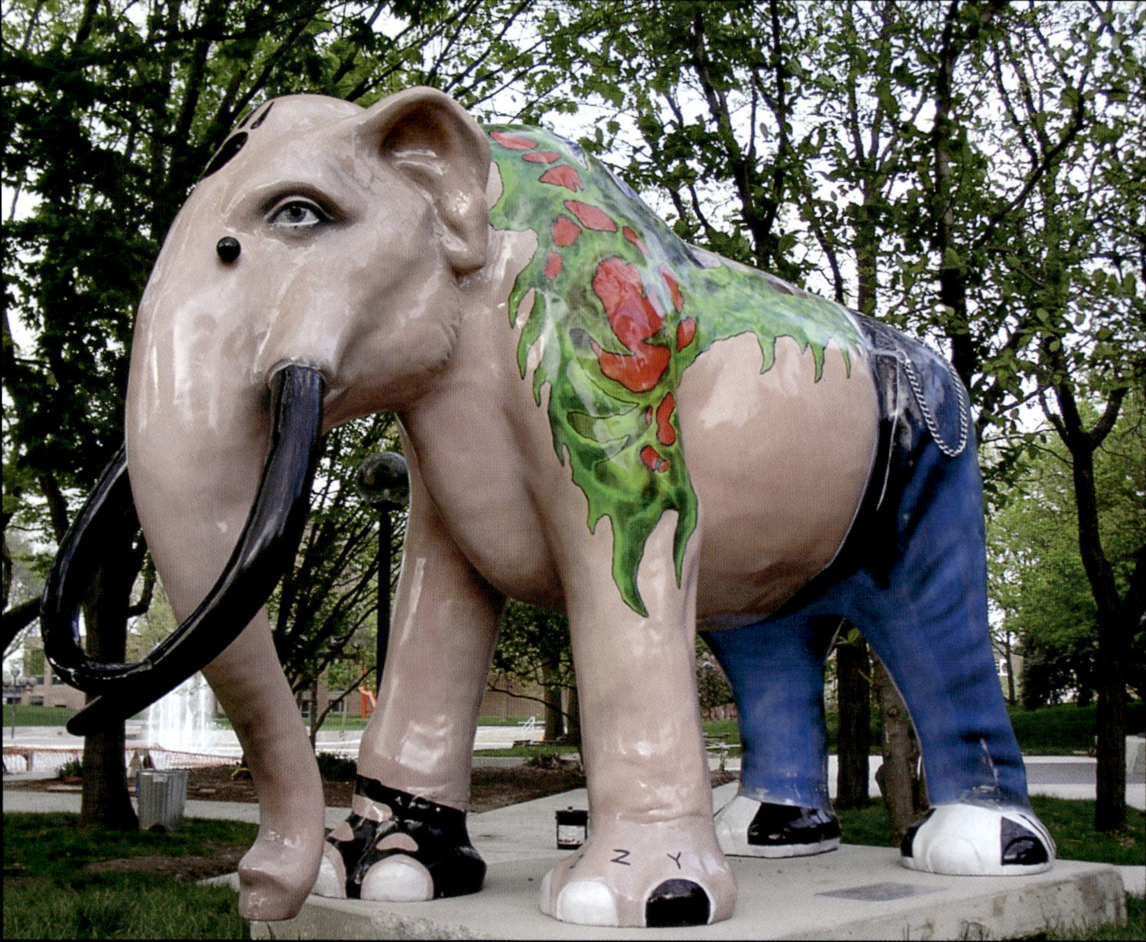

■ MAS-TAT-DON

Artist: Ryan Hadley

Sponsor: WBYR–98.9
The Bear

The Bear was instrumental in suggesting the concept of making the mastodon appear human. Painting the belly of the mastodon was the most difficult chore since I had to lie down and paint up. I was excited by the concept of working in a very different art medium. This project has inspired me to start showing artwork, especially paintings in oil and acrylic.

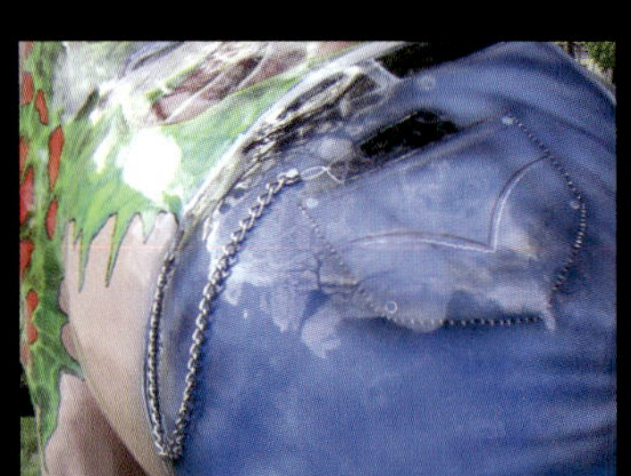

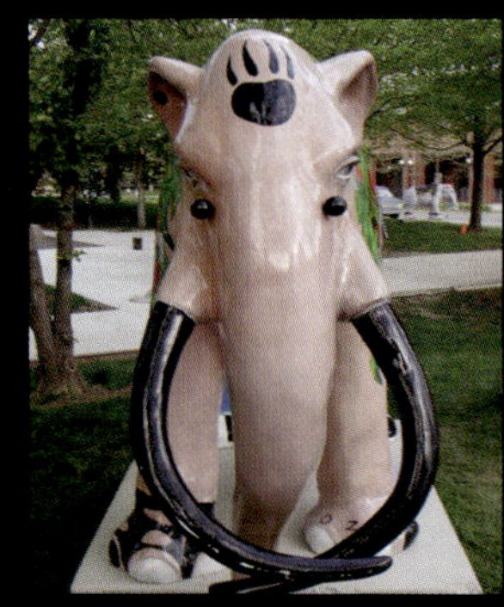

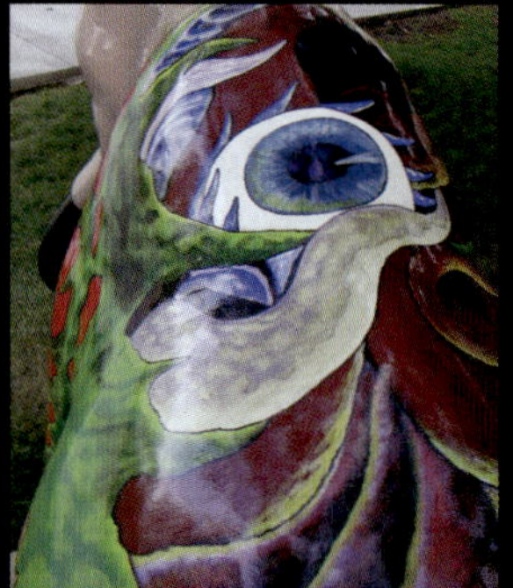

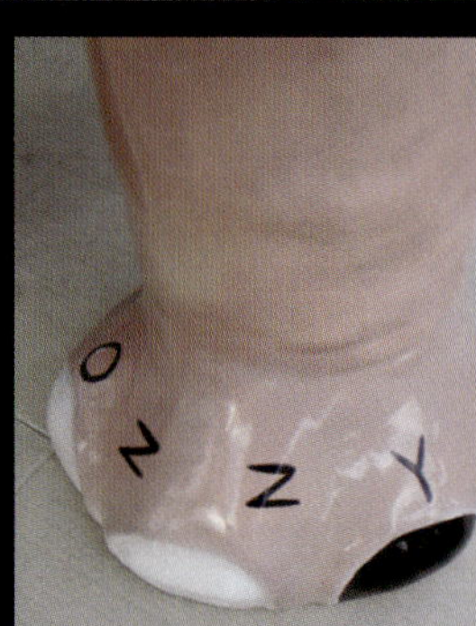

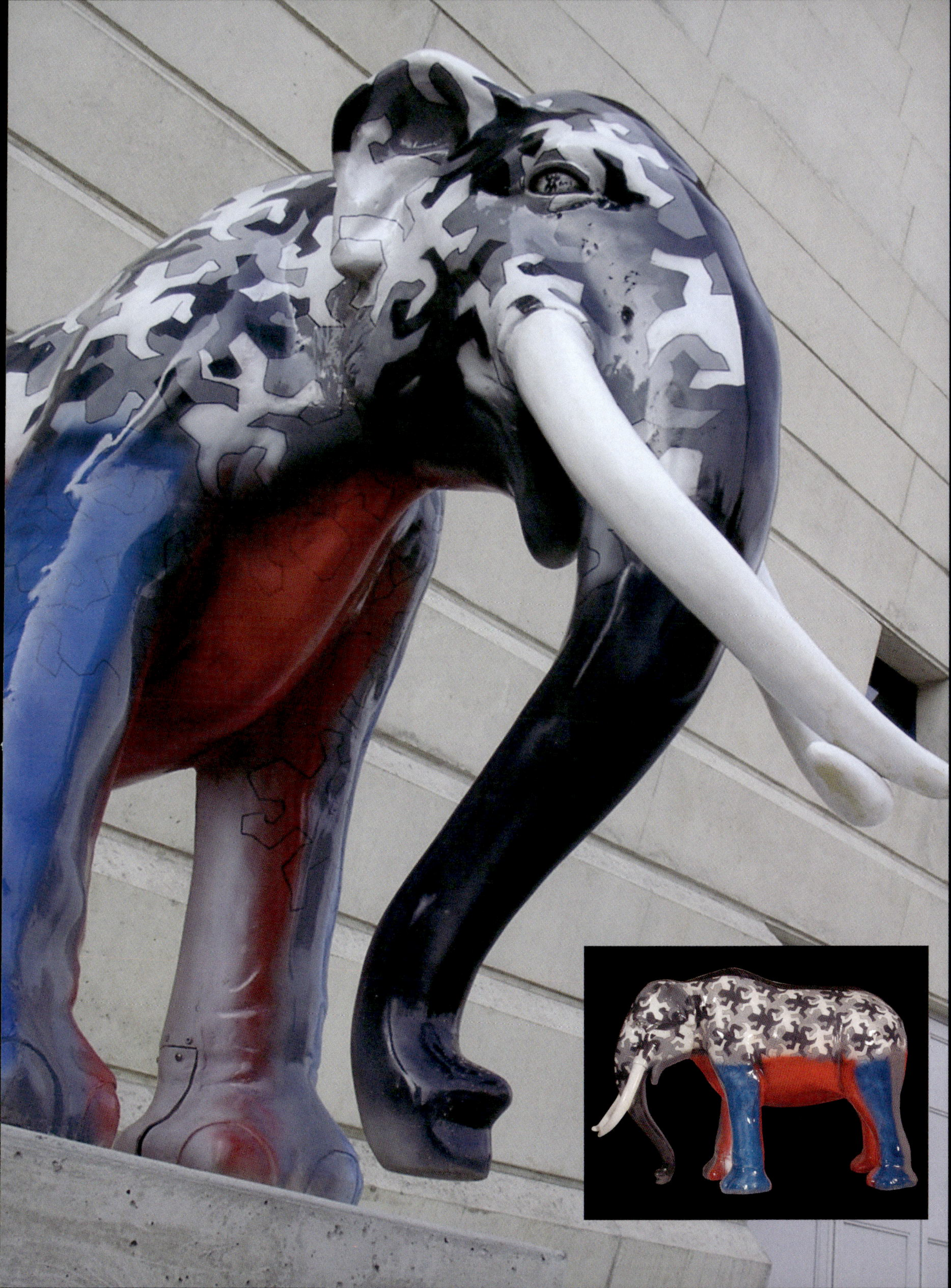

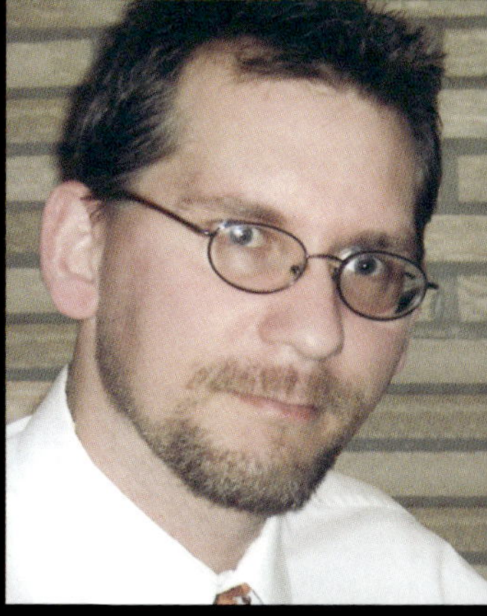

Artist: Don Jensen, The T.A.G. Art Company (*pictured*)

Eric Eisenberger, The T.A.G. Art Company

Sponsor: MSKTD & Associates Inc.

By Troy Ganser

Lizzadon is a tribute to artist M. C. Escher. Viewers will look at a mastodon but think "lizard, lizard, lizard" as they see a puzzle of reptiles teeming across the don's surface. Without question, our biggest challenge was to fit the pattern onto the statue's hide.

To be honest, a little fudging occurred. You may notice one or two lizards with an extra leg...or maybe a longer tail than the others. Nonetheless, the design stays consistent—even the pupils of our don's eyes are lizards!

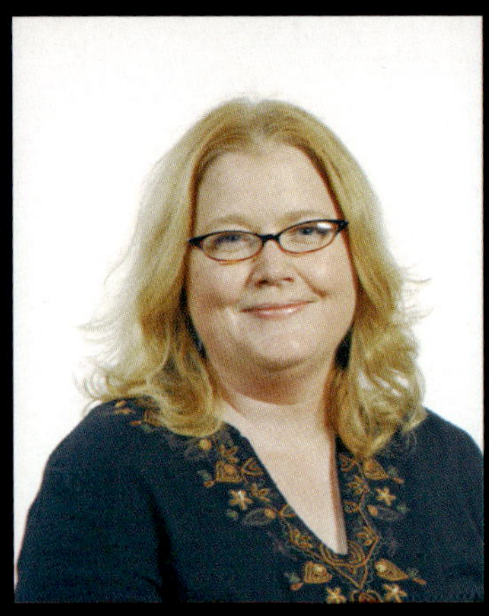

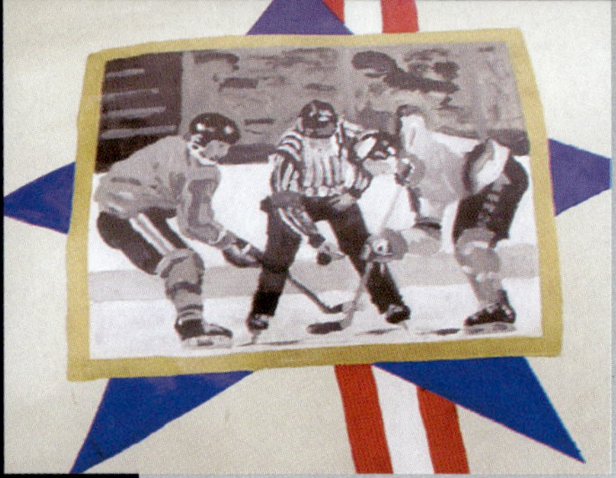

■ AMERICA'S LOVE OF SPORTS, LEISURE & ENTERTAINMENT

Artist: Pamela Turnbow, Whitley County artist

Sponsor: K&K Insurance Group, Inc.

Affectionately referred to as George, our don arrived on a cold January day. He was a lot larger than anticipated.

Overall, painting him was fun for the entire family, including the two dogs. My husband, Kent, was a big help with the project. He sanded and sprayed the primer coats. My biggest challenge was translating the design from paper to a 3-D mastodon.

George left the Turnbow home with a bit of drama as the limo sent to pick him up got stuck in the mud while trying to leave.

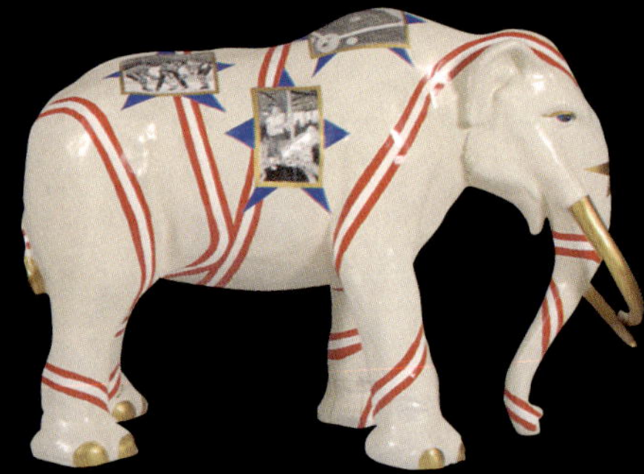

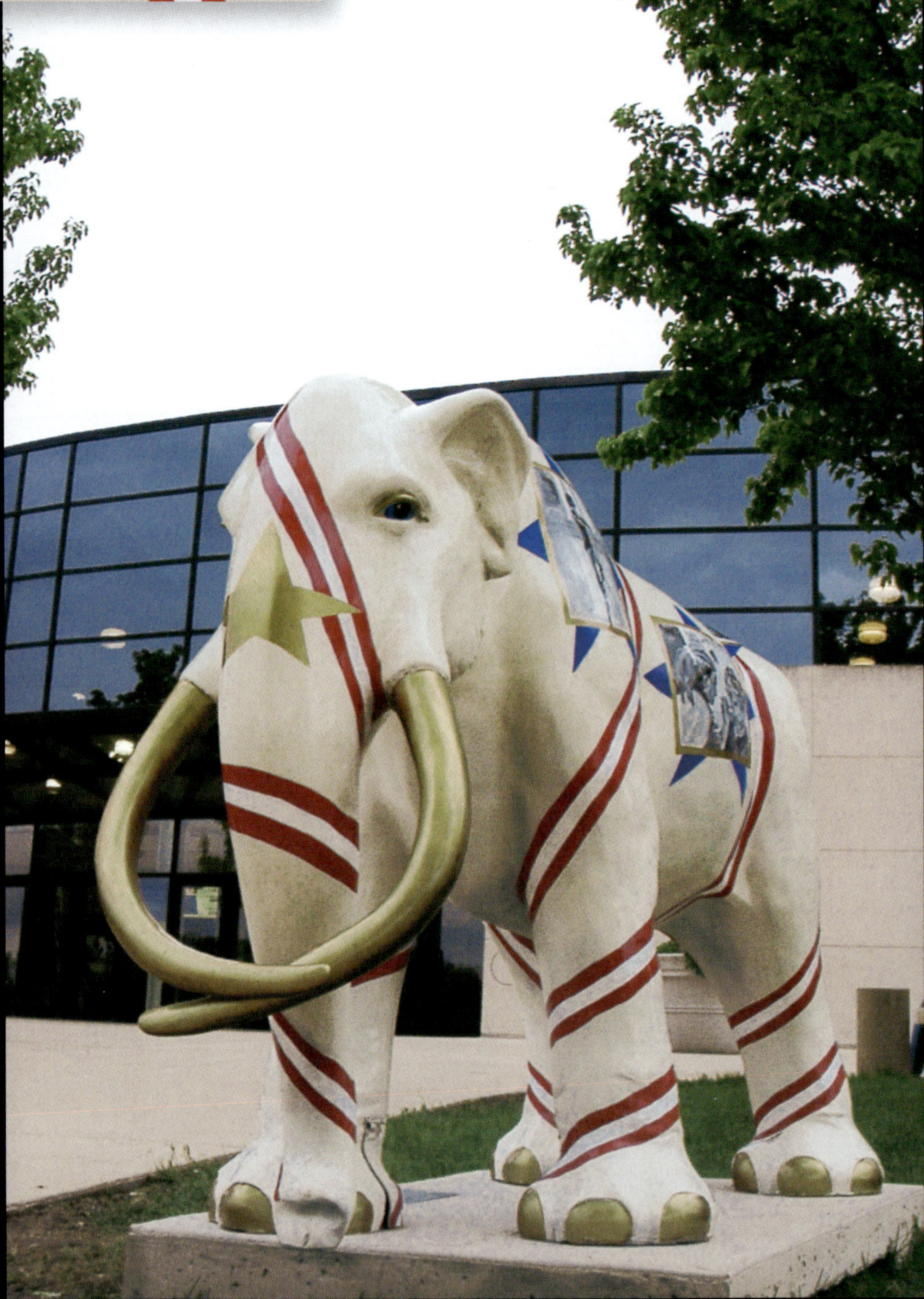

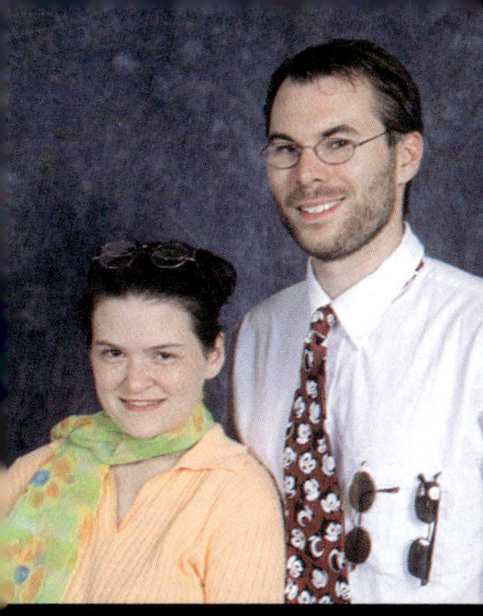

■ LEO

Artists: Jonna and Mark LeMieux,
professional artists, Platypus Productions
(pictured above, left to right)

Sponsor: Time Corners Lions Club

By Mark LeMieux

Bringing Leo to life has been a privilege
for both of us. He is a true work of the
heart. This fuzziest mastodon in the
herd took us over 250 hours to create,
including transit time. We live nearly
an hour from the warehouse where
he was stored.

We based Leo's design on the art style of
my favorite artist, Jim Henson. Our goal
was to come up with something fun, yet
artsy. He had to have character.

Jonna thinks he's our fourth child. She
cut over 3,240 feet of yarn for his
mane and hand tailored his vest while
I worked on his face.

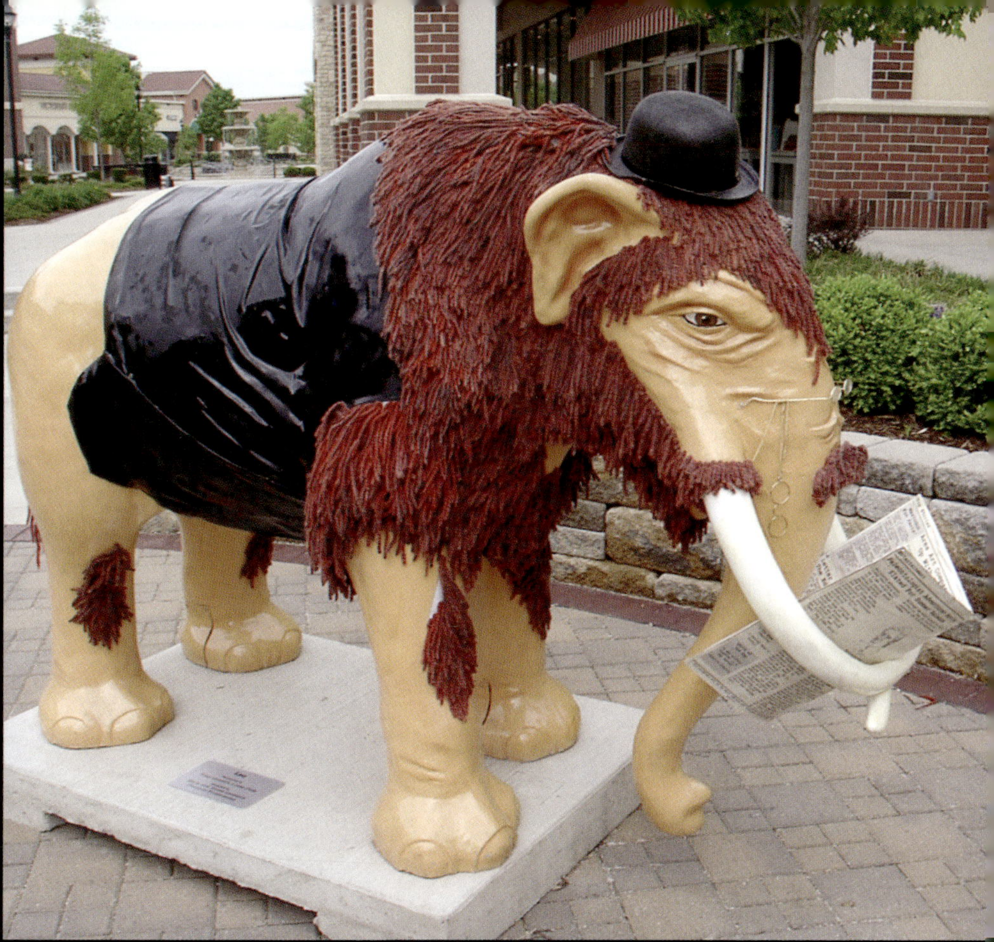

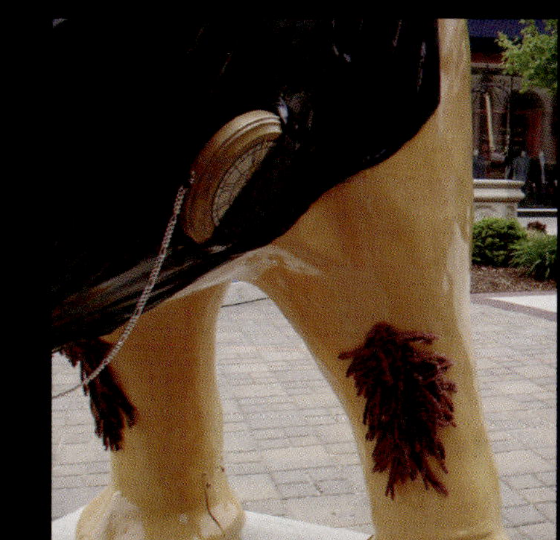

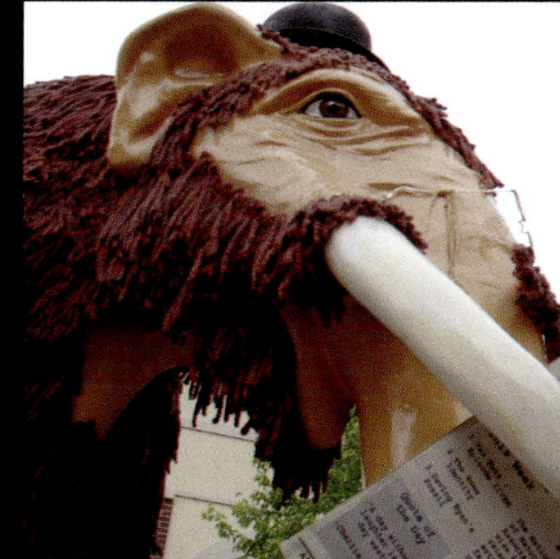

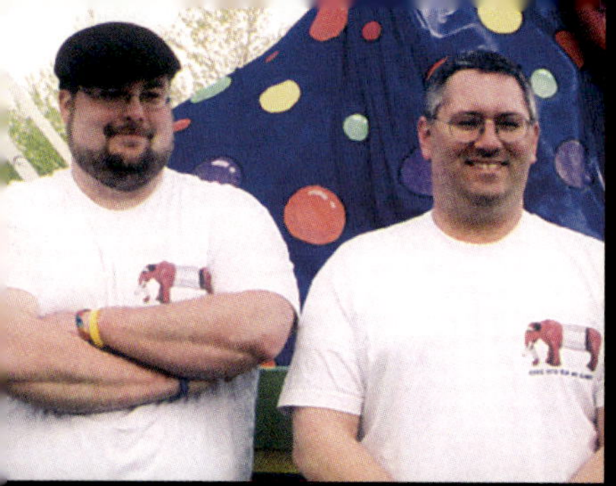

SLINKY DON

Artists: Larry Davis, graphic artist (*pictured left*)

Robert Gick, retired tool and die maker (*pictured right*)

Sponsor: Georgetown Square Shopping Center

By Larry Davis

My wife Tammy and I are both big kids. She is the one who inspired Slinky, our second mastodon.

Everyone wondered how we were going to pull off the spring. Once Robert came up with the rebar idea, everyone wondered how we were going to bend it. Richard Gick, my father-in-law, and Robert created a homemade bending bar.

That was the easy part. Making it sturdy and coating and painting it became our toughest obstacles. We ended up welding it and then having it plated. Slinky just didn't happen easily.

"It's kind of fun to do the impossible!"

— Walt Disney

"A spring, a spring, what a marvelous thing.
Everyone knows it's Slinky."

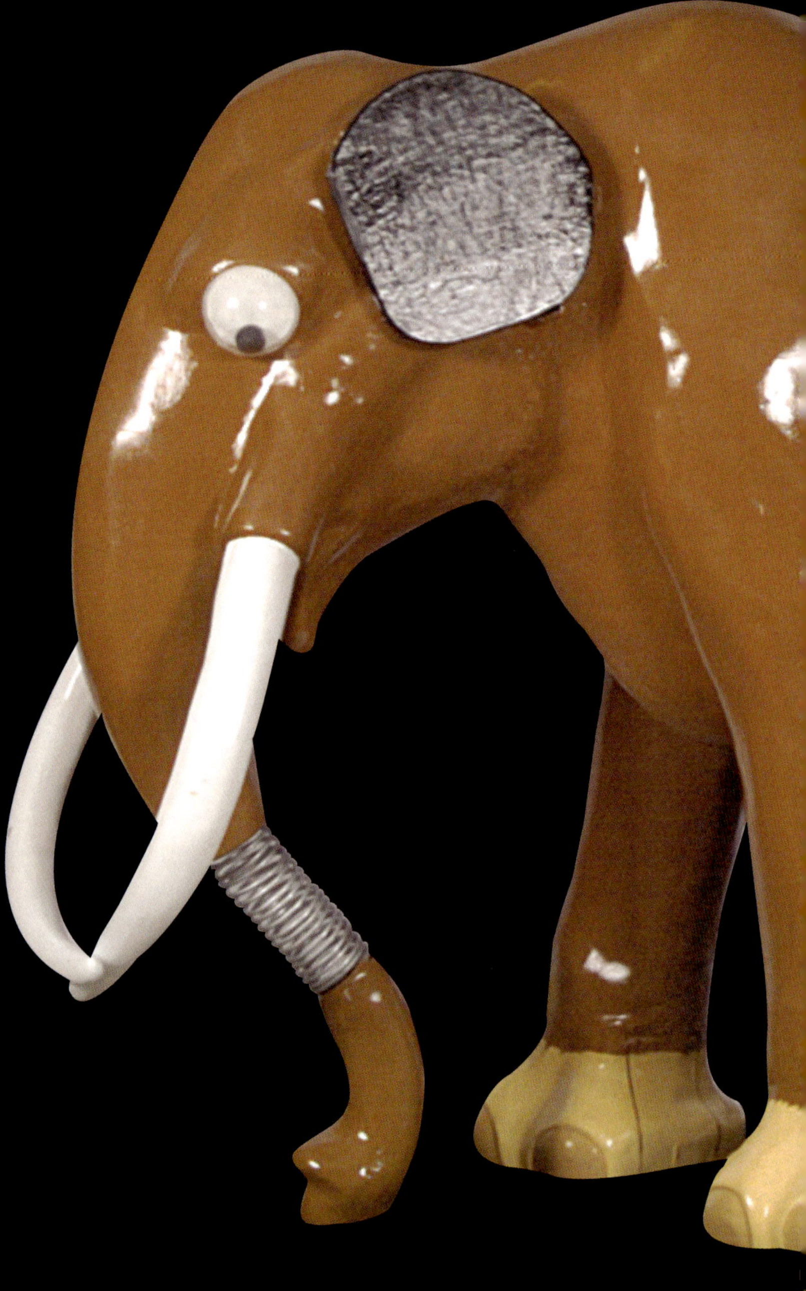

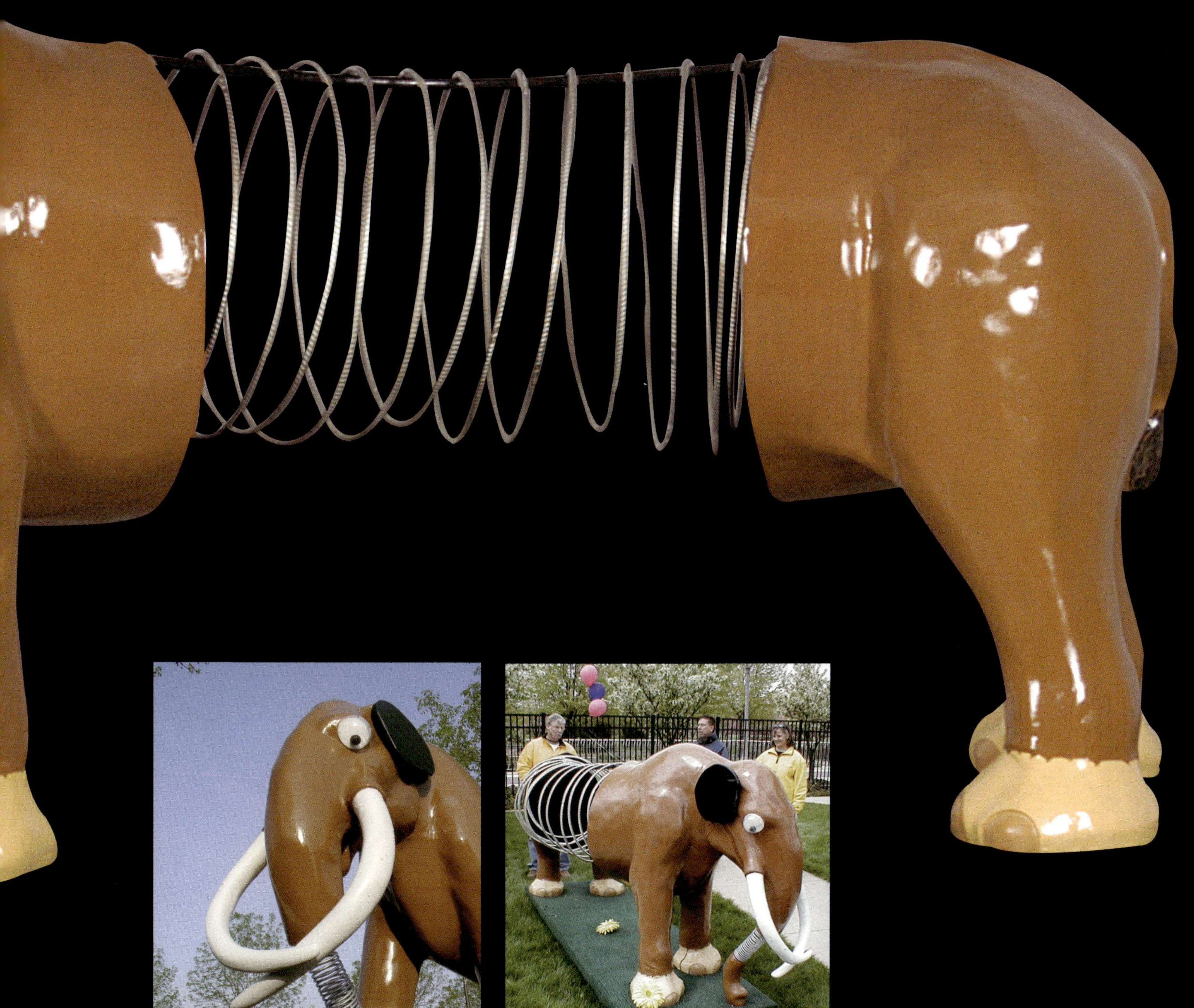

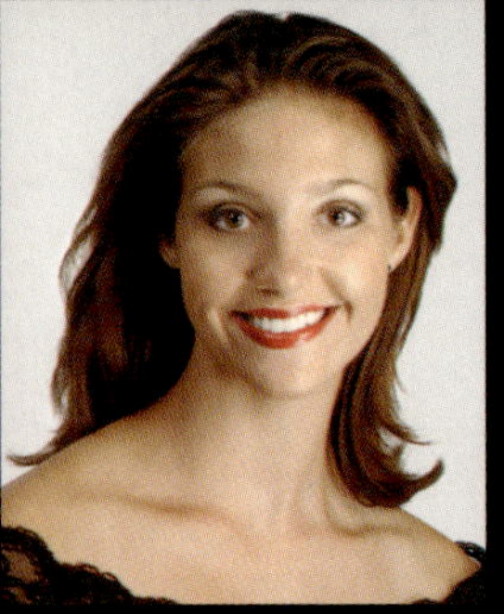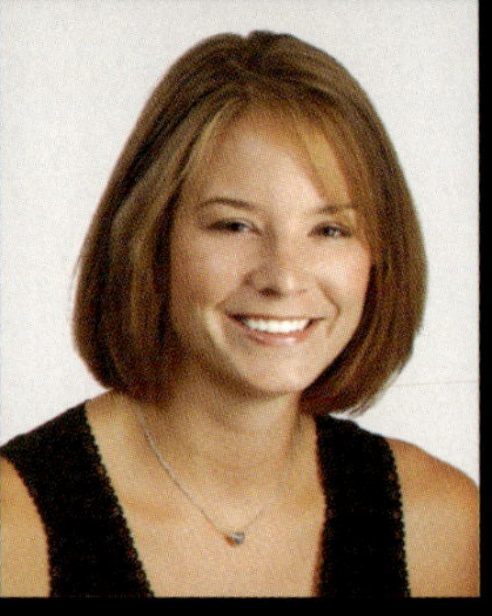

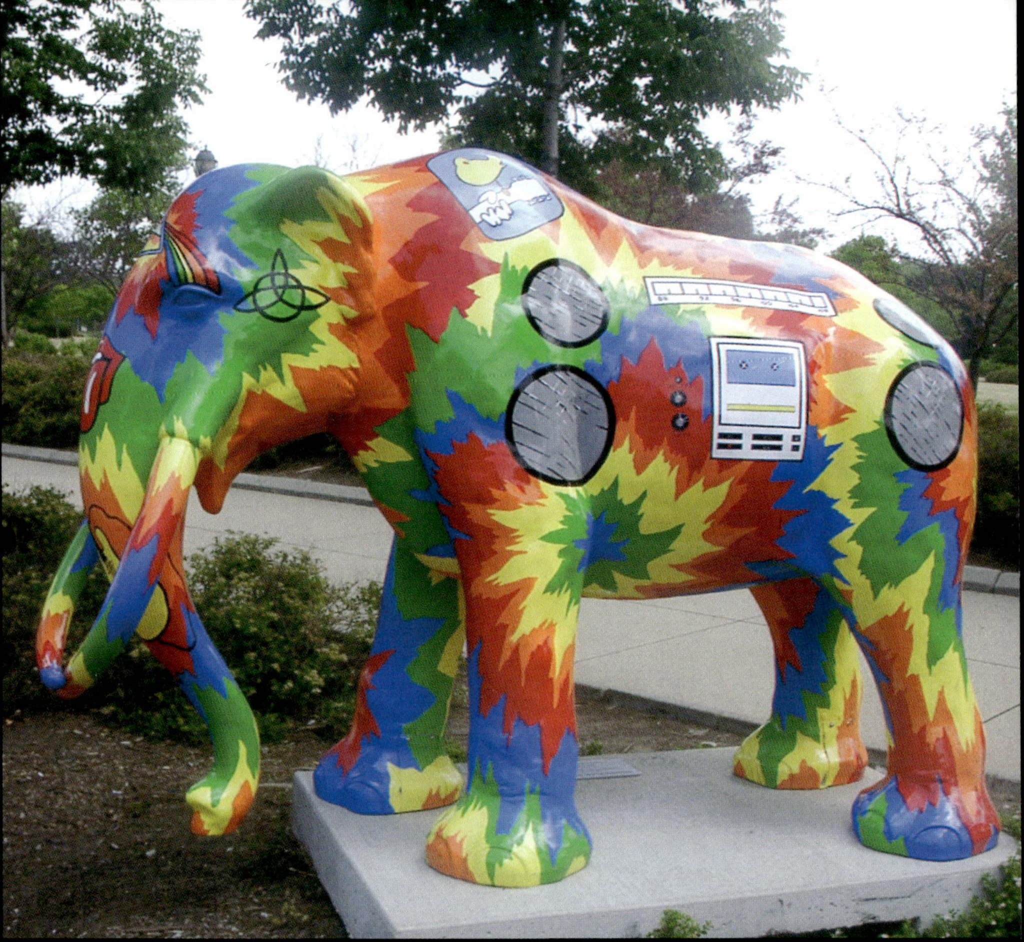

◼ CLASSIC ROCK O DON

Artists: Lyndsay Buesching,
IPFW art major (*pictured left*)

Jen Idle, IPFW art major (*pictured right*)

Sponsor: WFWI-92.3 "The Fort"

By Jen Idle

We are both art majors who were looking
for new artistic challenges. When
Chancellor Wartell approached us about
designing a mastodon for this community
project, we accepted.

The tie-dye concept arose through several
design submissions to our sponsor. The
actual design was inspired by musical
groups and trends of the classic rock era.
Look for rock band icons including the
Rolling Stones, Beatles, and Aerosmith.
Woodstock, that global phenomenon,
is also there.

The preparation phase took hours. The
actual painting was all full of color, fun, and
friendship. During the process there was
plenty of girl time, gossiping, listening to

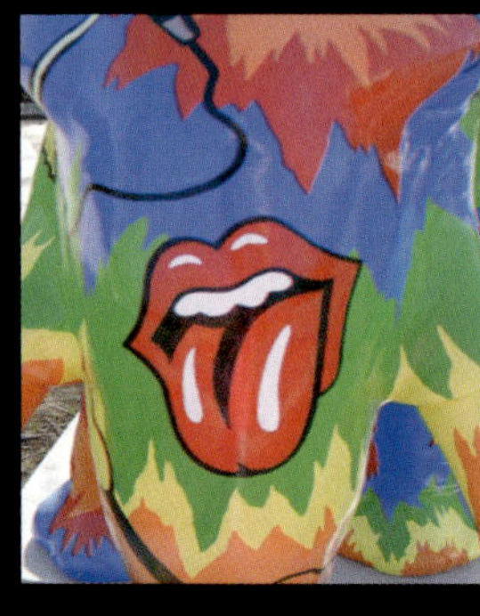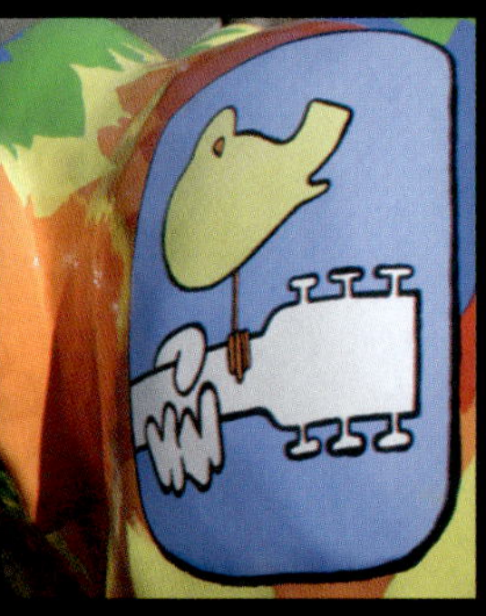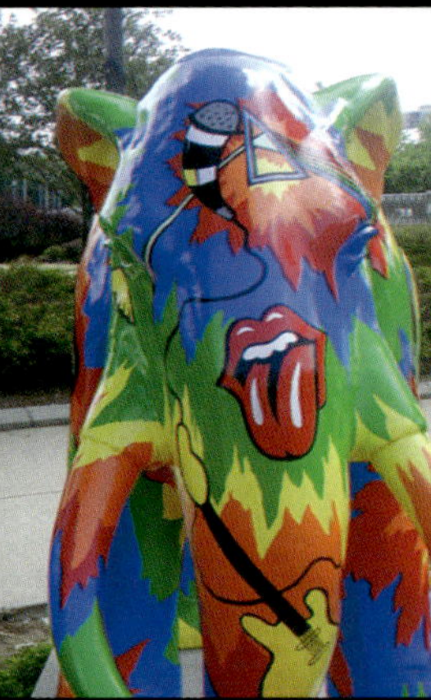

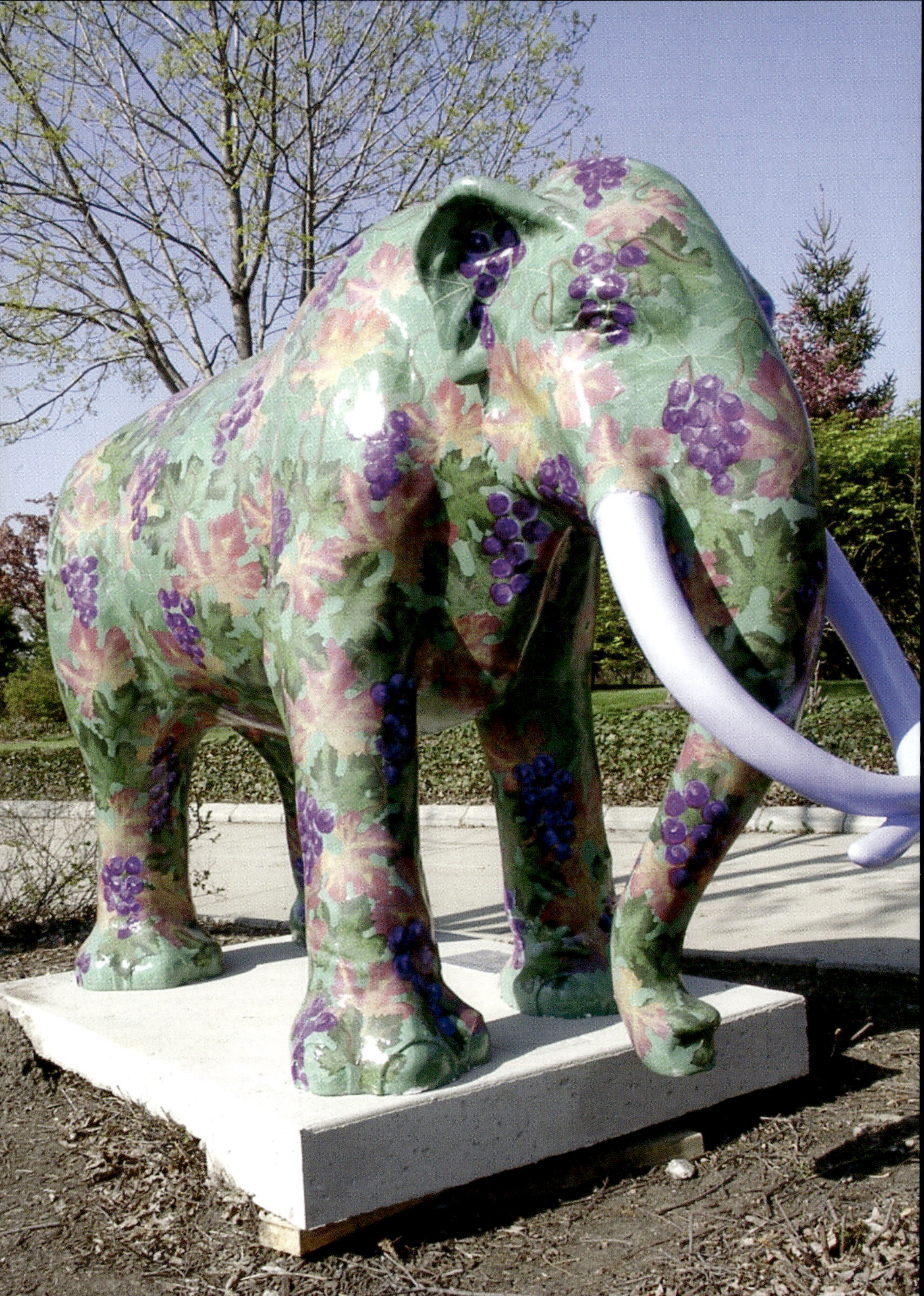

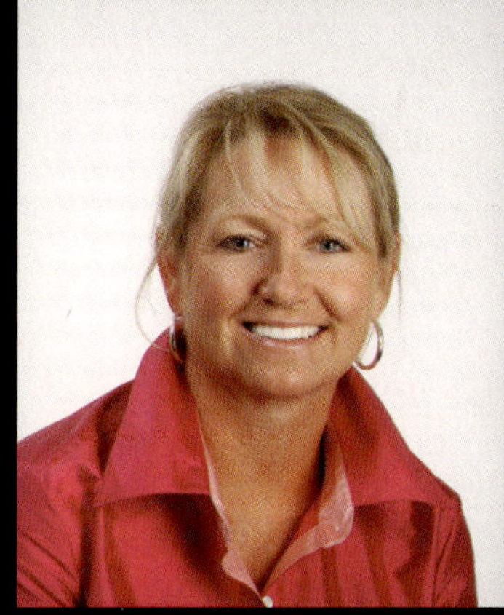

Artist: Flaim Cupp, commercial interior designer, IPFW Interior Design faculty

Sponsor: Lebamoff's Cap n' Cork

When first contacted about this project, I said, "No," since I didn't have a place to paint something that large. But once I learned that two other IPFW interior design professors were painting their mastodons in the engineering technology lab space, I asked if I could join them.

I tried to paint before and after class. It was fun having the students check on my progress.

I am so glad I finally said, "Yes." I am very proud of my hometown and thankful to have been a part of this wonderful experience!

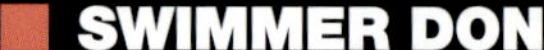

Artists: Boyden & Youngblutt, agency artists (*pictured right*)

Sponsor: Three Rivers Federal Credit Union

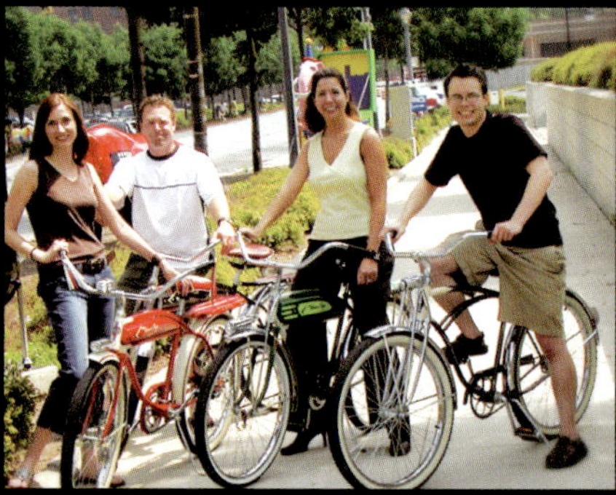

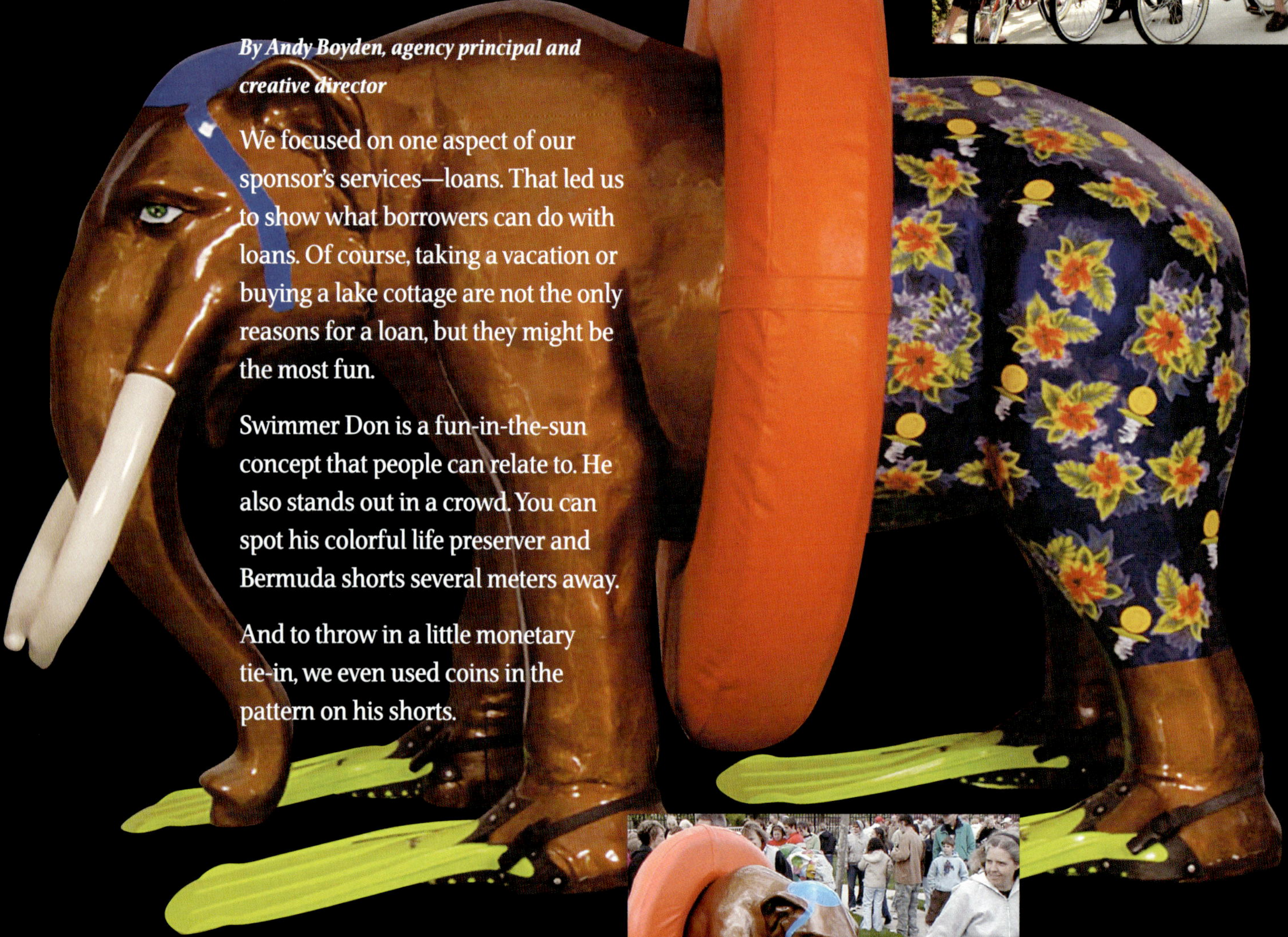

By Andy Boyden, agency principal and creative director

We focused on one aspect of our sponsor's services—loans. That led us to show what borrowers can do with loans. Of course, taking a vacation or buying a lake cottage are not the only reasons for a loan, but they might be the most fun.

Swimmer Don is a fun-in-the-sun concept that people can relate to. He also stands out in a crowd. You can spot his colorful life preserver and Bermuda shorts several meters away.

And to throw in a little monetary tie-in, we even used coins in the pattern on his shorts.

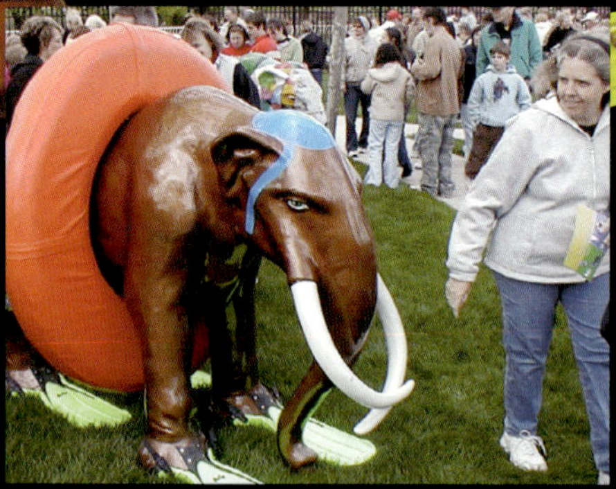

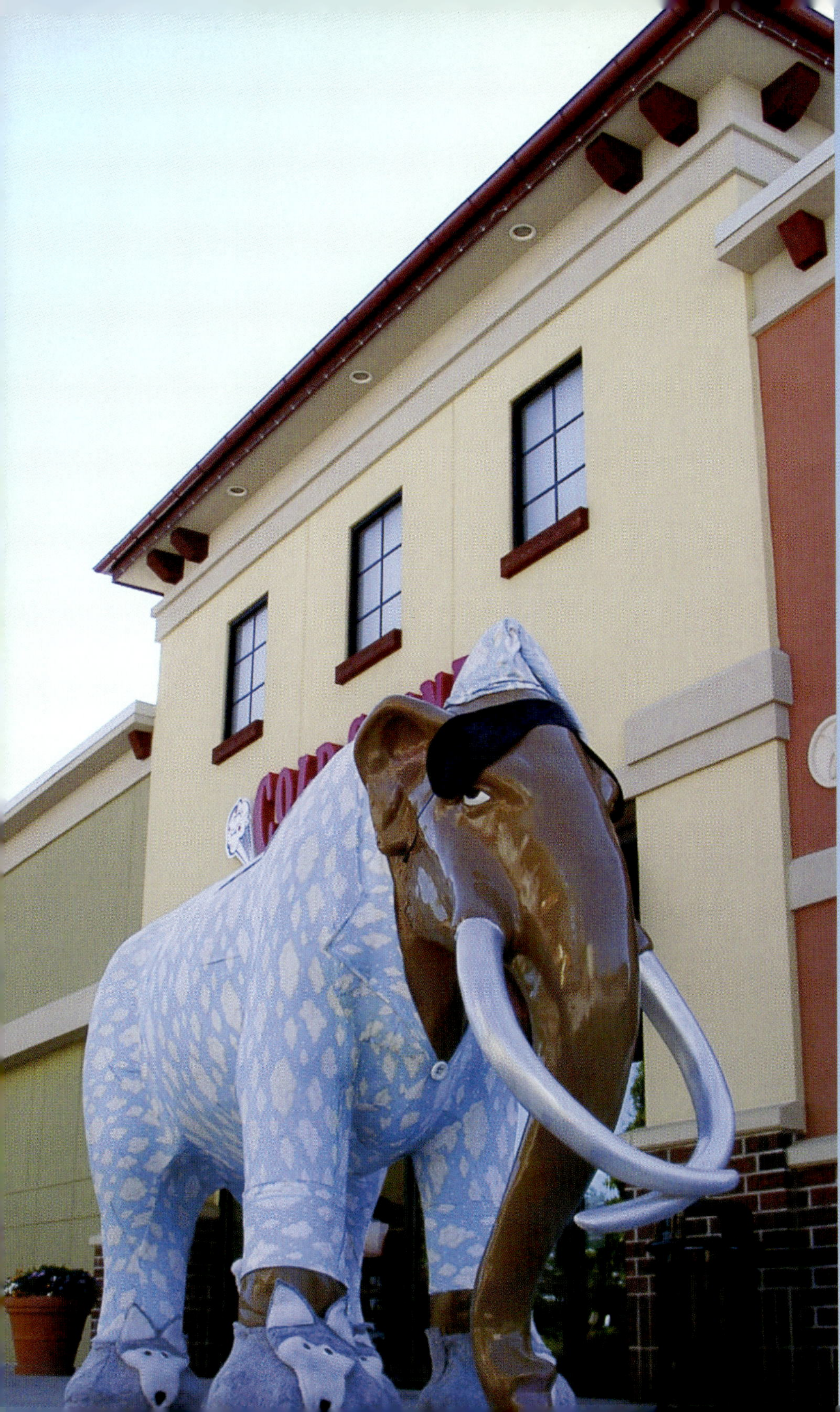

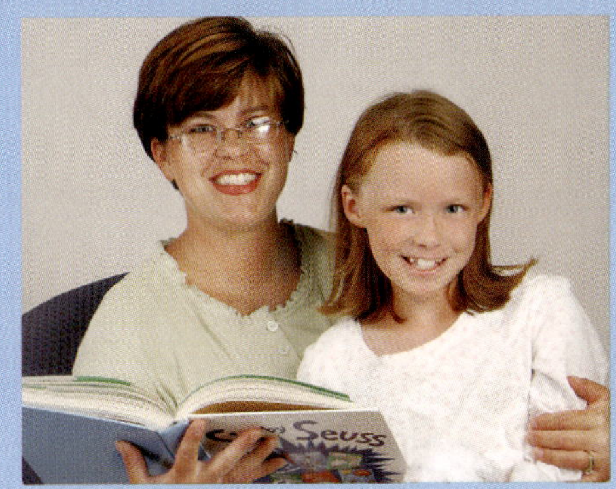

Artists: Melissa Adams, homemaker
(*pictured above, left*)

Catherine Adams, Melissa's daughter
(*pictured above, right*)

Sponsor: Wolf Corporation

By Melissa Adams

I asked my oldest, 8-year-old Catherine, what she would like to see on the mastodon. The pajama design started there. Then I said to myself, "I am more of a seamstress than a painter. I am not an artist. What was I thinking?"

But neighbors started stopping by my open garage, asking why a large fiberglass creature was there. Their positive feedback along with help from my husband, Brian, on things related to power tools made it become a "community" art project.

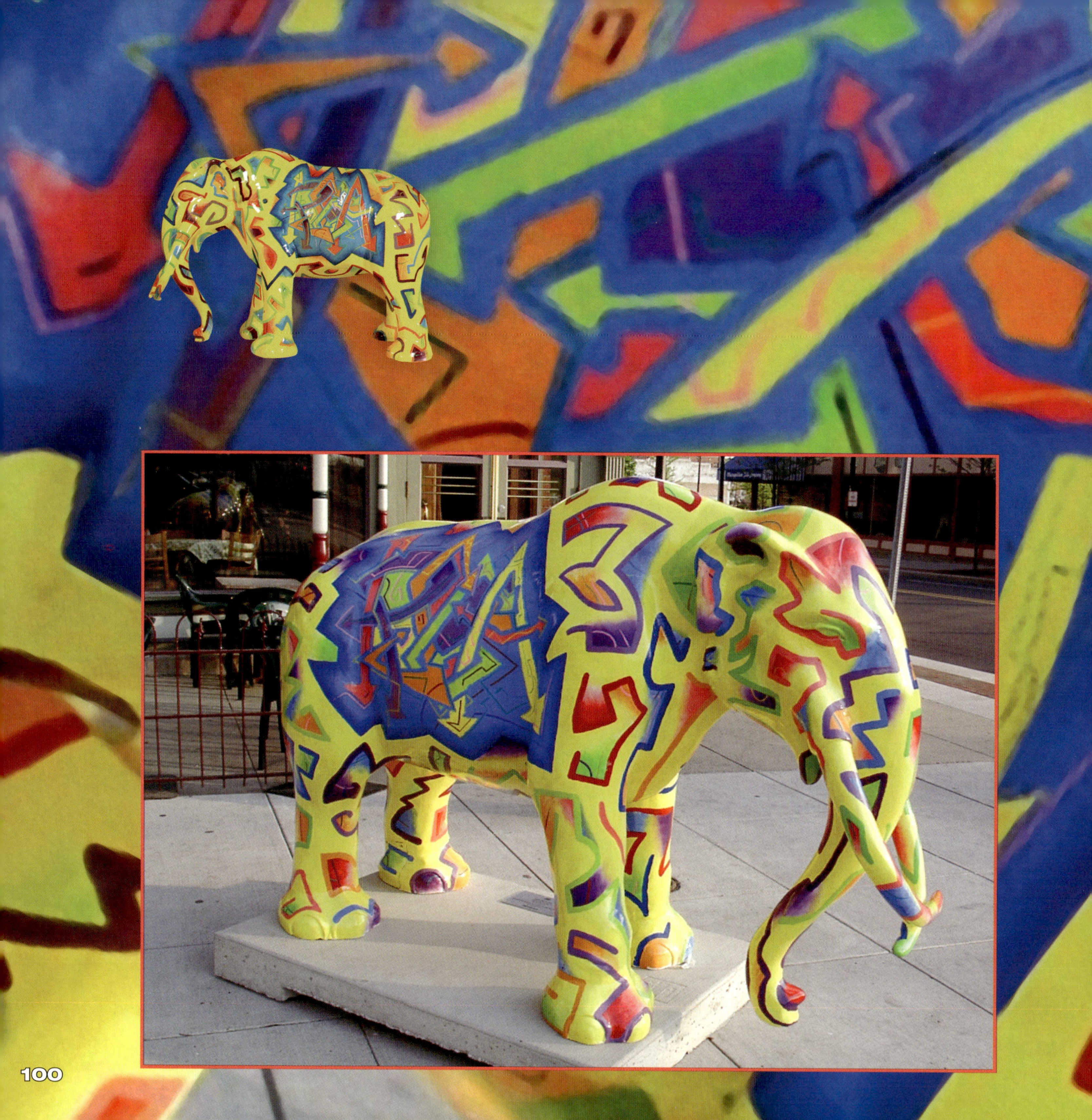

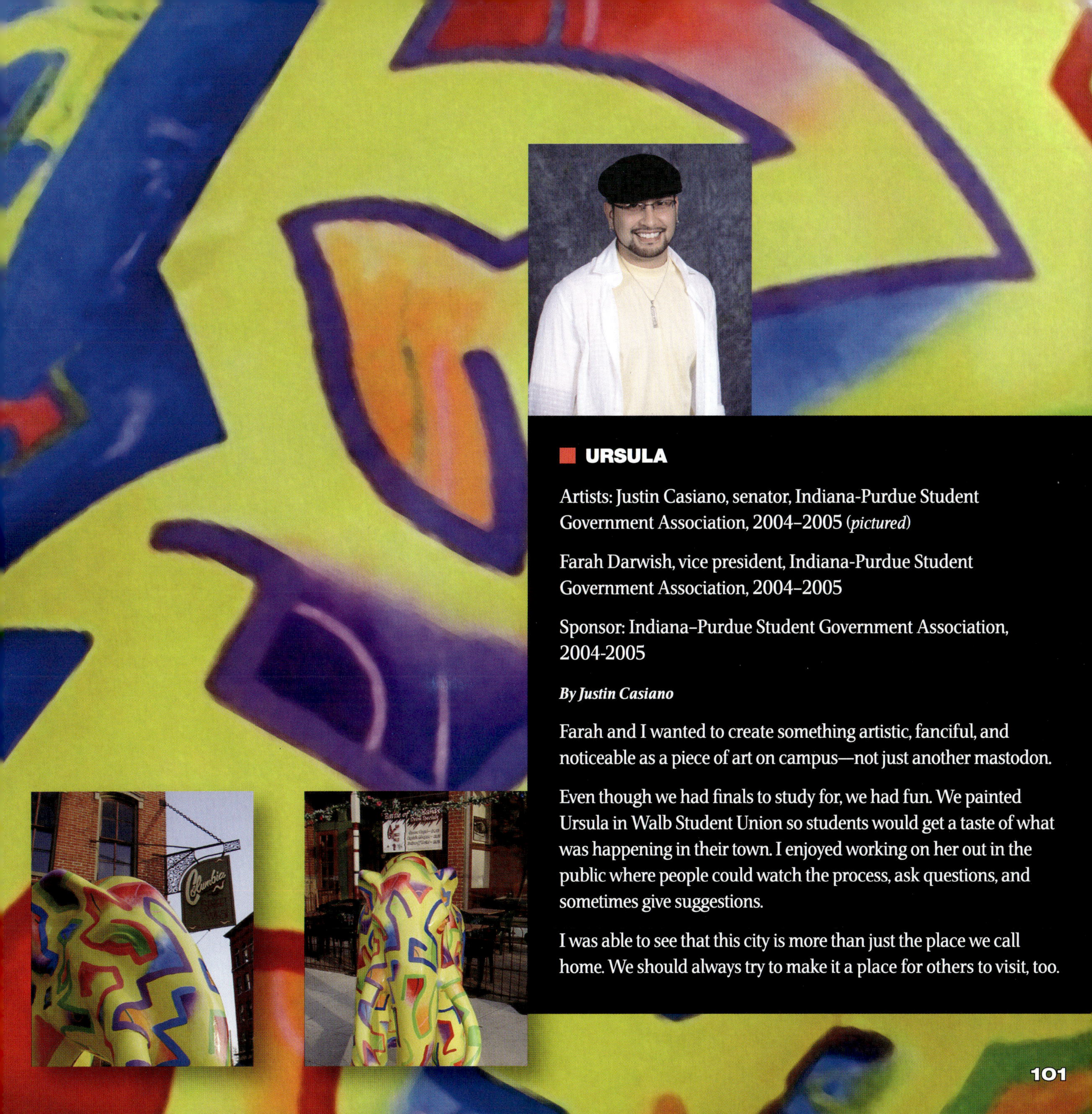

■ URSULA

Artists: Justin Casiano, senator, Indiana-Purdue Student Government Association, 2004–2005 (*pictured*)

Farah Darwish, vice president, Indiana-Purdue Student Government Association, 2004–2005

Sponsor: Indiana–Purdue Student Government Association, 2004-2005

By Justin Casiano

Farah and I wanted to create something artistic, fanciful, and noticeable as a piece of art on campus—not just another mastodon.

Even though we had finals to study for, we had fun. We painted Ursula in Walb Student Union so students would get a taste of what was happening in their town. I enjoyed working on her out in the public where people could watch the process, ask questions, and sometimes give suggestions.

I was able to see that this city is more than just the place we call home. We should always try to make it a place for others to visit, too.

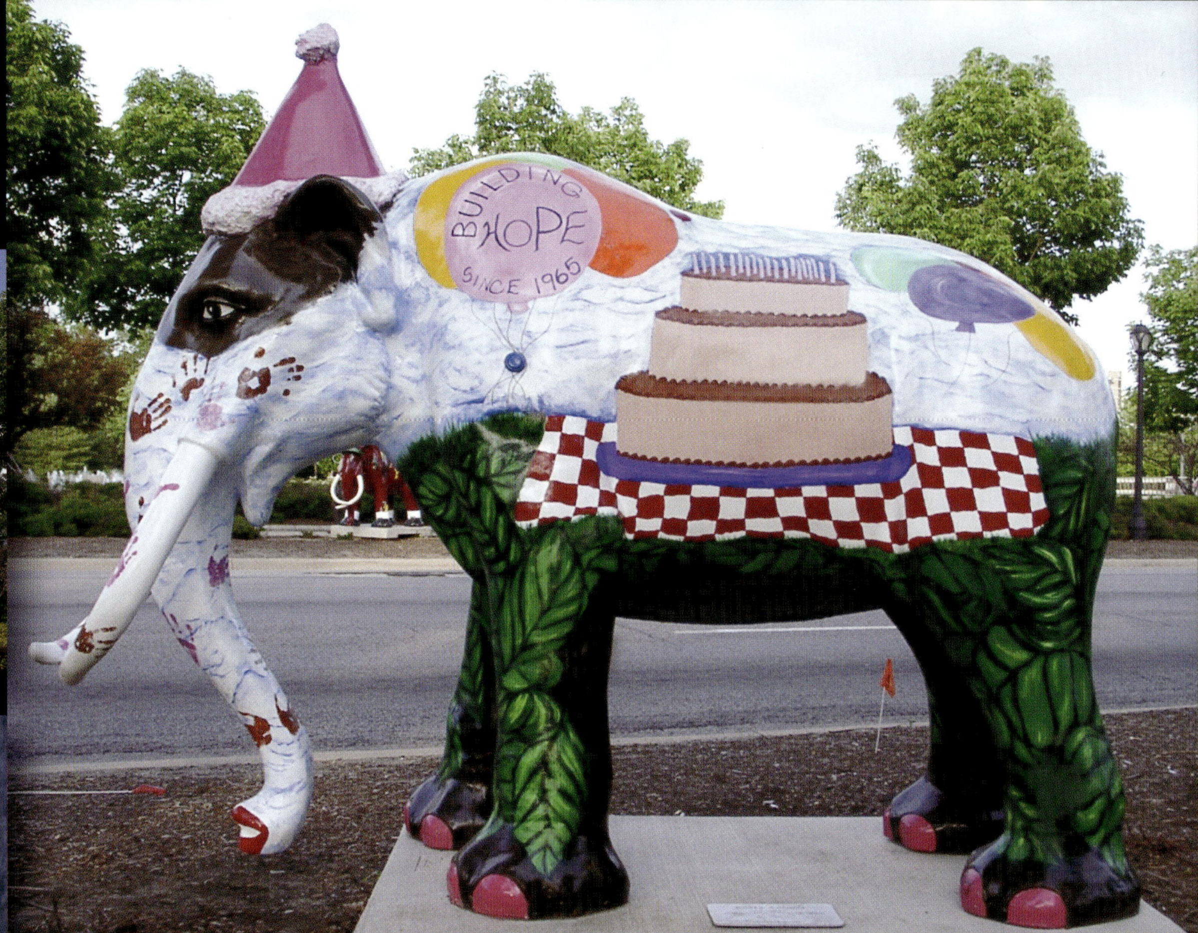

■ PARTY ANIMAL

Artist: Barbara Kuntz

Sponsor: Community Action of Northeast Indiana

My work on Party Animal was the first time I have participated in a project of such magnitude. The most rewarding result of my participation as a "Mastodonian" artist was the opportunity to be a member of an artistic community.

Working alongside Julia Meek, Gwen Gutwein, Palermo Galindo, and Drew Teague delighted me. They accepted me into their artistic community and inspired me.

I experienced complete satisfaction when I watched the public take immediate ownership of all 102 mastodons.

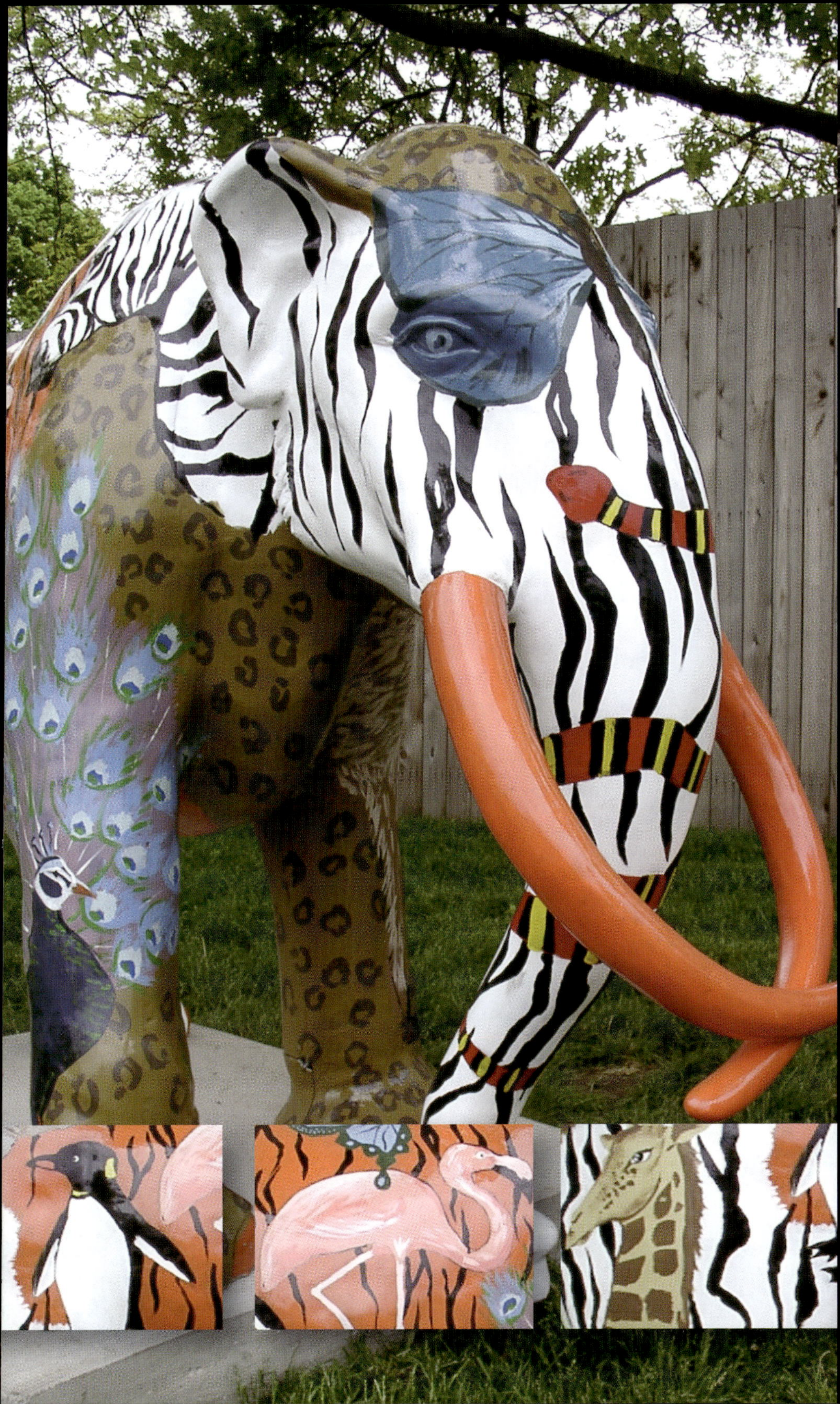

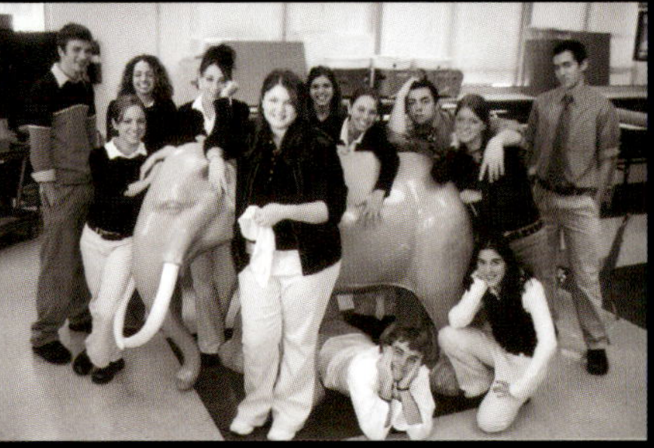

JUNGLE DON

Artist: Samantha Conrad, student,
Bishop Dwenger High School
(*pictured above, center*)

Sponsor: Needham and Associates

By Samantha Conrad

I thought doing an animal print on a mastodon would be fun. Then the final design just evolved into a collage of different animals. Getting Donald Trunk (the nickname all the kids at school gave him) into the art classroom was hard. We pushed him into the elevator, lifted him to the second floor, and then pushed him down the hall. Because he was so big, I had to work on him at school, which meant I was there a lot more than I liked to be. Some nights I worked till 10 p.m.

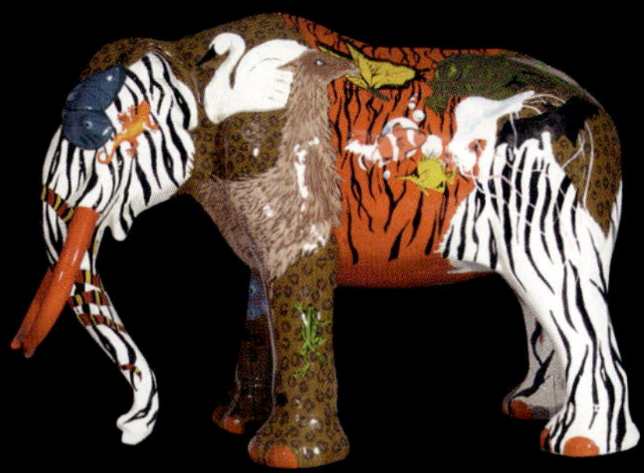

SplatoDon is a full-sized replica of the Mastodons on Parade project logo and serves as a community ambassador promoting the fun and excitement of Fort Wayne's first community art project.

With its freely applied splotches of paint, "Splat" represents the liberation of the artist's imagination on a most unusual canvas!

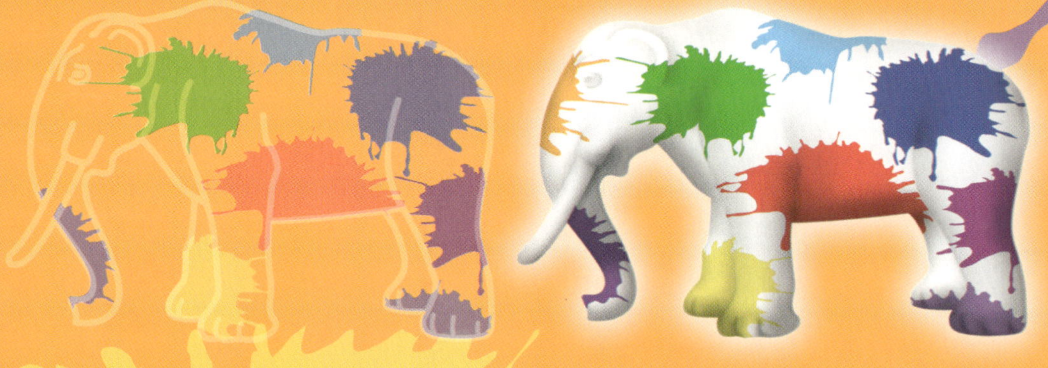

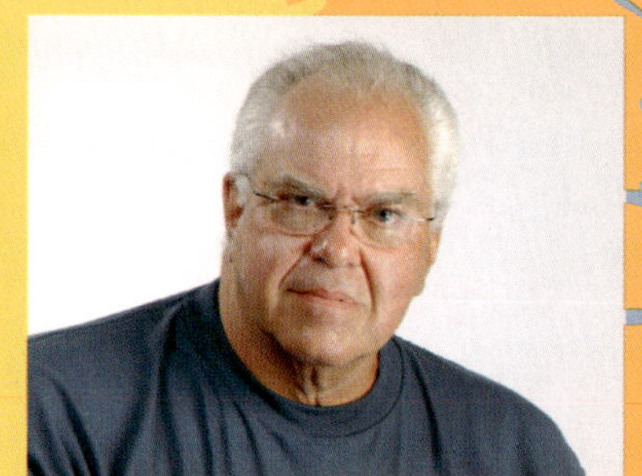

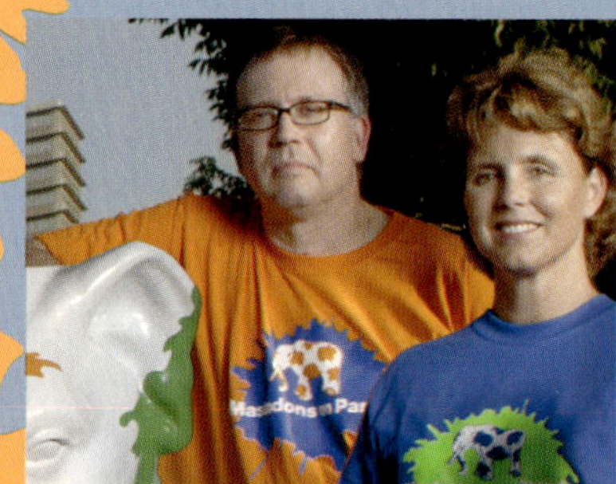

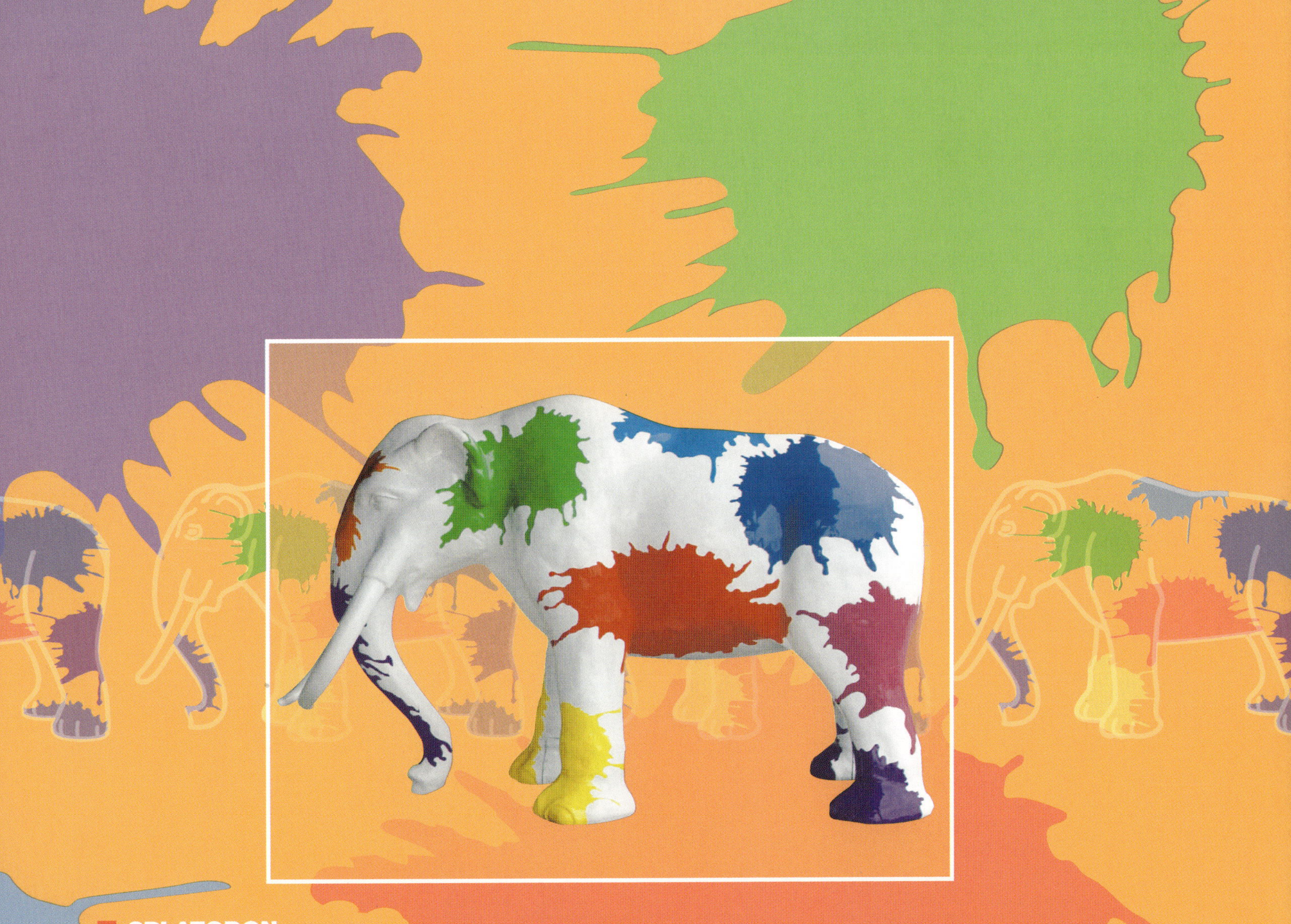

Artists: Barry Berggoetz, Superior Collision and Paint; Jim Studinski, retired auto detailer and painter (*pictured in far left photo*); John Paxson, Lea Ann Powers Gebhard (*pictured in right photo, left to right*)

Sponsor: IPFW University Relations and Communications

By Barry Berggoetz

I have been asked to paint a lot of unusual things, but to paint a mastodon—now that was a first! The mastodon went through a few identity crises from IPFW mascot to its current identity SplatoDon. It has been a challenge and yet fun to be a part of an event that has generated so much interest and excitement from the community.

I worked closely with IPFW Publications staff who participated in the design phase, and with Jim Studinski, an expert freehand vehicle painter and detailer.

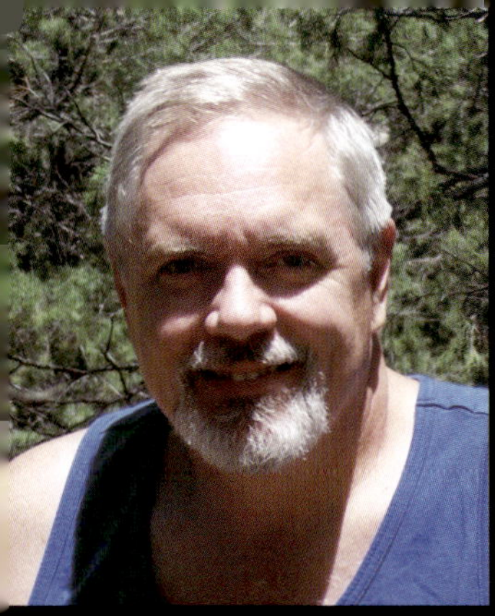

VORDERDON

Artist: Michael Schmid, art teacher, Southwest Allen County Schools

Sponsor: Vorderman Motor Werks

The mastodon is covered with a variety of bugs from around the world and my own imaginings. Since the sponsor is a Volkswagon dealer, I tried to play off the idea of the most easily identified image—the beetle.

My goal was to make this a fun and interesting piece that would make people laugh and think kindly of the VW image. I worked on the project at school so my students could see the entire creative process in action, from original concept to final project.

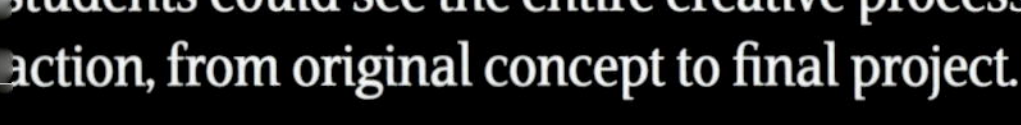

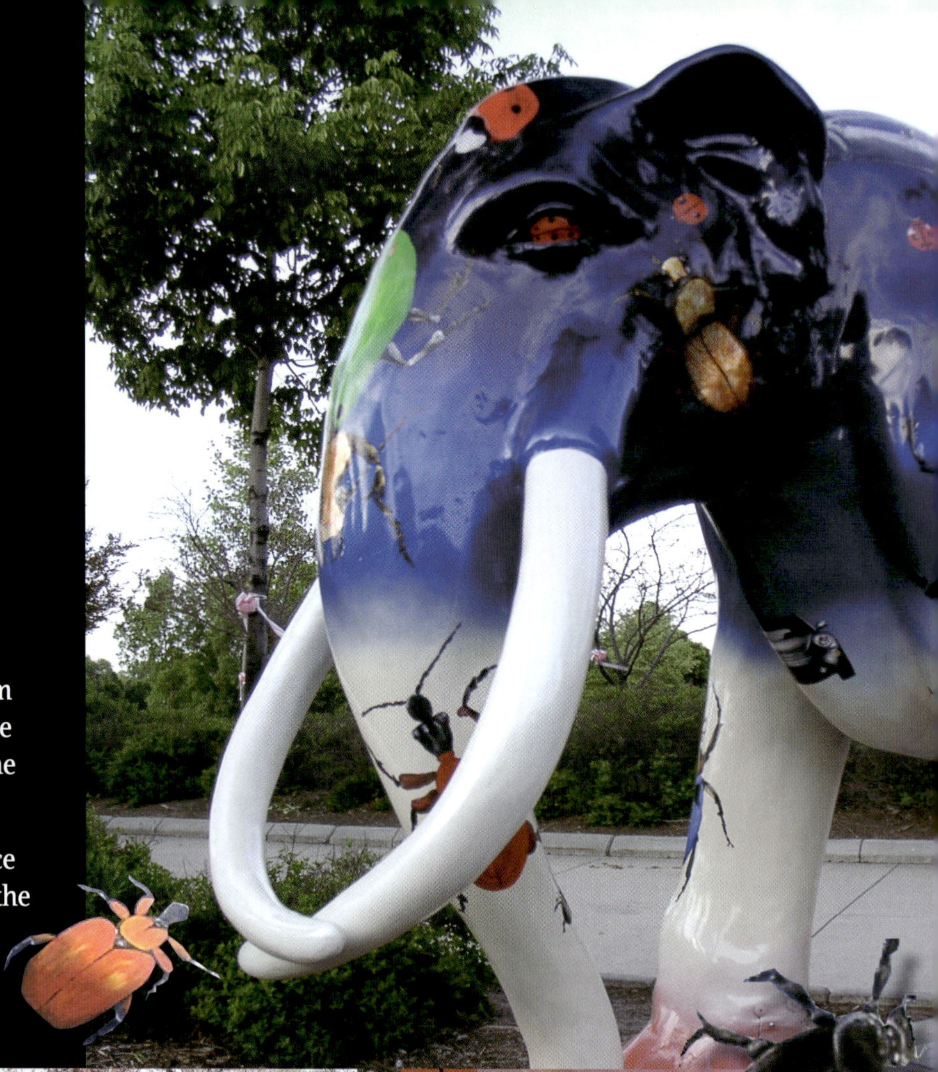

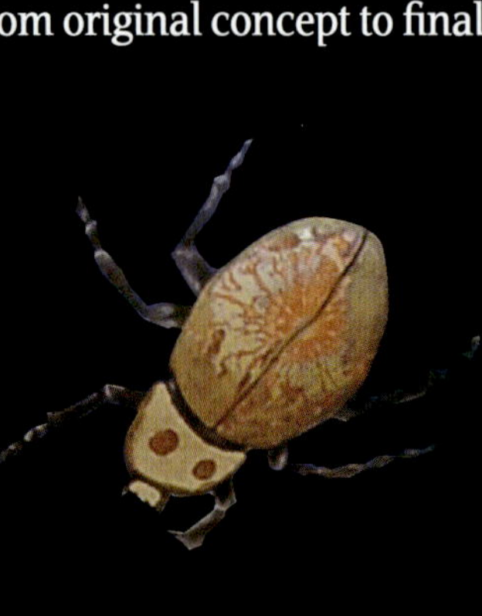

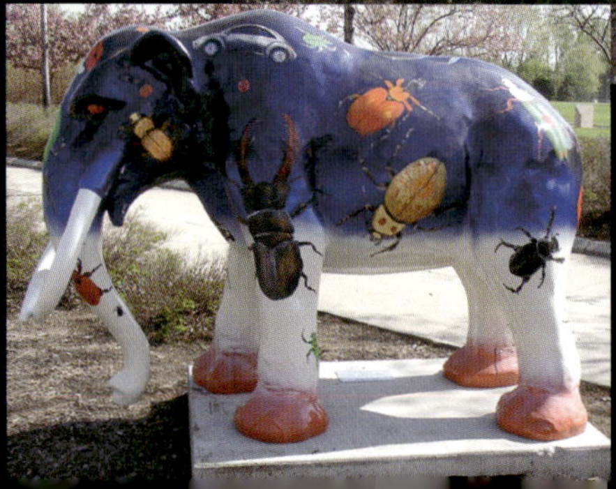

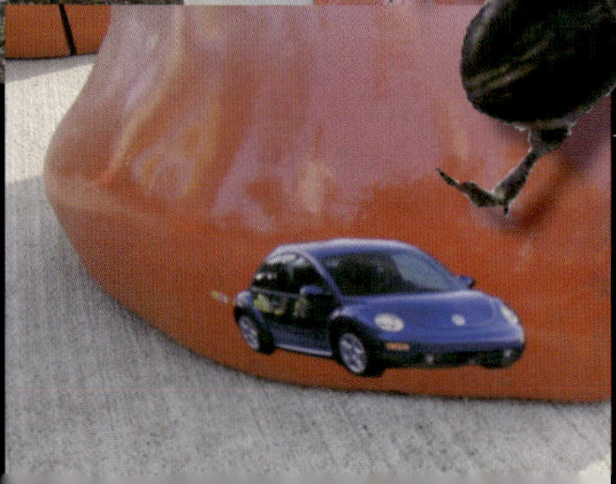

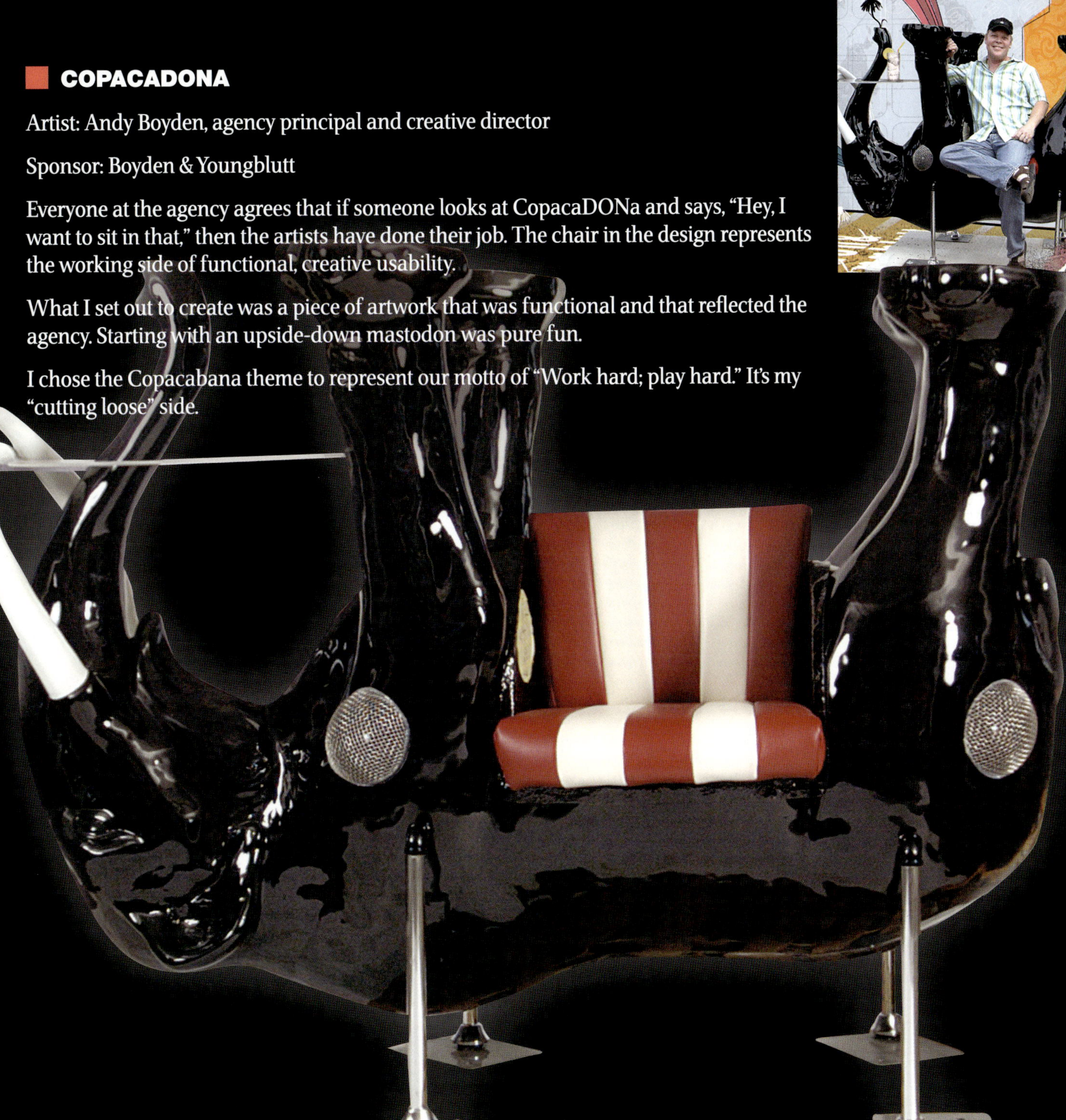

COPACADONA

Artist: Andy Boyden, agency principal and creative director

Sponsor: Boyden & Youngblutt

Everyone at the agency agrees that if someone looks at CopacaDONa and says, "Hey, I want to sit in that," then the artists have done their job. The chair in the design represents the working side of functional, creative usability.

What I set out to create was a piece of artwork that was functional and that reflected the agency. Starting with an upside-down mastodon was pure fun.

I chose the Copacabana theme to represent our motto of "Work hard; play hard." It's my "cutting loose" side.

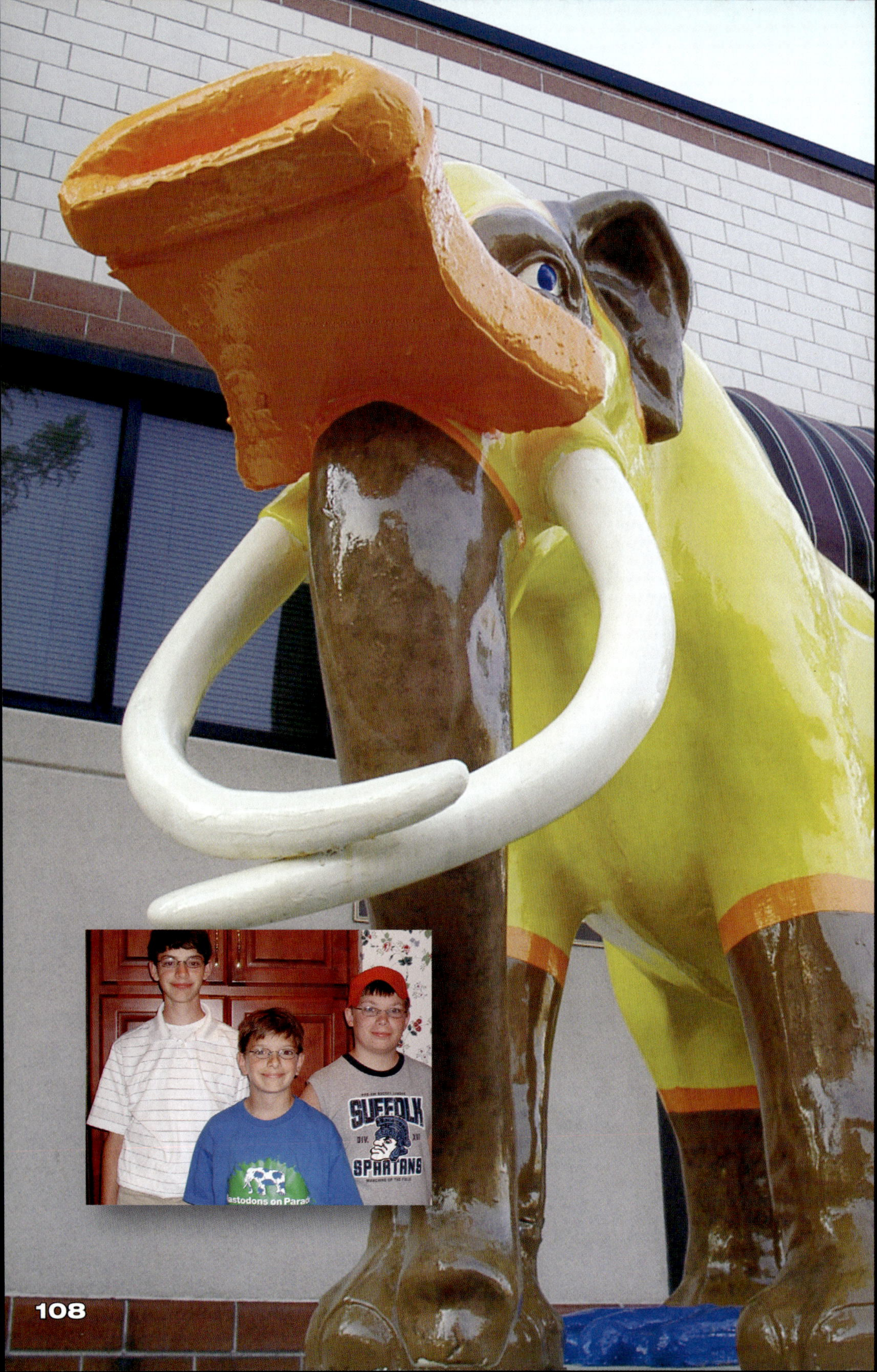

■ MASTODUCK

Artists: Scott Nill

Marshall Nill

Seth Boyden
(*pictured below, left to right*)

Sponsors: WMEE 97.3 and SCAN

By Seth Boyden

My father, Andrew Boyden, designed four mastodons. His ideas and enthusiasm encouraged me. I have always had an interest in styles of art that look amusing or simply ridiculous. For me, it was an enormous task to finish a mastodon with a duckbill and webbed feet in only several weeks.

By Marshall Nill

I am Seth's illustrious partner and friend. My mom learned about the Mastodons on Parade, and I really wanted to be involved. Seth and I had the daunting task of putting a mastodon in a duck suit. The designing process was child's play, but the duckbill and flipper feet were challenging.

We looked to my brother Scott for assistance. He gave up half his spring break to work on it. In our quest to perfect Mastoduck, we met kind, creative, and persevering people. We are grateful to all who helped us.

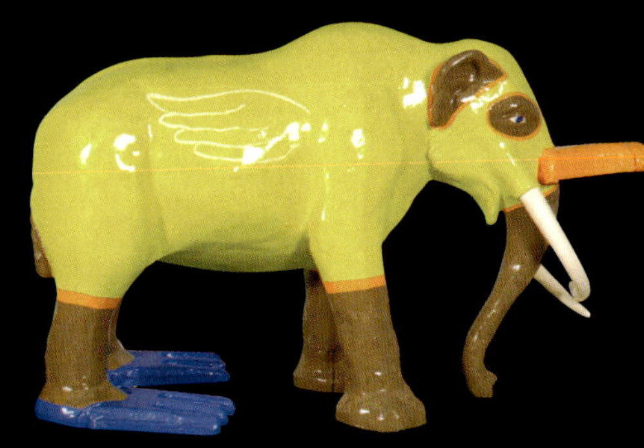

■ PARTY DON

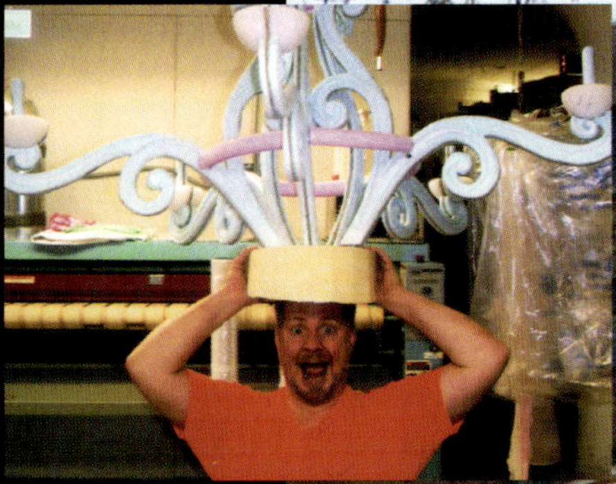

Artist: Ashton Prespentt, production artist, A Party Apart

Sponsor: A Party Apart

When Cheryl Brockmann, owner of A Party Apart, asked me to design Party Don, she said, "Go wild," and that's what I did!

The biggest challenge was to create the chandelier hat. I had never worked with fiberglass resin before, and that was a challenge in itself. We were also worried that the chandelier hat might be vandalized.

We even tried to simplify the design to make it less tempting. In the end, I decided to put my faith in the community of Fort Wayne, and they didn't let me down. Our original design has weathered the public extremely well.

So far this has been my first community art project, and I had a blast!

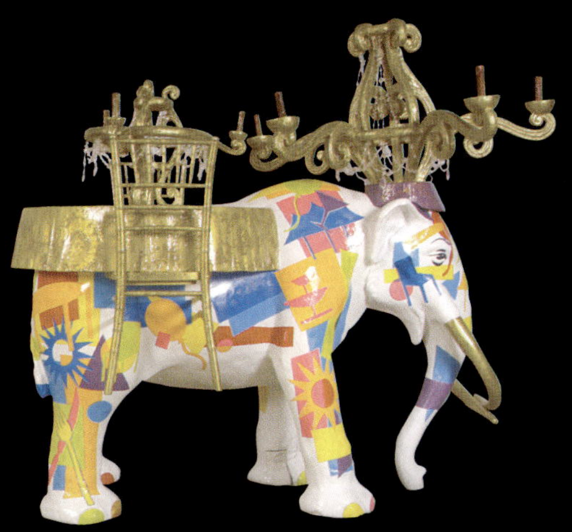

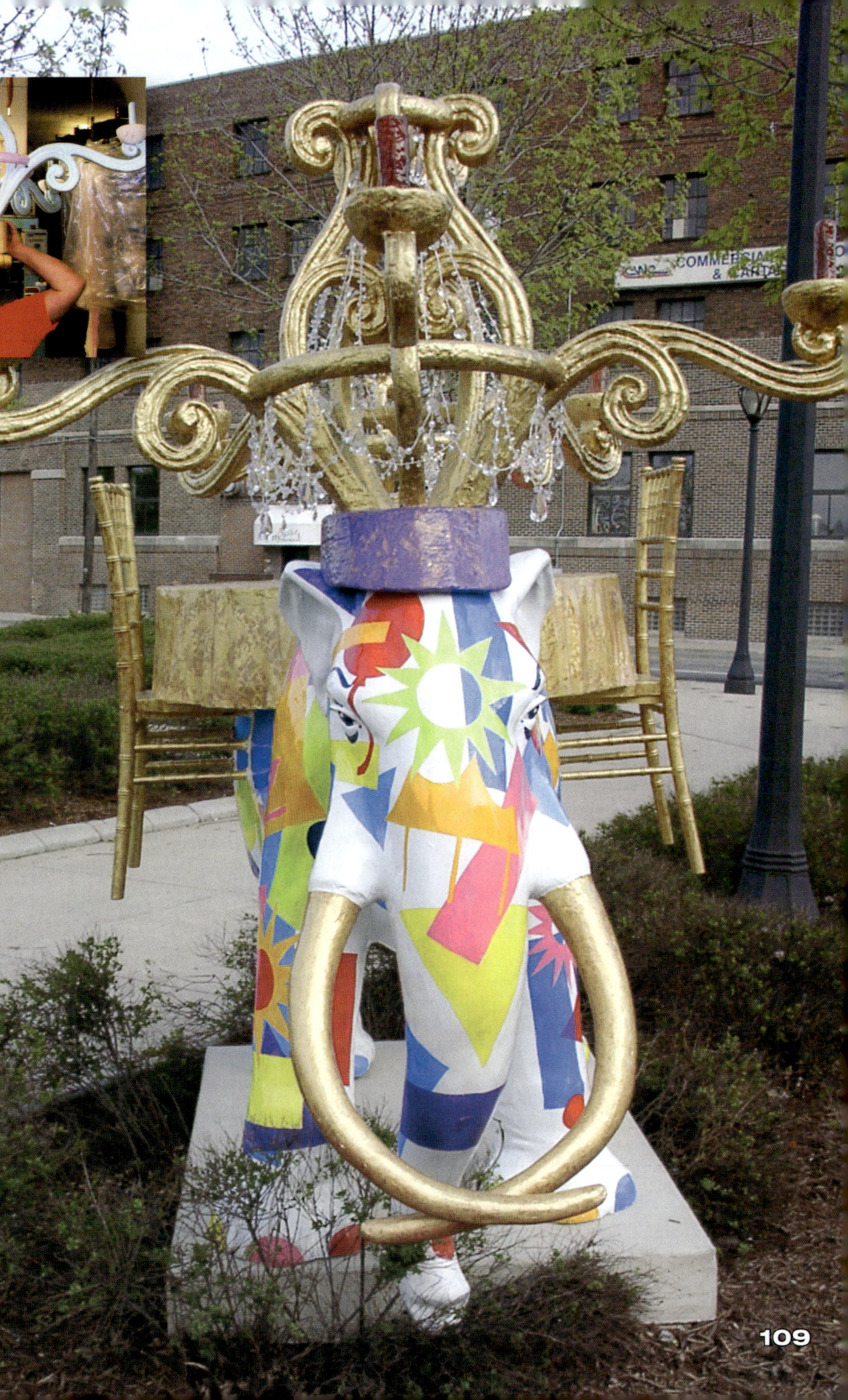

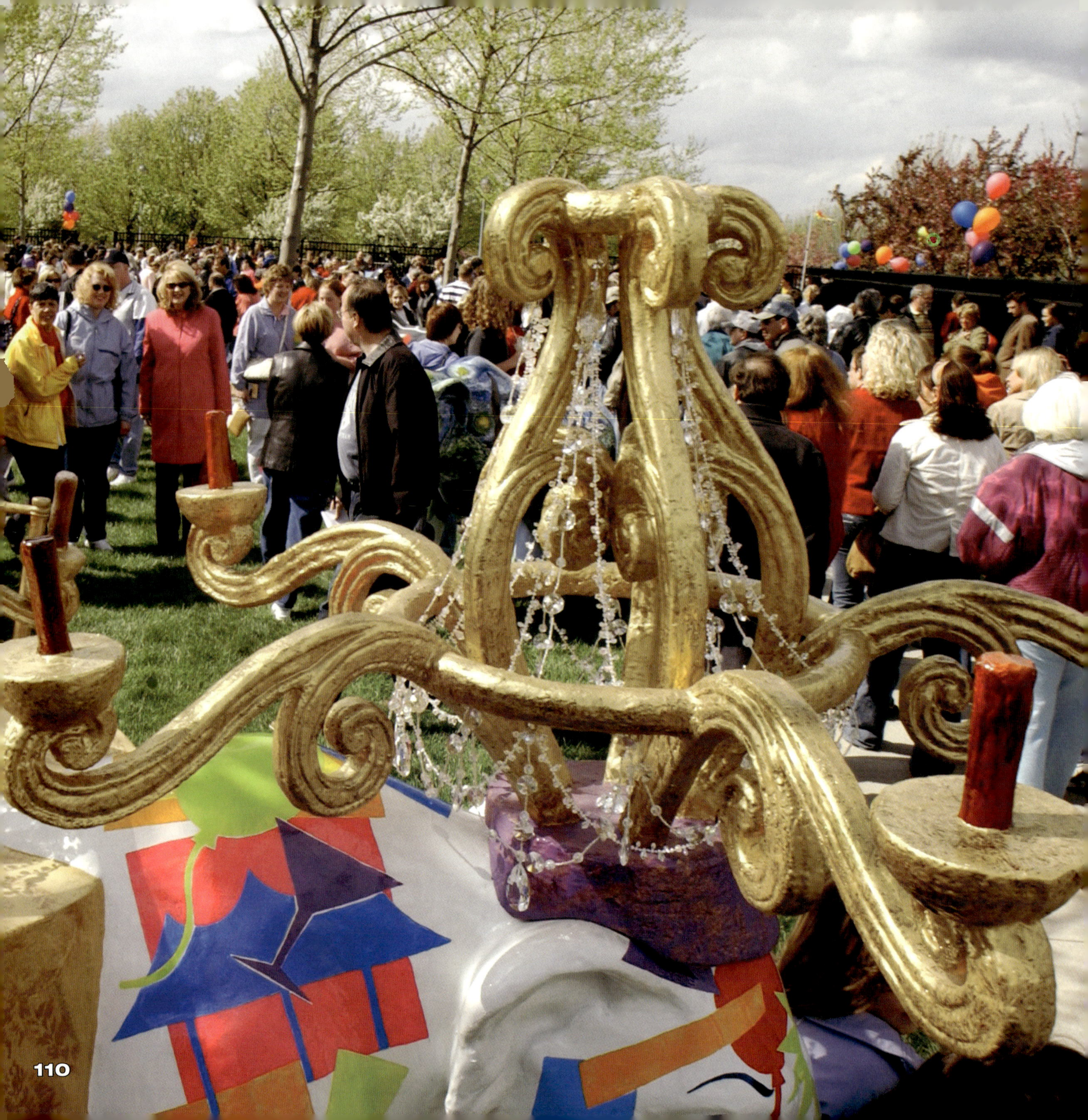

Mastodons on Parade

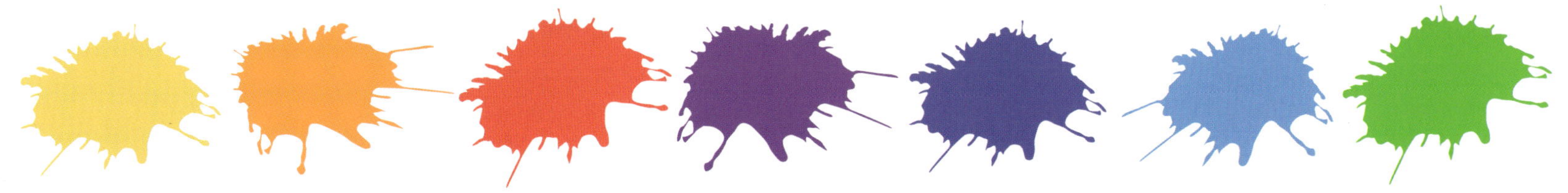

Dons Out and About

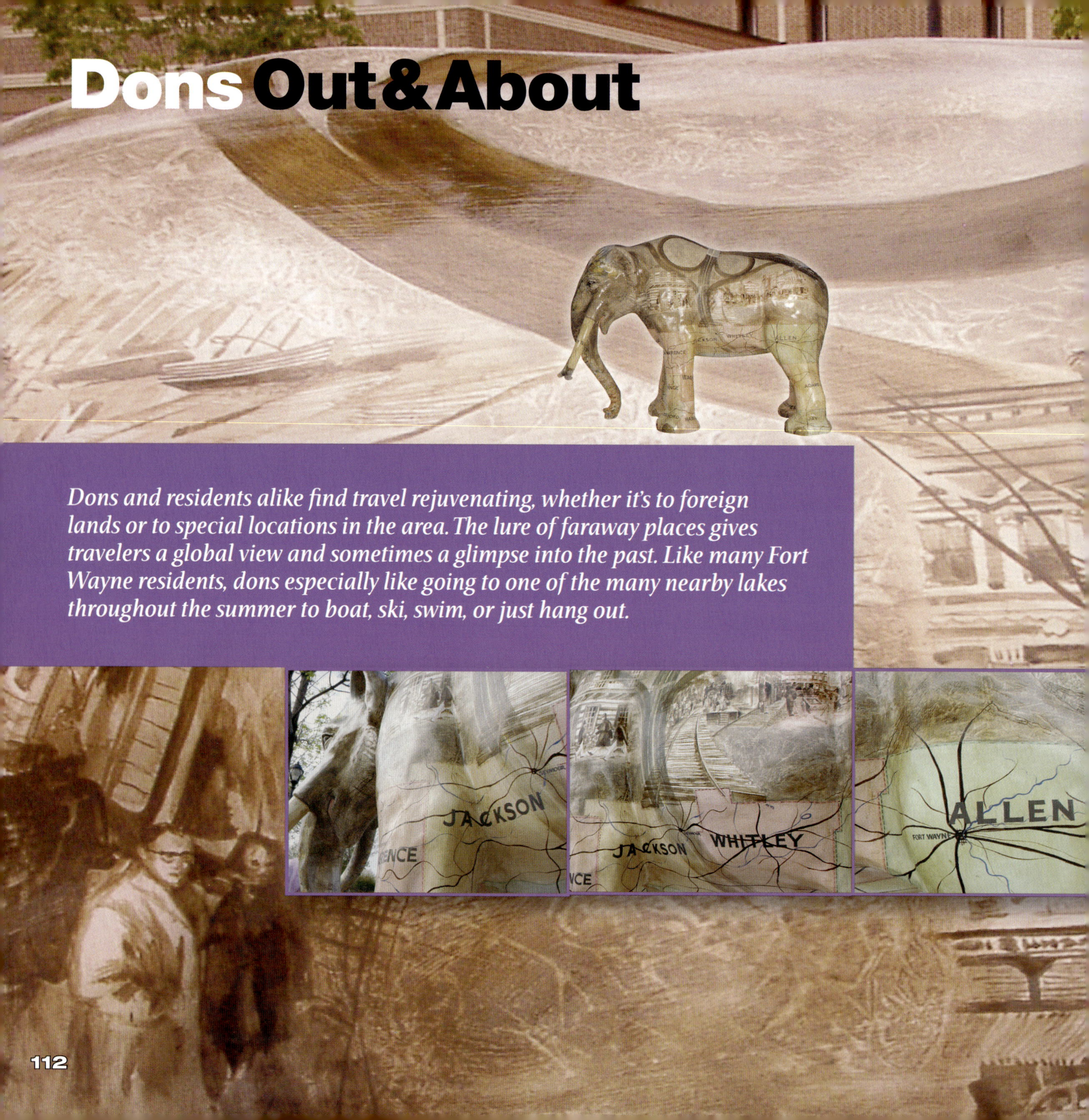

Dons Out & About

Dons and residents alike find travel rejuvenating, whether it's to foreign lands or to special locations in the area. The lure of faraway places gives travelers a global view and sometimes a glimpse into the past. Like many Fort Wayne residents, dons especially like going to one of the many nearby lakes throughout the summer to boat, ski, swim, or just hang out.

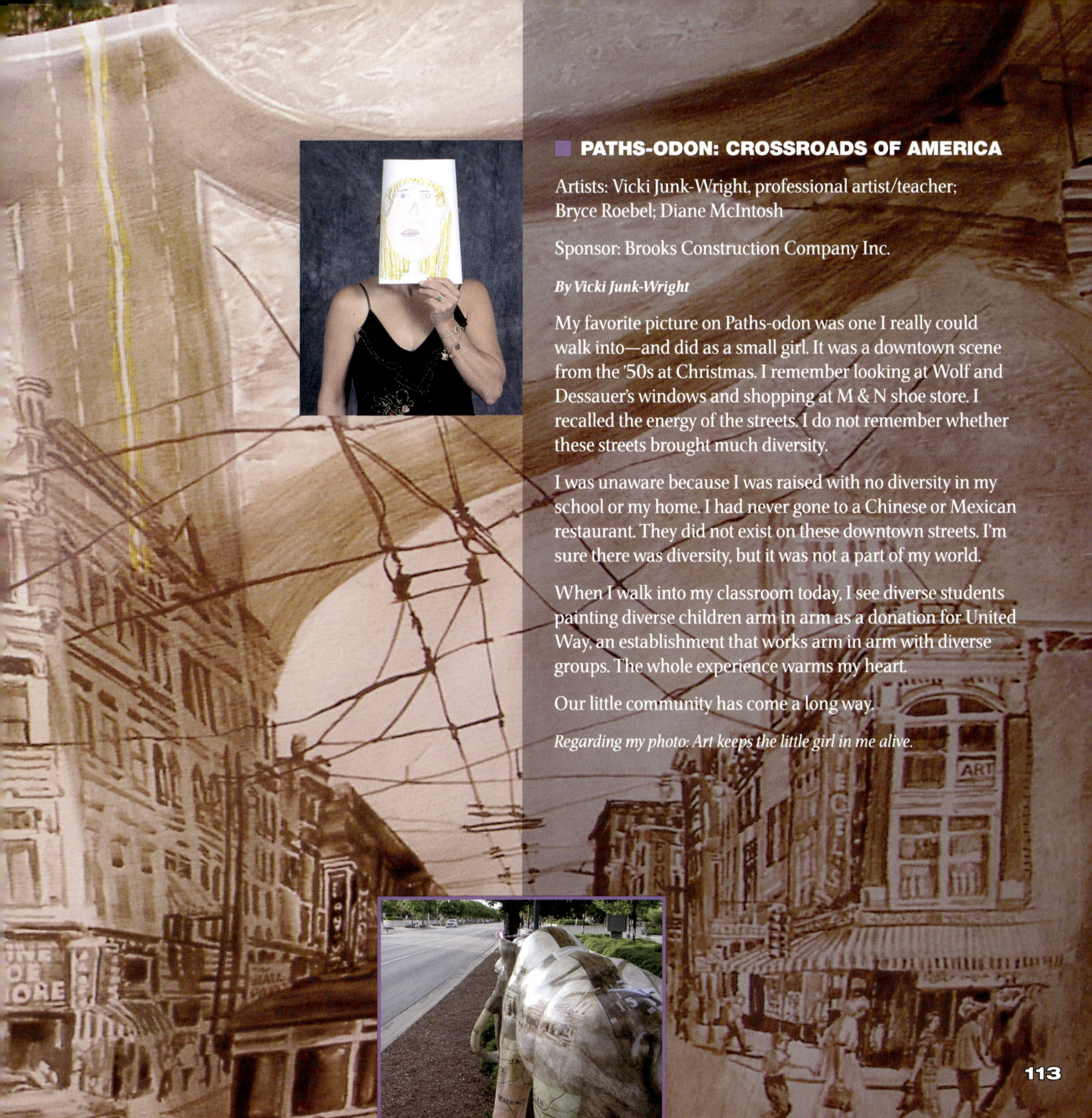

■ PATHS-ODON: CROSSROADS OF AMERICA

Artists: Vicki Junk-Wright, professional artist/teacher;
Bryce Roebel; Diane McIntosh

Sponsor: Brooks Construction Company Inc.

By Vicki Junk-Wright

My favorite picture on Paths-odon was one I really could walk into—and did as a small girl. It was a downtown scene from the '50s at Christmas. I remember looking at Wolf and Dessauer's windows and shopping at M & N shoe store. I recalled the energy of the streets. I do not remember whether these streets brought much diversity.

I was unaware because I was raised with no diversity in my school or my home. I had never gone to a Chinese or Mexican restaurant. They did not exist on these downtown streets. I'm sure there was diversity, but it was not a part of my world.

When I walk into my classroom today, I see diverse students painting diverse children arm in arm as a donation for United Way, an establishment that works arm in arm with diverse groups. The whole experience warms my heart.

Our little community has come a long way.

Regarding my photo: Art keeps the little girl in me alive.

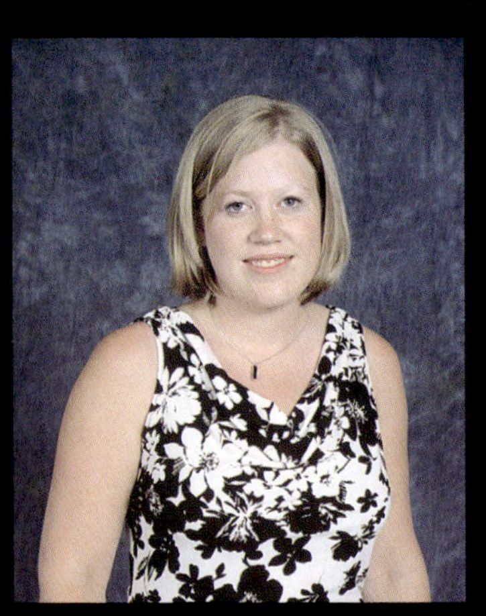

■ MIDEASTODON

Artist: Deb Washler, artist and arts administrator

Sponsor: Grand Wayne Center

When I heard about the mastodon project, I decided to pick up a paint brush. My design is based on line drawings that have a very Middle Eastern feel.

With my work in arts administration, I have the opportunity to participate in art activities and to work each day to make the arts available to our community.

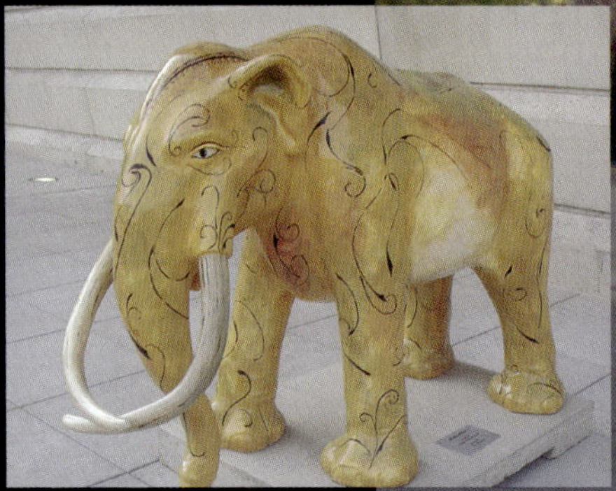

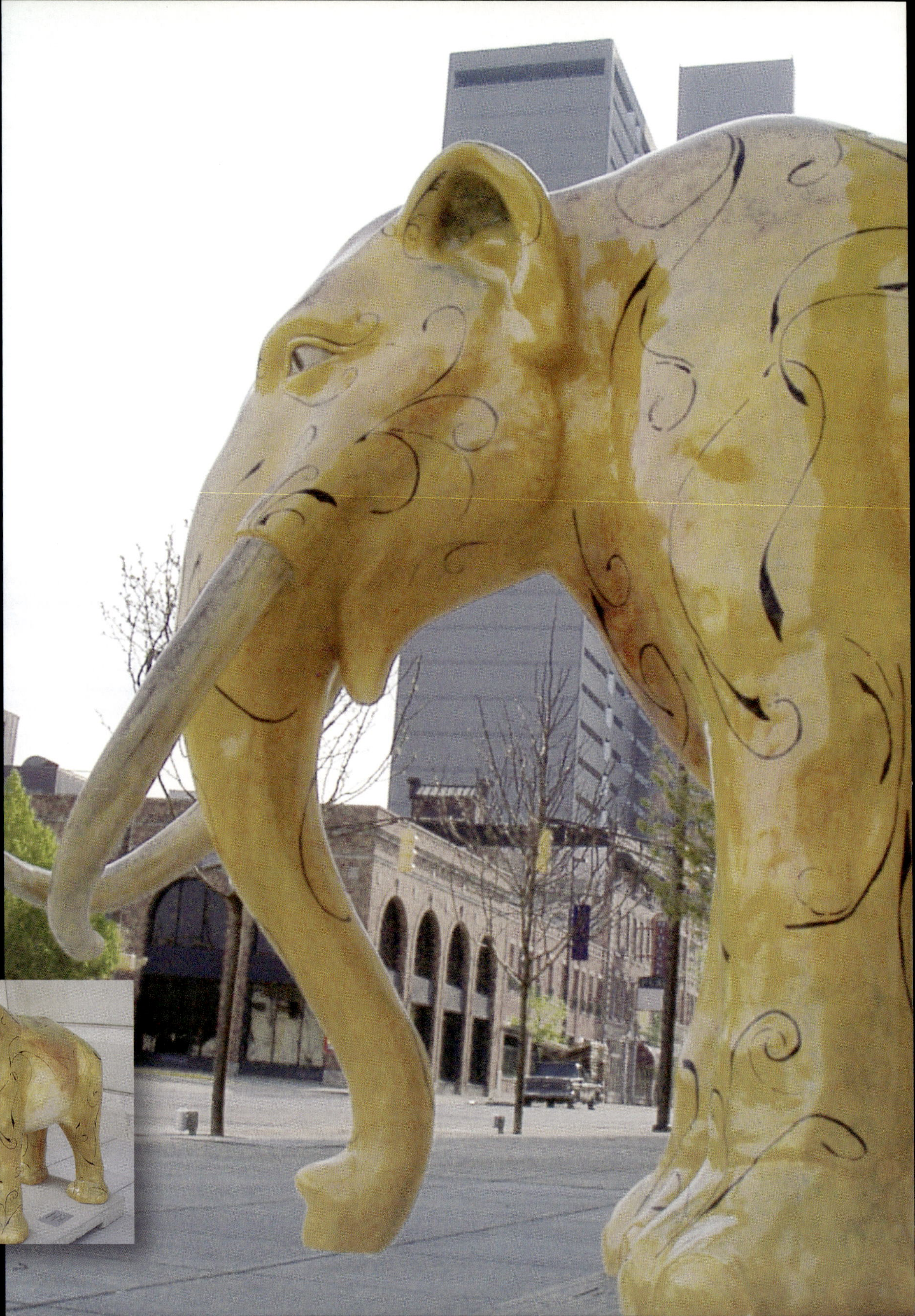

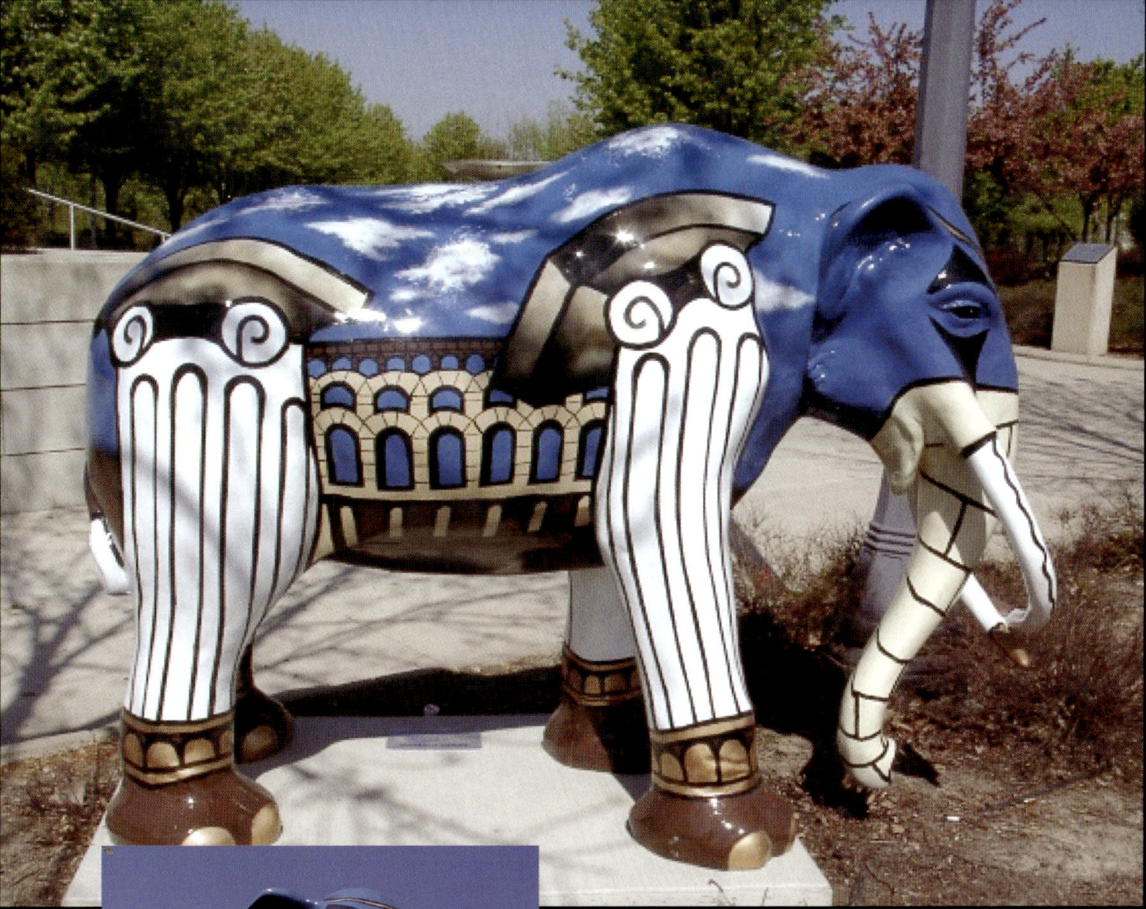

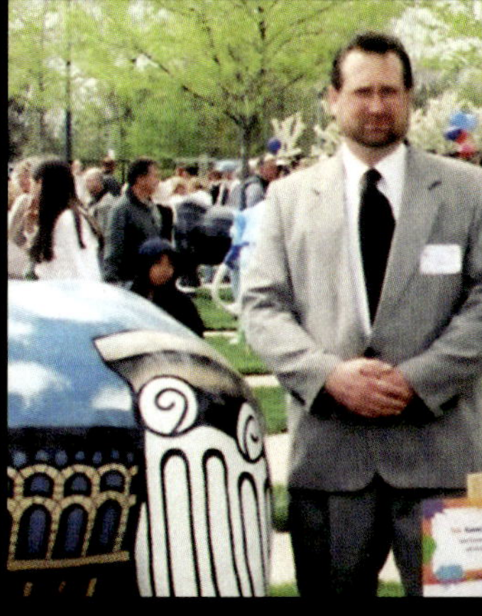

ROMAN COLISEUM

Artist: Jeff Johnston

Sponsor: Steel Dynamics Inc.

It was my wife, Krissy, who really kept me motivated and inspired to finish the project on time during the cold of winter in a garage with no heat. She and I did the cloud painting together, and after that, it was done.

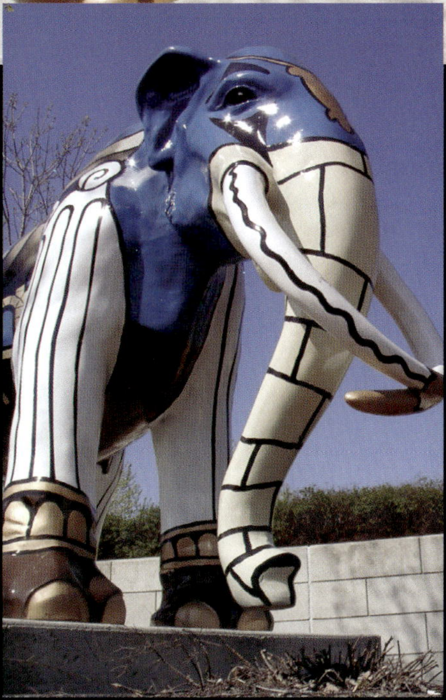

When I first heard about the project from other artists, I thought it would be a great way to support the arts in Fort Wayne and hopefully get the community some recognition.

I decided to get involved. The beast arrived in January, and I began the sanding and prep work. That took two weeks. Then it was time to mask and spray. My inspiration for the design probably came from experiences I had as a student in Florence, Italy.

Nearing the deadline, I worked every night and weekend for two weeks. The whole experience was wonderful from start to finish.

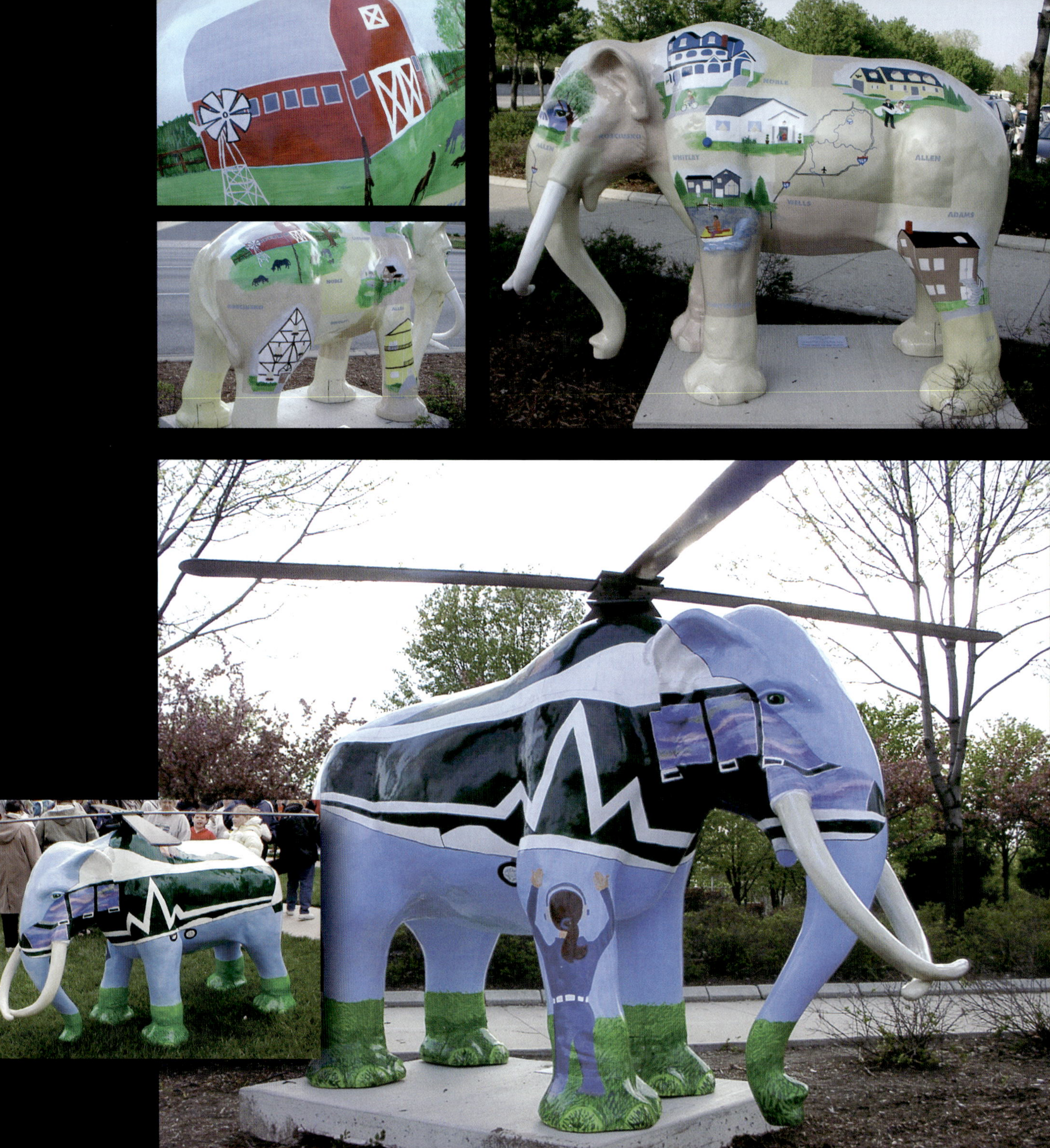

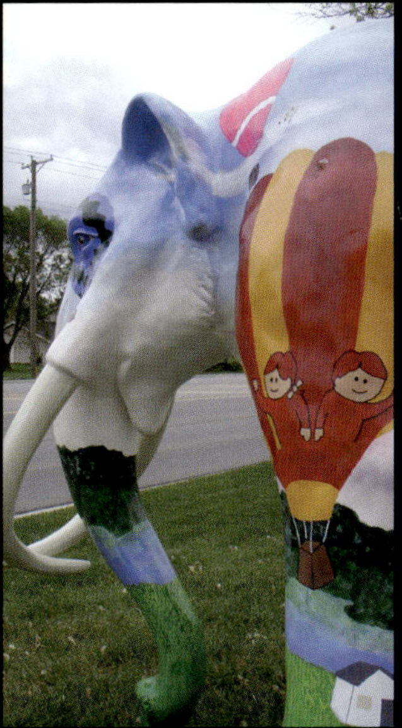

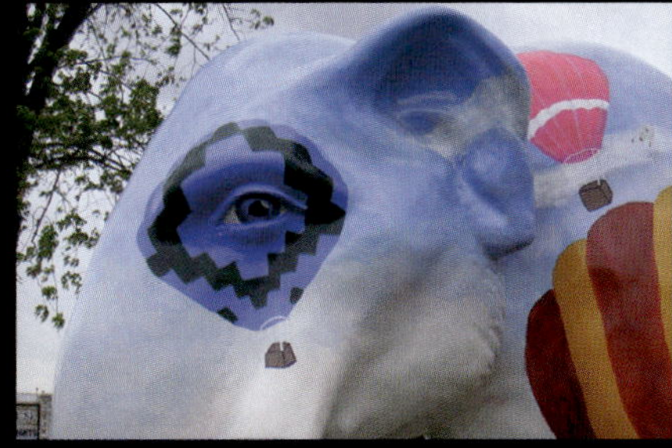

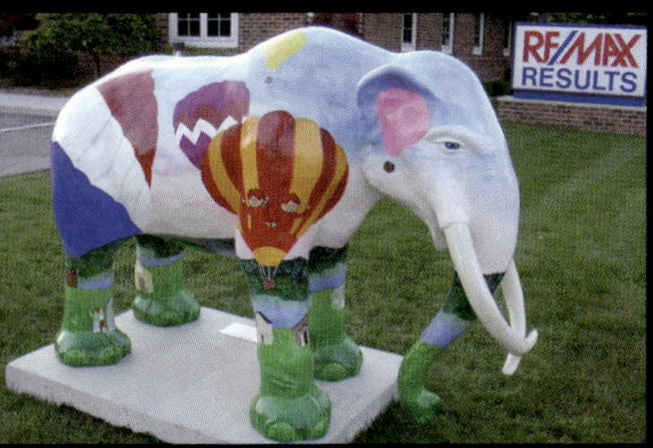

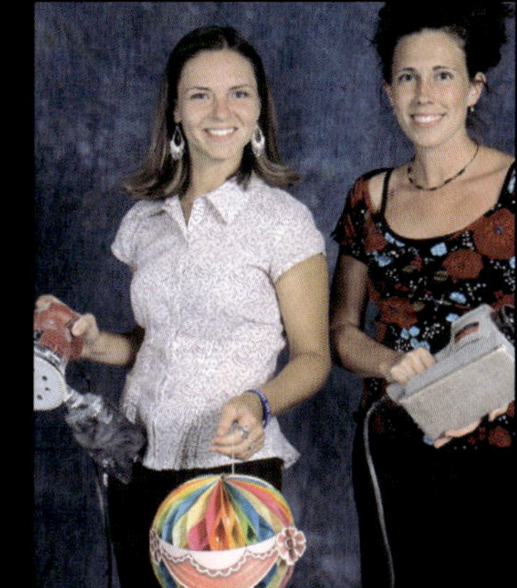

◼ RE/MAX-TODON

Sponsor: RE/MAX Results

◼ SAMARI-DON

Sponsor: Parkview Hospital

◼ WWW.REALTOR.DON

Sponsor: Fort Wayne Area
Association of REALTORS

Artists: Jennifer Clements, IPFW student
Erin Palmer, IPFW student (*pictured above, left to right*)

By Jennifer Clements

We have been best friends for the past 15 years—ever since the third grade. When we heard about the community art project, we thought it would be a good idea to submit some of our designs.

RE/MAX was our first mastodon. We never thought about doing more than one, but Parkview Hospital liked our design for the Samaritan helicopter, and we accepted a second project.

When the mastodons arrived, we learned quickly that each one was a couple of toes too wide to walk through the door. Luckily, our office window was easily removable and we air-lifted them in. Then two months into the project, we insanely agreed to add www.REALTOR.Don as the third member of our herd. Before they were all complete, we worked through several all-nighters and made many trips to a Chinese take-out restaurant. We finished our dons with seconds to spare.

We feel so lucky to be a part of Fort Wayne's first community-wide art project. When we started, somebody asked, "Are you sure you want to do this together?" We agree that we would not have had it any other way. We spent as much time strengthening our friendship as we did working our hearts out.

Our herd will forever be part of us!

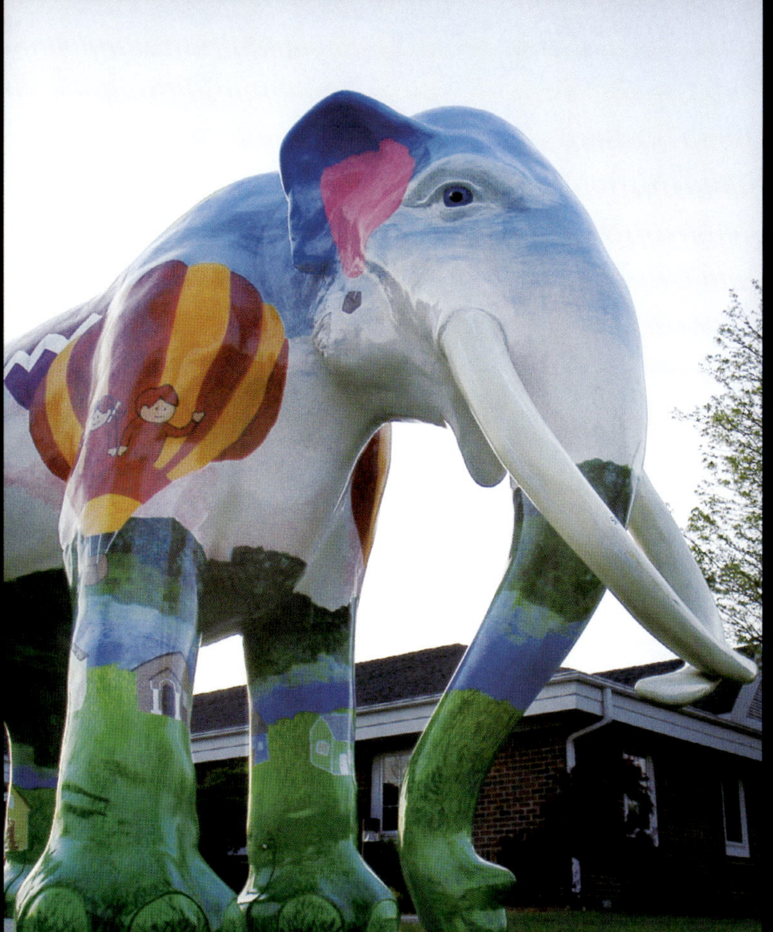

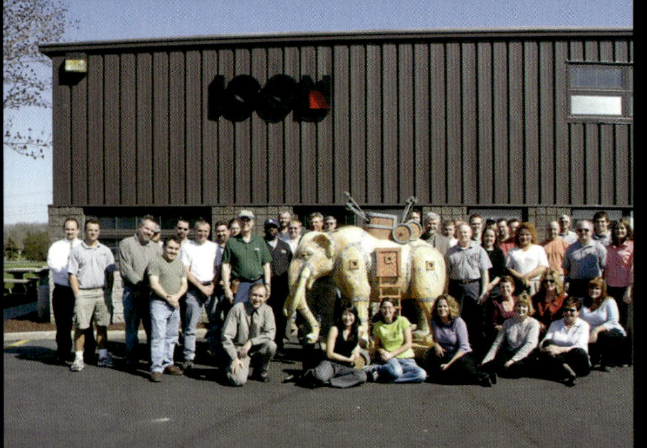

■ TROJAN DON

Artists: Associates of ICON Exhibits
(*pictured left*)

Sponsor: ICON Exhibits

We wanted Trojan Don to be solidly built and creative. Those spearheads look sharp and strong, but they are really made of sculpted styrofoam for safety purposes. The metal parts also look like burnished metal, but they are mostly paint, wood, and paper.

People are asking what we put inside. Maybe they are expecting toy soldiers? Our Trojan Don is on a mission to overwhelm our city, but it's not with soldiers. Our secret weapon is our creativity and craftsmanship.

Among many project contributors were Peter Baranowski for the idea, Marvin Hagen for painting, and Dave Disler for the structural and dimensional components.

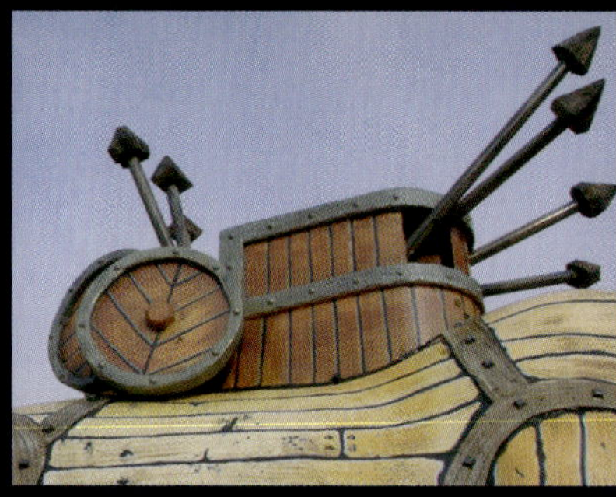

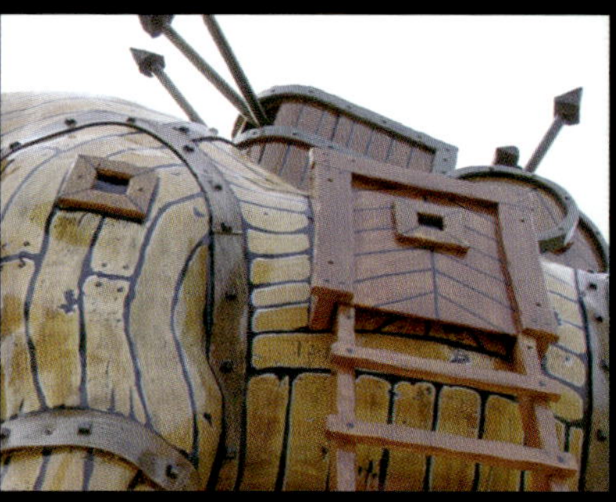

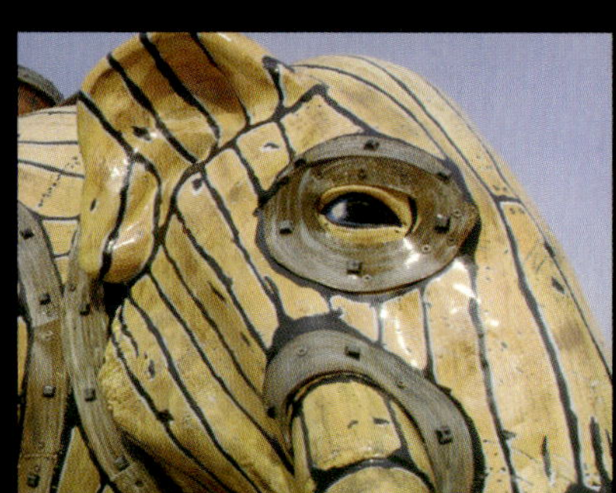

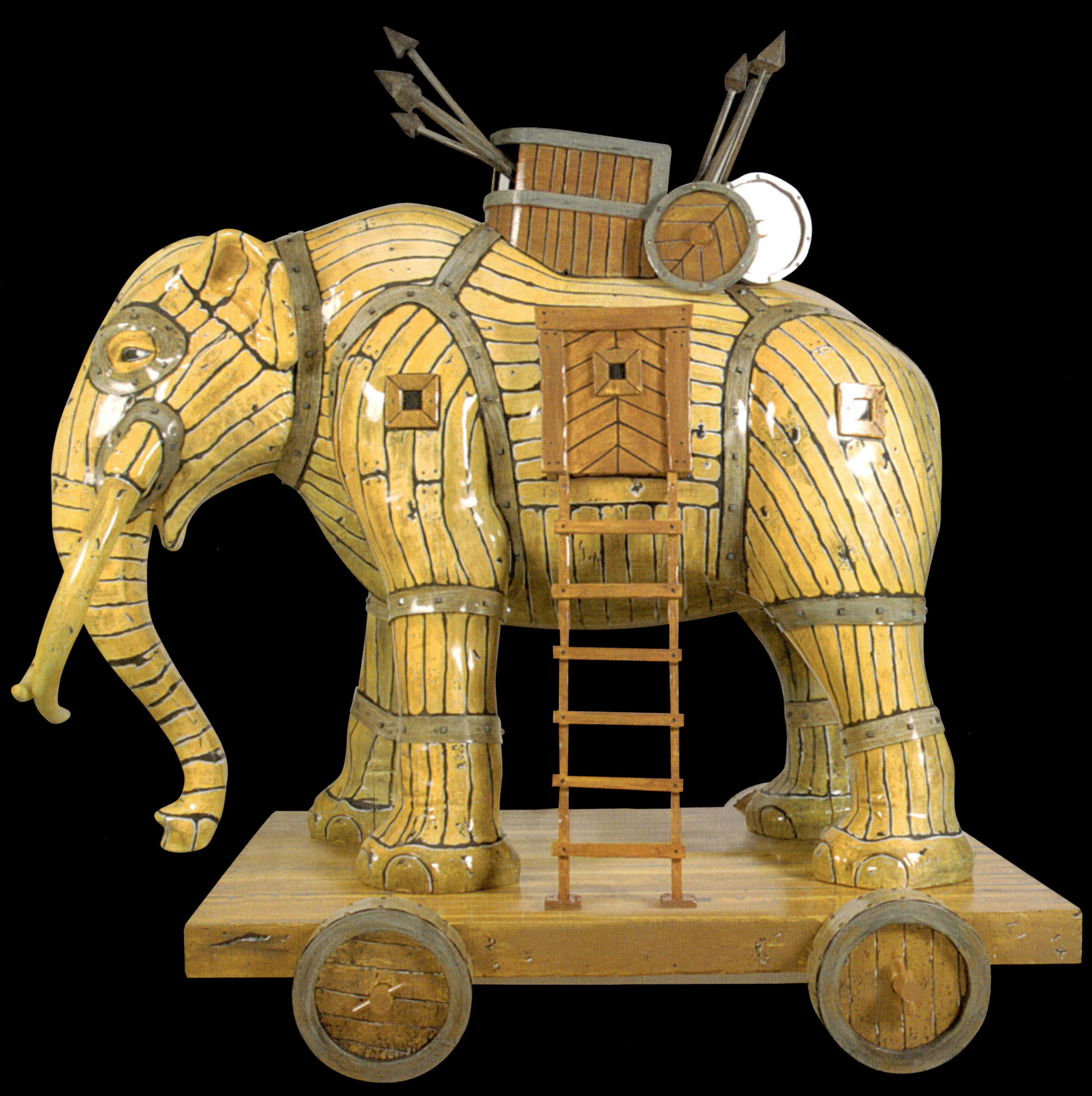

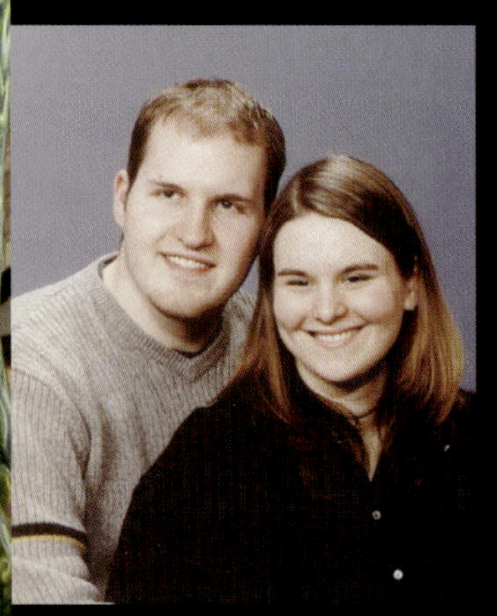

■ WALKODON

Artists: Emily Peters, computer artist,
Dragon Enclave Studios
(*pictured above, right*)

Josh Jones, professional artist,
Dragon Enclave Studios
(*pictured above, left*)

Sponsor: Summit City Fitness

By David Peters, Summit City Fitness

Walkodon encourages people to exercise for their heath and well being. Our don's design shows people walking, biking, and jogging along the River Greenway paths. It's an area where the real mastodons of some 10,000 years ago walked.

Walkodon has adopted a section of the Greenway through the Mayor's "Adopt a Greenway" program. We maintain and clean it. Walkodon's message is: "Don't become extinct. Exercise more and enjoy life."

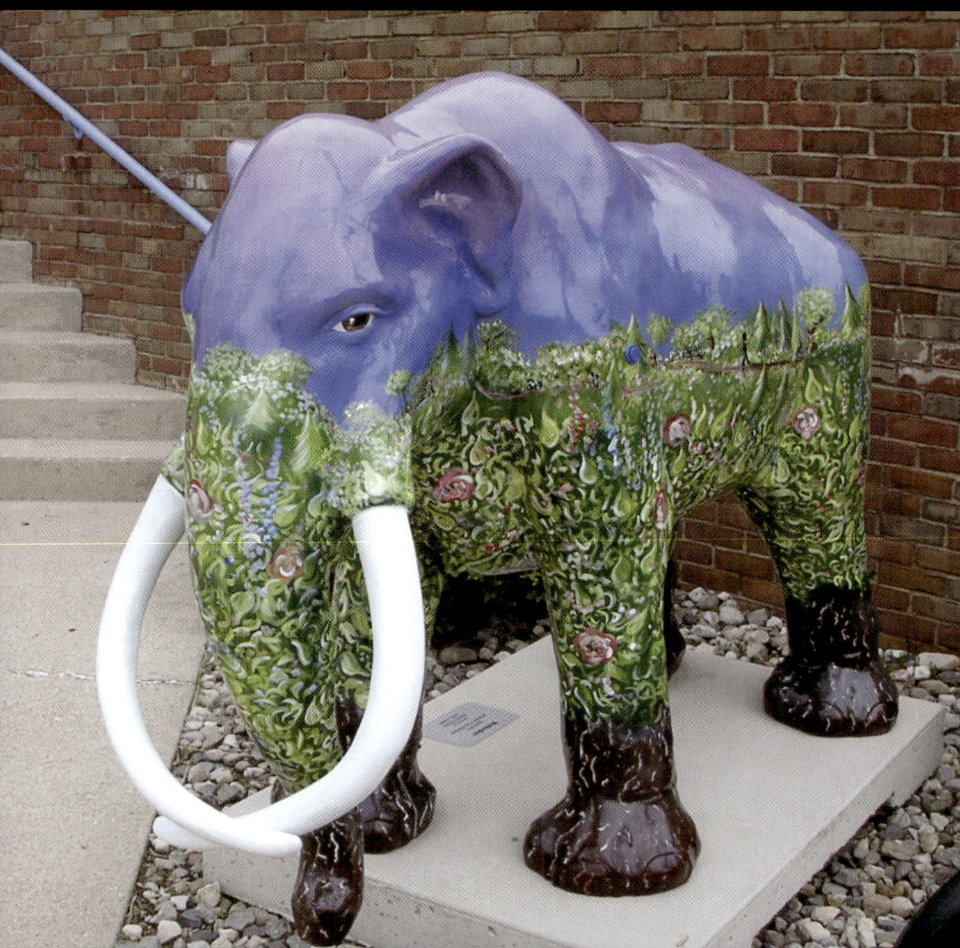

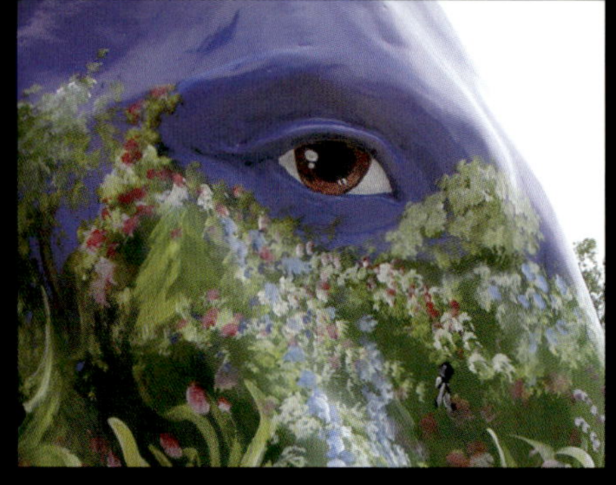

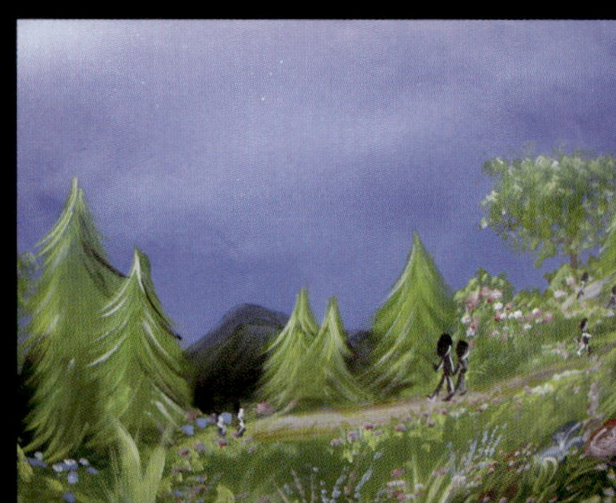

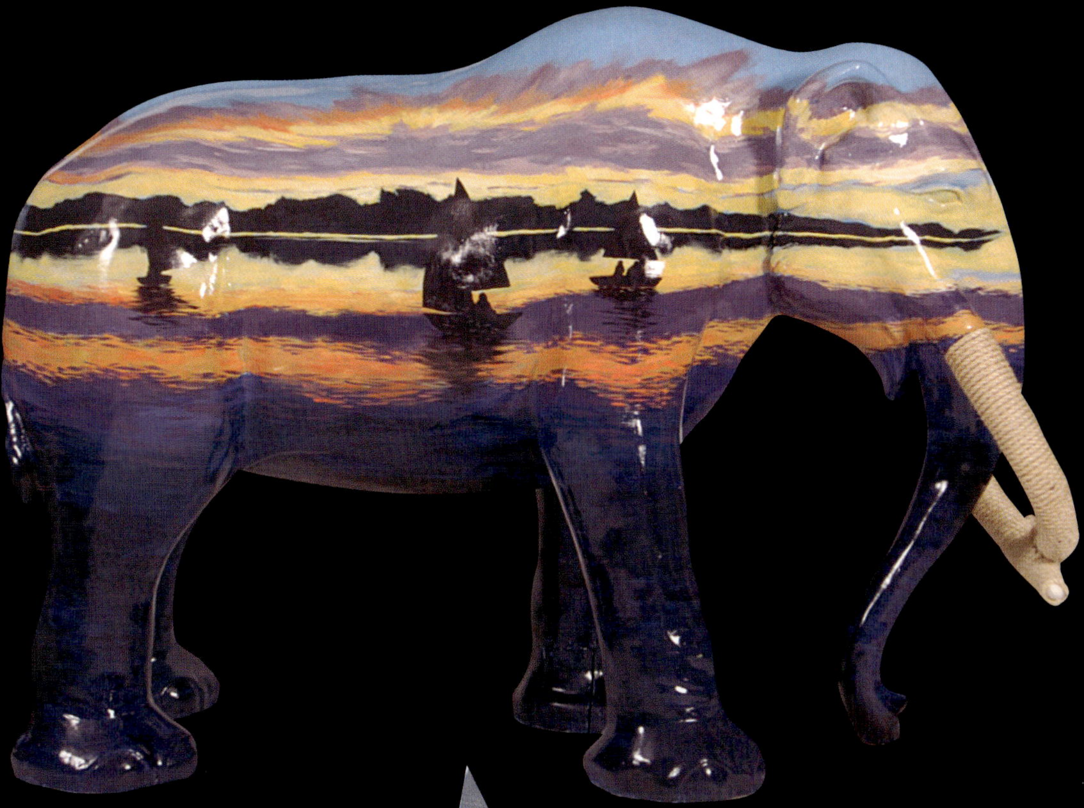

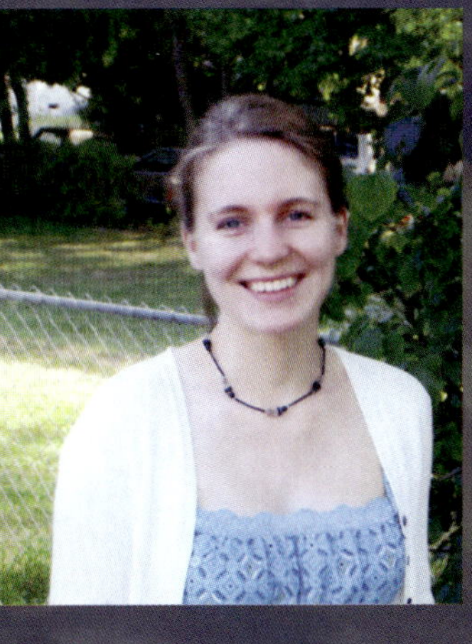

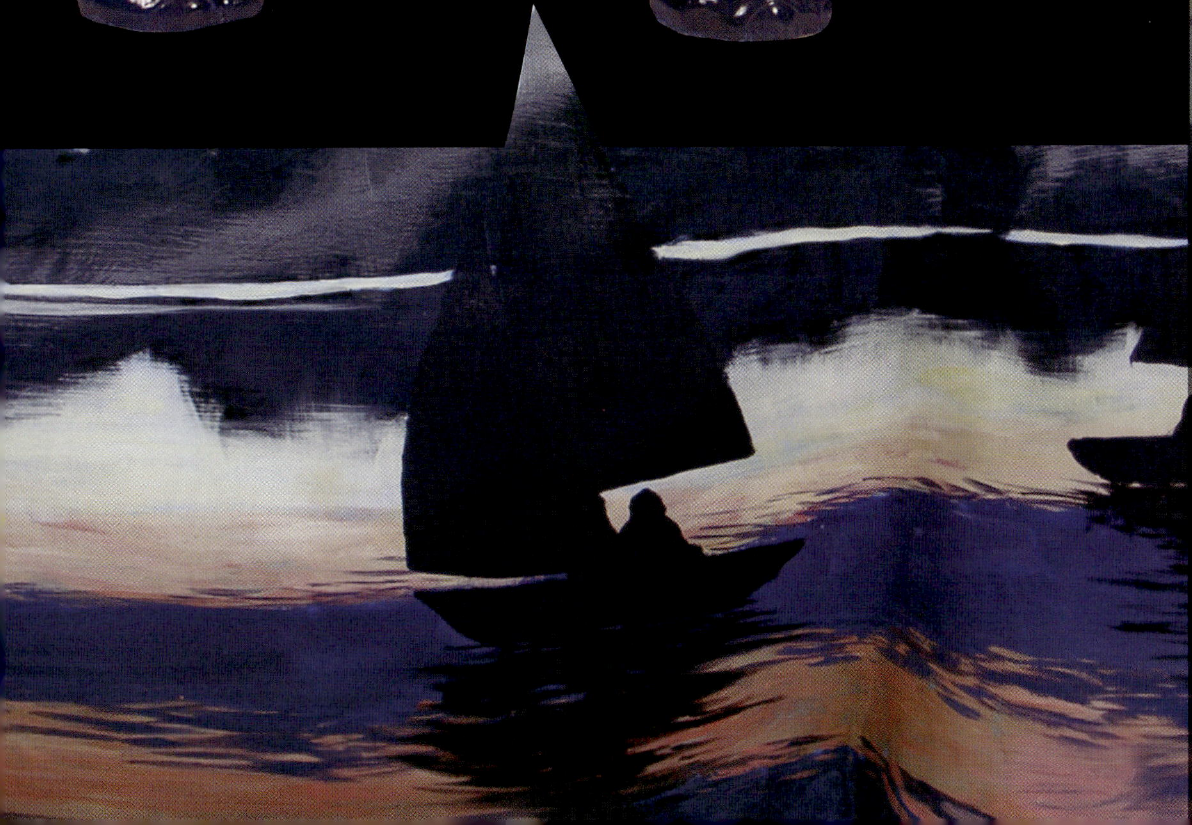

■ MAST AT DAWN

Artist: Lisa Timblin,
freelance artist

Sponsor: Lake City Bank

I'm originally from Canada, but right now my German-American husband, Mike, and I live in Warsaw, Ind.

I typically paint in oil on canvas, so it seemed only natural to me to treat the mastodon as if it were a flat surface. Prepping for paint and having to endure hours of very cold weather in my garage were my greatest challenges.

Being able to paint a sky in vibrant colors, always a pleasure for me, was the highlight.

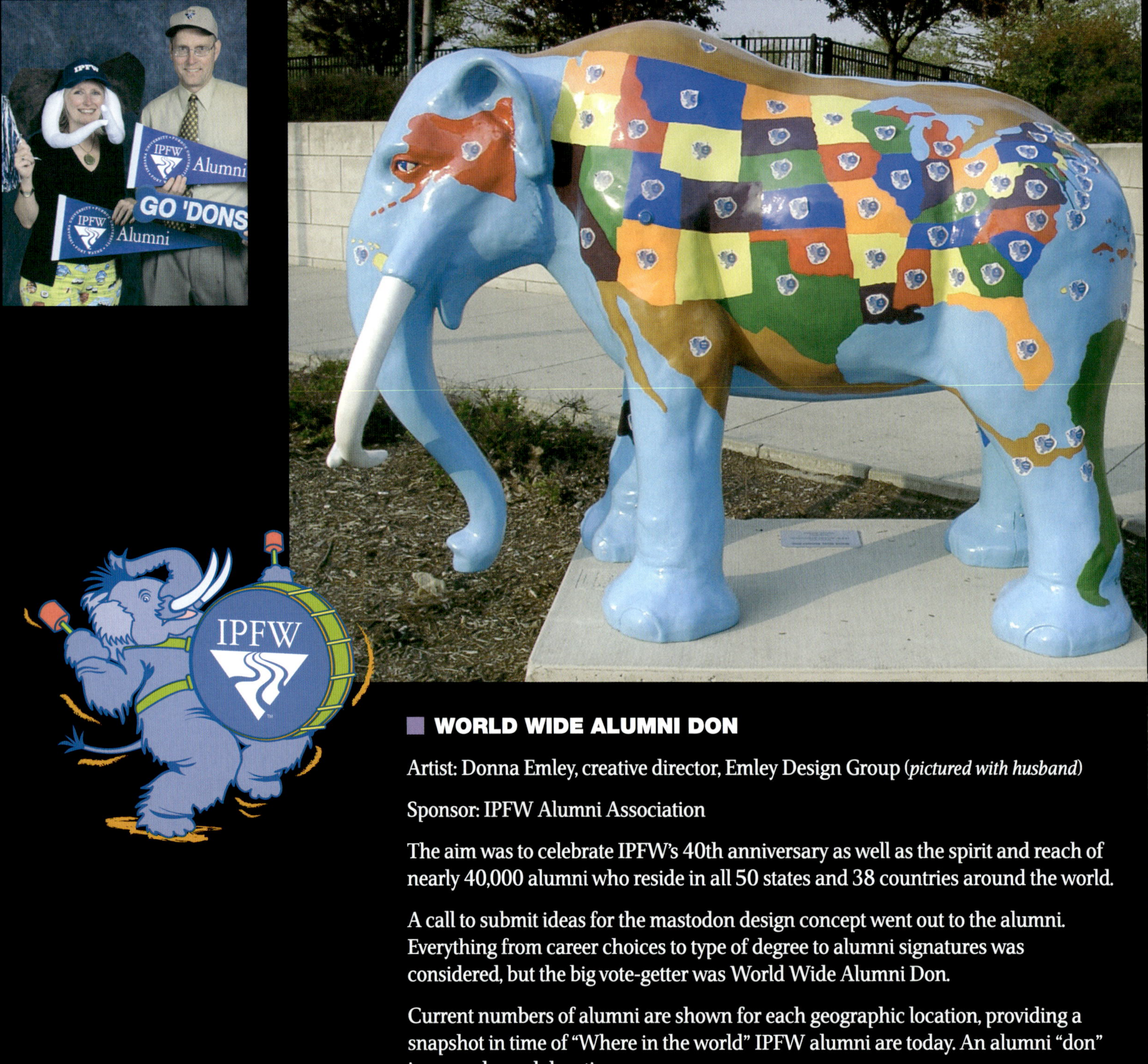

■ WORLD WIDE ALUMNI DON

Artist: Donna Emley, creative director, Emley Design Group (*pictured with husband*)

Sponsor: IPFW Alumni Association

The aim was to celebrate IPFW's 40th anniversary as well as the spirit and reach of nearly 40,000 alumni who reside in all 50 states and 38 countries around the world.

A call to submit ideas for the mastodon design concept went out to the alumni. Everything from career choices to type of degree to alumni signatures was considered, but the big vote-getter was World Wide Alumni Don.

Current numbers of alumni are shown for each geographic location, providing a snapshot in time of "Where in the world" IPFW alumni are today. An alumni "don" icon marks each location.

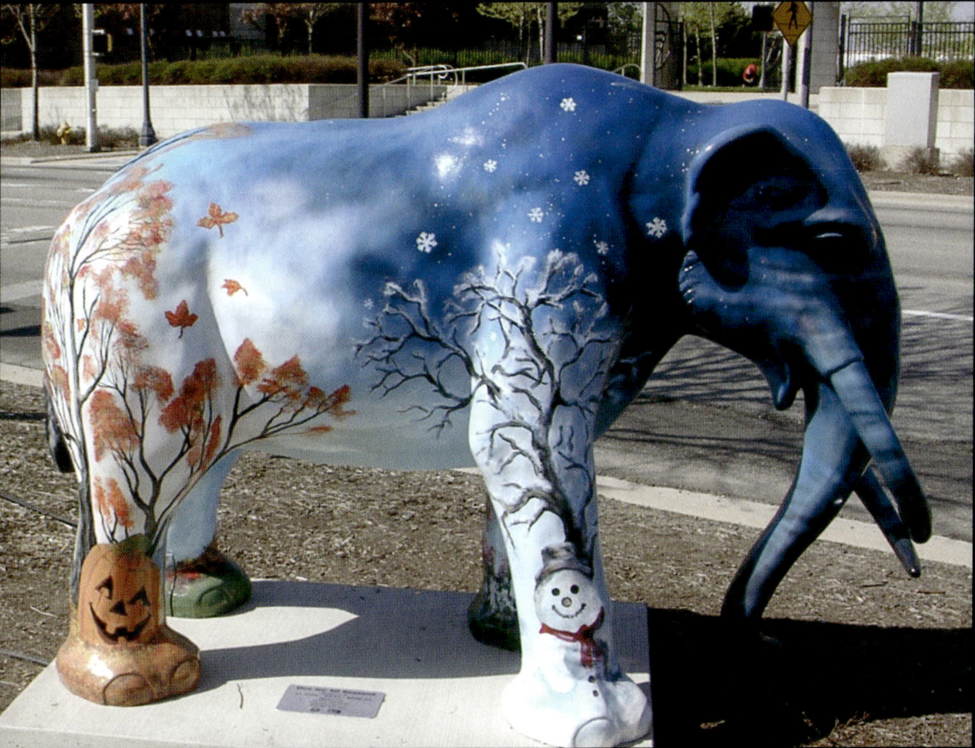

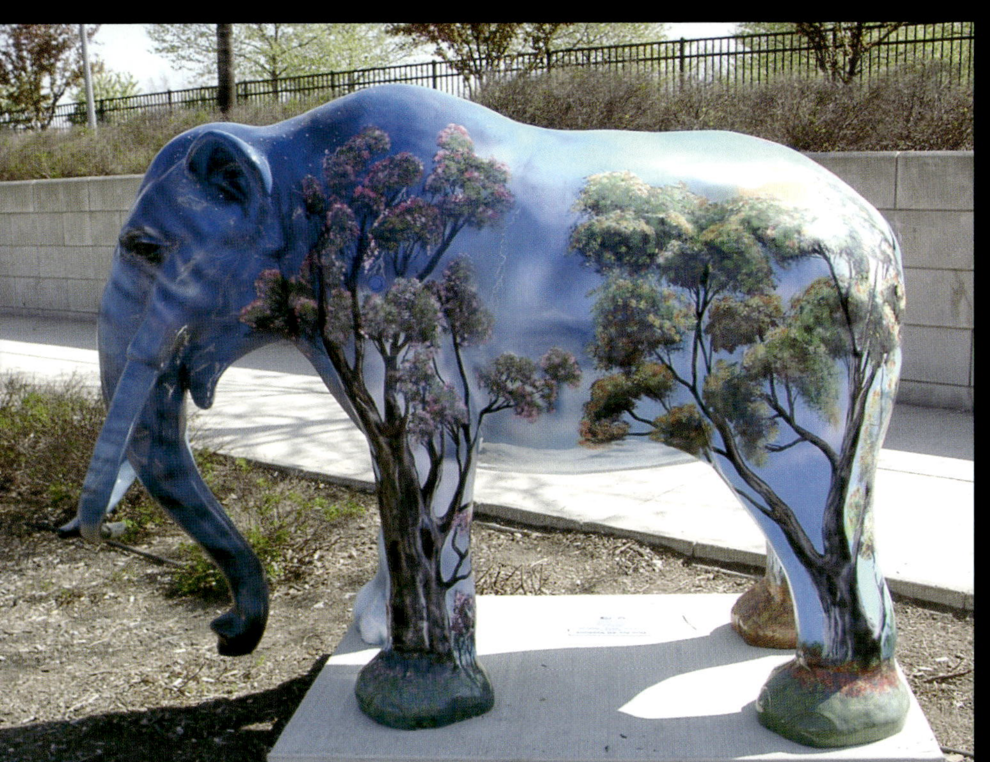

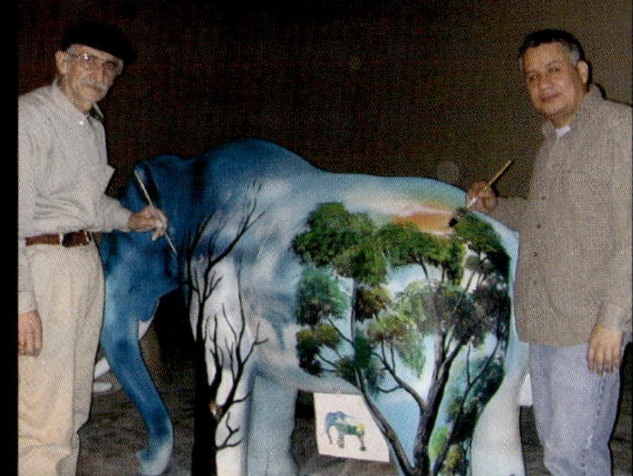

■ DON FOR ALL SEASONS

Artists: Palermo Galindo, photographer, IPFW Multicultural Services (*pictured above, right*); Adolfo Gardner, artist (*pictured above, left*); Denise Antoine, WPTA/WISE graphic designer

Sponsor: 21 Alive—WPTA/WISE 33

By Palermo Galindo

We worked together on a design Denise created. The objective was to celebrate our Don for All Seasons with brilliant and deep colors. We also wanted to equal the work on the Chicago cows and San Antonio longhorn bulls which I had seen earlier.

I utilized paint and brushes in executing our plan. Adolfo did the wonderful airbrushing with help from his son, Herman.

In fact, it was the help from Herman and my children (Iztaccihuatl, Palermo, and Alena) that made our don seem to come alive.

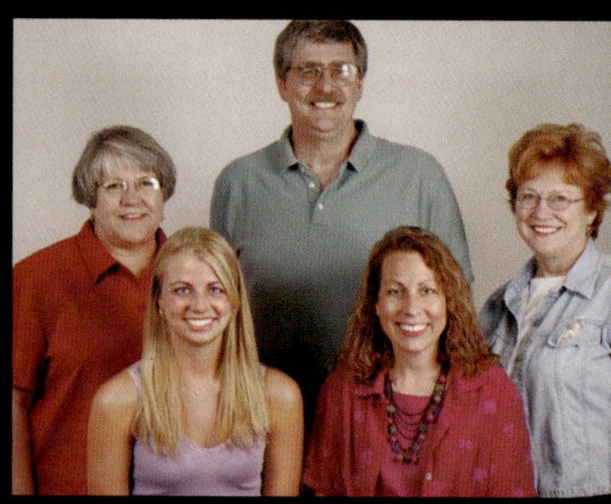

■ MAST-O-GREEN BUILD INITIATIVE

Artist: Northeast Indiana Green Building Coalition (*pictured above*)

Sponsor: Moake Park Group

By Regina Leffers, for the coalition

A few weeks before deadline for completing the mastodons, Steve Park called. The people from Moake Park Group were buried. He asked if we could take on the project.

Although our purpose is to raise the awareness of residents in the area of green building and sustainable living, we thought we could manage a mastodon.

I said, "Sure, we can do it."

Brenda Betley and I sketched in the design. Our most dedicated artist, Brenda, stopped by on her way to interviews, pulled coveralls over her suit, immersed herself in paint for awhile, took off the coveralls, and left, looking like a million bucks!

Other artists included Tim Hearld, Ann Helmke, Mike Michmerhuizen, Ann Beeching, Marjorie Havens, Steve Park and his daughter Ashley, and me.

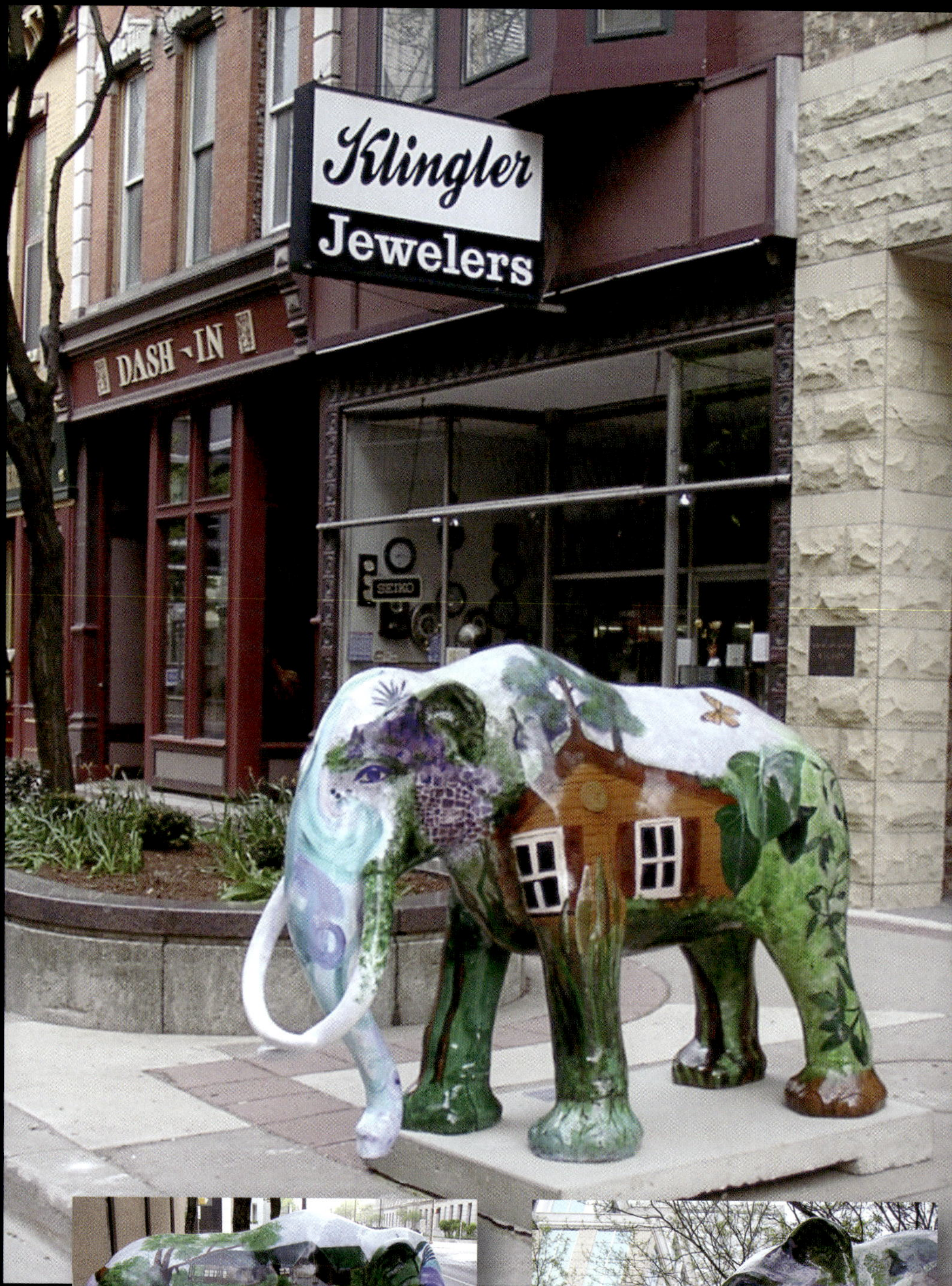

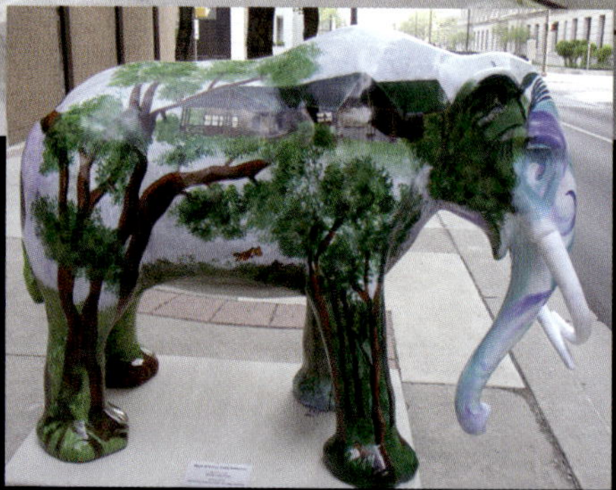

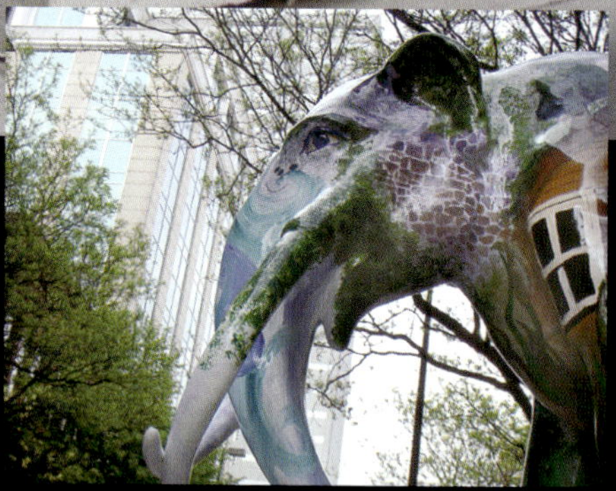

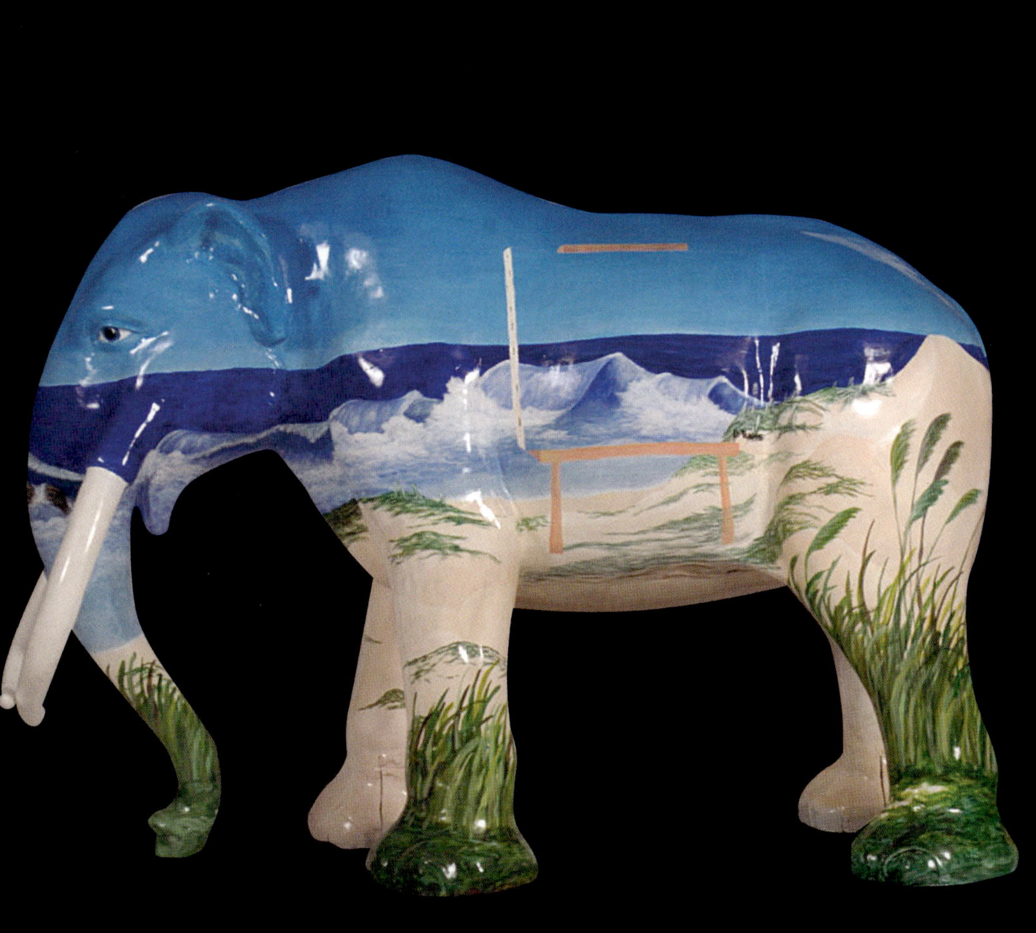

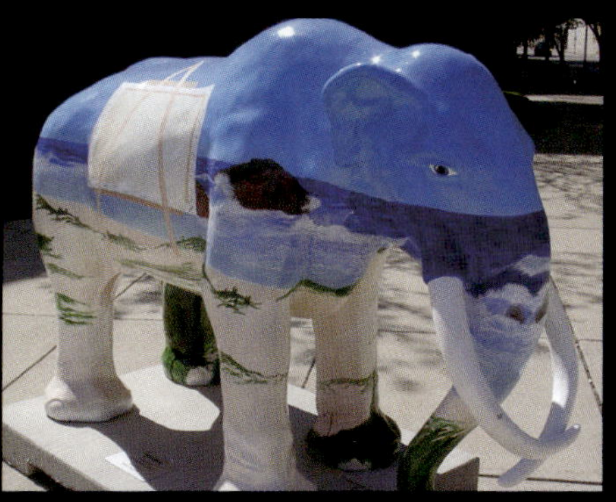

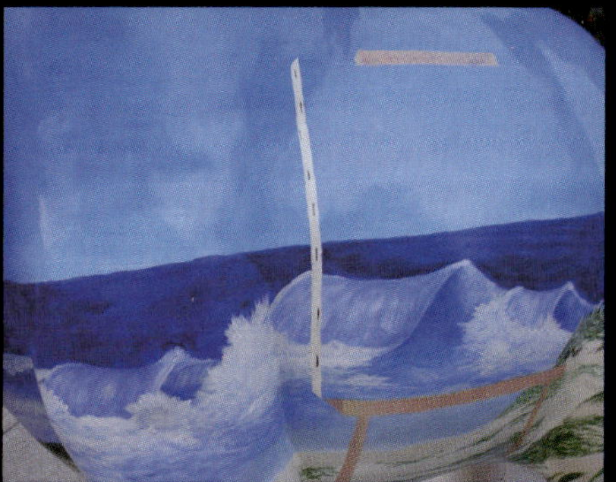

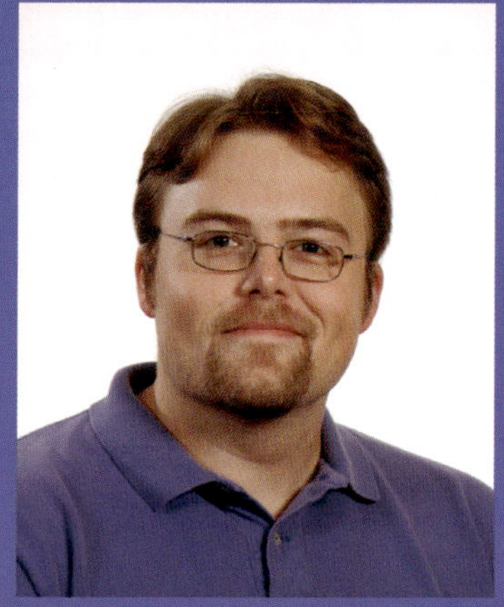

■ iMAGiDON

Artist: Drew Teague,
IPFW anthropology student

Sponsor: FourthWave LLC

iMAGiDON was conceived to invoke a sense of wonder in the viewer. I was inspired by the thought-provoking surrealist art of René Magritte. Magritte constructs his paintings in a highly realistic style, exaggerating an element to inspire imaginative thought.

For iMAGiDON, the imaginative element is the canvas and easel, as if the entire scene were frozen long enough for the artist to paint it. The exact moment waves crash onto the shore is captured on the canvas—even as it happens.

The artwork is the visual representation of an idea. The moment it is thought, the idea comes to life on the canvas of the mind.

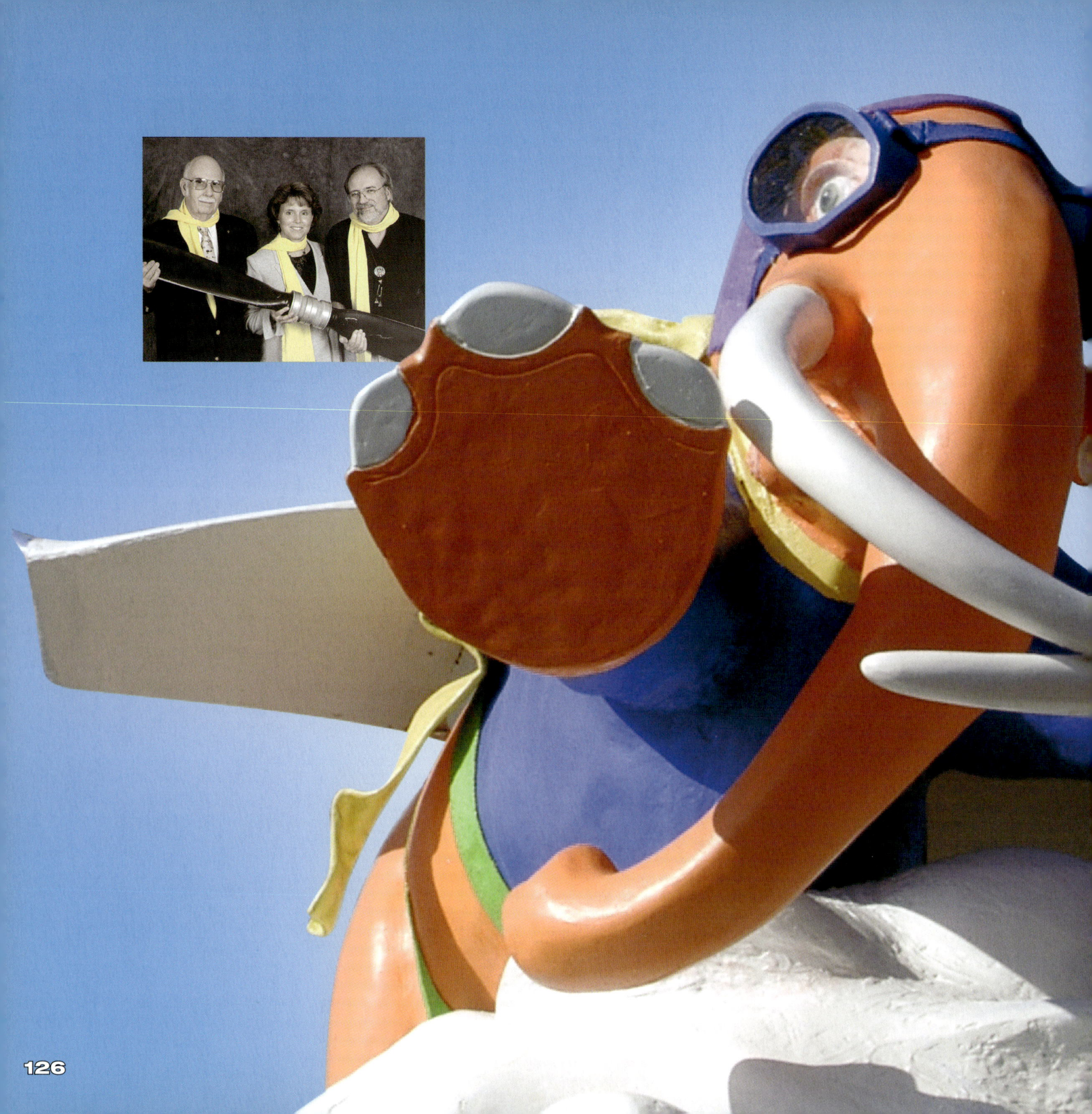

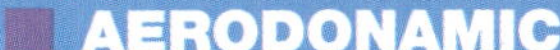

AERODONAMIC

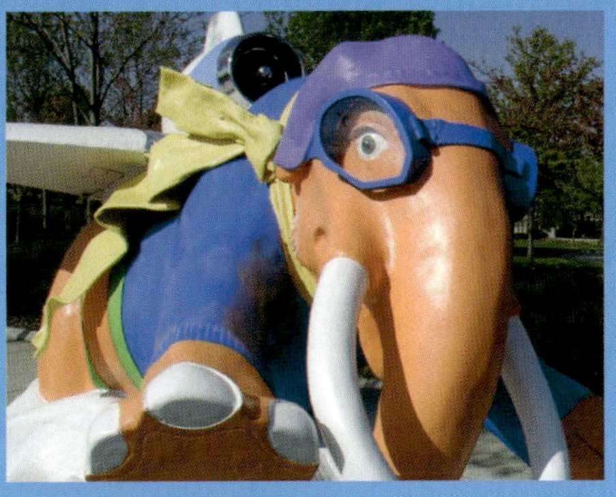

Artists: Lea Ann Powers Gebhard, artist, designer, and painter (*pictured, center*)

Ron Mitchell, industrial sculptor (*pictured, right*)

Sponsor: Fort Wayne-Allen County Airport Authority

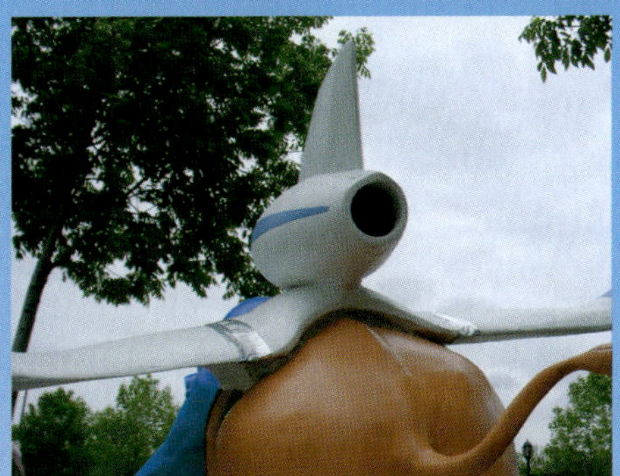

By Lea Ann Powers Gebhard

Without challenges in life, we would not feel the exhilaration of accomplishment. AeroDONamic was definitely a challenge. I got a crash course in welding, fiberglass, and the use of power tools so I could help Ron turn my design from a two-dimensional drawing into a 500-pound flying mastodon. Giving Aerie (as we like to refer to him) wings tested all the skills I had just learned.

Aerie wouldn't have lifted off without the help of our right-hand helper Larry Murphy (pictured left). He also wouldn't have had a hangar without the generosity of Chris Timmerman and his family, who allowed us to use their garage as a studio. Finally, thanks to the Fort Wayne-Allen County Airport Authority for its support and trust that this project would take off.

It's been a wonderful opportunity to be a part of this community event that has brought diverse backgrounds and experiences together. It's been rewarding to see the joyful smiles on people's faces.

By Ron Mitchell

I liked the design concept (that Lea created) very much. It was animated and lots of fun. I also liked the challenge of recreating the original model and wanted to work on a project that pushed the limits. I was proud to be involved in a Fort Wayne project, especially one that has been so well received.

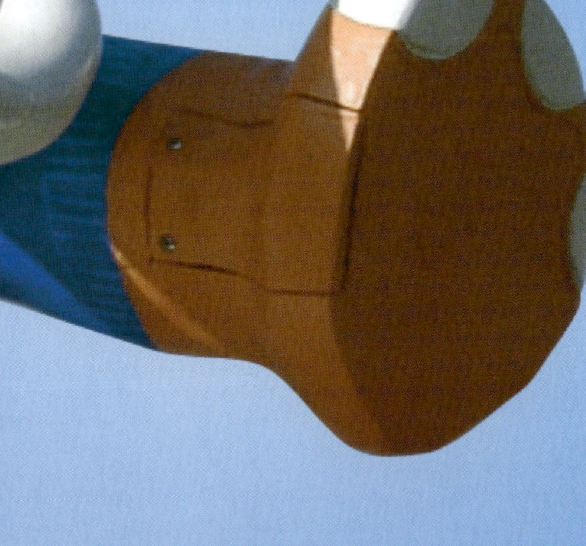

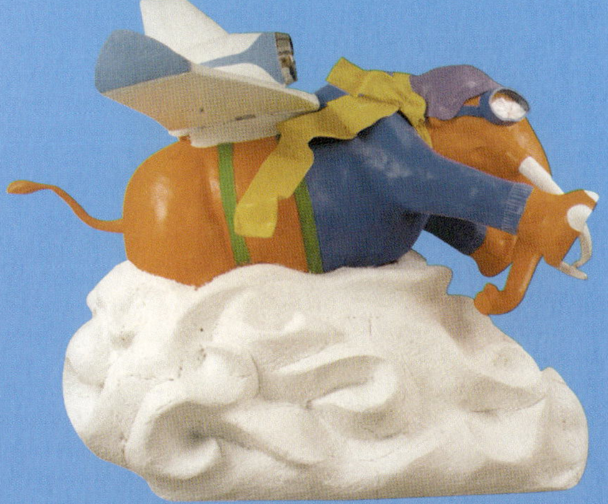

■ FORT WAYNE-O-DON

Artists: Andrea Snyder, interior designer; Tami Mizzell, artist; Lori Boester, artist; Sarah Boester, artist; Emily Guerrero, artist; Aaron Guerrero, artist

Sponsor: *Fort Wayne Business Journal*

By Andrea Snyder

Our creative families decided to let photos tell the story of Fort Wayne. Our list of places to include started small but kept growing and made each of us more appreciative of our city's attractions, architecture, and art.

There were memories of the first summer ice cream at Zesto's and memories of days playing in our parks. We enriched each other's lives as we shared our stories. This project really brought our two generations together.

The response from the community has been awesome. It's so neat to see families enjoying the mastodons and to see the children running around yelling their names.

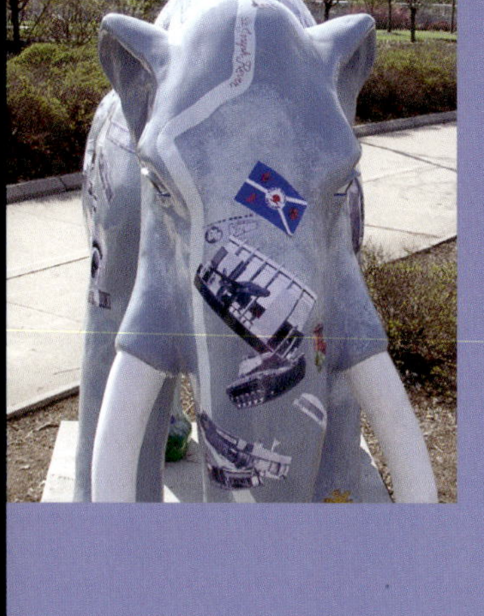

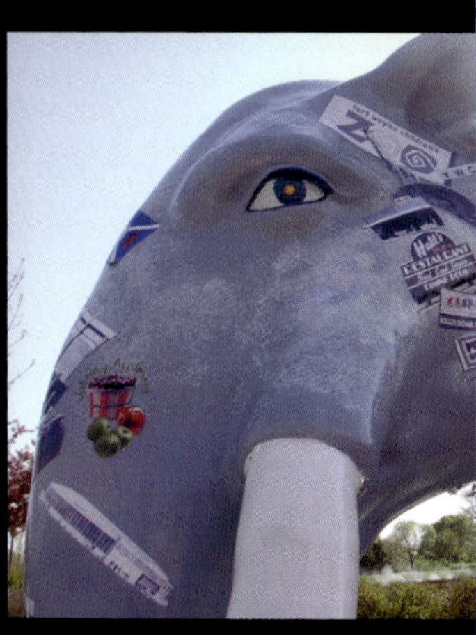

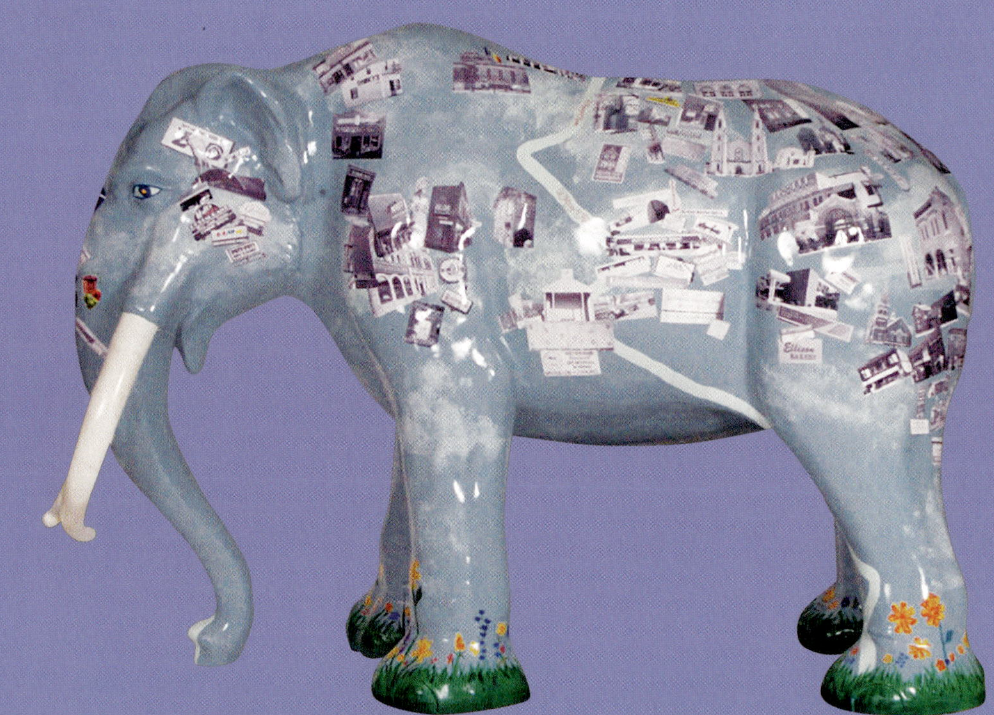

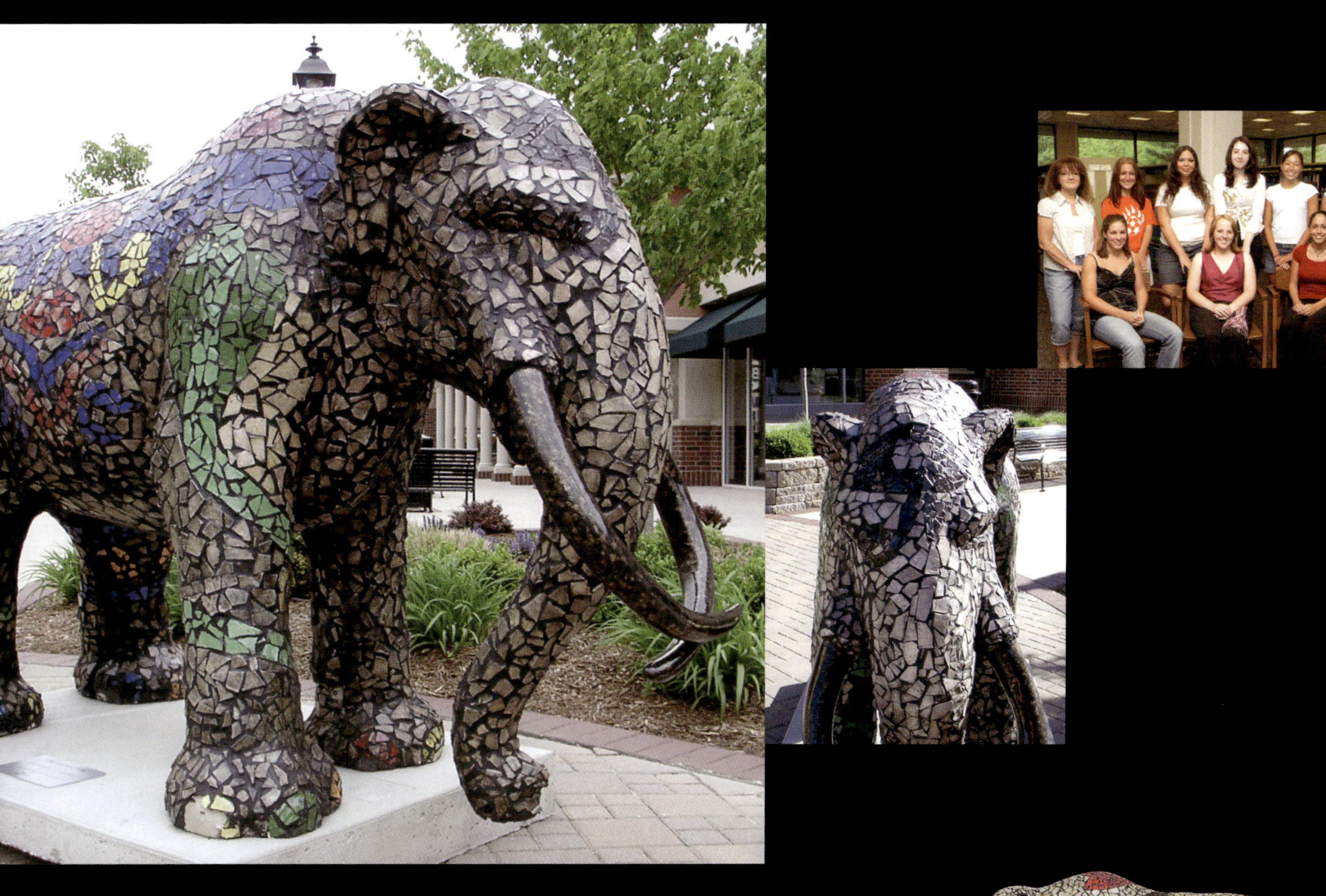

EGYPTIAN DON

Artist: Art Club, Northrop High School   Sponsor: Professional Federal Credit Union

By Becky Griswold, Northrop art teacher

Everybody in the art club submitted designs, but it finally came down to a choice between a Peyton Manning mastodon representing Indiana and an Egyptian Don depicting art history. Being an art club, students voted for Egyptian Don.

Using clay we had on hand, the students made tiles and then took a hammer to them to create the small pieces for a mosaic. Closer to deadline, they worked all hours of the day, got splattered, and ruined some clothes.

Finally, 10 students from a bodybuilding class moved Egyptian Don into a well-lighted main hall where it was easy to see all the grout that had been missed. It took a 12" screwdriver and hammer to chip it all away.

Those who worked on this project were: Brittnie Arroyo, Andrea Case, Ariel Case, Becky Griswold, Ejecta Isbell, Tsion Kisle, Stacy Makridakis, Hoa-Nau Pham, Mindy Shull, Latricia Stults, Shelby Vorndran, Alyssa Welles, and Lisa Wilson.

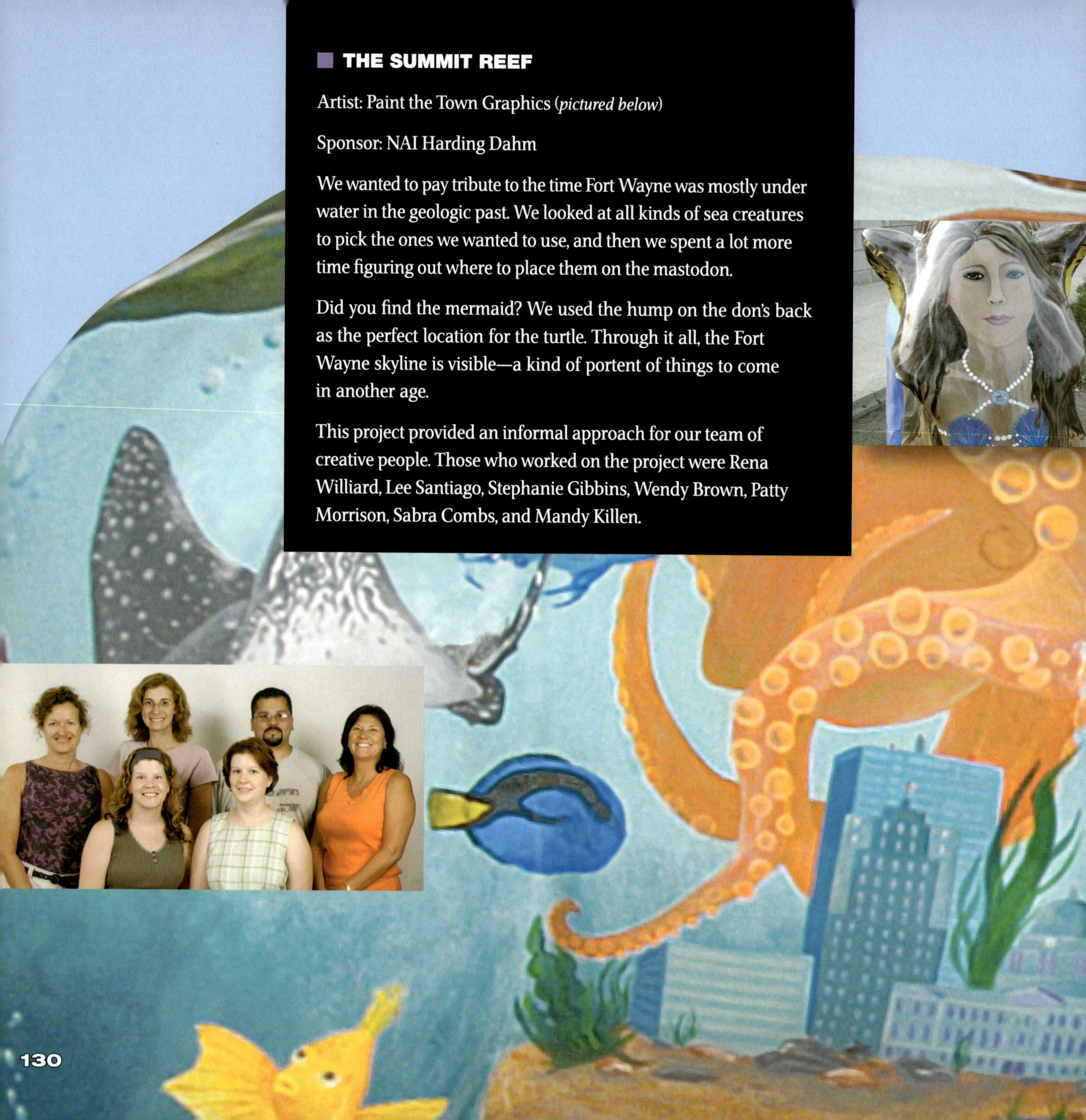

■ THE SUMMIT REEF

Artist: Paint the Town Graphics (*pictured below*)

Sponsor: NAI Harding Dahm

We wanted to pay tribute to the time Fort Wayne was mostly under water in the geologic past. We looked at all kinds of sea creatures to pick the ones we wanted to use, and then we spent a lot more time figuring out where to place them on the mastodon.

Did you find the mermaid? We used the hump on the don's back as the perfect location for the turtle. Through it all, the Fort Wayne skyline is visible—a kind of portent of things to come in another age.

This project provided an informal approach for our team of creative people. Those who worked on the project were Rena Williard, Lee Santiago, Stephanie Gibbins, Wendy Brown, Patty Morrison, Sabra Combs, and Mandy Killen.

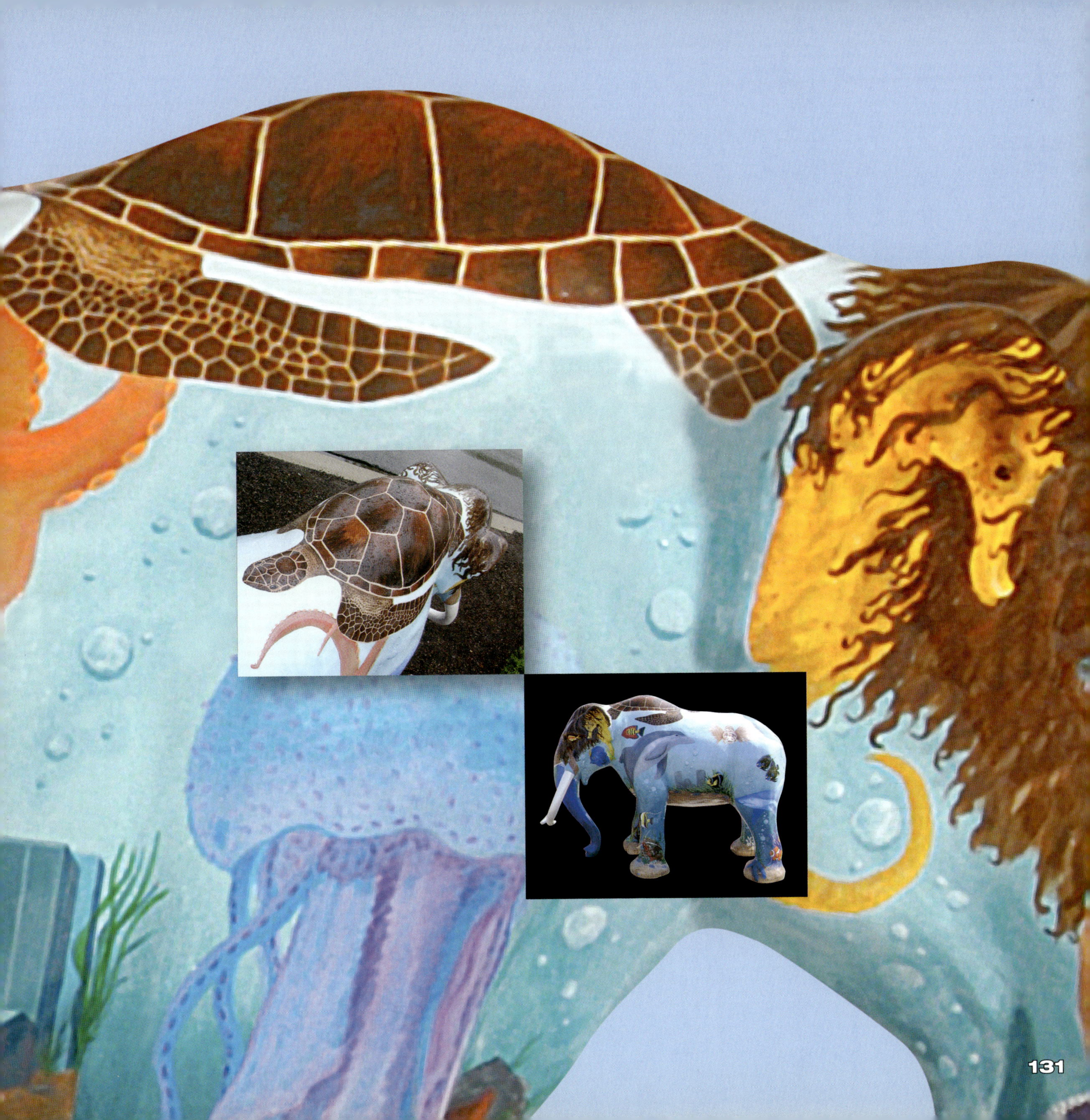

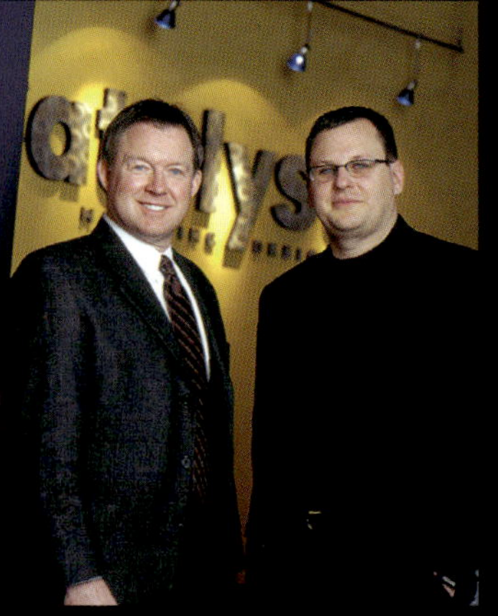

THE MASTODON EXPRESS

Artists: Catalyst Marketing Design's Richard Gripp and Ted Kucinsky (*pictured above left to right*)

Sponsor: Wells Fargo Bank

Our art directors developed many concepts incorporating the Wells Fargo brand into the design. Finally, we arrived at a stagecoach design which told the story and was, at the same time, visually interesting and a bit whimsical.

Our design called for more than just a paint job. We purchased actual wagon wheels from a supplier and had to integrate them into the mastodon's legs. We also custom built a stagecoach body and mounted it on top of the mastodon's back. Following painting, we installed wheels and applied detailing and antiquing effects.

This project required the entire team to exercise all its talents: imagination, collaboration, creativity, artistry, craftsmanship, attention to detail, timelines, cooperation, and hard work.

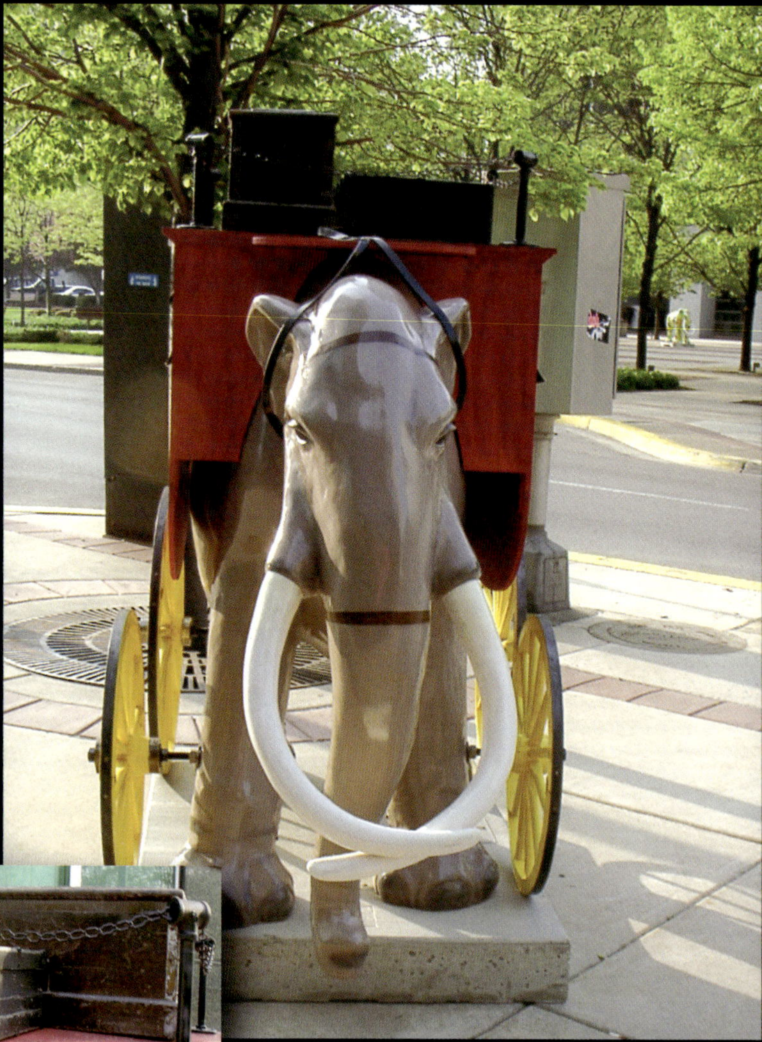

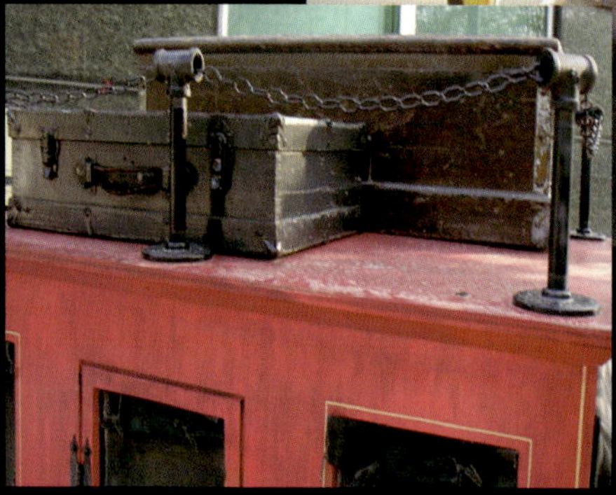

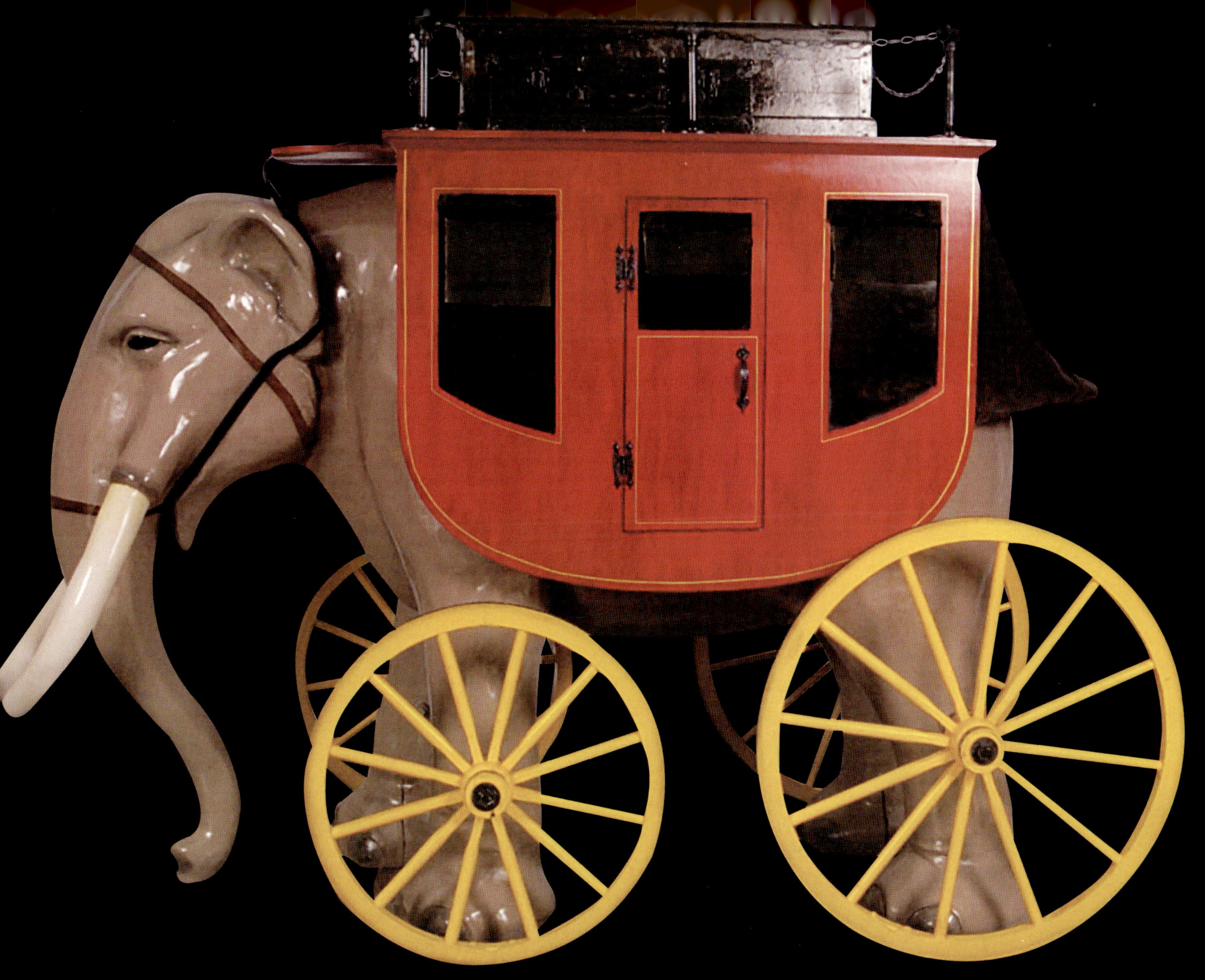

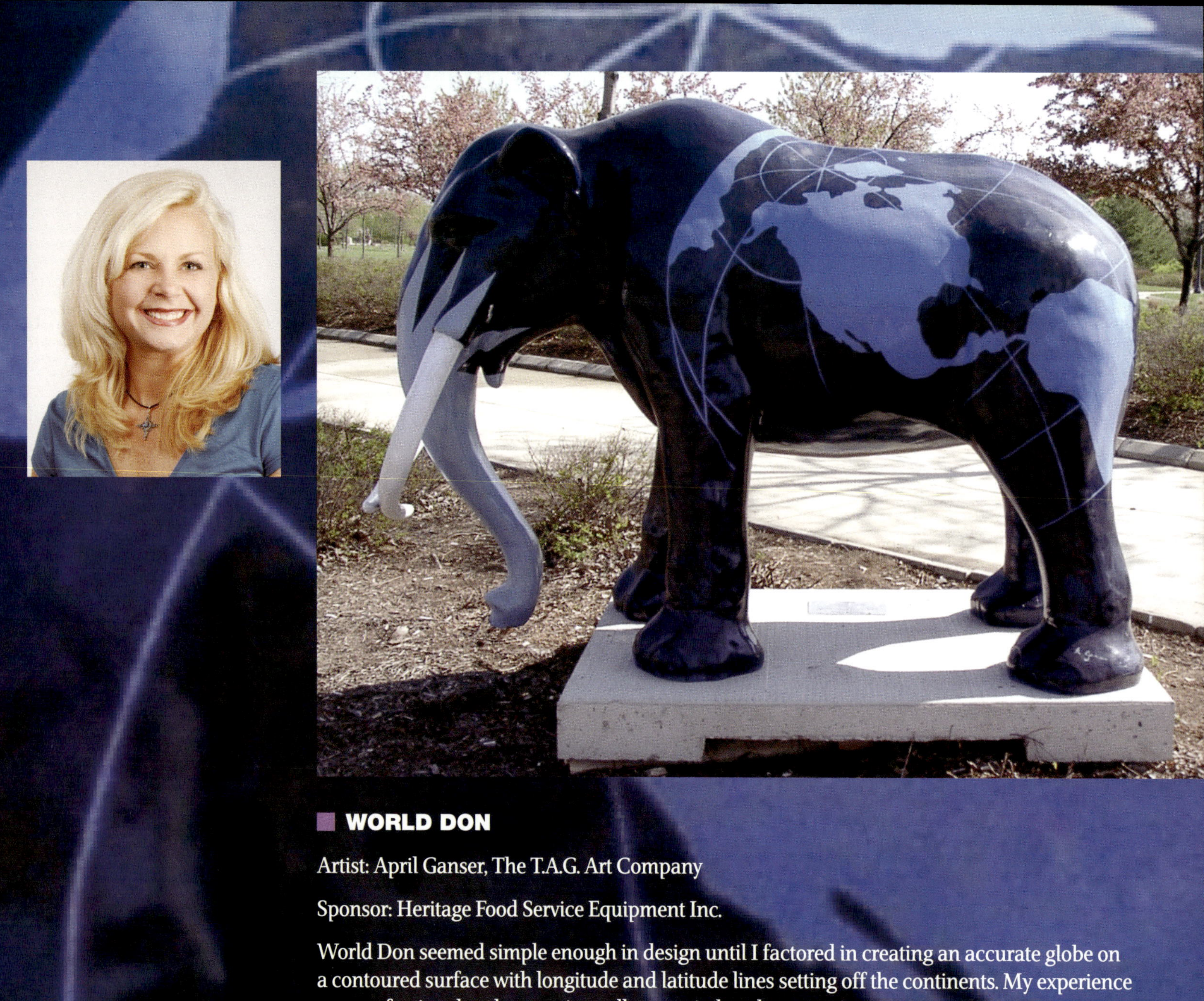

WORLD DON

Artist: April Ganser, The T.A.G. Art Company

Sponsor: Heritage Food Service Equipment Inc.

World Don seemed simple enough in design until I factored in creating an accurate globe on a contoured surface with longitude and latitude lines setting off the continents. My experience as a professional makeup artist really came in handy.

It took a lot of late night tweaks to ensure quality. The resultant work is actually the third draft in fine-line detail. The final clear coat covering was to maximize shine.

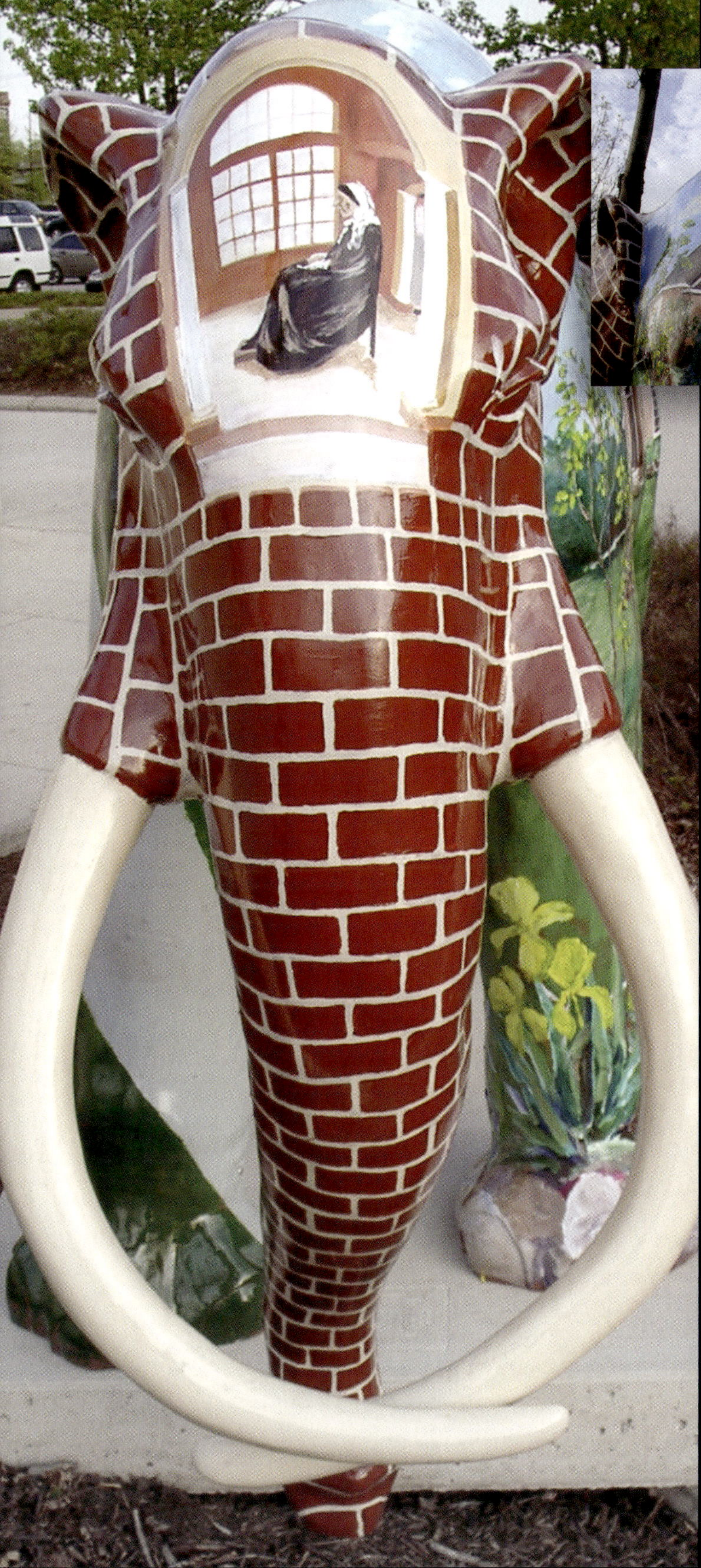

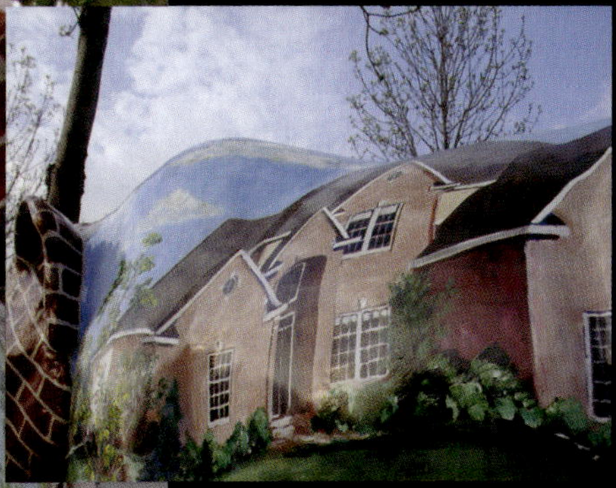

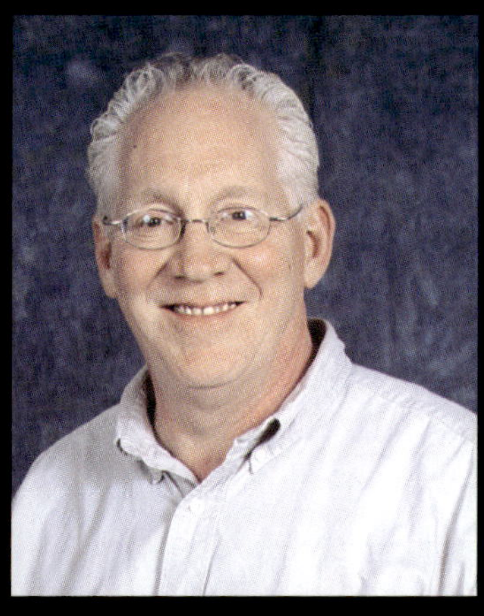

THE ALL AMERICAN DREAM O DON

Artist: James Jur, Artisan Gallery

Sponsor: All American Homes Store

There was quite a flurry of interest while I was painting my mastodon in our gallery window. People stopped by to check out my progress.

The most fun part for me was adding Whistler's Mother. Seated in the interior of one of the homes depicted, she is located squarely on Dream o Don's forehead and represents the permanence and stability of home life in Fort Wayne.

I am proud to have been part of Mastodons on Parade.

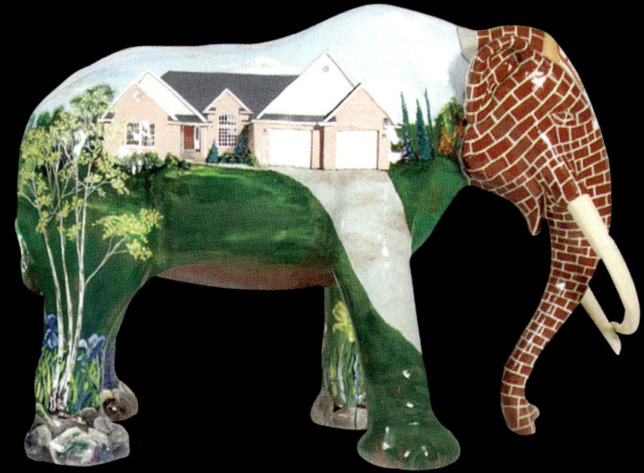

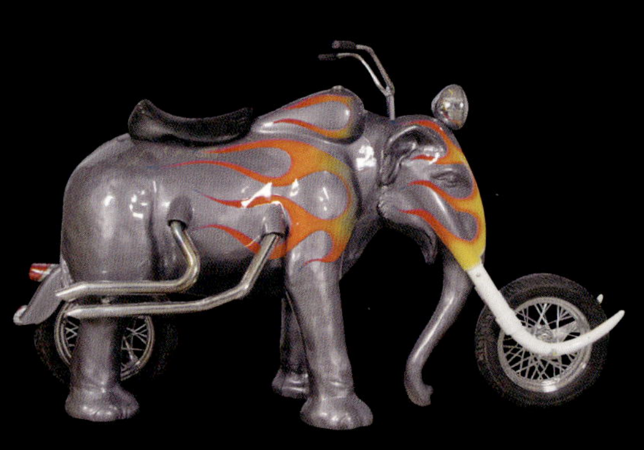

■ CHOPPER DON

Artists: Bob Kiel, art director, Ferguson Advertising (*pictured, left*); Ed Rost, Oakland Body Shop (*pictured right*)

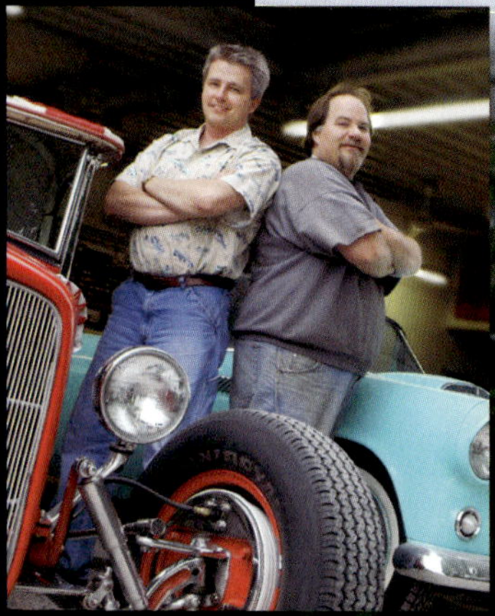

Sponsor: Jim Bailey's Harley-Davidson/Buell

By Bob Kiel

Friends since our days together at Bishop Luers High School, we have maintained a mutual interest in anything cars and cool. Still, the process of turning a pachyderm into a motorcycle was an interesting challenge.

Our sponsor said he wanted something "that looked like a Harley and was cool." So, inspired by George Barris, the famous Hollywood car customizer who created the Batmobile, and Paul Teutel from the *American Chopper* TV show, we came up with Chopper Don. Armed with parts salvaged from old Harleys, we spent our weekends cutting, sanding, sketching, and improvising to build something unique.

Mastodons on Parade shows that Fort Wayne is a very creative city. We would definitely be involved in another project like this. It was good for us and good for the city.

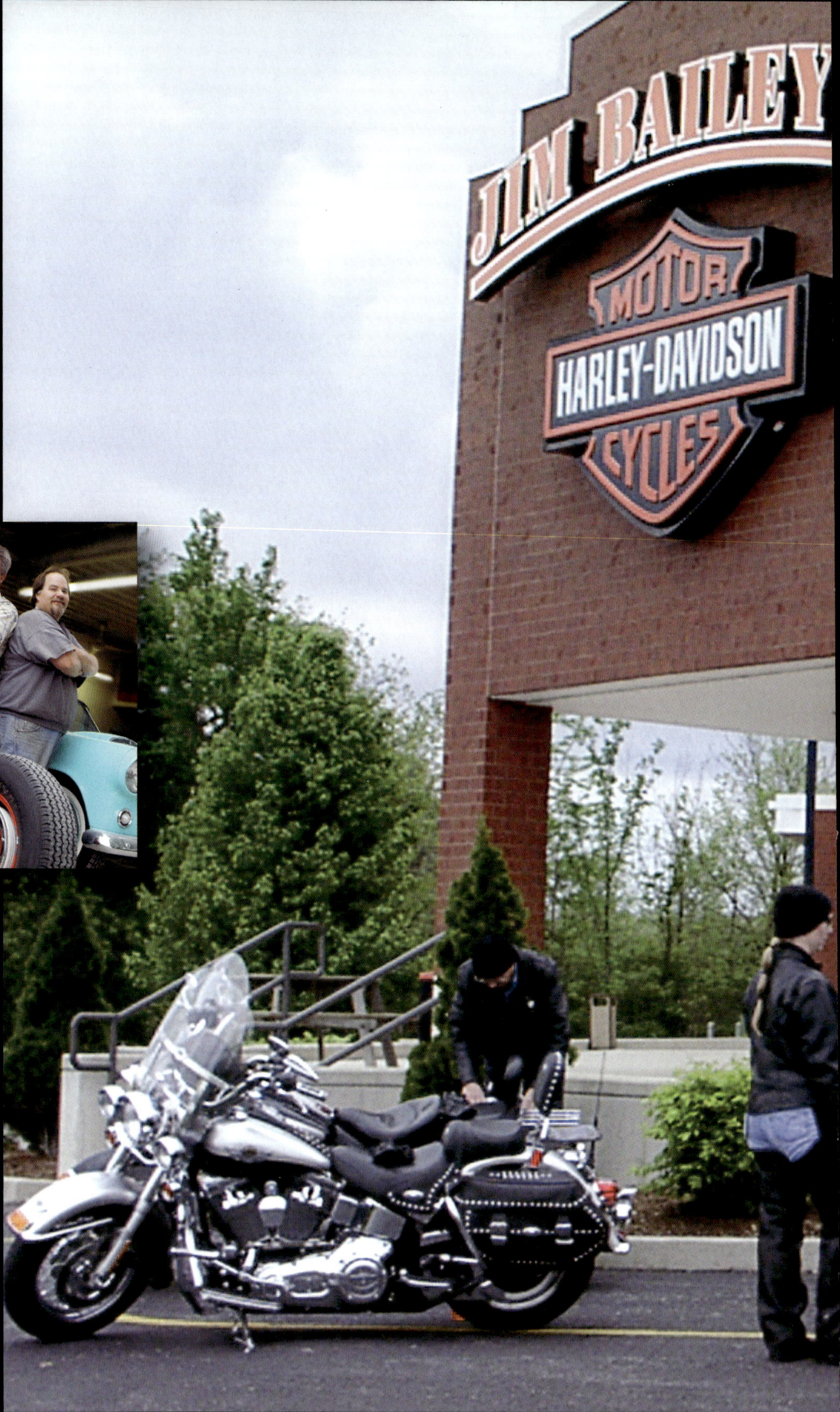

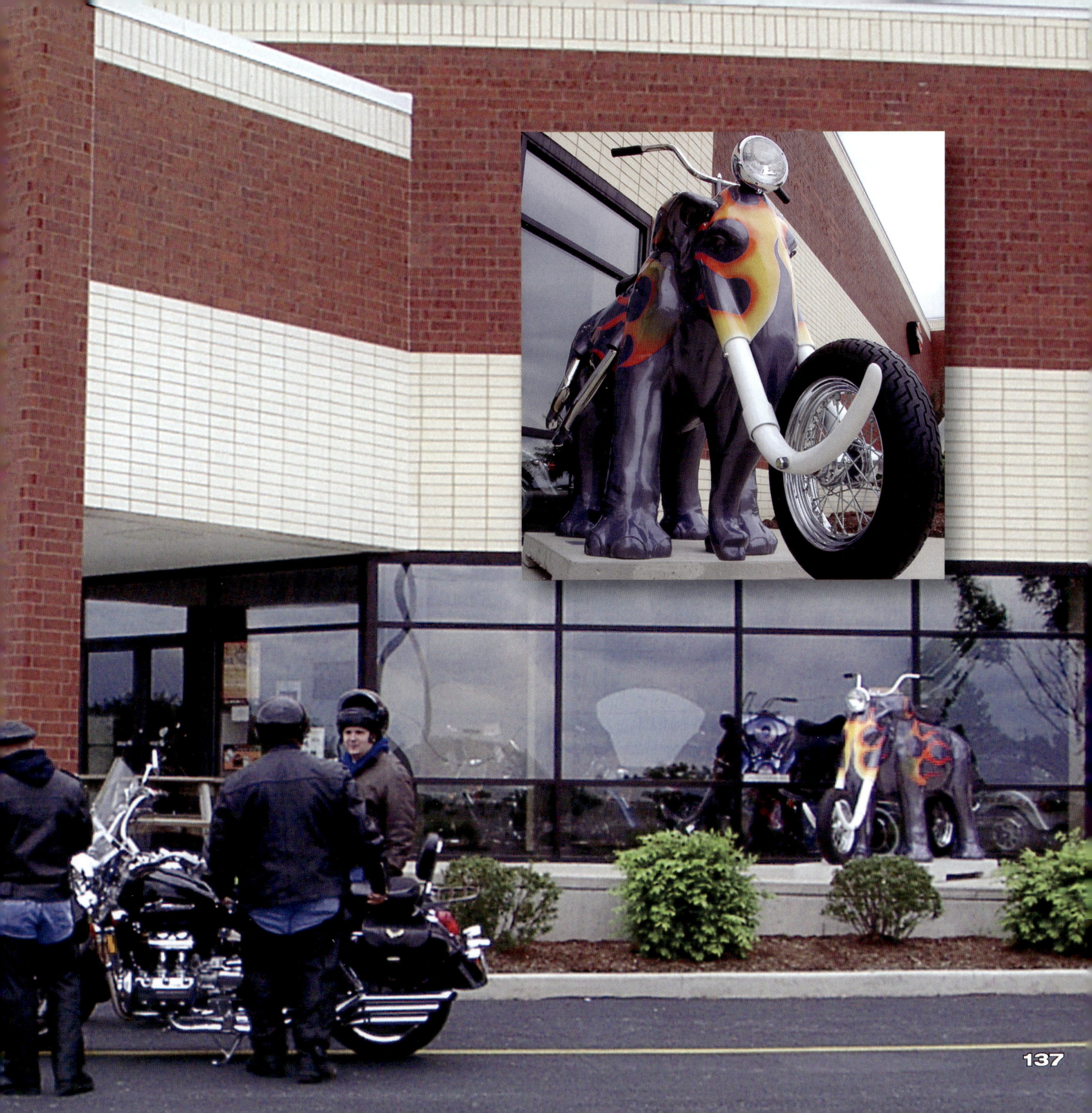

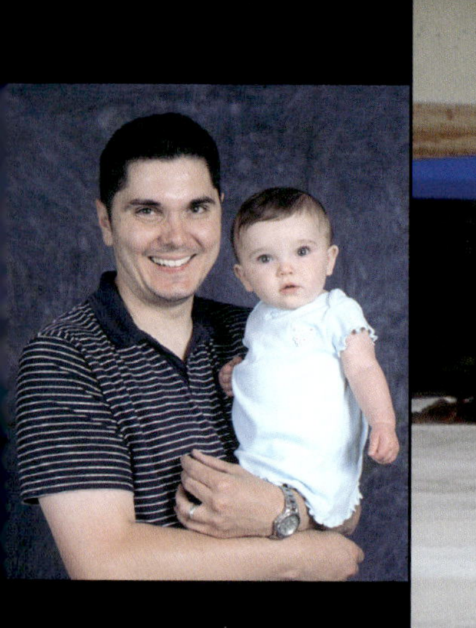

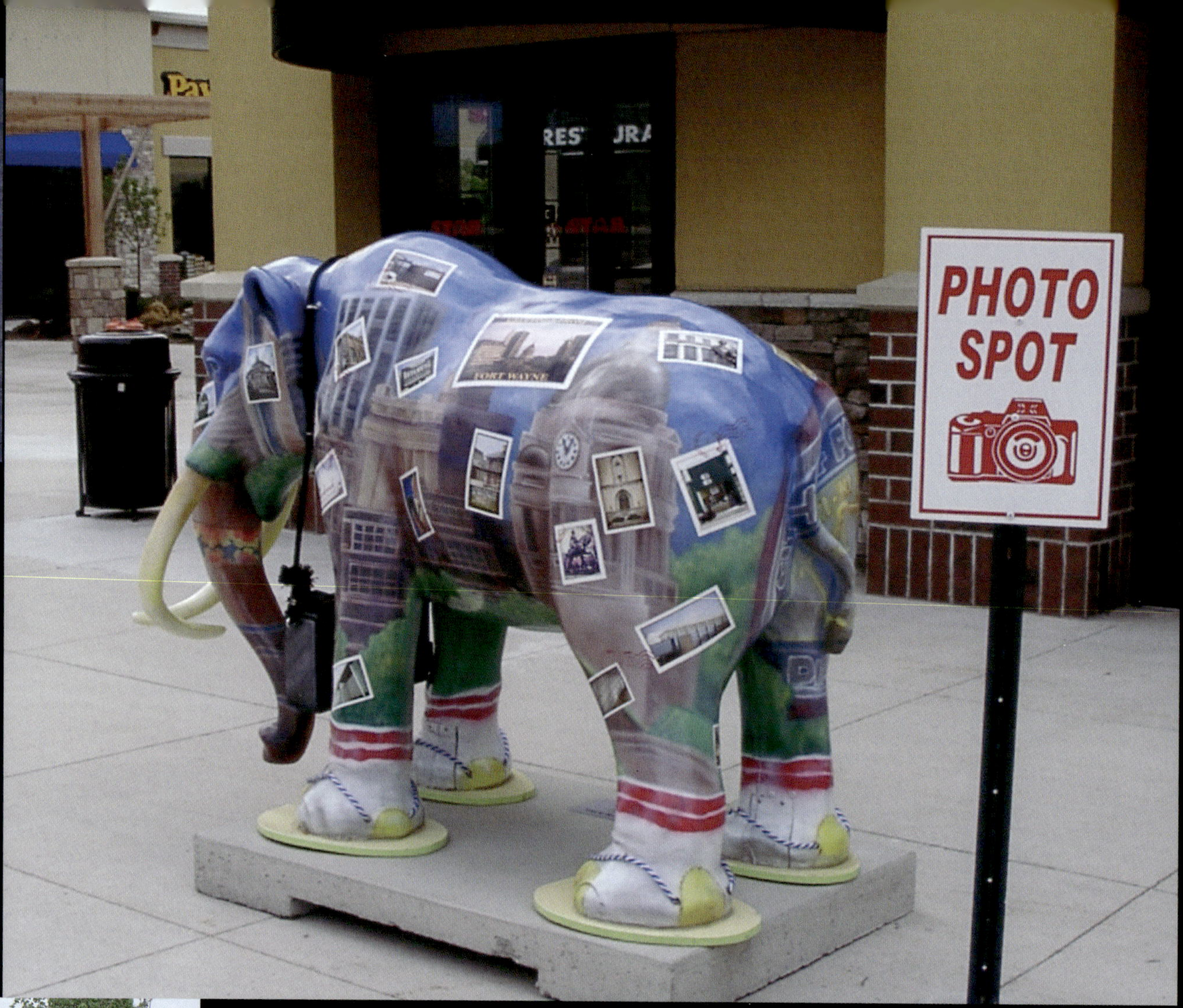

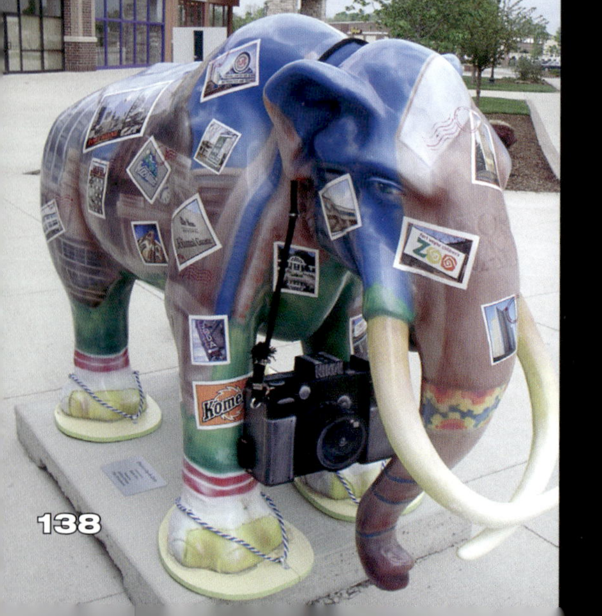

■ PHOTO-OP-A-DON

Artists: Jeffrey Crane, professional photographer (*pictured with daughter*)
Tim Brumbeloe, professional photographer and artist

Sponsor: Bank One

By Jeffrey Crane

Have you ever been on vacation and seen one of those signs telling you where a great place to take a family photo is? That's where the inspiration came from for Photo-Op-A-Don.

As a photographer and a painter, I wanted to be able to showcase all that Fort Wayne has to offer. We created postcards of such Fort Wayne landmarks as Cindy's Diner and Main Street Coney Island.

After all the body work was done, we built the camera, added some flip-flops, and Photo-Op-A-Don was born.

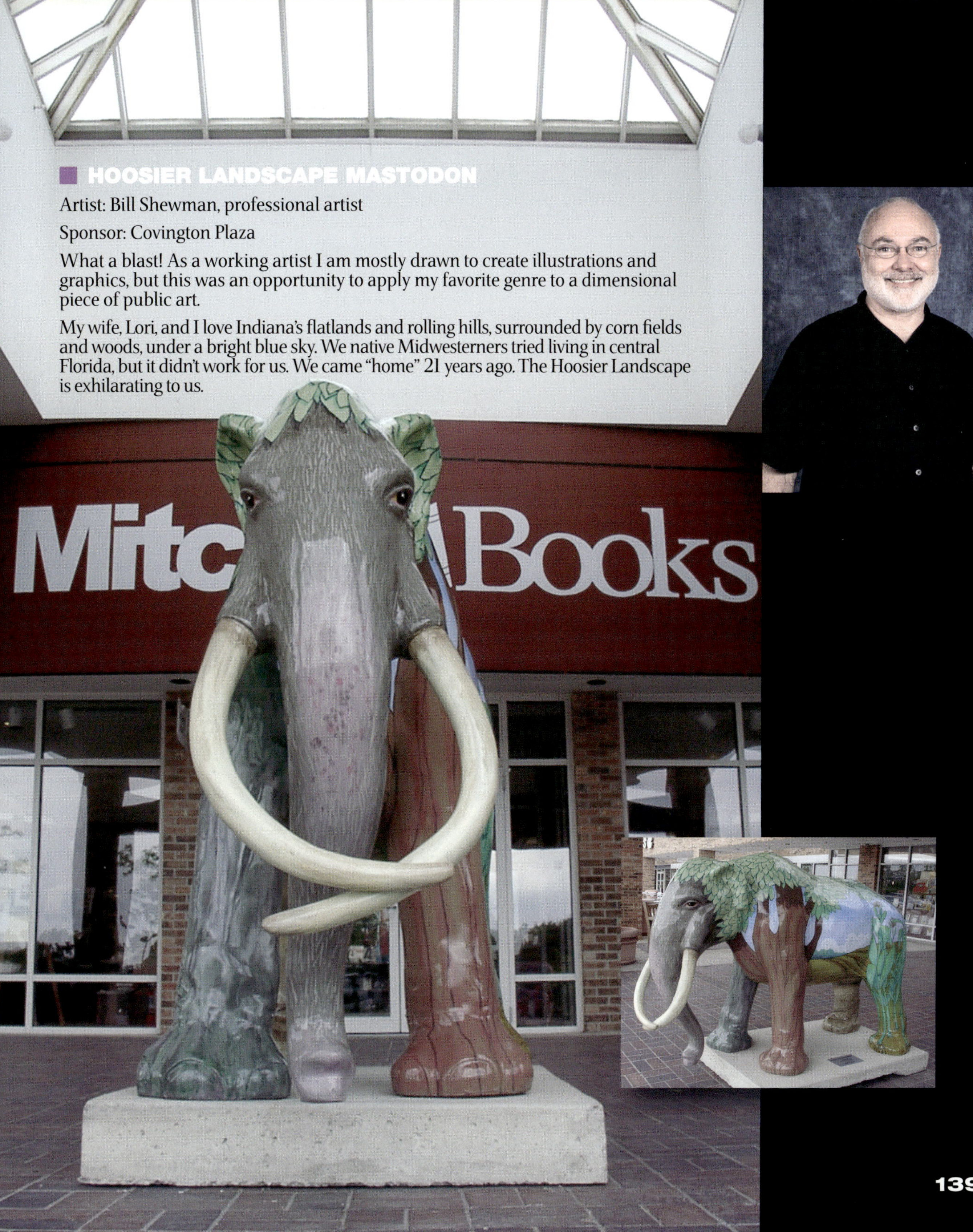

◼ HOOSIER LANDSCAPE MASTODON

Artist: Bill Shewman, professional artist

Sponsor: Covington Plaza

What a blast! As a working artist I am mostly drawn to create illustrations and graphics, but this was an opportunity to apply my favorite genre to a dimensional piece of public art.

My wife, Lori, and I love Indiana's flatlands and rolling hills, surrounded by corn fields and woods, under a bright blue sky. We native Midwesterners tried living in central Florida, but it didn't work for us. We came "home" 21 years ago. The Hoosier Landscape is exhilarating to us.

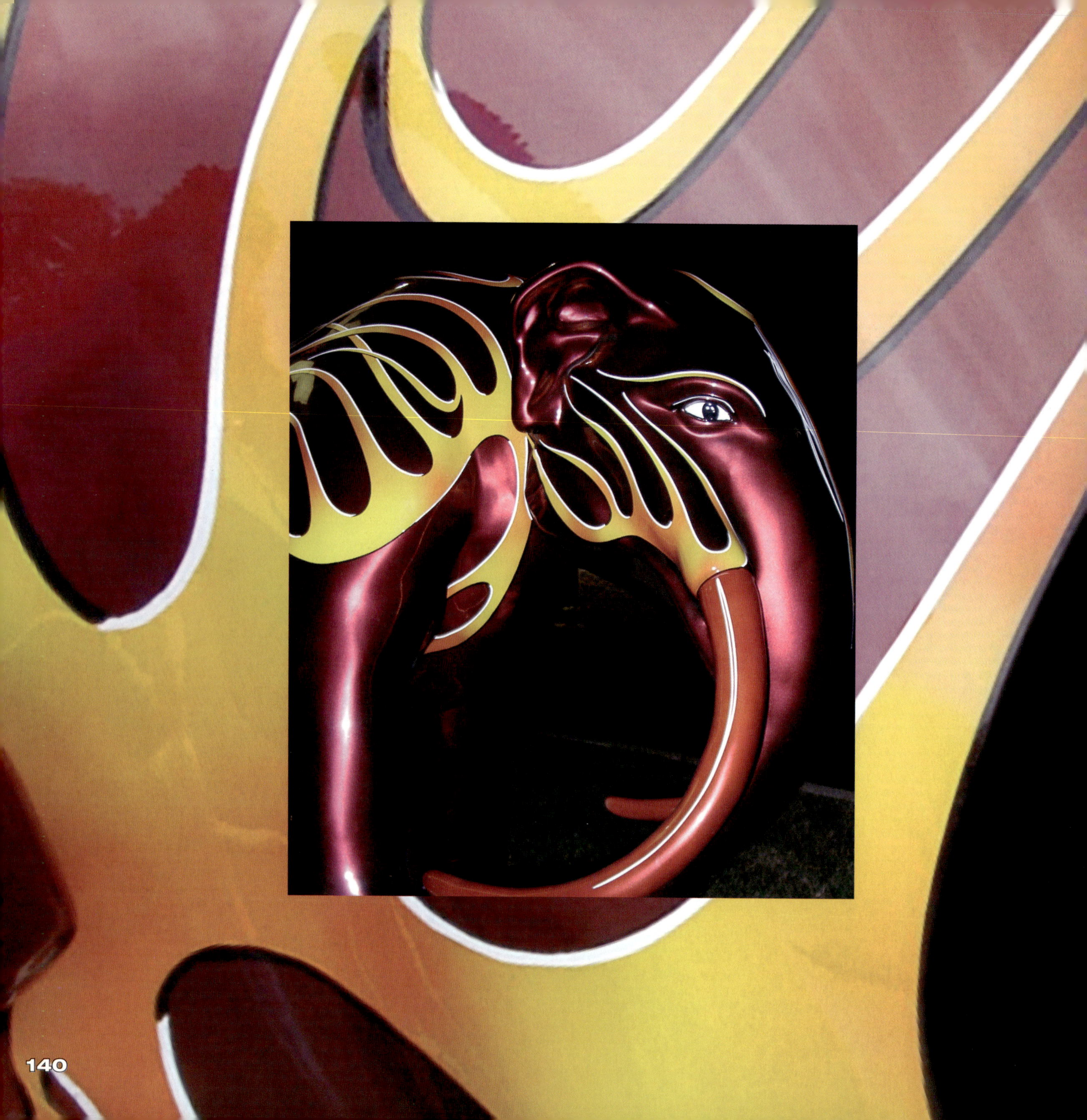

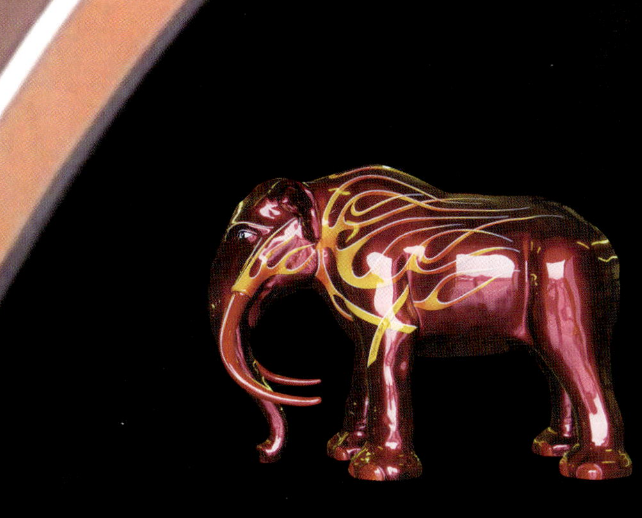

■ AUTO DON

Artist: Jim Studinski, automotive graphics, detailing professional

Sponsor: Auto Collision Service

I designed Auto Don as a refinished don because the sponsor is all about auto refinishing. We completely sanded and smoothed our model to ensure a perfect surface for the custom finish paint. This gave Auto Don a sleek, high-speed appearance.

Then it was time to add the custom flames. I don't use computer–aided graphics. The flames, which lead into a "Support Our Troops" ribbon, are hand-painted.

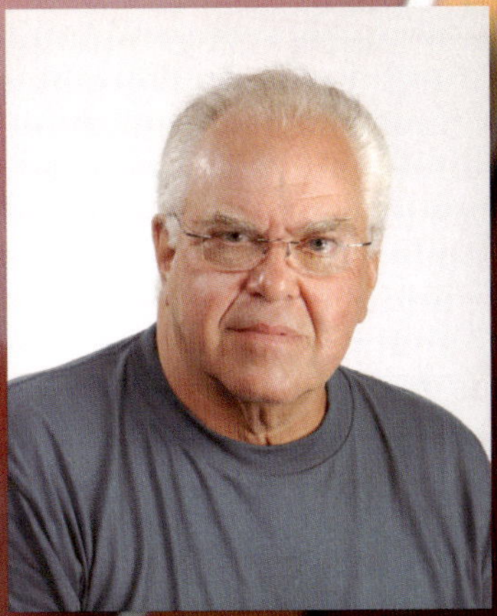

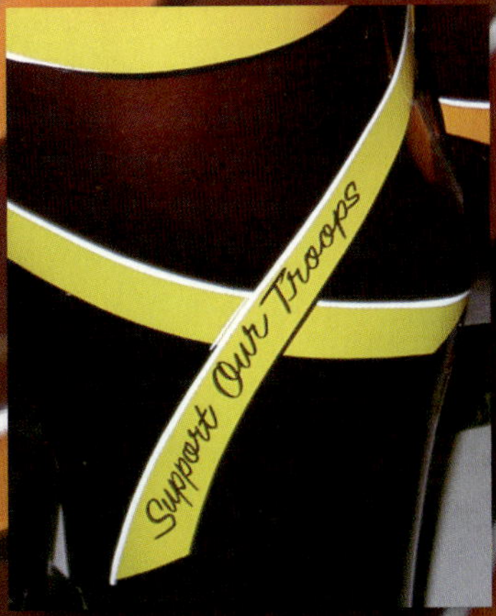

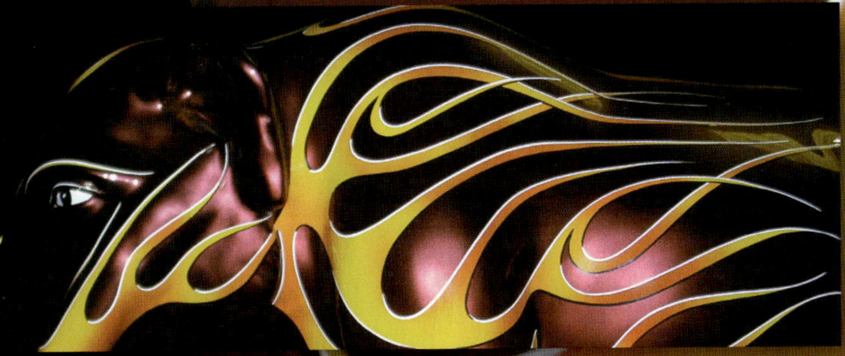

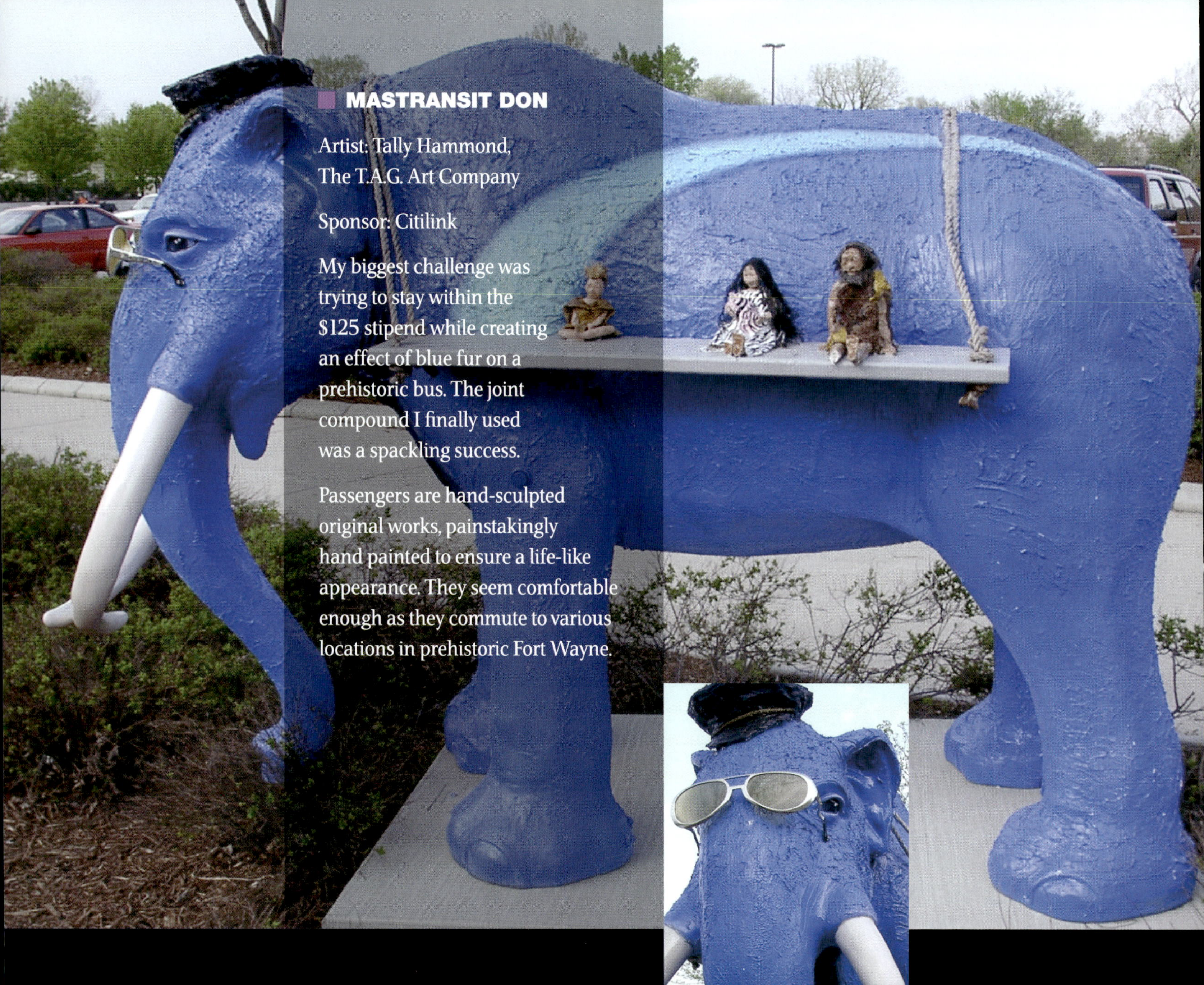

MASTRANSIT DON

Artist: Tally Hammond,
The T.A.G. Art Company

Sponsor: Citilink

My biggest challenge was
trying to stay within the
$125 stipend while creating
an effect of blue fur on a
prehistoric bus. The joint
compound I finally used
was a spackling success.

Passengers are hand-sculpted
original works, painstakingly
hand painted to ensure a life-like
appearance. They seem comfortable
enough as they commute to various
locations in prehistoric Fort Wayne.

Mastodons on Parade

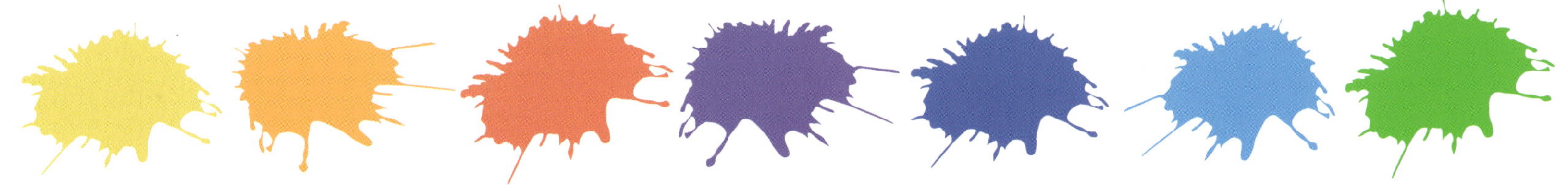

Dons in the Community

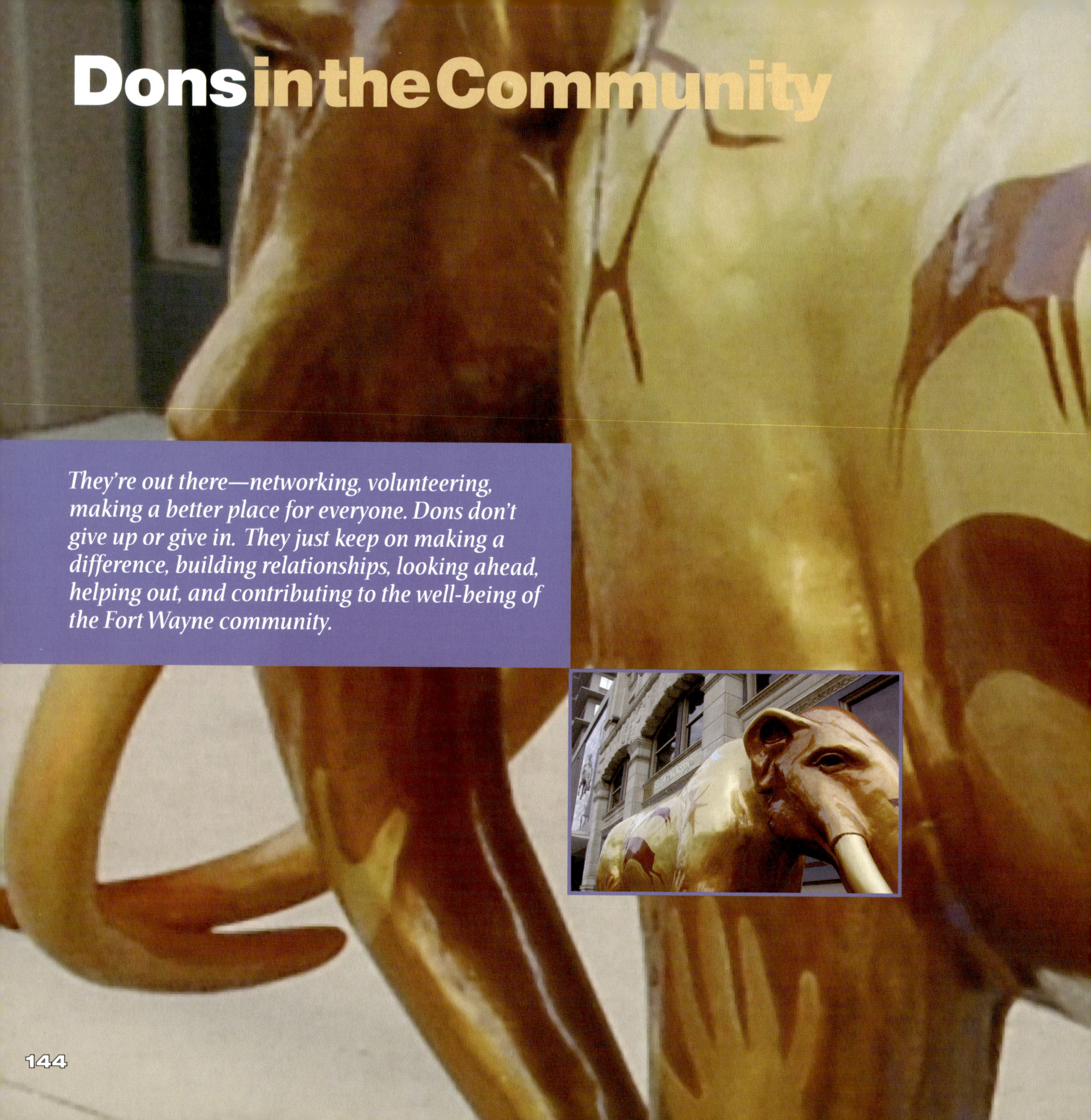

Dons in the Community

They're out there—networking, volunteering, making a better place for everyone. Dons don't give up or give in. They just keep on making a difference, building relationships, looking ahead, helping out, and contributing to the well-being of the Fort Wayne community.

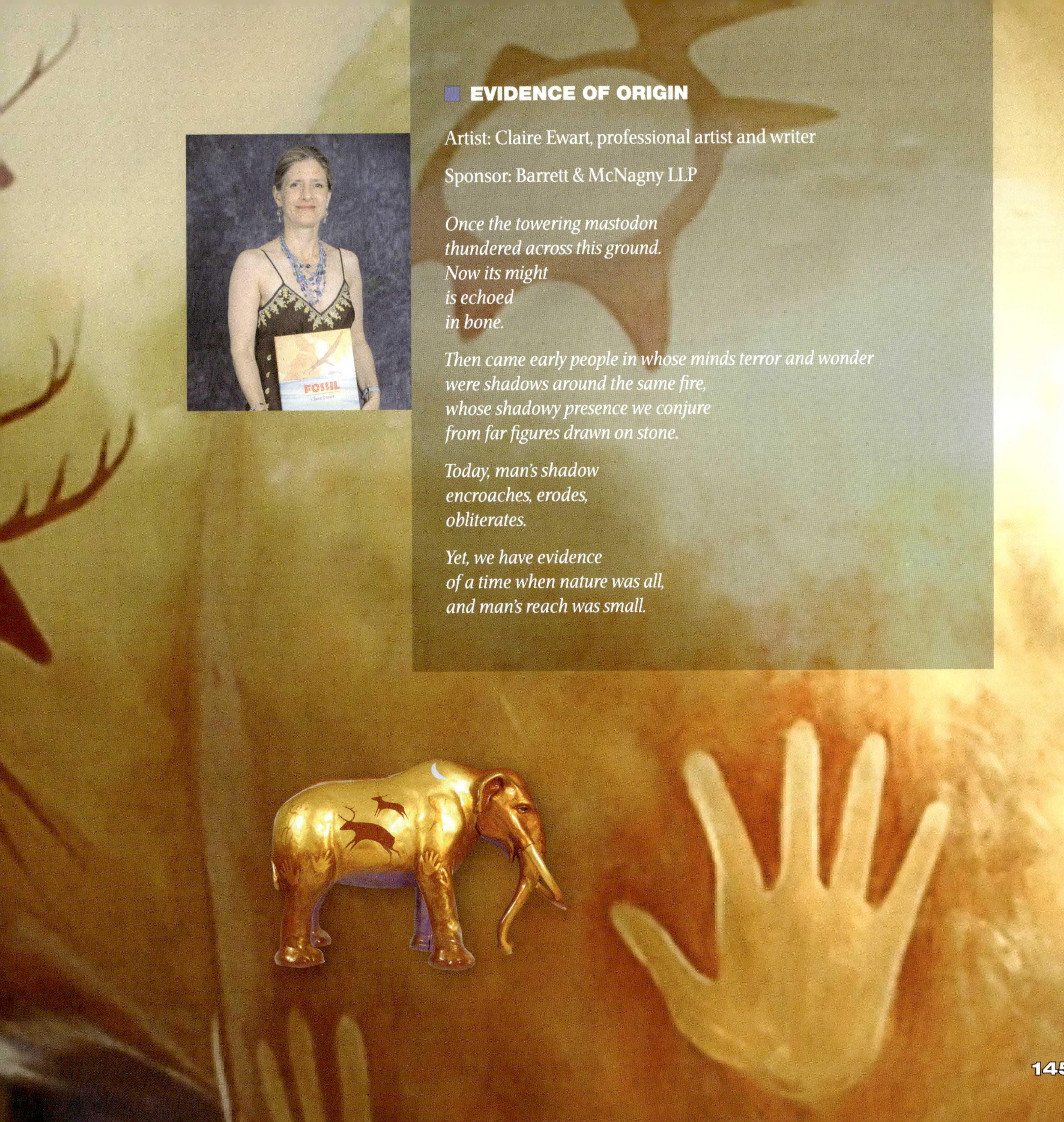

▪ EVIDENCE OF ORIGIN

Artist: Claire Ewart, professional artist and writer

Sponsor: Barrett & McNagny LLP

Once the towering mastodon
thundered across this ground.
Now its might
is echoed
in bone.

Then came early people in whose minds terror and wonder
were shadows around the same fire,
whose shadowy presence we conjure
from far figures drawn on stone.

Today, man's shadow
encroaches, erodes,
obliterates.

Yet, we have evidence
of a time when nature was all,
and man's reach was small.

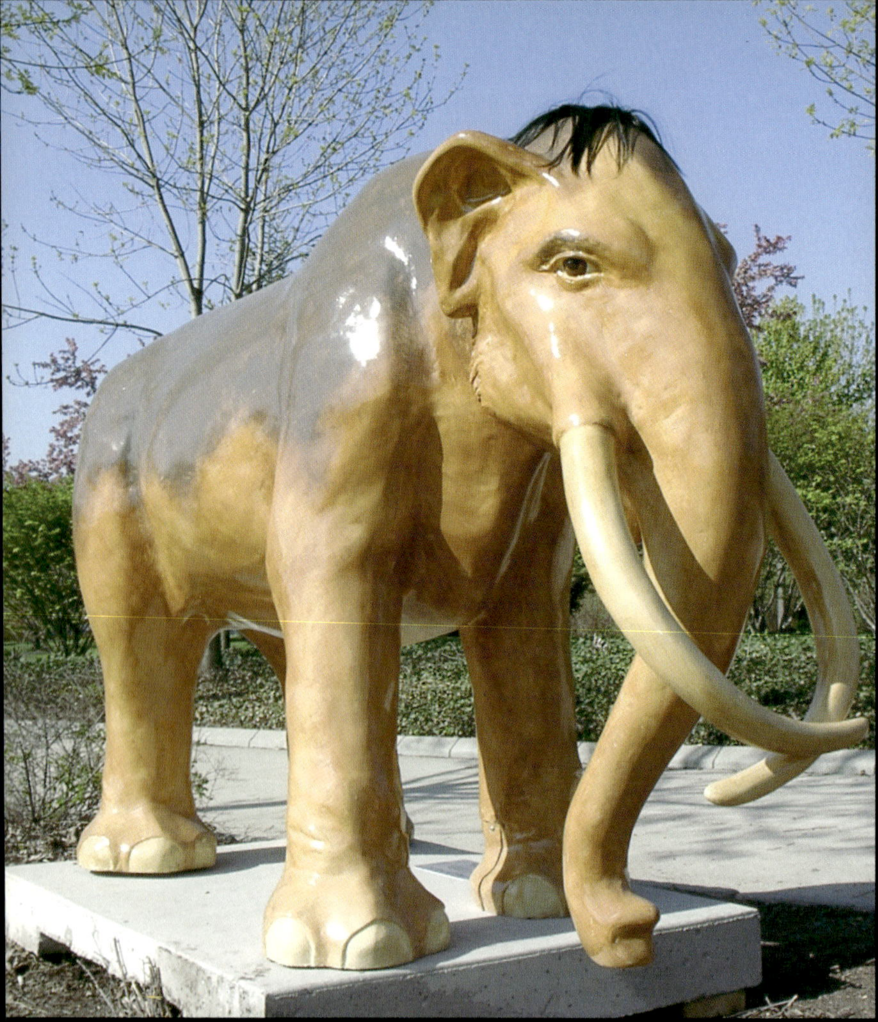

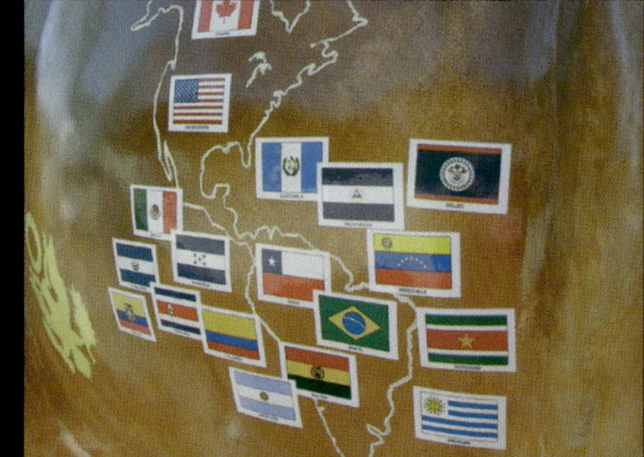

■ MIGUEL THE MASTODON

Artist: Bridgett Santiago, owner, Restoration International

Sponsor: The Greater Fort Wayne Hispanic Chamber of Commerce

In English, the name Miguel represents "Michael the Messenger." Our Miguel is a passport to education. He displays flags of the countries the mastodon migrated to before becoming extinct. It is hoped he can be used as a teaching tool for children.

I enjoy restoring a variety of art media including plaster, terra cotta, porcelain, and oil paintings. It's a challenge to make things look as they were originally intended. It's not surprising, then, that my mastodon looks like...well, a mastodon! Miguel also has a voice chip which communicates in English and Spanish.

Our stipend for materials was $125. Our costs added up to $124.93.

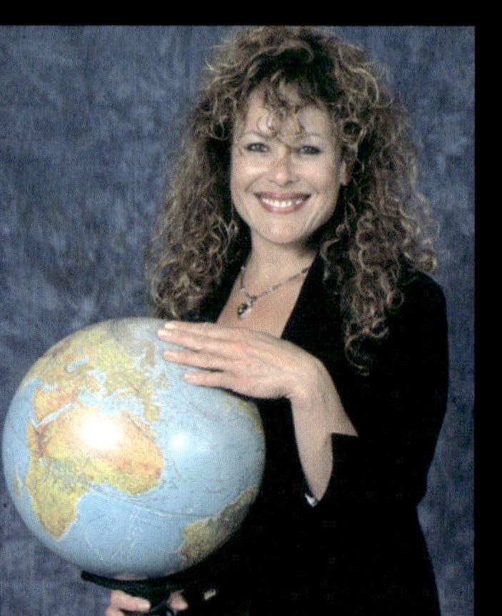

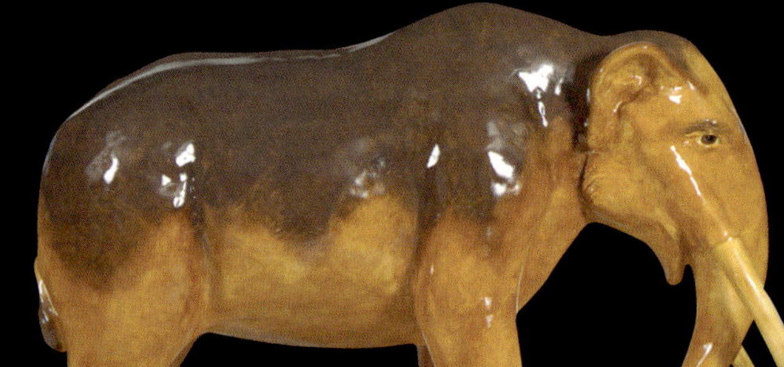

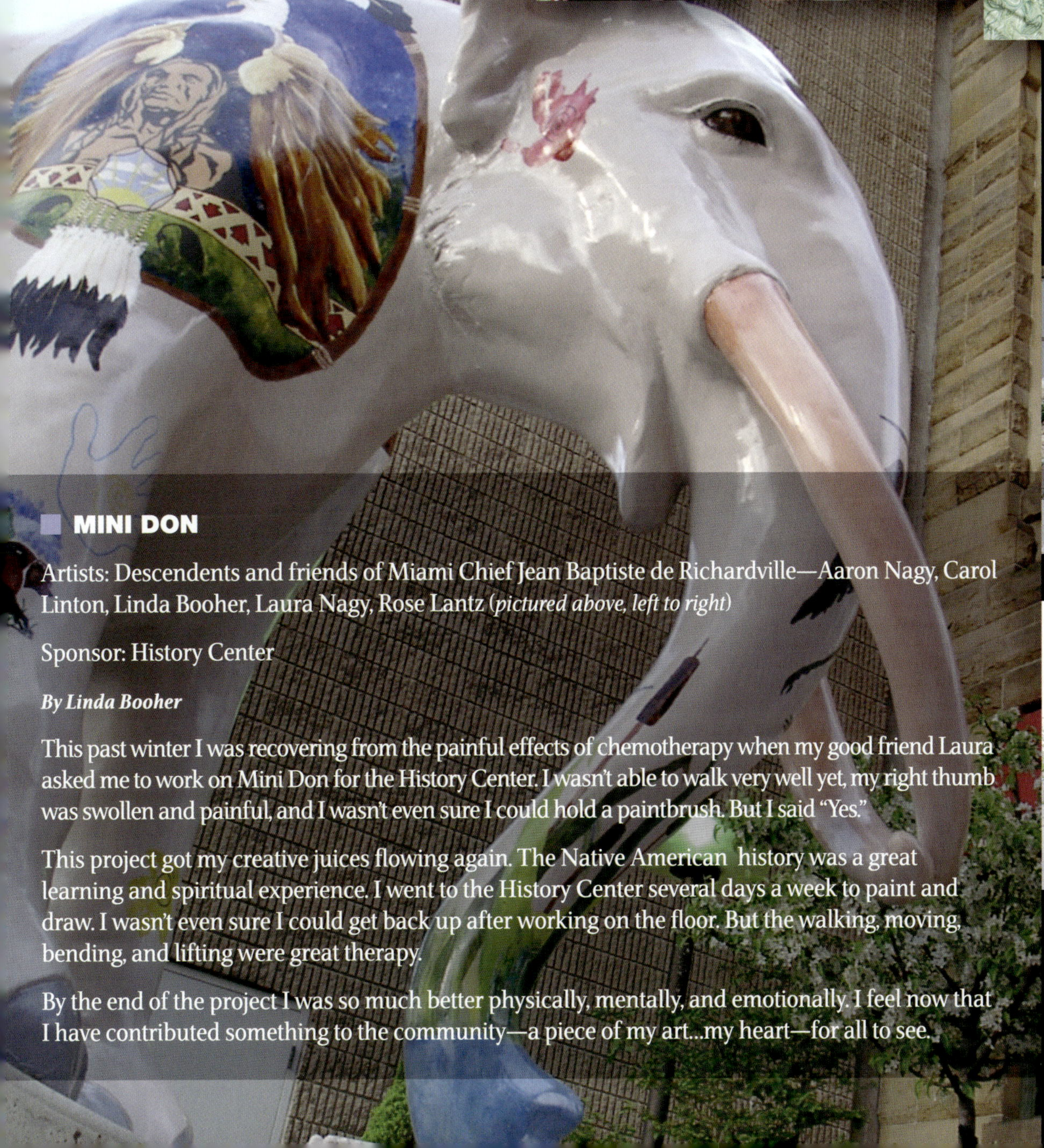

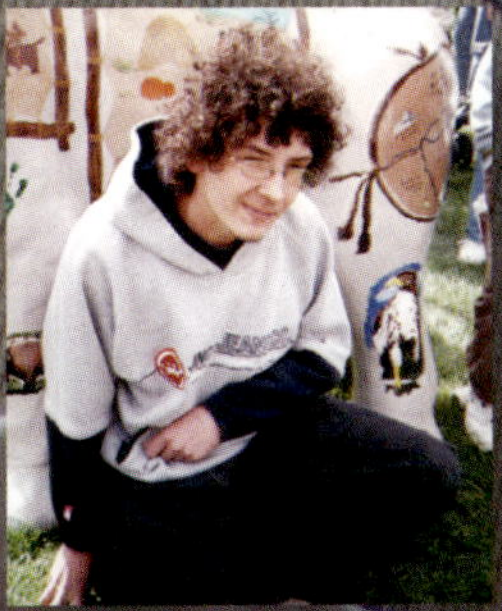

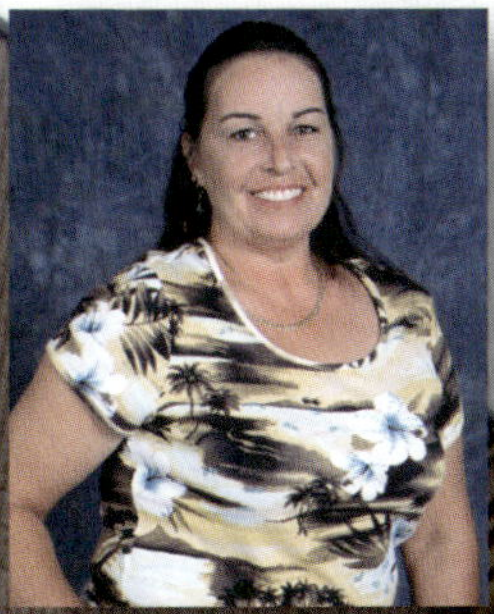

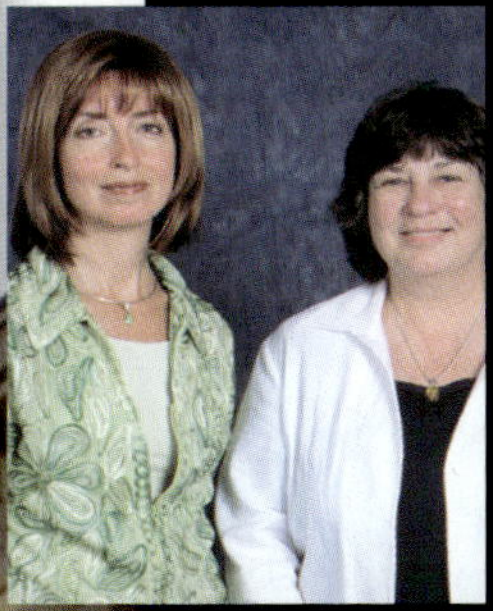

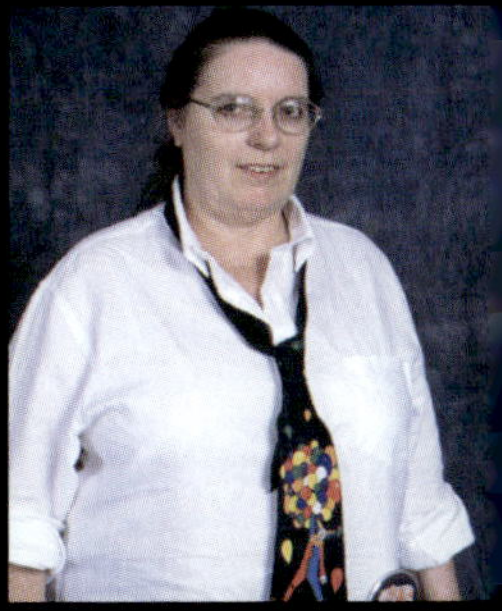

◼ MINI DON

Artists: Descendents and friends of Miami Chief Jean Baptiste de Richardville—Aaron Nagy, Carol Linton, Linda Booher, Laura Nagy, Rose Lantz (*pictured above, left to right*)

Sponsor: History Center

By Linda Booher

This past winter I was recovering from the painful effects of chemotherapy when my good friend Laura asked me to work on Mini Don for the History Center. I wasn't able to walk very well yet, my right thumb was swollen and painful, and I wasn't even sure I could hold a paintbrush. But I said "Yes."

This project got my creative juices flowing again. The Native American history was a great learning and spiritual experience. I went to the History Center several days a week to paint and draw. I wasn't even sure I could get back up after working on the floor. But the walking, moving, bending, and lifting were great therapy.

By the end of the project I was so much better physically, mentally, and emotionally. I feel now that I have contributed something to the community—a piece of my art...my heart—for all to see.

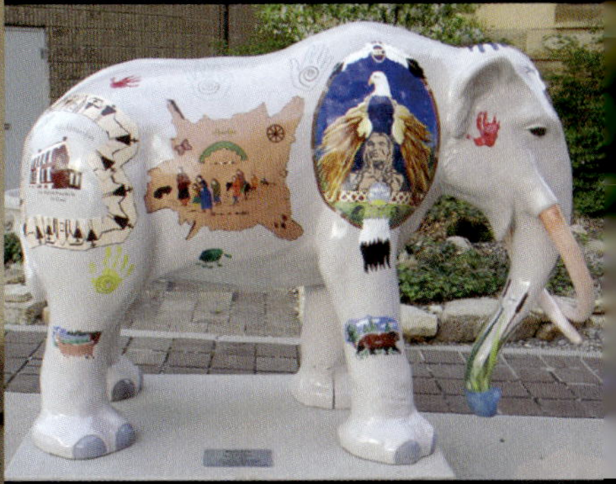

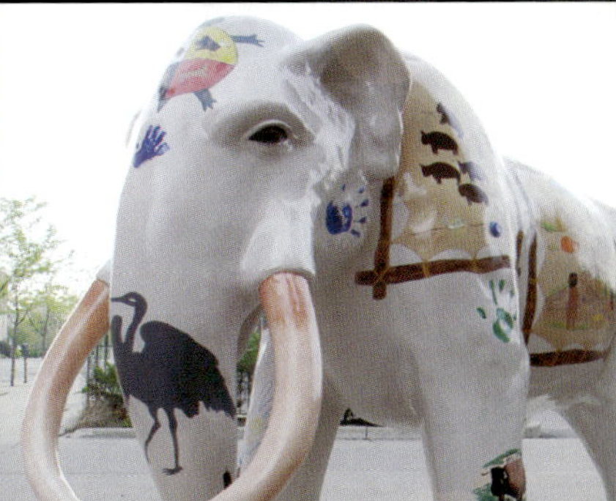

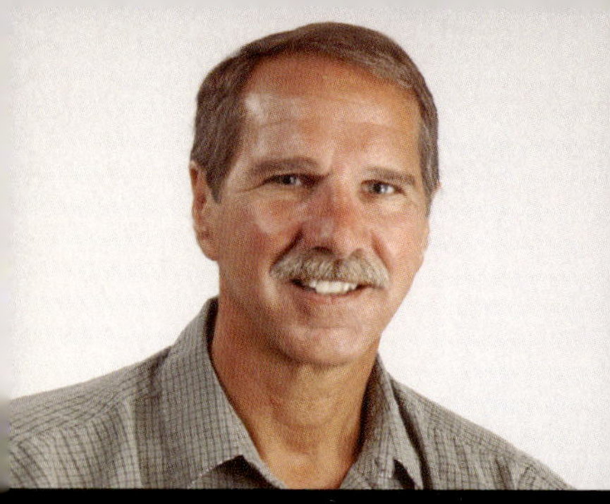

■ MASTO-DOWNTOWN 1794–PRESENT

Artist: Gregg Bender

Sponsor: *The Journal Gazette*

A coworker at *The Journal Gazette* volunteered me for the mastodon project. I thought it might be fun, but it was a lot of hard work. I based the theme on something I had done for a Three Rivers Festival Weekender cover from 2004.

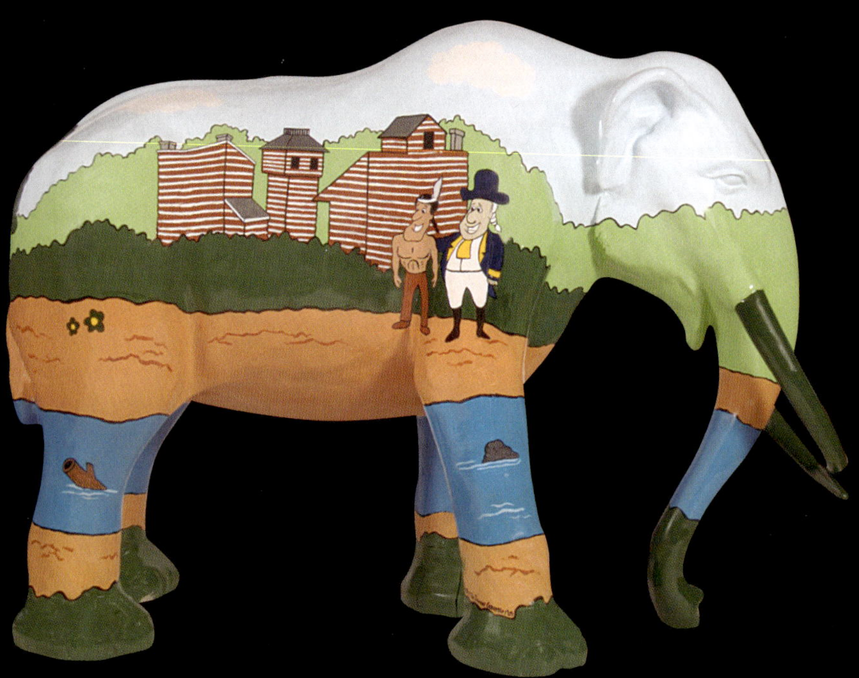

The task of getting that vision onto the side of a fiberglass mastodon proved more difficult than expected. I'm used to working with programs on a computer screen and electronically enhancing illustrations, but actually painting on the side of this beast was a bear.

With the help of volunteer Amanda Beglin, a copy editor, I was able to meet the deadline. I'd like to say "never again" to a project like this, but after seeing all the different mastodons, the hard work and talent that went into this production, and just how cool they look sitting around town, I would definitely try it again.

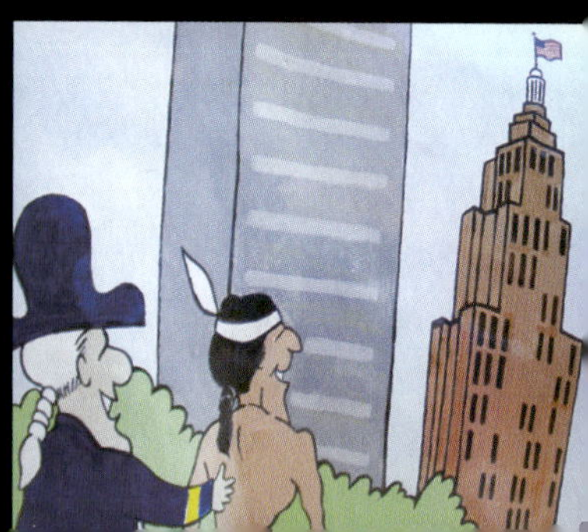

■ JUSTICE DON

Artist: Roger Hultquist, attorney, artist
(*pictured below*)

Sponsor: Haller and Colvin

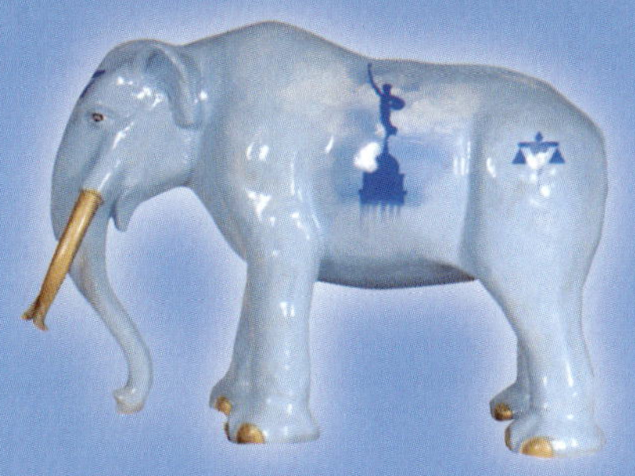

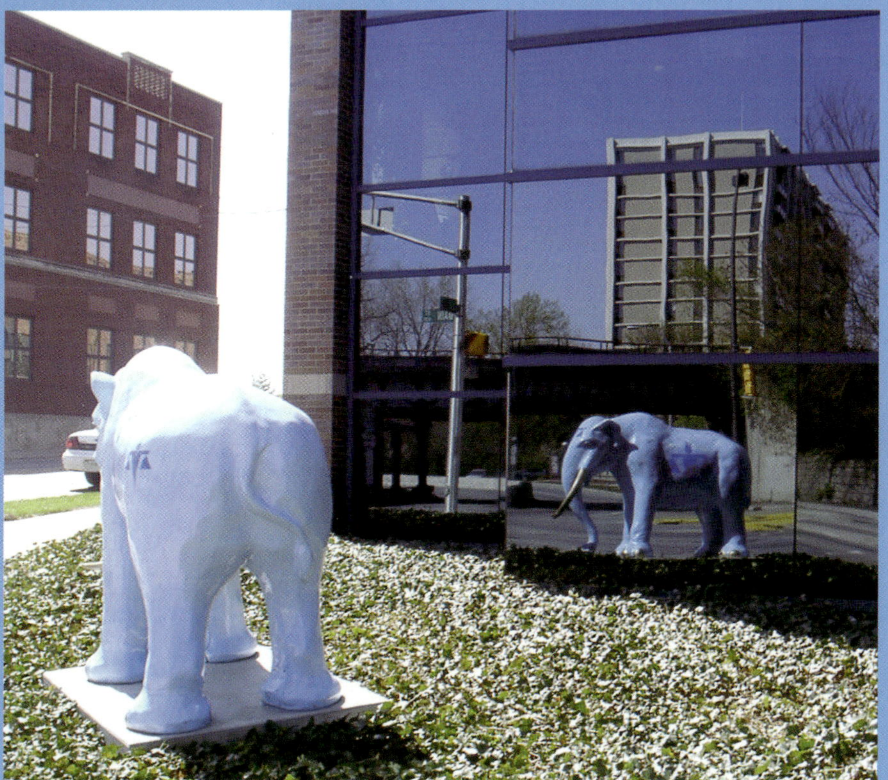

I felt Justice Don should have a minimalist design so that images could be read from cars passing at a busy corner. Lady Liberty atop the Allen County Courthouse and the scales of justice painted against a light blue background said what Justice Don, our gentle giant, needed to say.

Then vandals struck. I fashioned a healing bandage and added a crutch, ice bag, get-well card, and vase of flowers. The community responded with more flowers, a bottle of aspirin, and a lime-green teddy bear. Little children signed the get-well card.

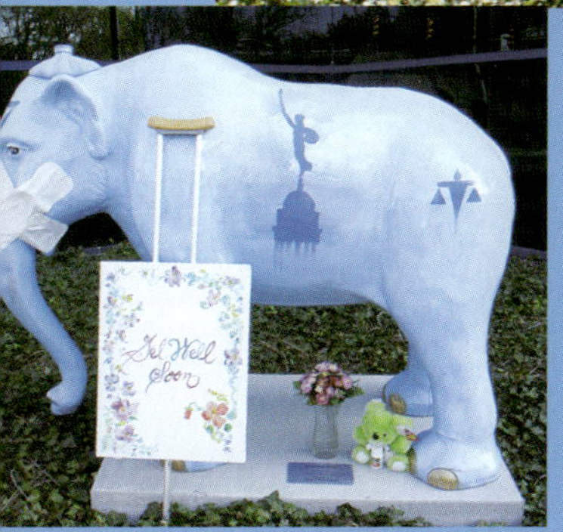

My little mastodon became the city's symbol of kindness and caring—the essentials of justice.

It was so much more than sympathy for broken fiberglass. These gestures were genuine expressions of caring in a larger sense and a message that an effort to destroy will always be met with a greater effort to heal and restore.

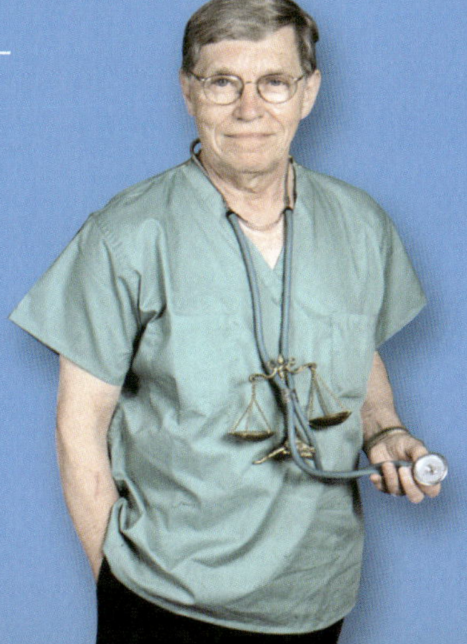

149

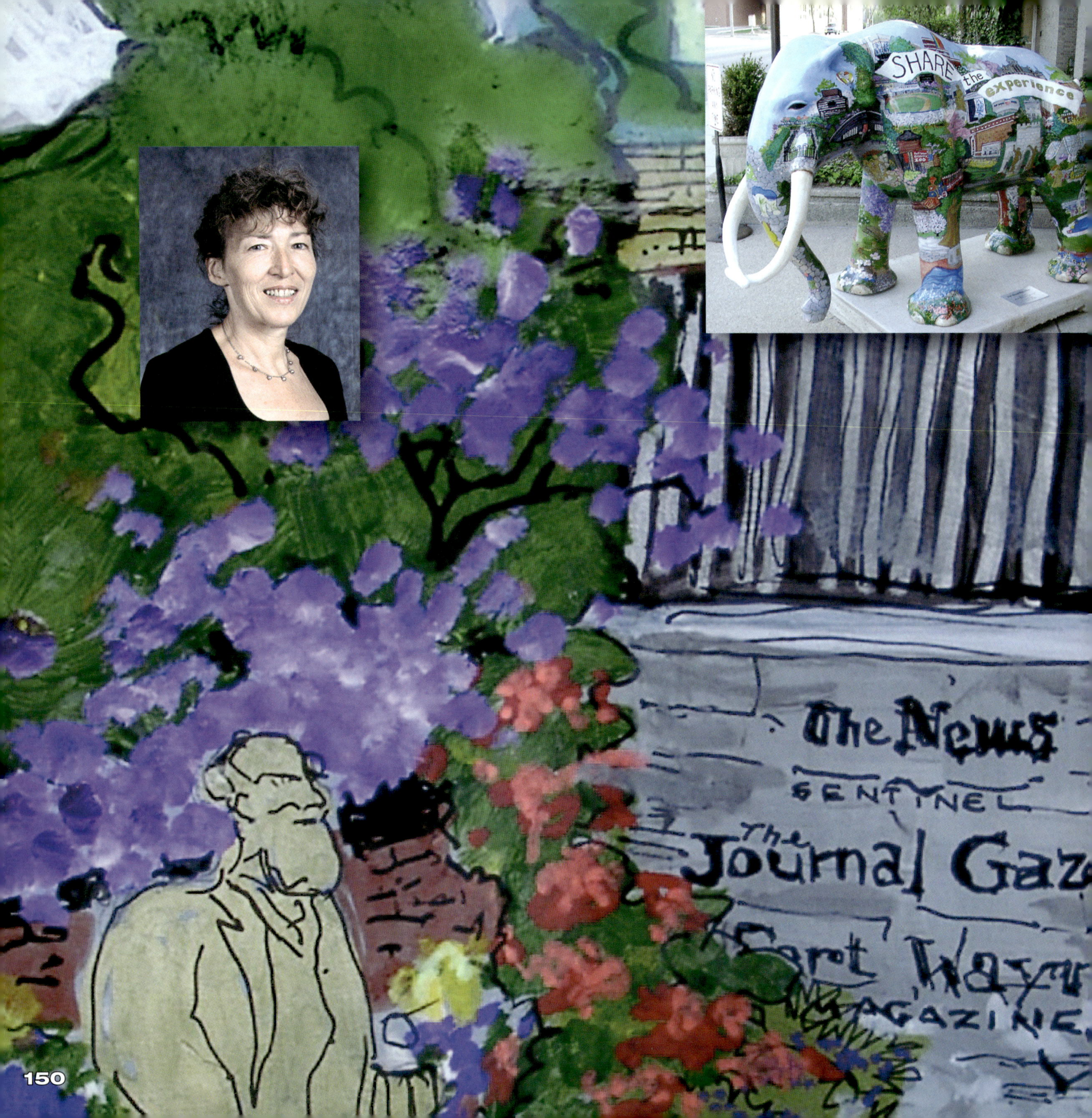
SHARE the experience
The News
SENTINEL
The Journal Gaz
Fort Wayn
Magazine

Artist: Julia Meek, professional artist

Sponsor: *Fort Wayne Magazine*

"Share the experience," the sponsor's theme, was my focal point. In a grand, kaleidoscopic style, I was prepared to share the experience of our past including our geographic past.

Keeping to my favorite illustration style, I depicted our parks, historic landmarks, a cityscape, iconic businesses, and even those wonderful building stones the crazy glaciations left us.

There are several personal treasures on the mastodon including my own garden, my mom's patio, and two treasured pieces of jewelry that artist Bob Bentz made.

It's always been my practice to write in names as I work large ink-lined spaces such as tree foliage. It's therapeutic—kind of like a Tibetan prayer wheel. So just about everyone I know and love is named somewhere on the piece—just don't expect me to remember where.

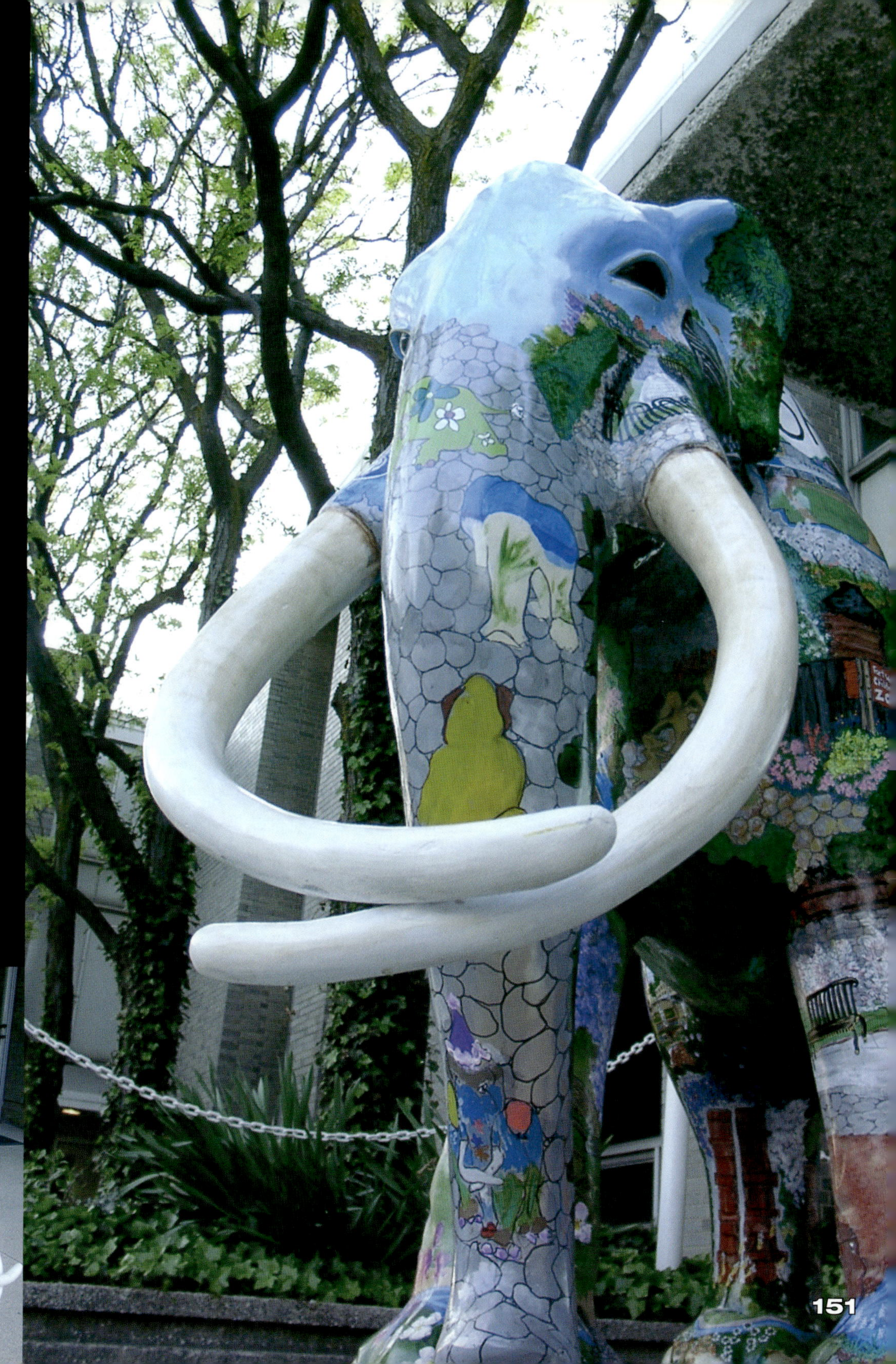

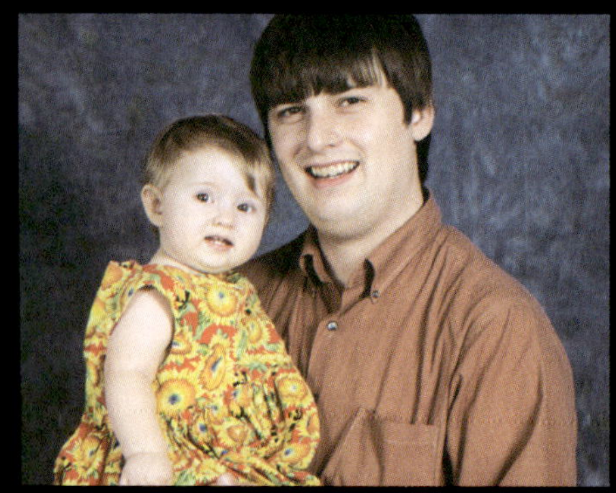

■ MAST-O-PIECE

Artist: Max Meyer, curator of children and family programs, Fort Wayne Museum of Art (*pictured above with daughter*)

Sponsor: Beckman Lawson LLP

We invited the public to participate in creating our mastodon in an effort to demonstrate how varied the artistic tastes are in Fort Wayne. Each participant was to choose an image from a large selection of art magazines and catalogs and suggest a location for placement on the mastodon.

About 140 people contributed to our Mast-O-Piece, including a 4-year-old named Lina (pictured below). She chose countless images and kept Mackenzie Ladd and Michael Johnson, artists who also helped with the project, busy.

We were all amazed that Lina stayed for four and a half hours at the Fort Wayne Museum of Art until Mast-O-Piece was finished. It felt really good to see her and the other contributors so excited about the project.

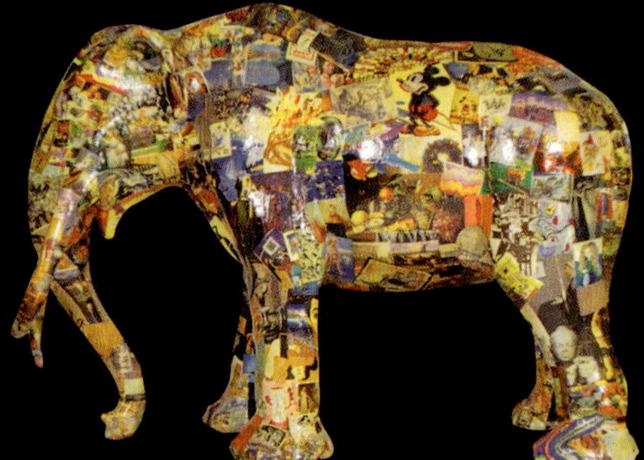

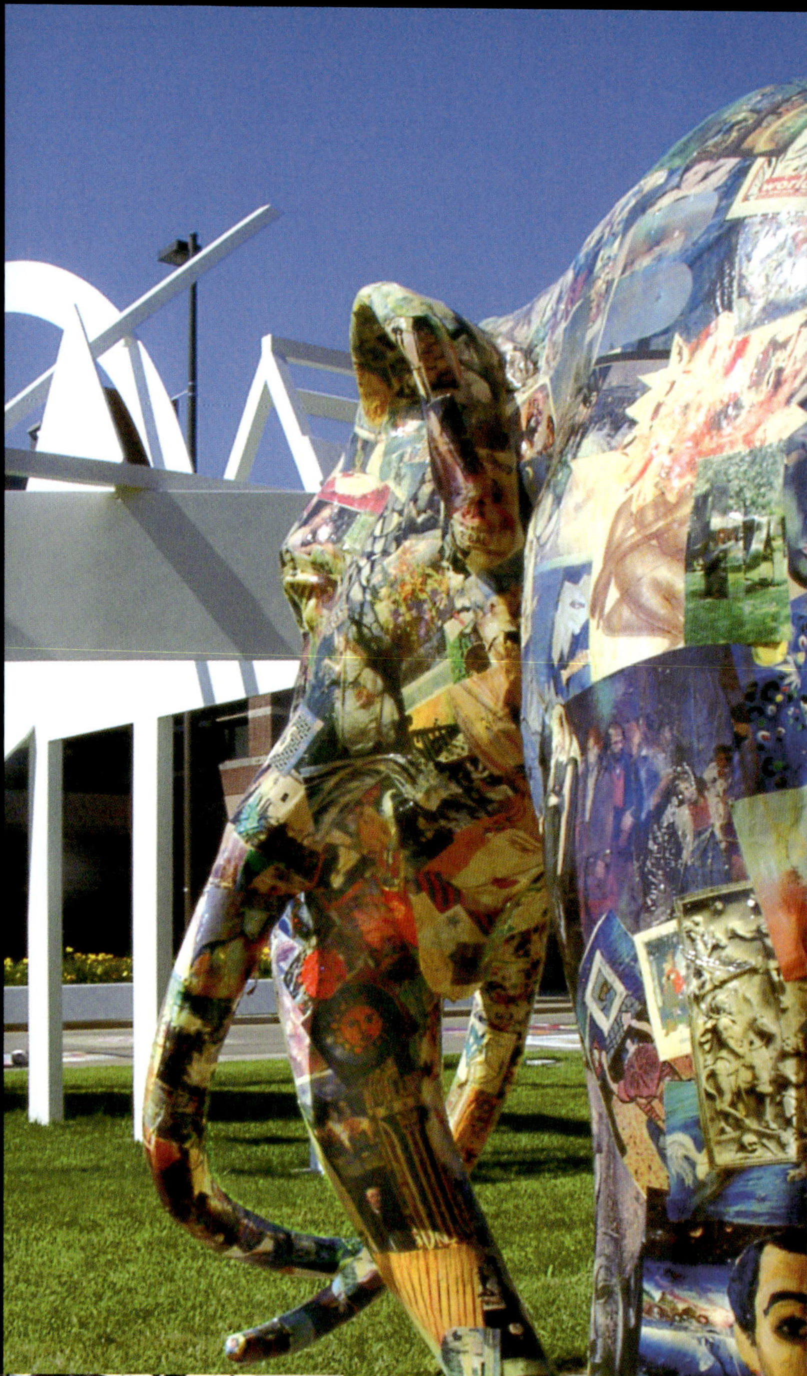

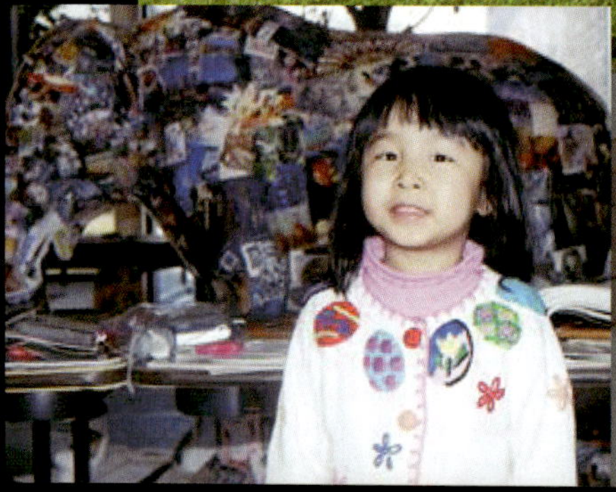

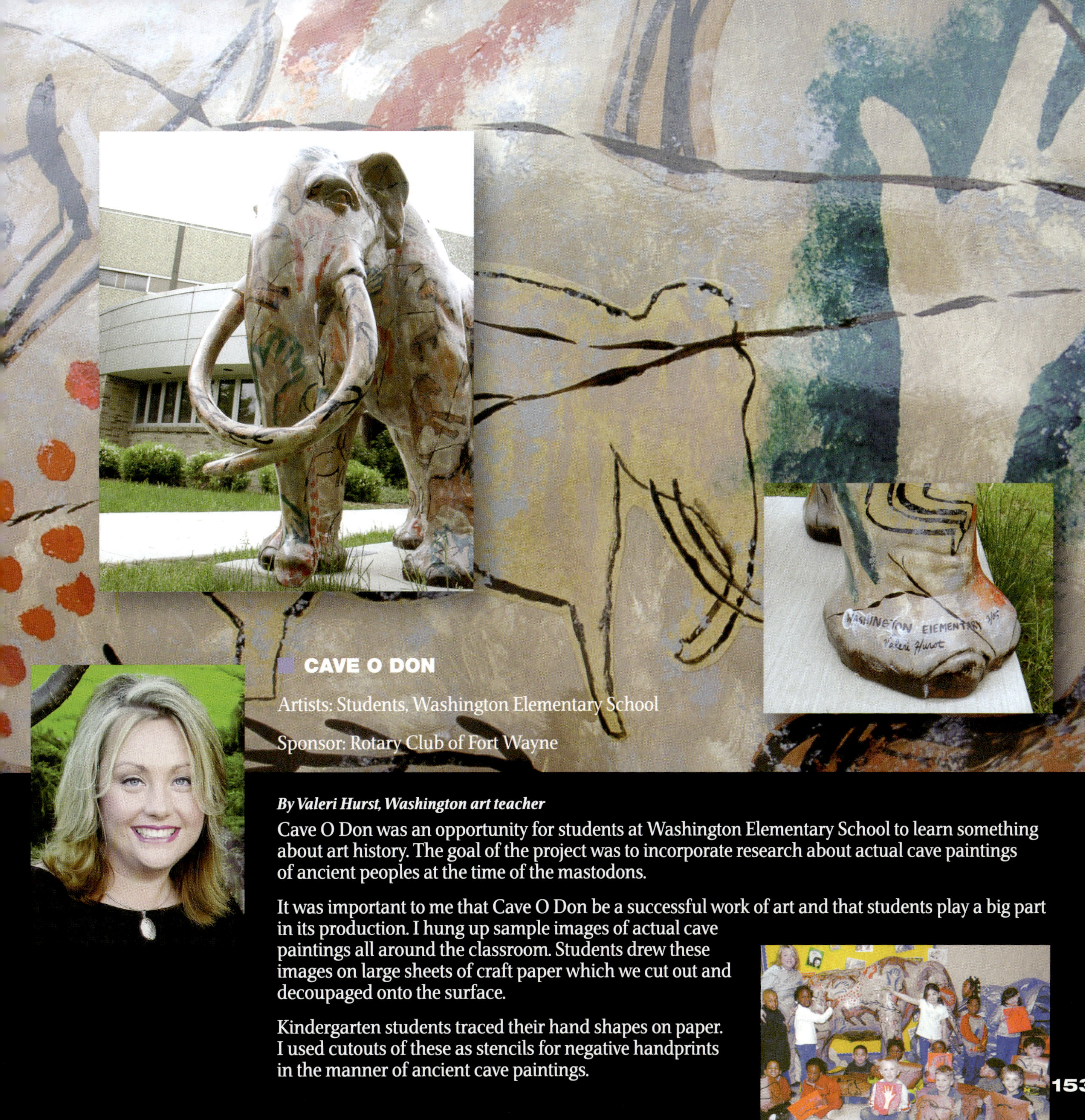

CAVE O DON

Artists: Students, Washington Elementary School

Sponsor: Rotary Club of Fort Wayne

By Valeri Hurst, Washington art teacher

Cave O Don was an opportunity for students at Washington Elementary School to learn something about art history. The goal of the project was to incorporate research about actual cave paintings of ancient peoples at the time of the mastodons.

It was important to me that Cave O Don be a successful work of art and that students play a big part in its production. I hung up sample images of actual cave paintings all around the classroom. Students drew these images on large sheets of craft paper which we cut out and decoupaged onto the surface.

Kindergarten students traced their hand shapes on paper. I used cutouts of these as stencils for negative handprints in the manner of ancient cave paintings.

153

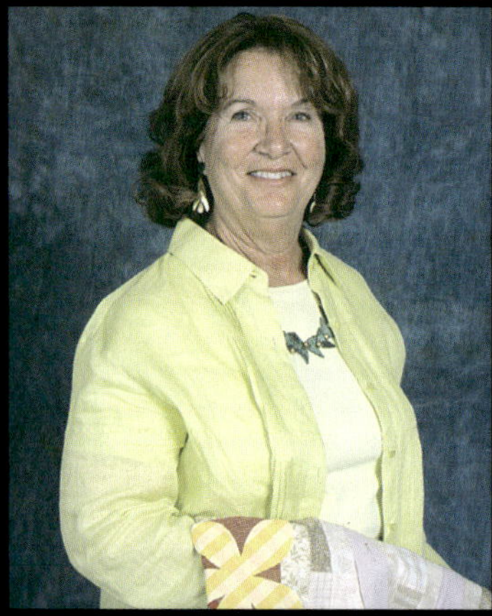

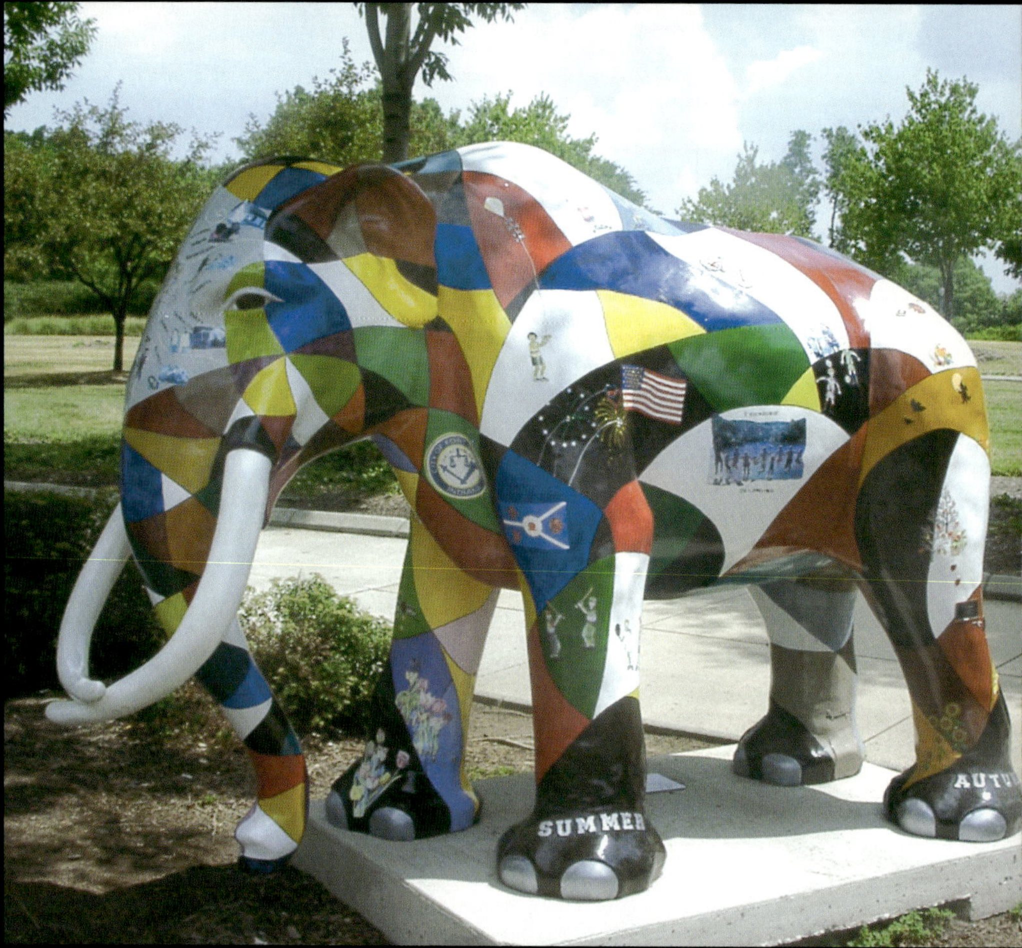

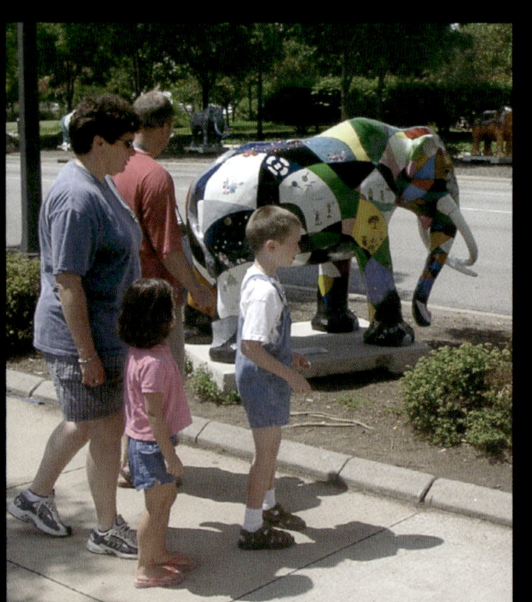

By Susan Schenkel

My husband, David, and I thought this would be a good project for the community and for the Youth Services Center. We gave copies of the mastodon shape to the children to develop their designs.

Then we sent their 34 designs to my architect son, Brad. He studied all the pictures and drew up a composite of the ideas.

We named our don It Takes a Village because that's what it takes to raise a child into a complete, confident, loving person.

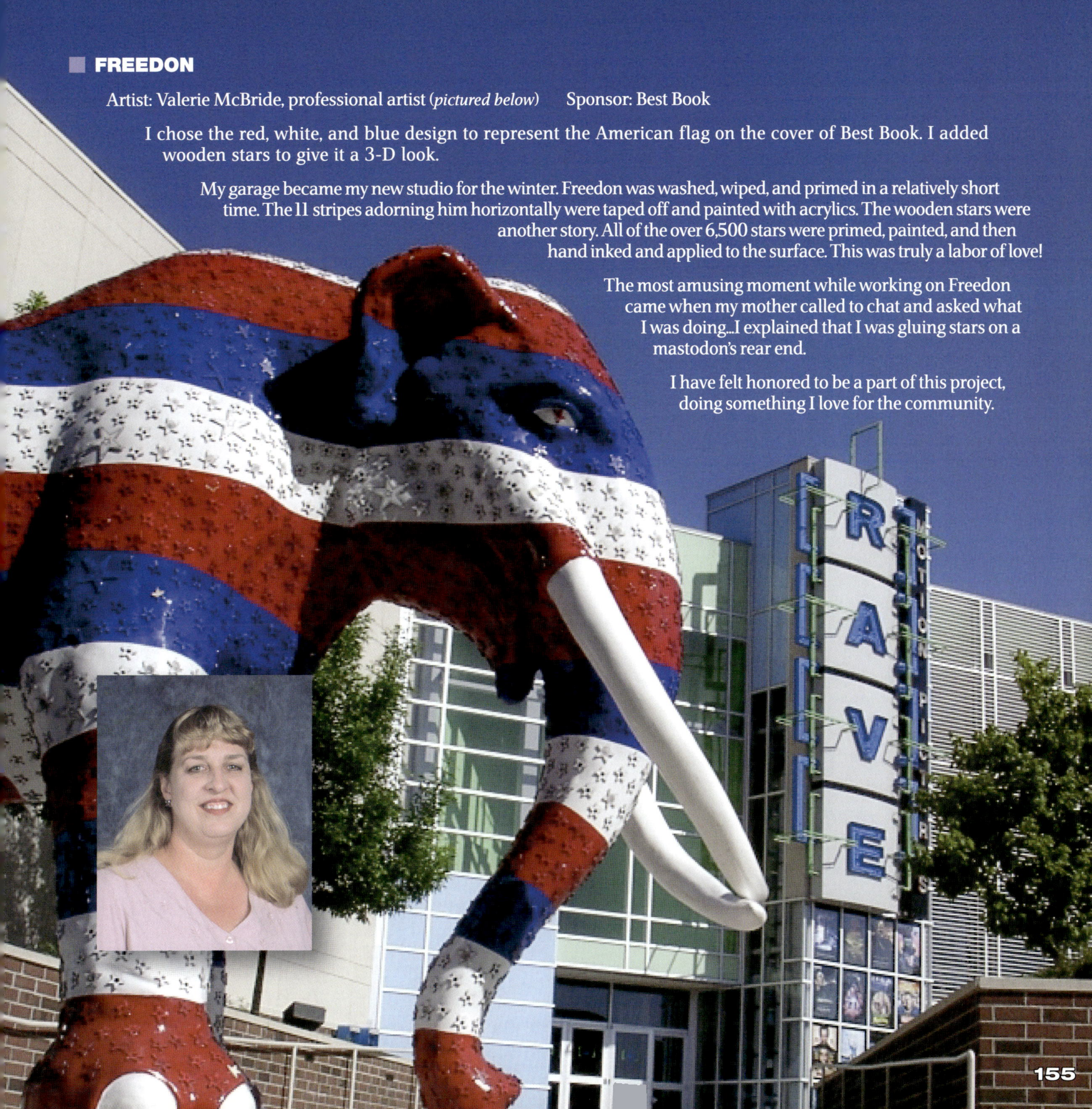

FREEDON

Artist: Valerie McBride, professional artist (*pictured below*)   Sponsor: Best Book

I chose the red, white, and blue design to represent the American flag on the cover of Best Book. I added wooden stars to give it a 3-D look.

My garage became my new studio for the winter. Freedon was washed, wiped, and primed in a relatively short time. The 11 stripes adorning him horizontally were taped off and painted with acrylics. The wooden stars were another story. All of the over 6,500 stars were primed, painted, and then hand inked and applied to the surface. This was truly a labor of love!

The most amusing moment while working on Freedon came when my mother called to chat and asked what I was doing...I explained that I was gluing stars on a mastodon's rear end.

I have felt honored to be a part of this project, doing something I love for the community.

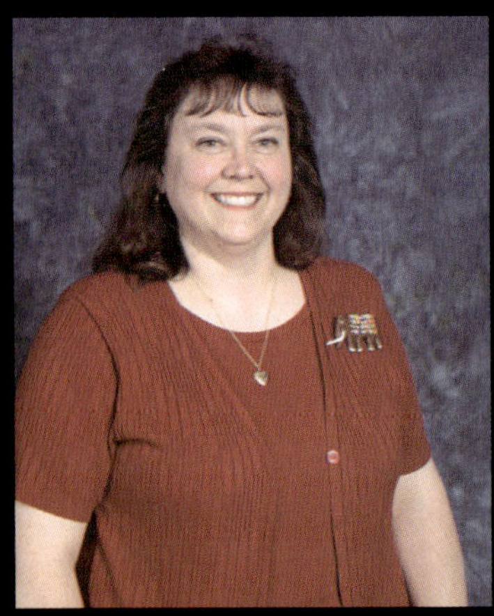

■ ARLI-DON

Artists: Fifth-grade students at
Arlington School

Sponsor: Brueggemann Lumber
Do-It-Center

By Janet Corah, Arlington art teacher
(pictured above)

When I heard about this project, I
knew that I wanted a mastodon for
my students. We chose a concept that
allowed each of them to paint the design
of their choice on a square of paper.

My husband, Joe, did lots of sanding
and patching before we began actual
painting. Following the final coat,
students decoupaged their individual art
squares onto Arli. They also took turns
painting his nails, eyes, and tusks.

Then Arli joined the herd at Headwaters.
It was a great surprise to everyone
when he returned for our fifth-grade
recognition program.

Arli-Don is now on display at
Brueggemann Lumber out in the
country where many Amish people live.
He is a curiosity to the horses at the
hitching post.

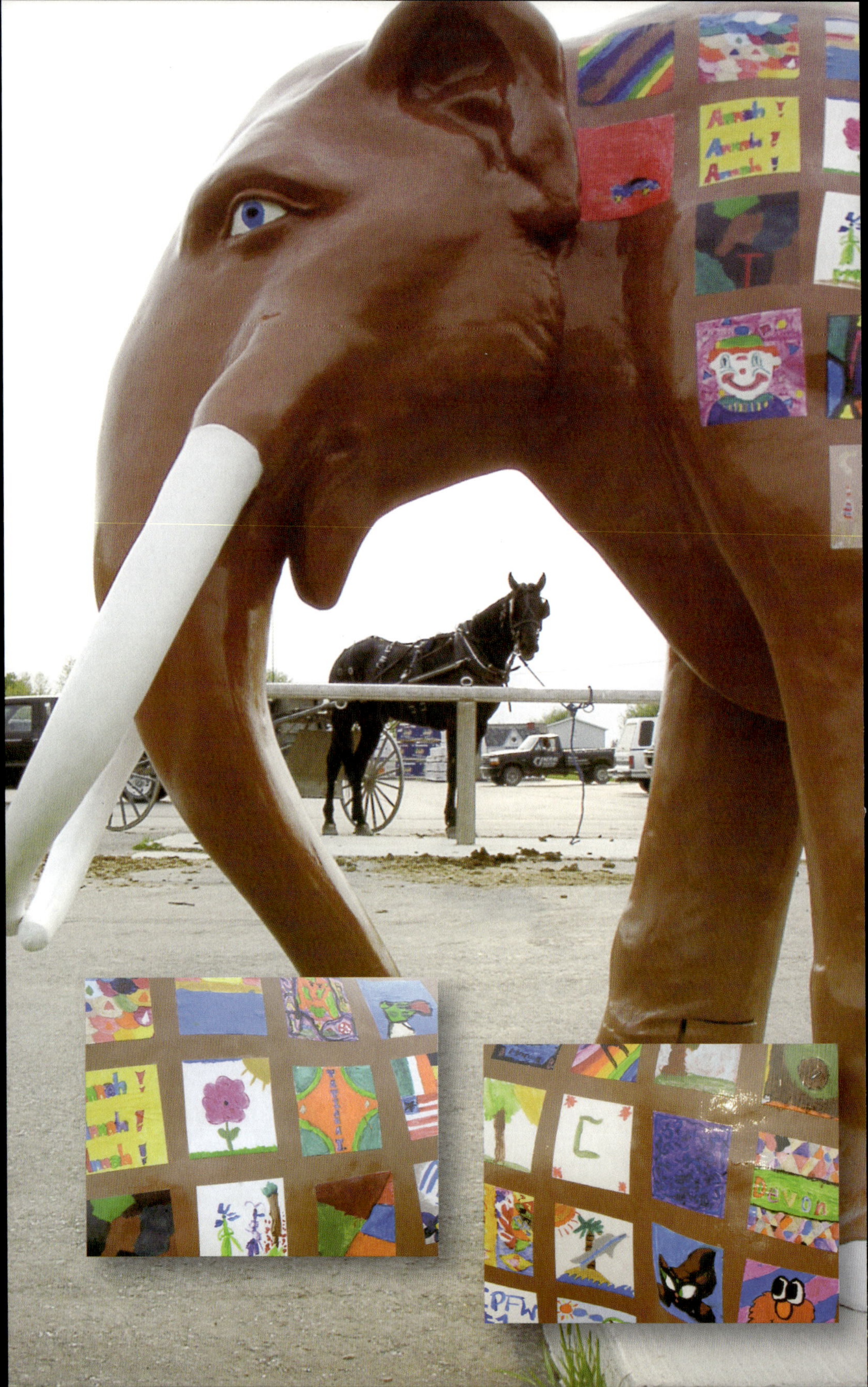

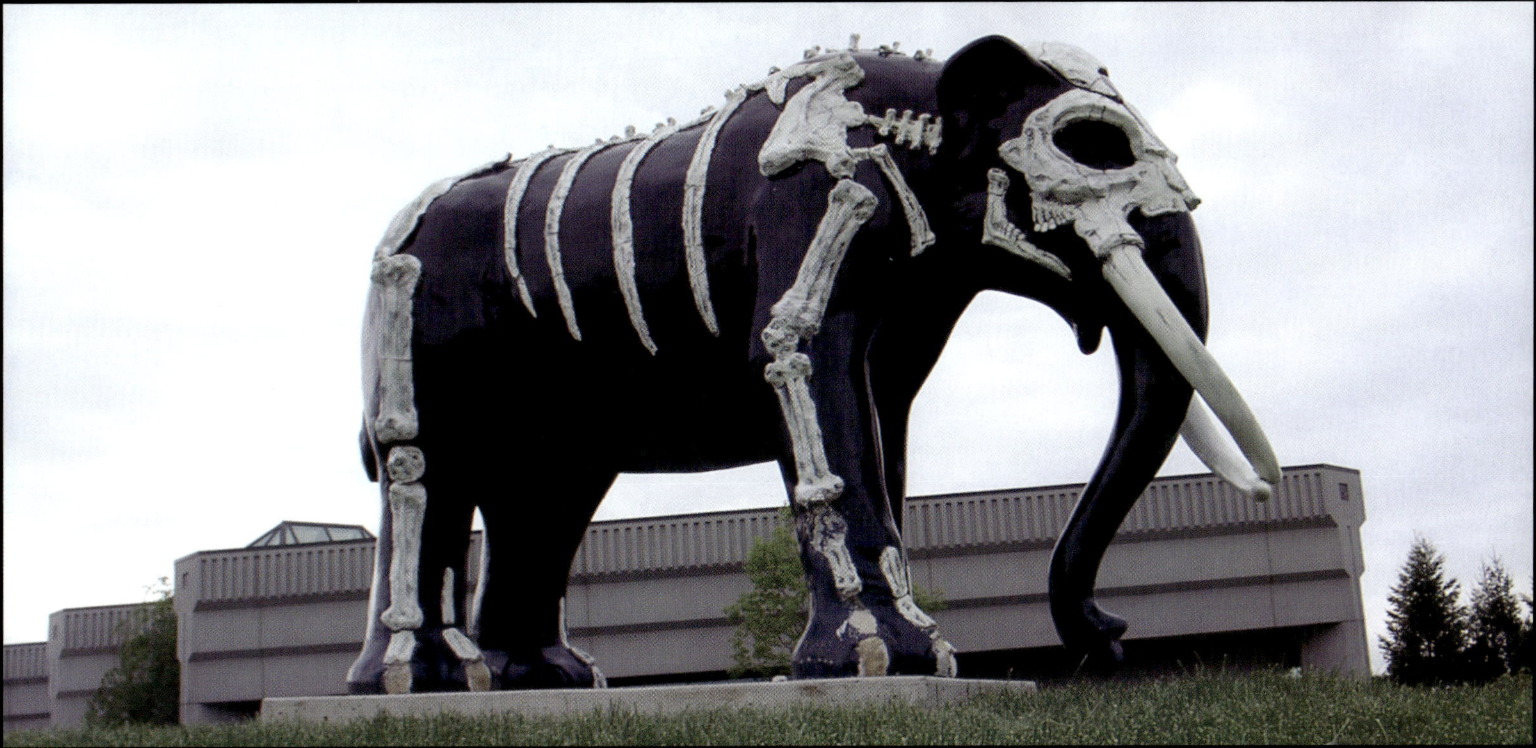

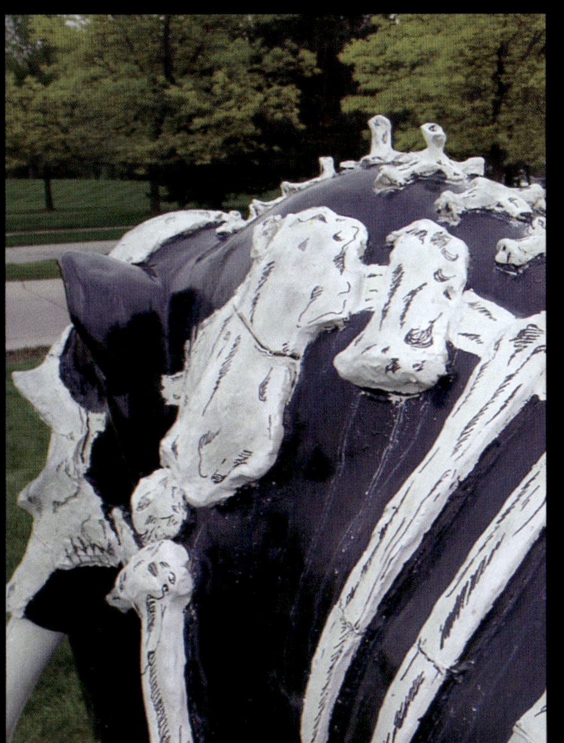

FOSSIL FUELS

Artist: Perry Lifsey, The T.A.G. Art Company

Sponsor: Petroleum Traders Corporation

The challenge was to get the bones to stay on! We used a self-hardening clay that cured to the same texture and weight as actual bone tissue. We experimented with epoxy, gorilla glue, and double-sided foam tape.

Ultimately, the material that worked best was hot glue. We used about 100 sticks. The bones were then sprayed with a fluorescent paint so that the skeleton would glow in the dark, giving the semblance of a floating skeleton!

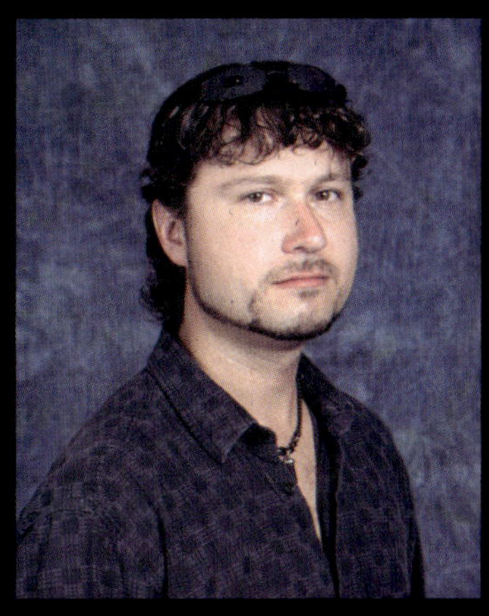

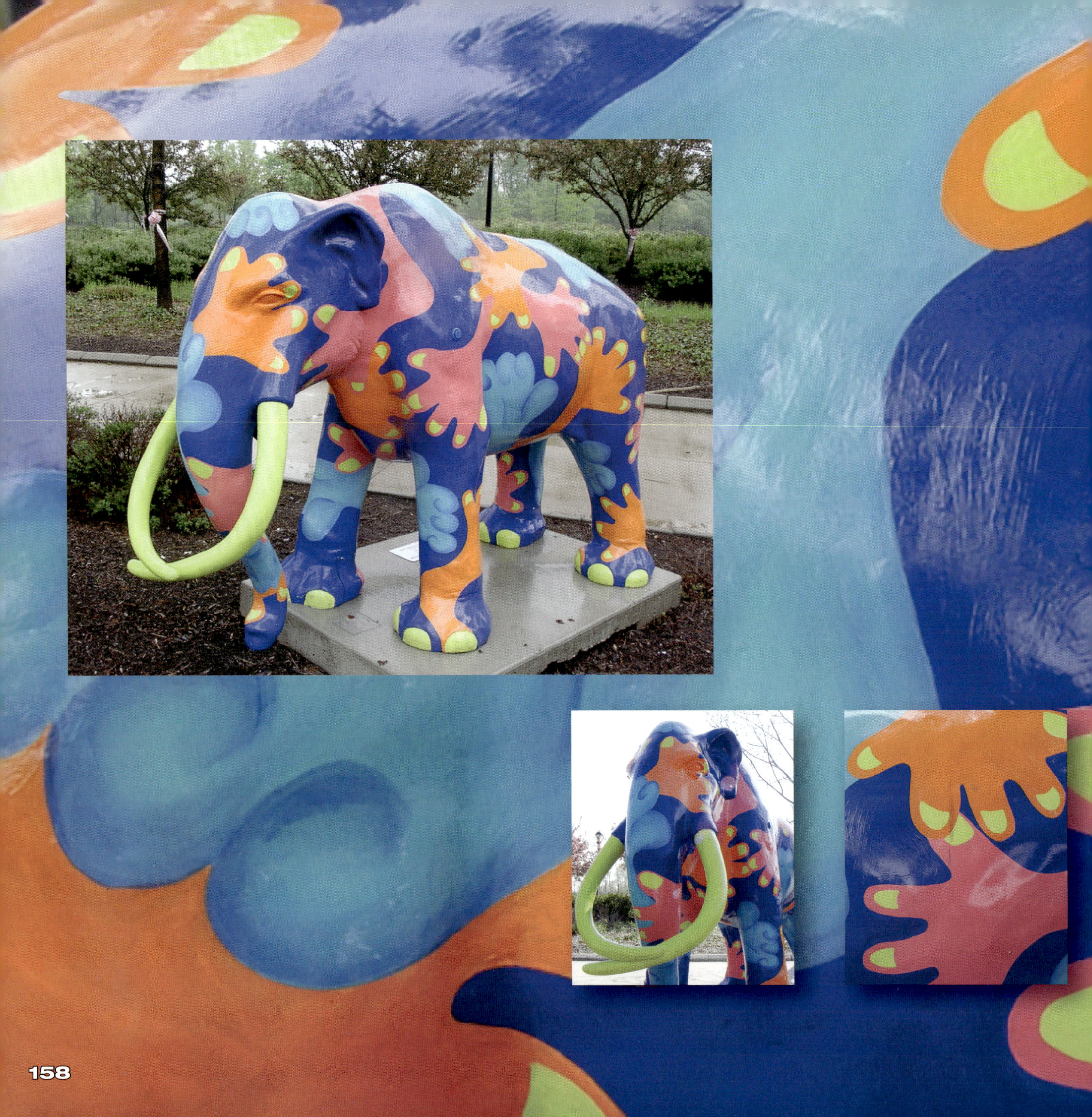

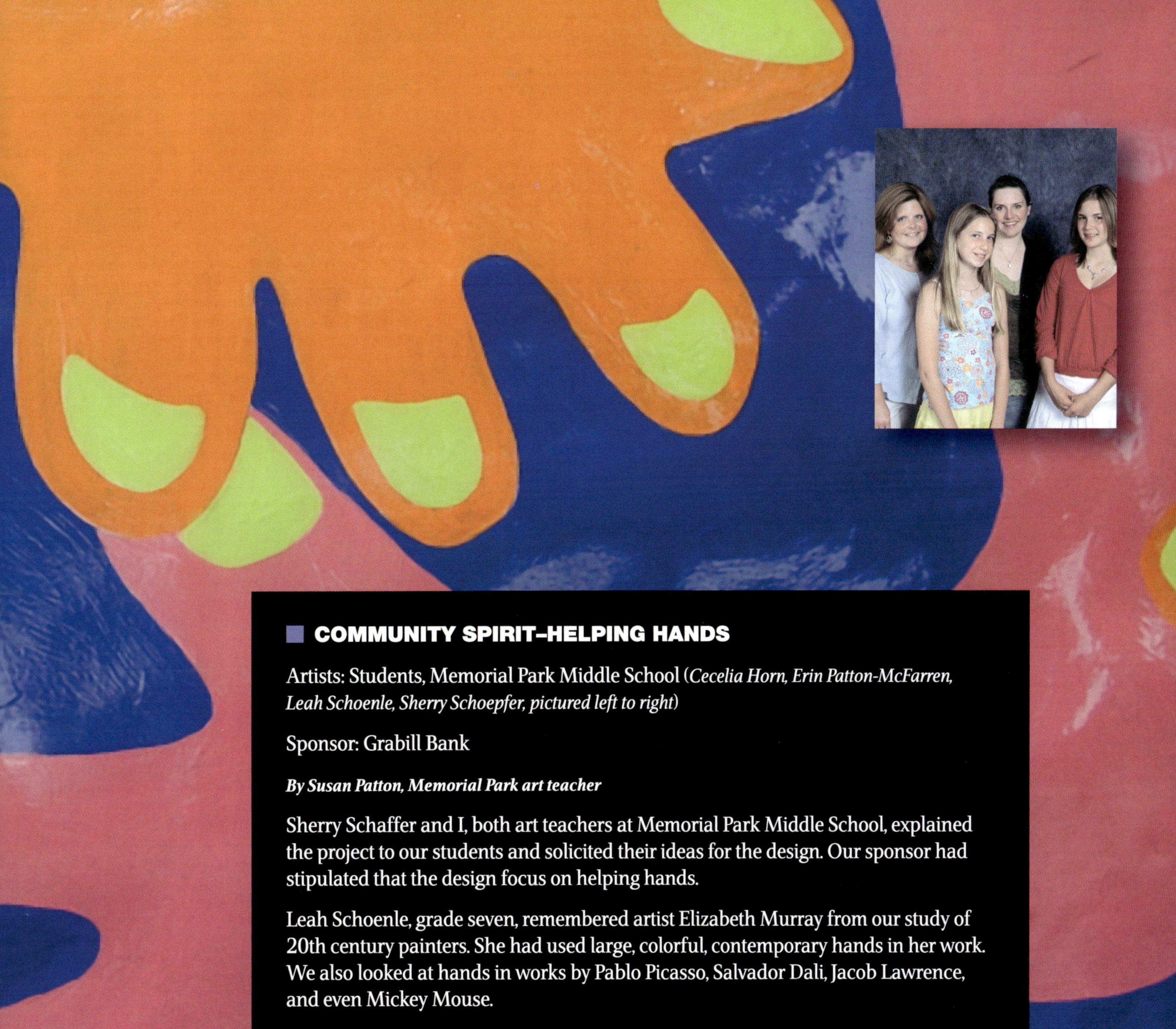

■ COMMUNITY SPIRIT–HELPING HANDS

Artists: Students, Memorial Park Middle School (*Cecelia Horn, Erin Patton-McFarren, Leah Schoenle, Sherry Schoepfer, pictured left to right*)

Sponsor: Grabill Bank

By Susan Patton, Memorial Park art teacher

Sherry Schaffer and I, both art teachers at Memorial Park Middle School, explained the project to our students and solicited their ideas for the design. Our sponsor had stipulated that the design focus on helping hands.

Leah Schoenle, grade seven, remembered artist Elizabeth Murray from our study of 20th century painters. She had used large, colorful, contemporary hands in her work. We also looked at hands in works by Pablo Picasso, Salvador Dali, Jacob Lawrence, and even Mickey Mouse.

I designed two types of hand shapes and overlapped the patterns until they covered the mastodon's body. Sherry developed the color scheme. Three students (Lauren Patton, Cecilia Horn, and Taylor Jaxtheimer) helped us paint the mastodon as did our media teacher, Erin Patton-McFarren.

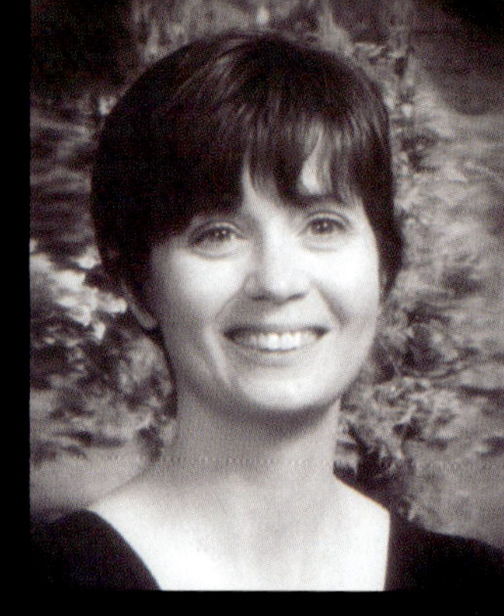

■ MANNY THE KEYSTONE MASTODON

Artists: Keystone School students; Sandra K. McCurdy, art teacher (*pictured right*)

Sponsor: Keystone Schools

By Dacia Willis, executive director, 4 D Education Foundation

A Keystone School second grader suggested Manny as the name for the school's mastodon. Short for Emmanuel, it was a perfect fit to highlight our school's core pillars of spiritual formation, academic rigor, physical development, and life experiences.

Sandra McCurdy believes her work in a nondenominational Christian school is a rewarding mission and worked with the high school students on a final design. They incorporated glass tile, paint, fabric, decoupage, stained glass, and actual items such as books, balls, and even a basketball net. The entire student body joined in when it came time to apply the various media. Look closely. Students even used their handprints for stars on the American flag.

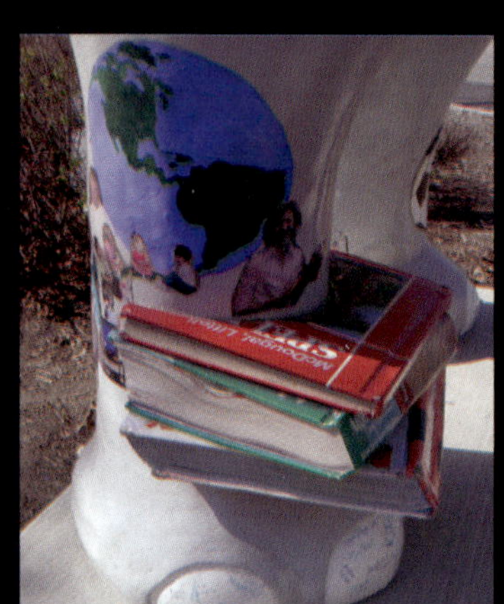

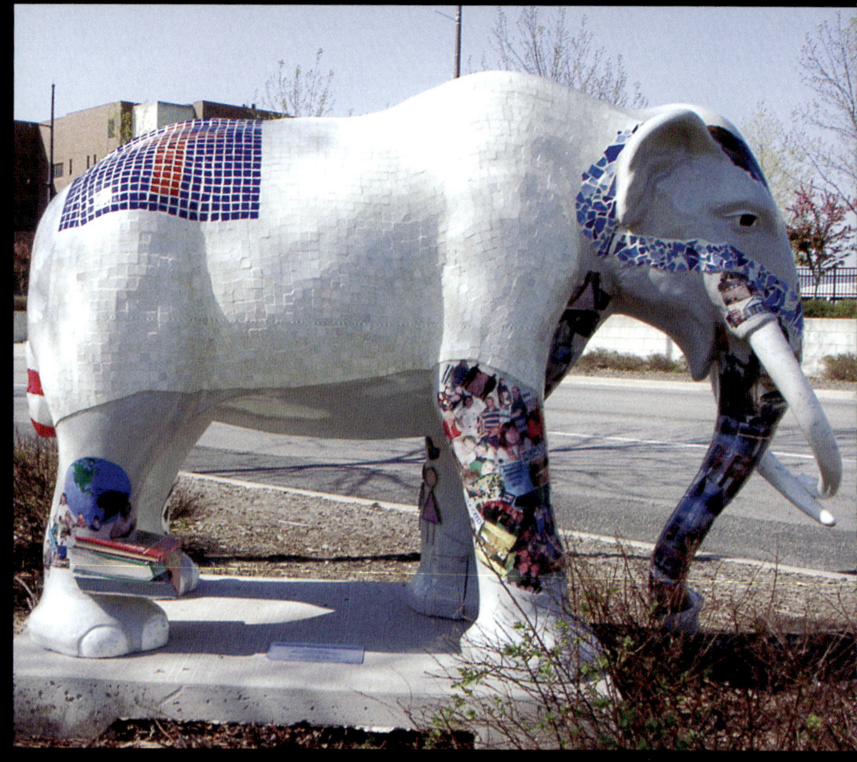

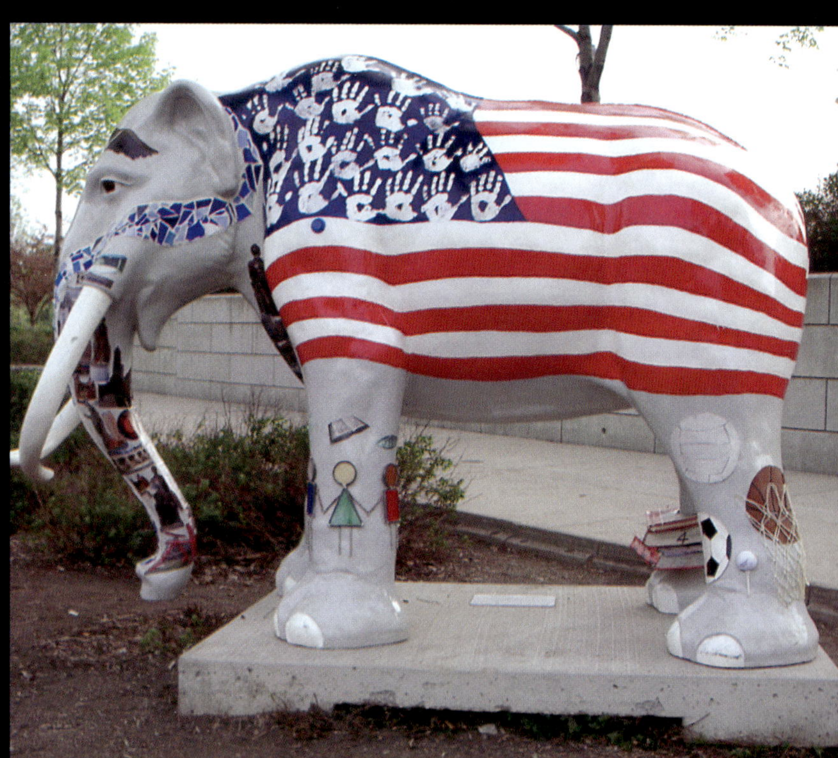

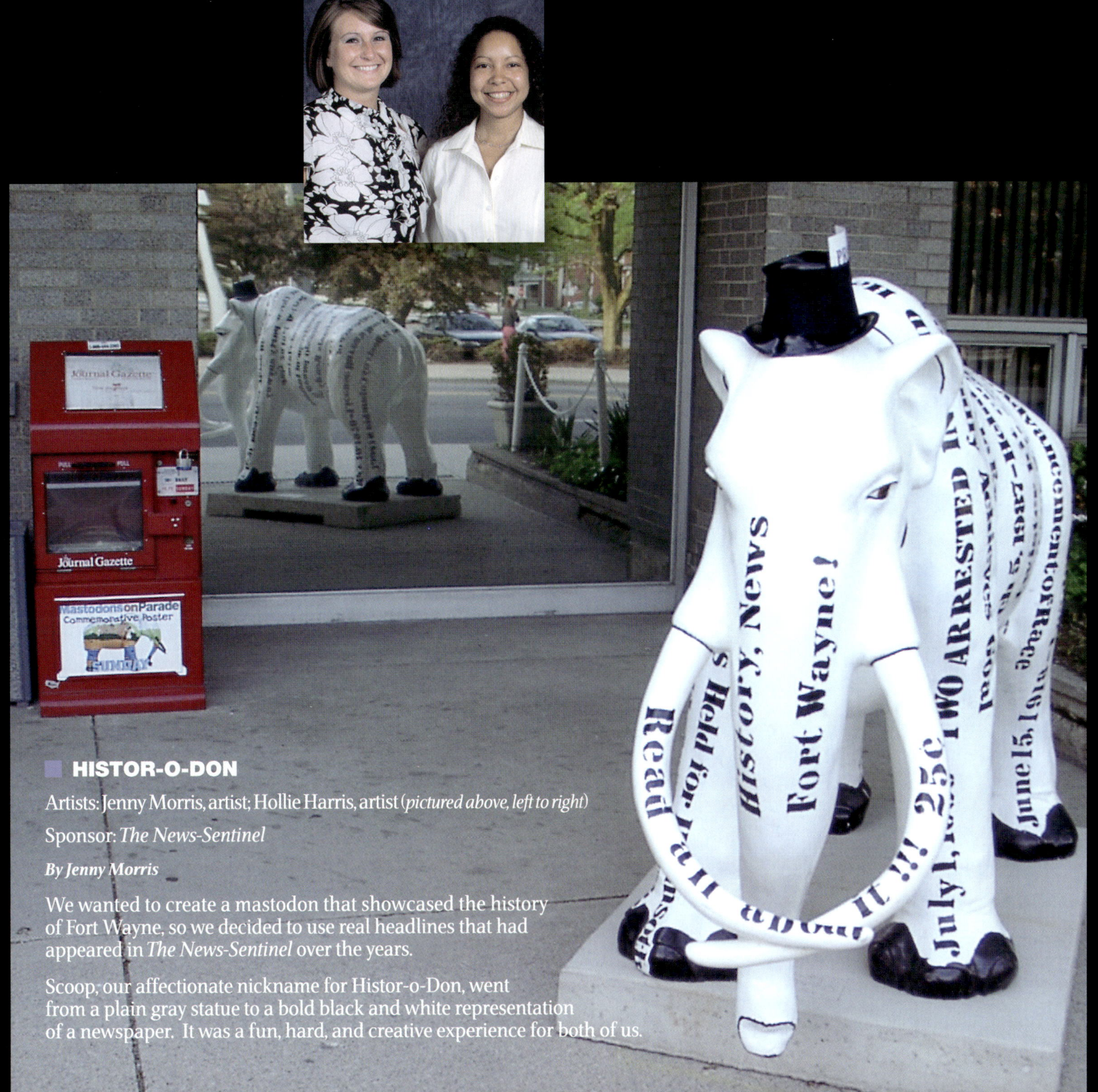

HISTOR-O-DON

Artists: Jenny Morris, artist; Hollie Harris, artist (*pictured above, left to right*)

Sponsor: *The News-Sentinel*

By Jenny Morris

We wanted to create a mastodon that showcased the history of Fort Wayne, so we decided to use real headlines that had appeared in *The News-Sentinel* over the years.

Scoop, our affectionate nickname for Histor-o-Don, went from a plain gray statue to a bold black and white representation of a newspaper. It was a fun, hard, and creative experience for both of us.

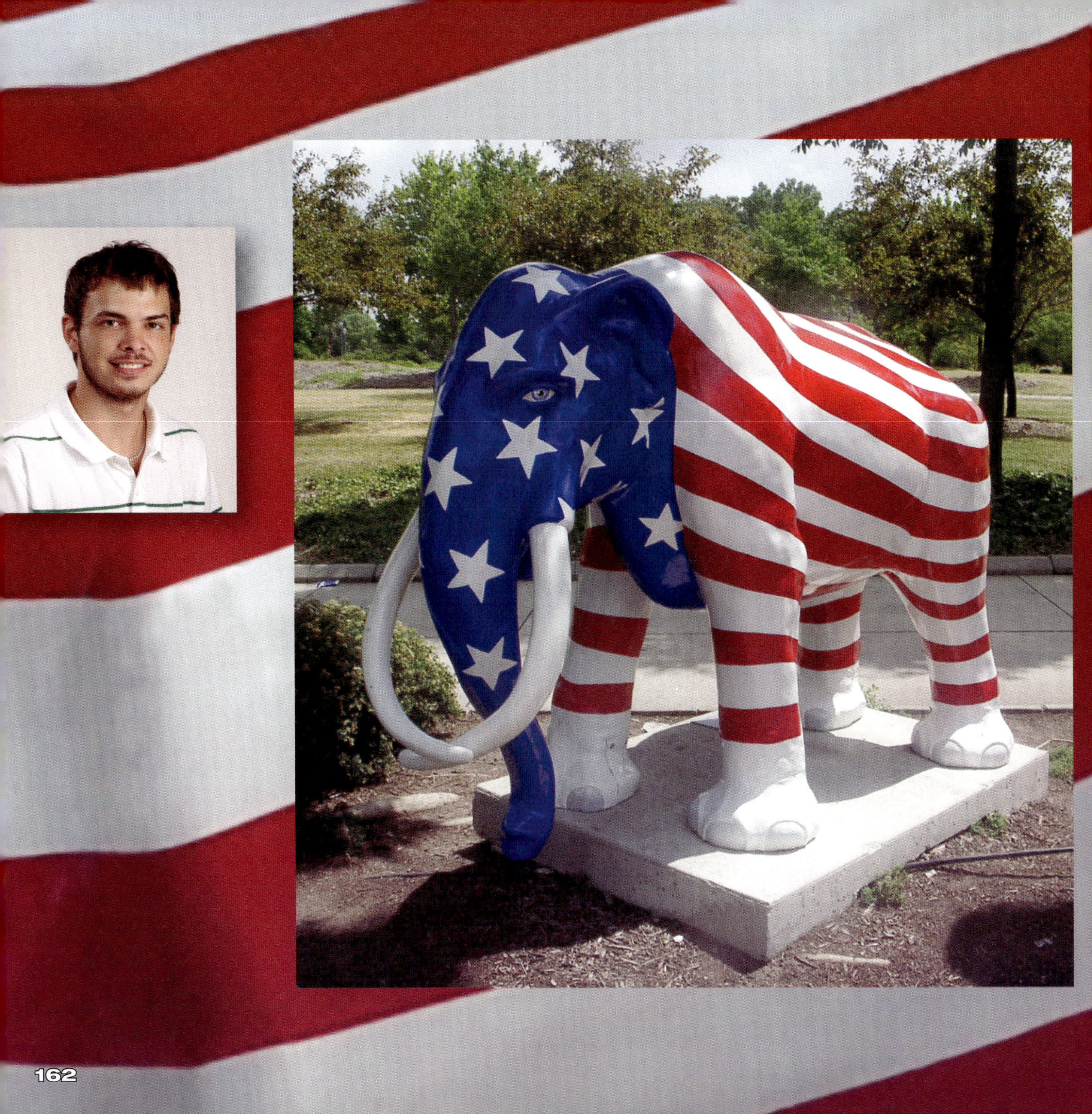

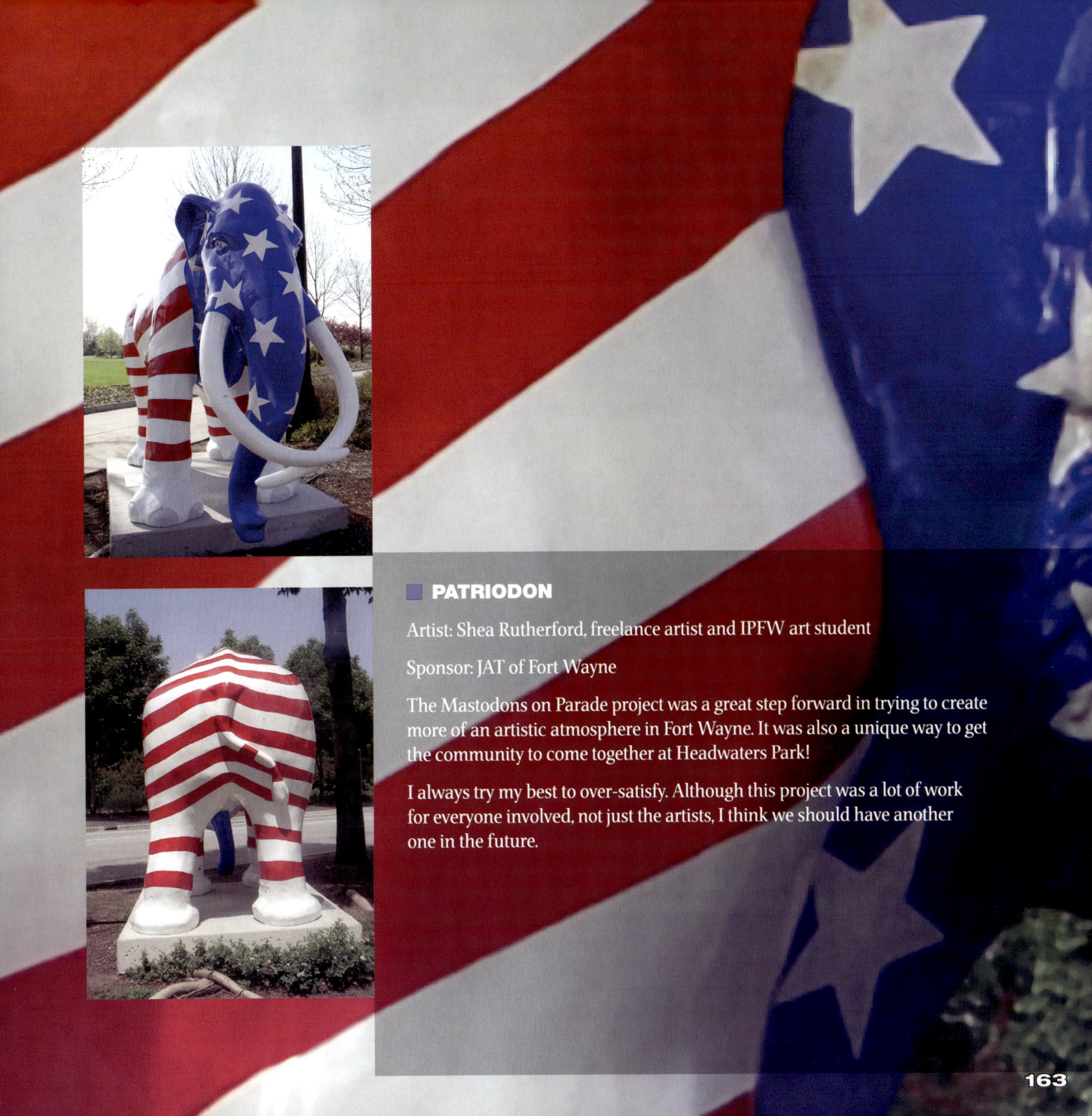

■ PATRIODON

Artist: Shea Rutherford, freelance artist and IPFW art student

Sponsor: JAT of Fort Wayne

The Mastodons on Parade project was a great step forward in trying to create more of an artistic atmosphere in Fort Wayne. It was also a unique way to get the community to come together at Headwaters Park!

I always try my best to over-satisfy. Although this project was a lot of work for everyone involved, not just the artists, I think we should have another one in the future.

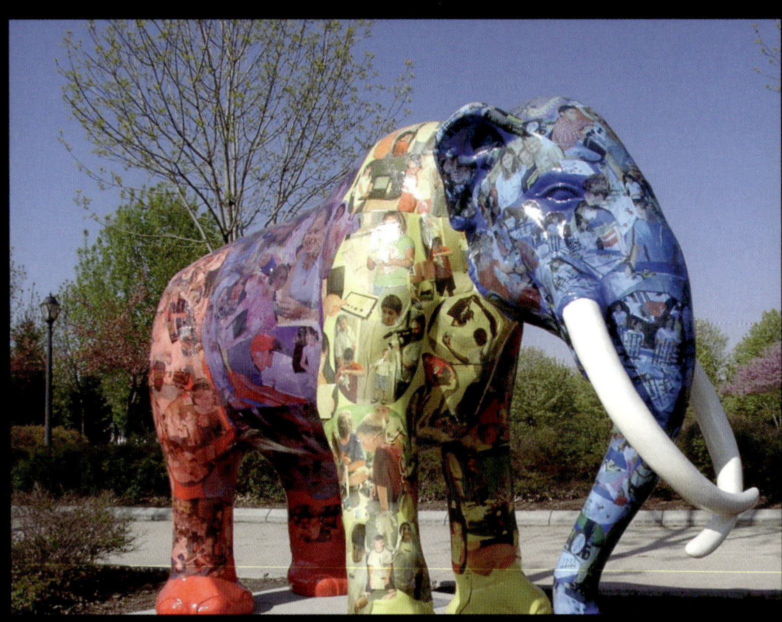

■ MASTER CAMP-ODON

Artist: Donna Emley, creative director, Emley Design Group

Sponsor: MASTer Camp

The surface of our mastodon is a photographic and illustrative collage/montage of images of students in the MASTer Camp learning environment. Color bands or tints represent the four disciplines of music, art, science, and technology.

It was exciting to share the camp experience while creating this mastodon and to watch as the education process tapped into each individual child's potential, piqued interest, and generated such a great enthusiasm for learning.

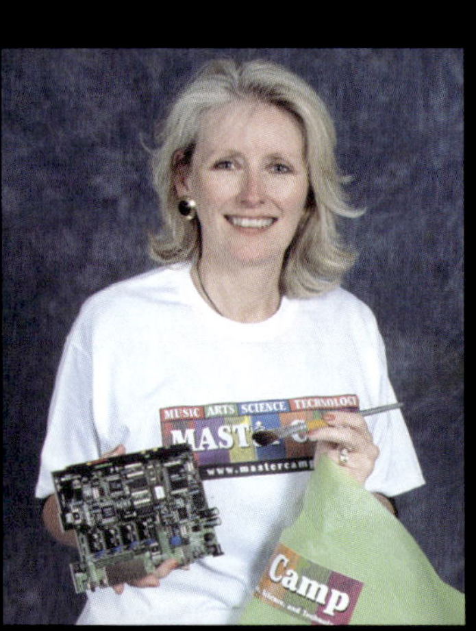

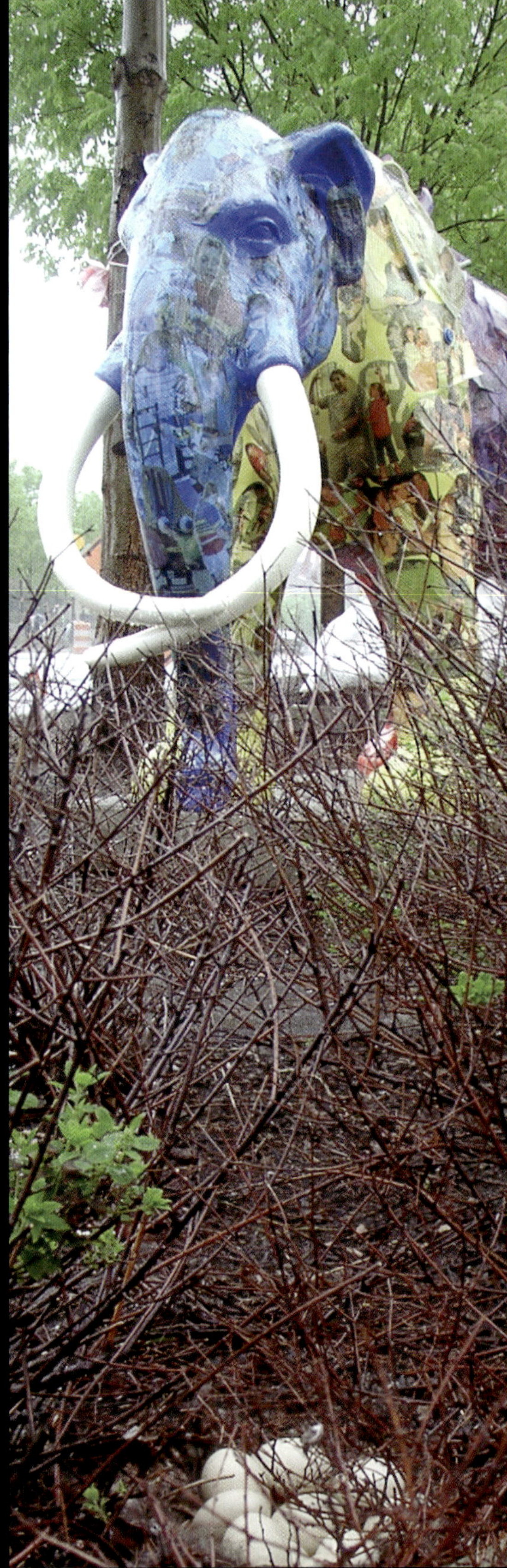

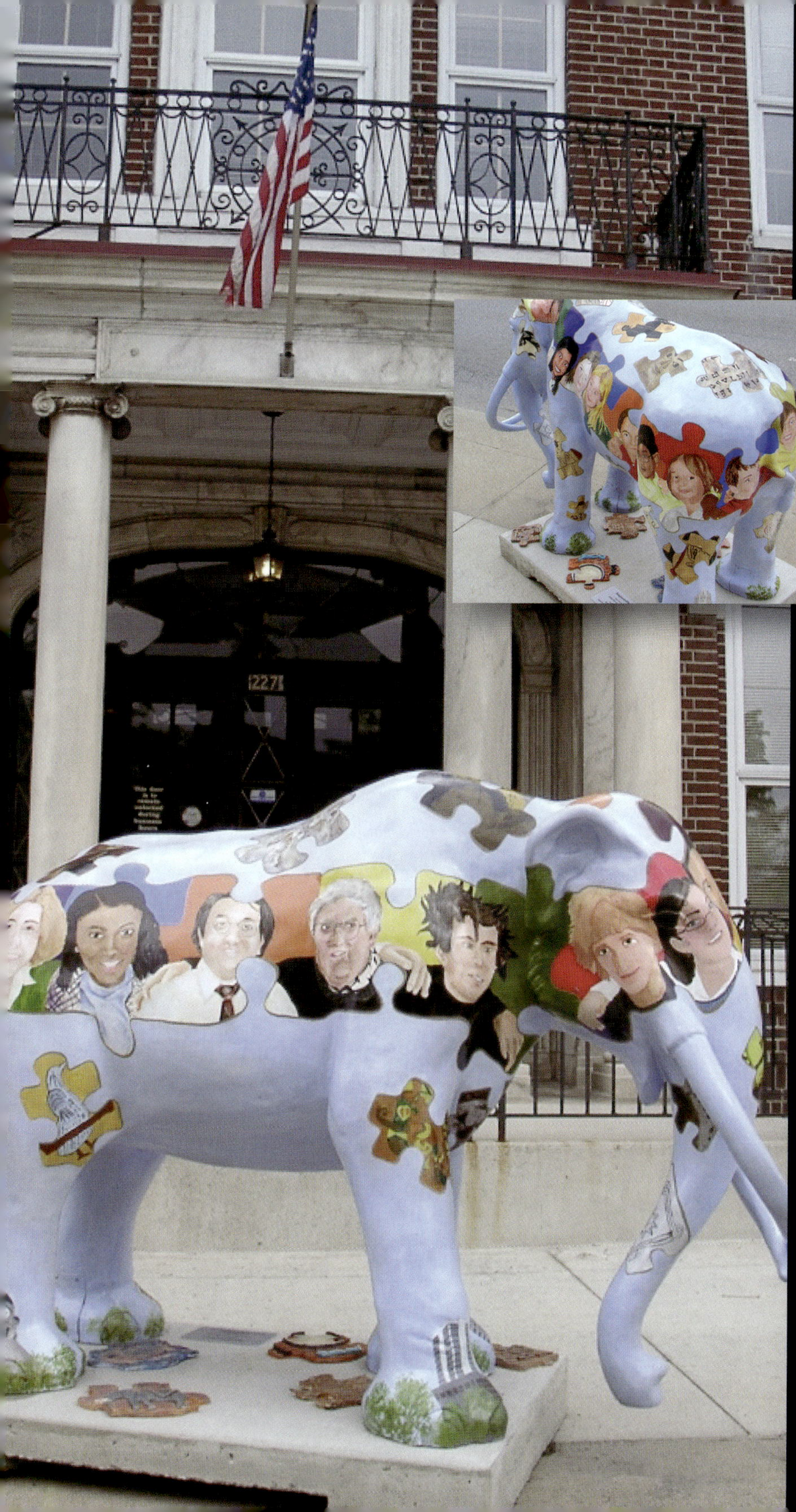

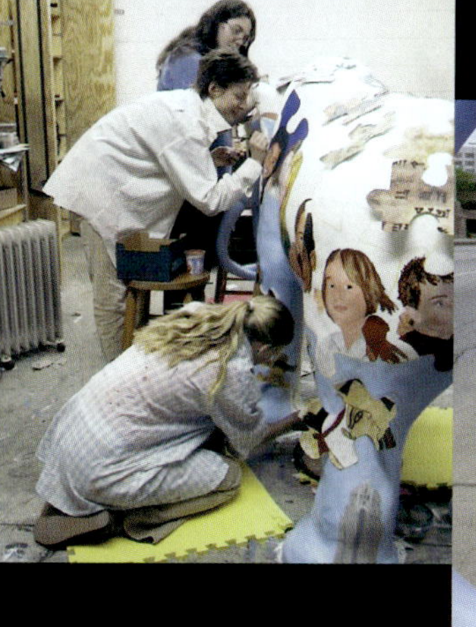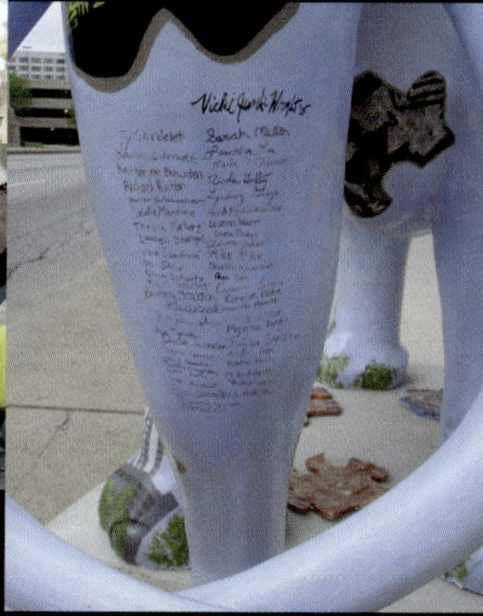

■ IMPACTODON

Artists: Vicki Junk-Wright, professional artist, teacher; Students, Canterbury High School (*pictured above*)

Sponsor: United Way of Allen County

By Vicki Junk-Wright

Before I knew it, I had taken on the challenge of painting two mastodons. I spent mornings painting sepia-toned images of our community through historic times and my afternoons helping a very diverse group of students to paint images of people from many ethnic backgrounds.

I realized the first school in our community was made up of 10 English, six French, one African American, and eight Native American children. It was a very diverse community, but it had a dark side. Soldiers used Native Americans as pawns in their land grab.

In my classes today, we work in harmony with children of every skin color, making a positive statement about unity. I feel glad that something special is happening. And this time, there is no dark side.

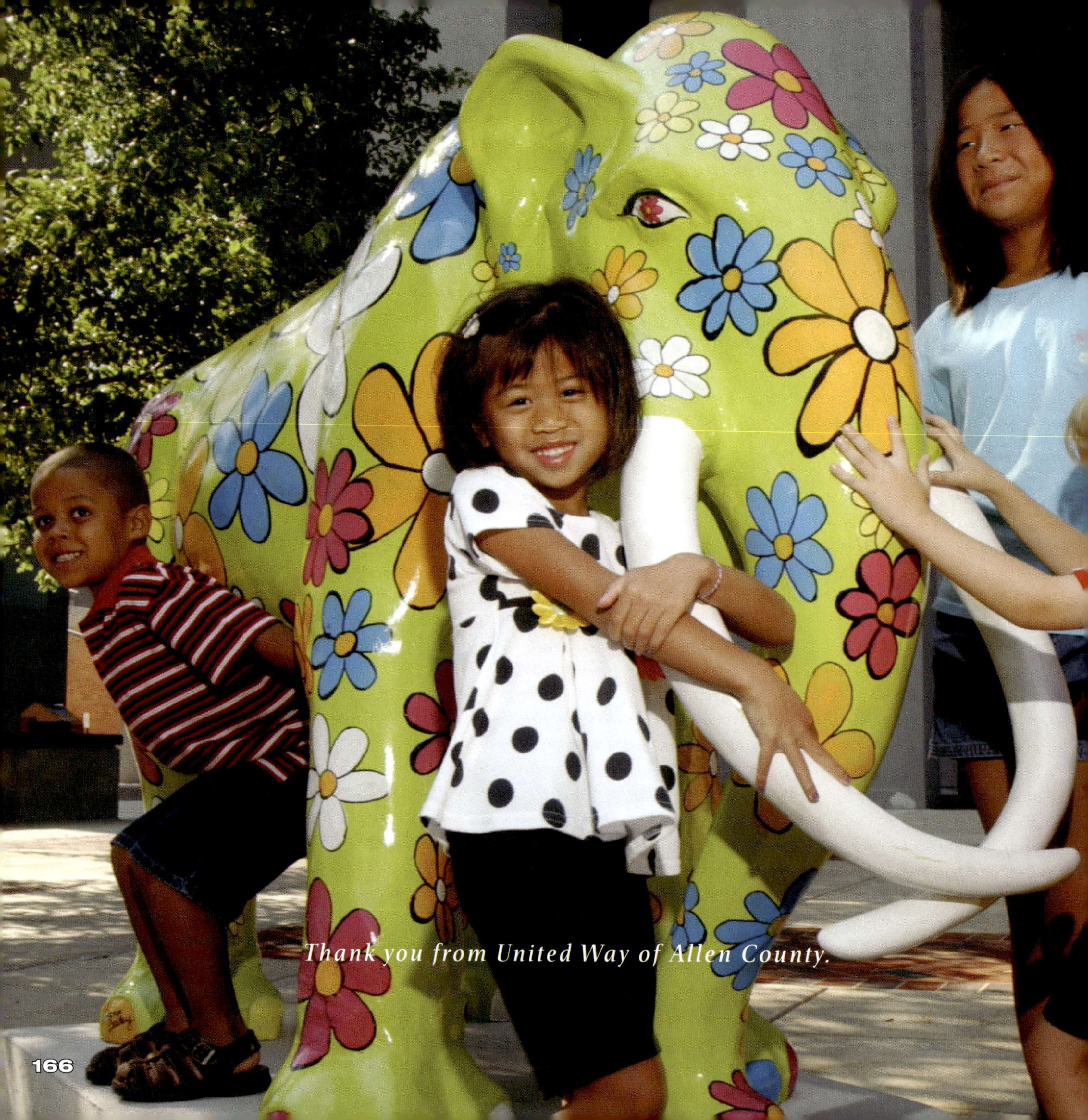
Thank you from United Way of Allen County.

Artifacts

Many of the artists incorporated scenes from Fort Wayne's history in the designs for their mastodons. Collectively, these artists have redefined for us all what it means to live in Fort Wayne. They have conjured up memories of our past. They have shown us pivotal moments in our history that led us to become what we are today. They have painted the lingering magic of personal memories into this particular place where three rivers meet.

Such memories do not rely on the history printed in fifth-grade textbooks nor on the lectures of high school social studies teachers and college professors. The artists have given us a new sense of place. It is personal and meaningful. It is prideful. Look carefully at what they chose to commemorate.

Information from the following sources: John Beatty, Bibliographer and Reference Librarian, Allen County Public Library; *Fort Wayne Bicentennial Heritage Trail Guide Map; Fort Wayne Favorite Historic Buildings* (ARCH); *Illustrated Guide to the Allen County Court House* (Bond and Fenton); Tower Bank Archives. Mastodon art has been taken from Vince FAME-O-DON, www.REALTOR.Don, The Summit Reef, Masto-Downtown 1794–Present, Fort Wayne Mag-a-Don, Photo-Up-A-Don, Broadcastodon.

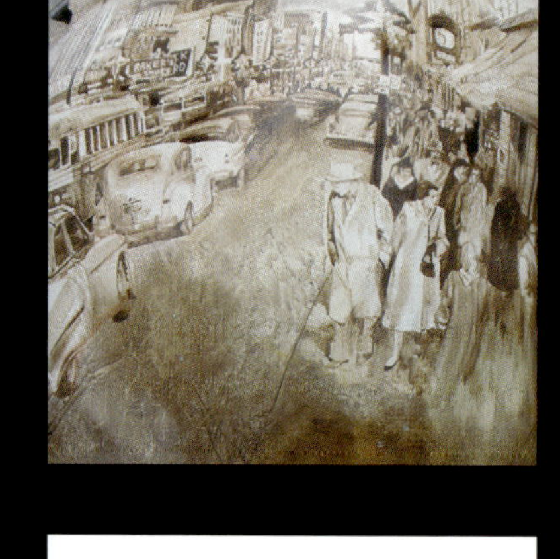

◀ Before the advent of the retail malls, people spent Saturdays shopping downtown. Who didn't look forward to the animated, winter holiday windows and lighted Santa display at Wolf and Dessauer department store? Who didn't get new shoes at M & N Shoe Store or buy meat at Tapps? Who didn't stop at Lenkendofer Coffee Ranch for candy before catching the trolley for home? Downtown was a happening place.

Chief Little Turtle, known to the Miami people as Meshekinnoquah, was one of the most feared and respected Indian leaders during the frontier wars of the 1790s. Following military victories over the Americans, he became a peacemaker and negotiator for his people, meeting with three U.S. presidents to improve the conditions of the Miamis. His grave is located on Lawton Place off Spy Run Avenue. ▶

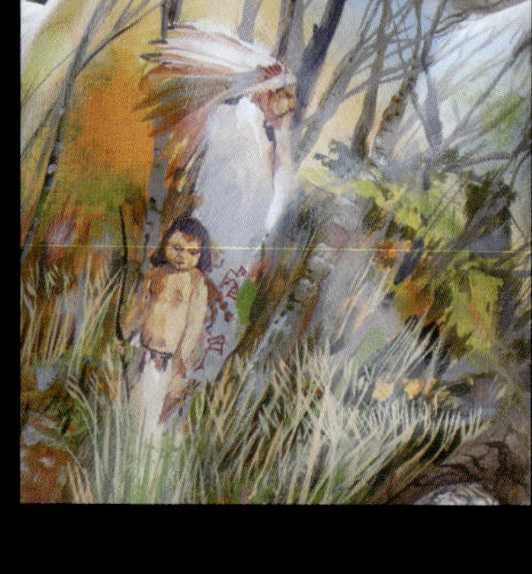

Originally a trail leading to the western edge of town, The Landing (Columbia Street) has been noted for its fine hotels including the Randall and the Rosemarie. Due to heavy canal warehousing activity between 1830–1870, the block was known as The Docks. Today The Landing sports one of the few remaining clusters of buildings from the 19th and early 20th centuries. ▶

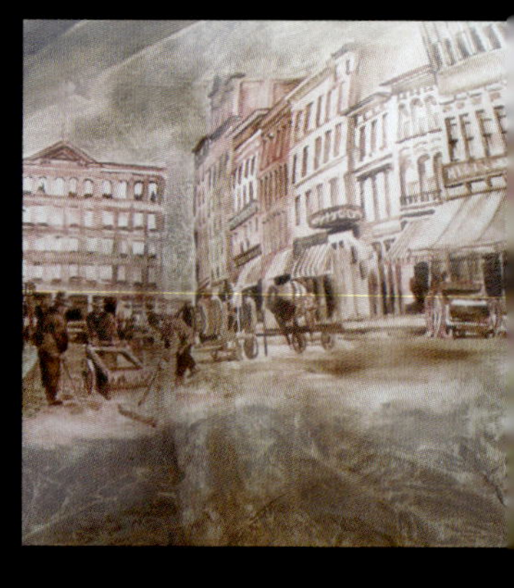

◀ John Chapman arrived in Fort Wayne with a load of apple seeds in the 1820s at Pirogue Landing. It was a spot on the St. Joseph River where dug-out canoes (pirogues) landed with trade goods, travelers, and military supplies. A preacher, Chapman earned the Appleseed nickname by planting apple trees wherever he went. He is buried in Johnny Appleseed Park off Parnell Street.

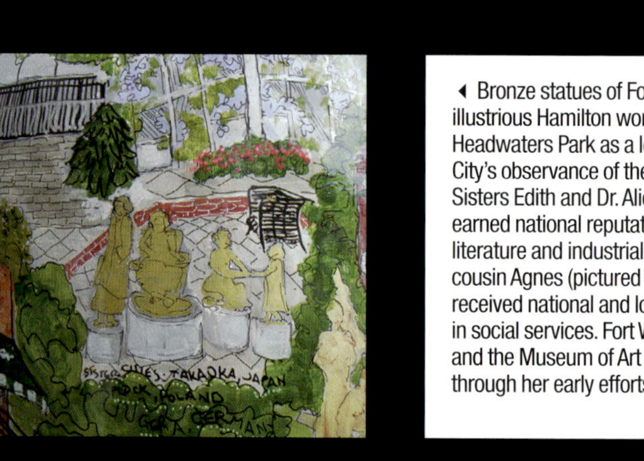

◀ Bronze statues of Fort Wayne's illustrious Hamilton women stand in Headwaters Park as a legacy of the City's observance of the new millennium. Sisters Edith and Dr. Alice Hamilton earned national reputations in classical literature and industrial medicine. Their cousin Agnes (pictured with a child) received national and local recognition in social services. Fort Wayne's YWCA and the Museum of Art were founded through her early efforts.

The Wabash & Erie Canal, the longest canal in North America, had its beginnings in Fort Wayne. As the highest point on the route connecting Lake Erie to the Ohio River, the town was labeled The Summit City. Throughout its history, the city has served as a transportation hub, first for the fur trappers and traders, then during the canal period, and later as a railway center. ▶

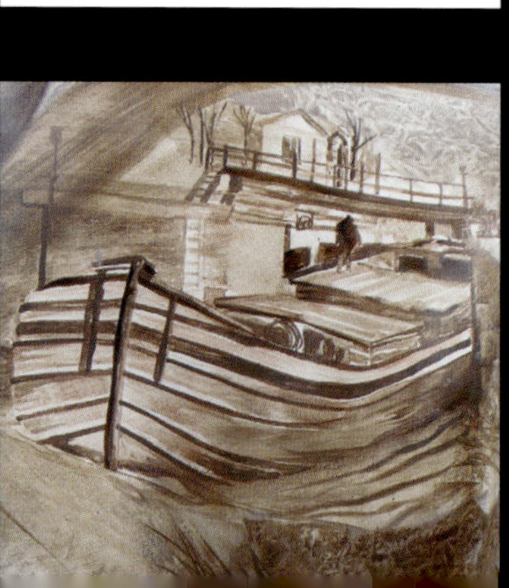

Any town situated at a confluence of three rivers must pay attention, of necessity, to its bridges or transportation will stop. The Wells Street Bridge was designed by A.J. Stewart in 1884 and remains one of the few iron truss bridges left intact. Traffic across the St. Mary's River near Wells Street today has been rerouted, leaving the Wells Street Bridge for pedestrian traffic only. ▶

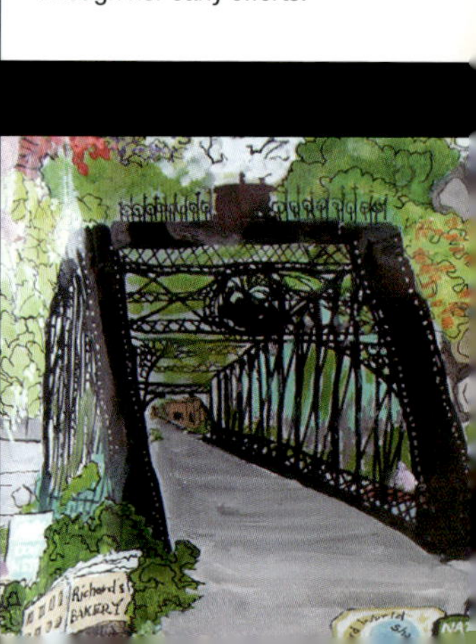

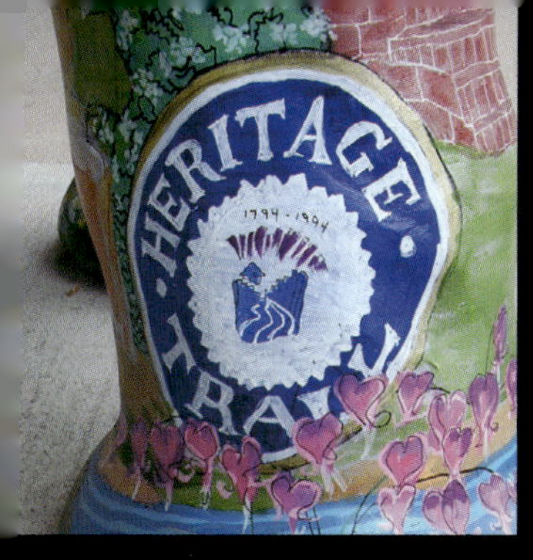

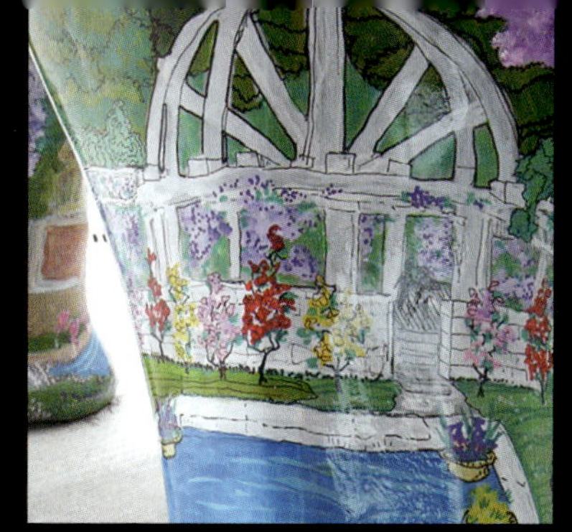

◀ The Heritage Trail is a lasting legacy to the community, developed as part of the 1994 Fort Wayne Bicentennial Celebration. It organizes 51 significant historical sites in the heart of the city. Tours include trails for both walkers and drivers. Interpretive markers stand at a number of sites, providing information about the location. Maps are available at the Fort Wayne/Allen County Convention and Visitors Bureau.

◀ Lakeside Park, long noted for its spectacular rose gardens, is part of the city's extensive system of public parks. Two ponds on the grounds provide fishing and ice skating opportunities for adults and children. A pergola faces a reflecting pond, making it a popular location for garden weddings and family celebrations. Over 2,000 plants (225 varieties) stud the grounds.

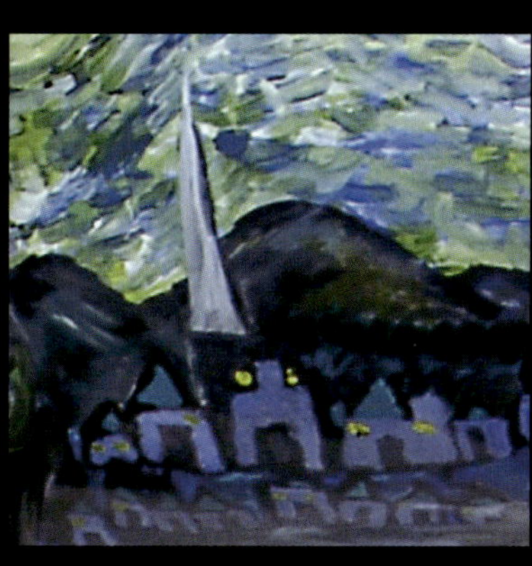

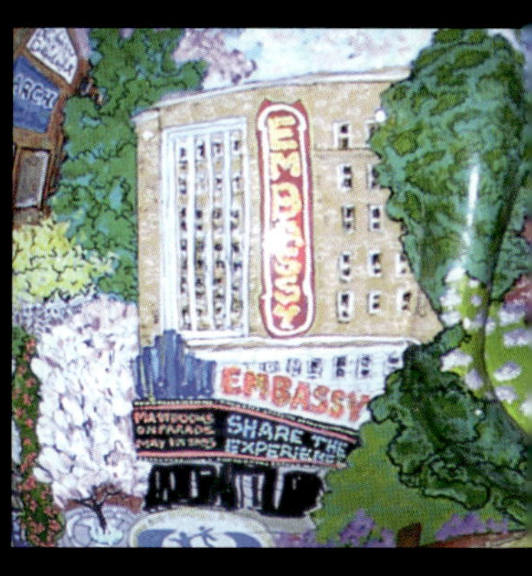

While the first church building in Fort Wayne may have been a crude frame church named St. Mary's erected sometime between 1834 and 1835 on present Cathedral Square), the Presbyterians built the first permanent church building in this "City of Churches" in 1837. Soon many other Christian denominations built churches, and in 1848 the state's first Jewish congregation, Achduth Vesholom, was organized. ▶

Save the Embassy, the 1972 campaign to restore the ornate Embassy Theatre, was the city's most dramatic volunteer effort. It resulted in restoration of the auditorium, lower level, and lobby. Later additions to the stage areas have made Broadway productions possible. Home of the Fort Wayne Philharmonic, the Embassy is one of the few remaining movie palaces of the early 20th century. ▶

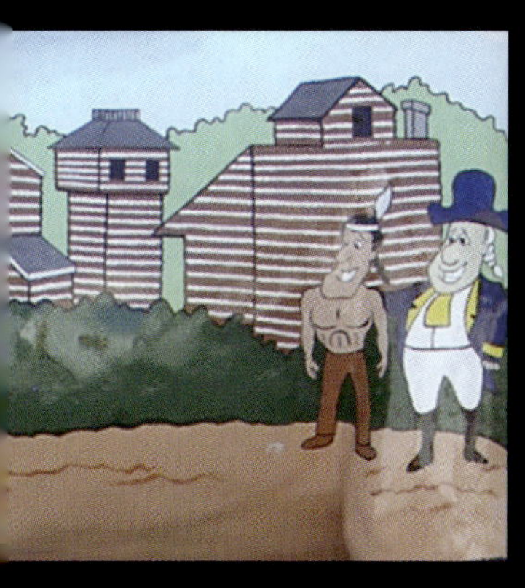

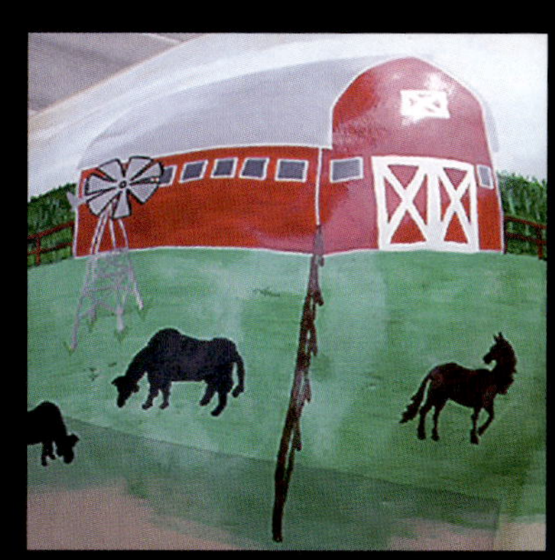

◀ Kekionga (Miami for "blackberry patch") was a battleground for dominion over the wilderness. Under Chief Little Turtle, the Miami Confederacy fought back the U.S. Army through 1790 and 1791. Although they won stirring victories, the Miami were ultimately overwhelmed. On Oct. 22, 1794, General "Mad" Anthony Wayne dedicated a fort in his own name—Fort Wayne.

◀ The Little Red Barn, one of WOWO's most popular radio programs, featured announcer Jay Gould with the farm news. He gave daily livestock and grain market reports, weather, and bits of human interest. Gould said he liked "irritating people to think for themselves." In 1930, the station was the first anywhere to broadcast a basketball game. By mid-century, WOWO was a powerful 50,000-watt station.

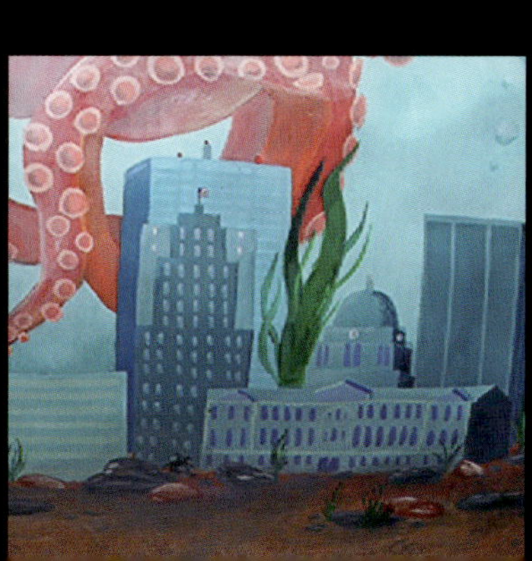

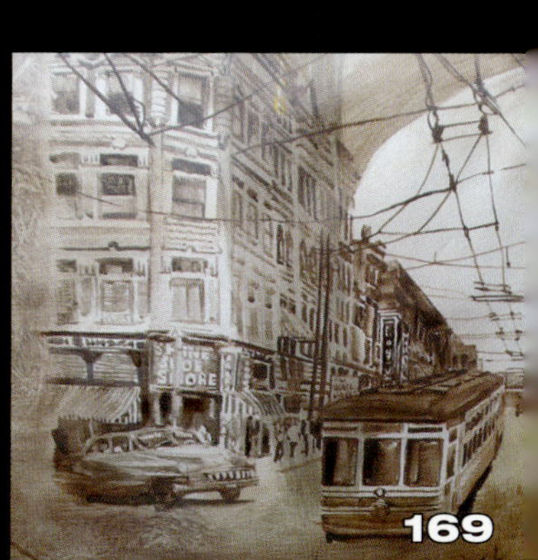

Built in the late 1800s, the Allen County Courthouse is an outstanding example of the Beaux-Arts style. Across the street stands the Lincoln Tower, Indiana's first skyscraper, which is the best known example of Art Deco architecture in Fort Wayne. Also nearby (right of Courthouse) is National City Bank. It contains a parking garage within its footprint, responding to needs of a mobile population. ▶

Transfer Corner (intersection of Main and Calhoun) was the hub of Fort Wayne's public transportation from 1890 to 1960. Folks walked from there to the annual lighting of the city's Christmas tree. They bought donuts from G. C. Murphy Co.'s dime store before catching the trolley or bus home. On summer weekends in the early years, they "took the interurban" to Robison Park, Fort Wayne's popular amusement park. ▶

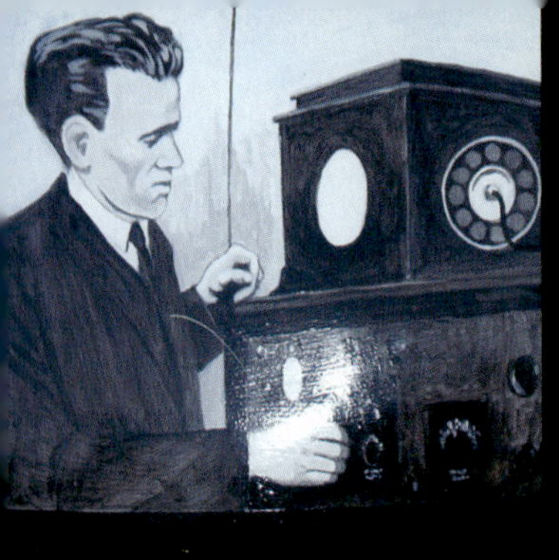

◀ Fort Wayne inventors changed the world. They have given us handheld calculators and video games. Philo T. Farnsworth, who started Farnsworth Radio and Television Company (now ITT), invented the television tube. Other inventions of note include baking powder, the mechanical washing machine, and the modern refrigerator. The city is also known for its magnet wire industry.

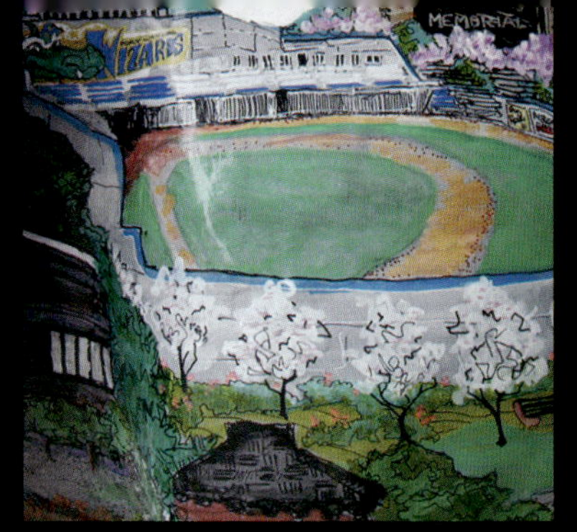

◀ With a rich sports tradition, the city today patronizes the Fort Wayne Wizards (baseball), Fort Wayne Freedom (football), and Fort Wayne Komets (hockey). In 1871, it sponsored one of the first professional baseball league games and one of the first night games in 1883. The Zollner Pistons basketball team was part of the birth of the NBA (1949), and the Daisies women's pro baseball team earned kudos for women's athletics.

A classic 50s diner with white steel panels and lots of chrome, Cindy's Diner can serve all of Fort Wayne–15 at a time. Garbage, a popular dish of eggs, ham, cheese, onions, and hash browns, is a menu favorite. On Dr. Suess' birthday, the diner serves Green Eggs and Ham. Donuts are made in the famous machine from G. C. Murphy Co.'s dime store. ▶

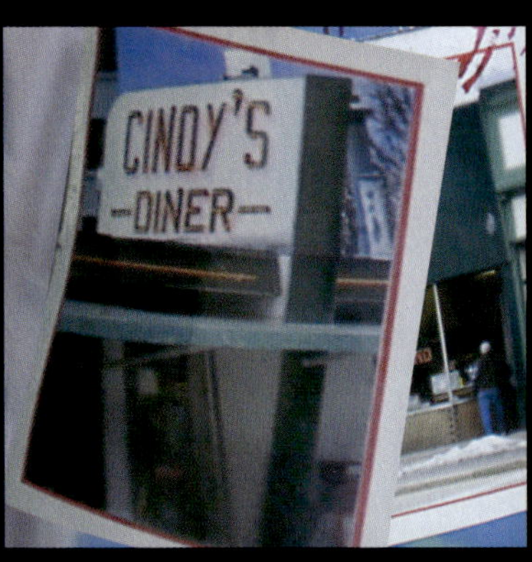

The Allen County Public Library holds one of the nation's top two genealogy collections. It consistently ranks among the nation's top libraries measured by circulation and visitation, size of collections, and services available. Now undergoing a major expansion, the library also includes a number of branch sites throughout the county to serve citizens. ▶

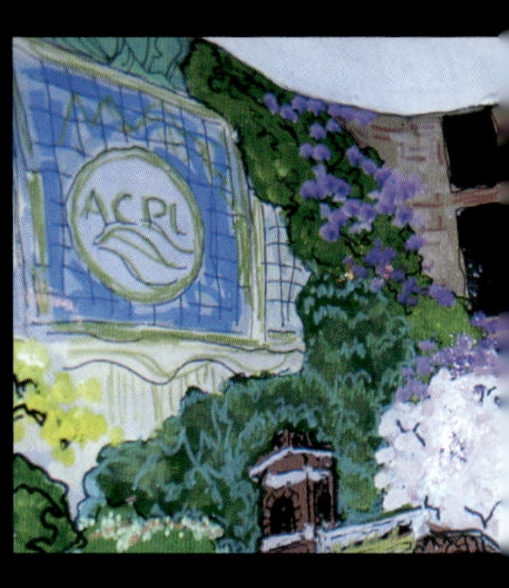

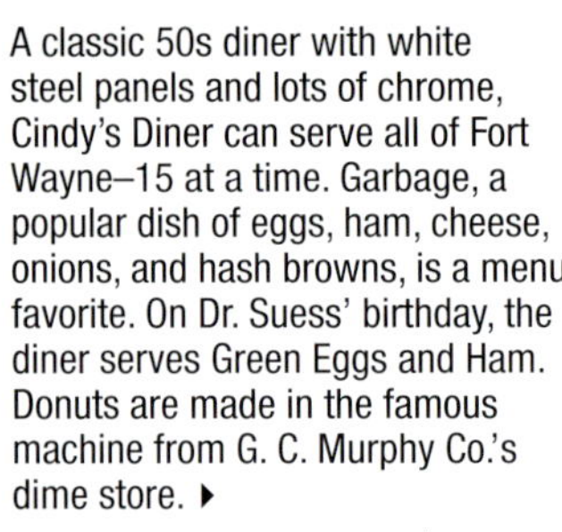

◀ Science Central is a hands-on facility which provides youth with opportunities to build an understanding of science concepts. Children learn about the physical sciences and math in a variety of interactive exhibitions and play stations. The skull of a baby mastodon from the Routsong farm is on permanent display. Initially, the building was owned by City Light and Power.

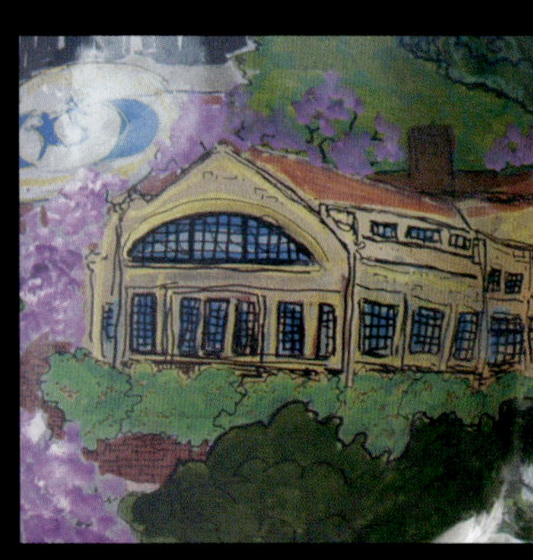

◀ Built in 1914, The Pennsylvania Railroad Station (commonly know as the Baker Street Station) is no longer used as a central terminal. Renovated by an architectural firm it now houses several businesses and provides a venue for a variety of community functions. When railroads originally came through Fort Wayne, the city billed itself as the Altoona of the West. Following World War II, highways and the airport replaced reliance on trains.

The city is noted for its exemplary arts programs. ARTLINK, one of 10 member groups of Arts United of Greater Fort Wayne, focuses on contemporary art. An umbrella group that assists with funding, Arts United also includes: ARCH (historic preservation), Fort Wayne Ballet, Cinema Center, Civic Theatre, Dance Collective, Fort Wayne Museum of Art, Fort Wayne Philharmonic, Fort Wayne Youtheatre, and the Allen County–Fort Wayne Historical Society. ▶

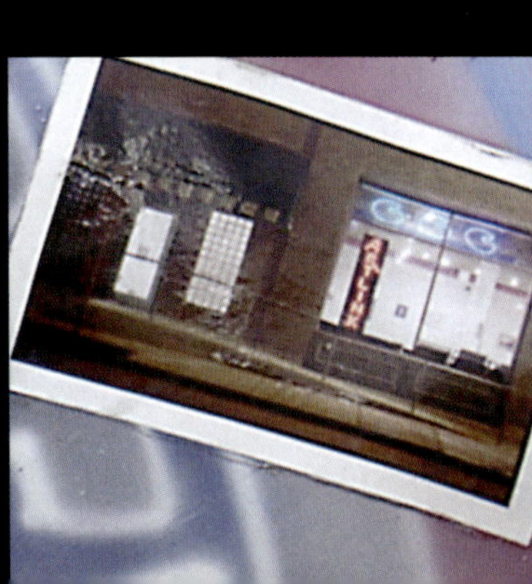

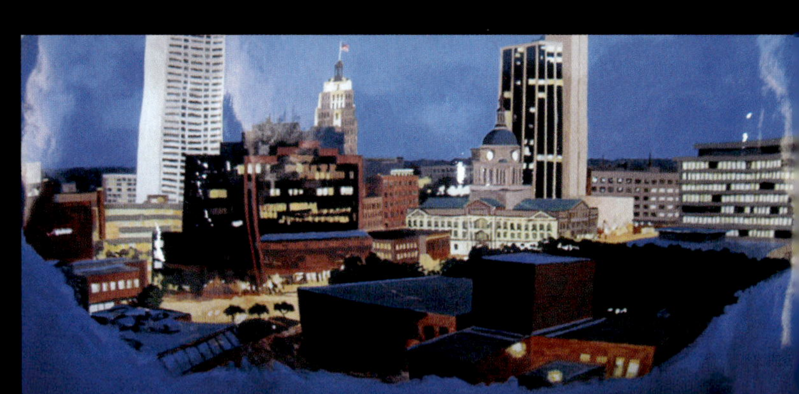

Mastodons on Parade

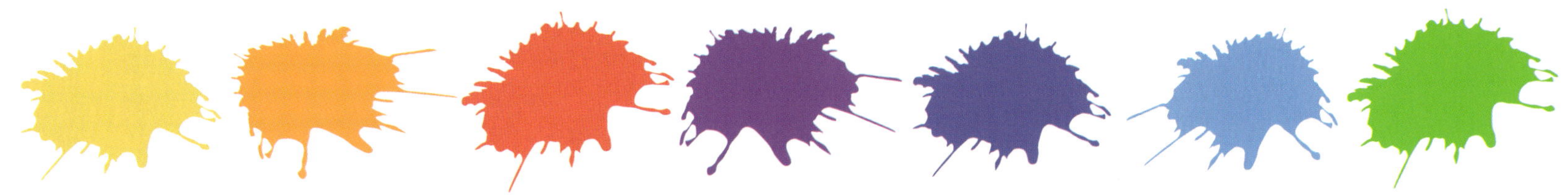

Mastodon Montage

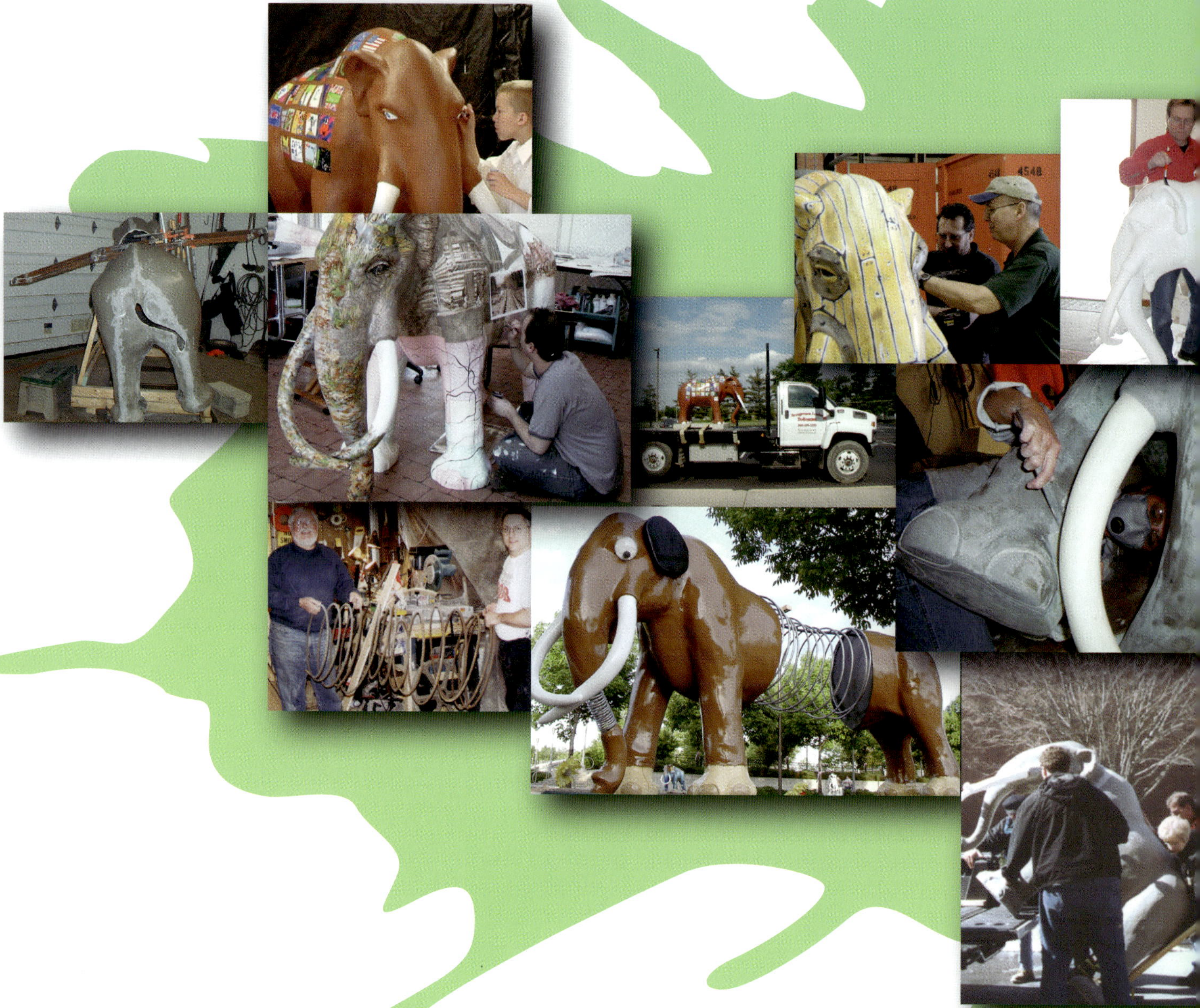

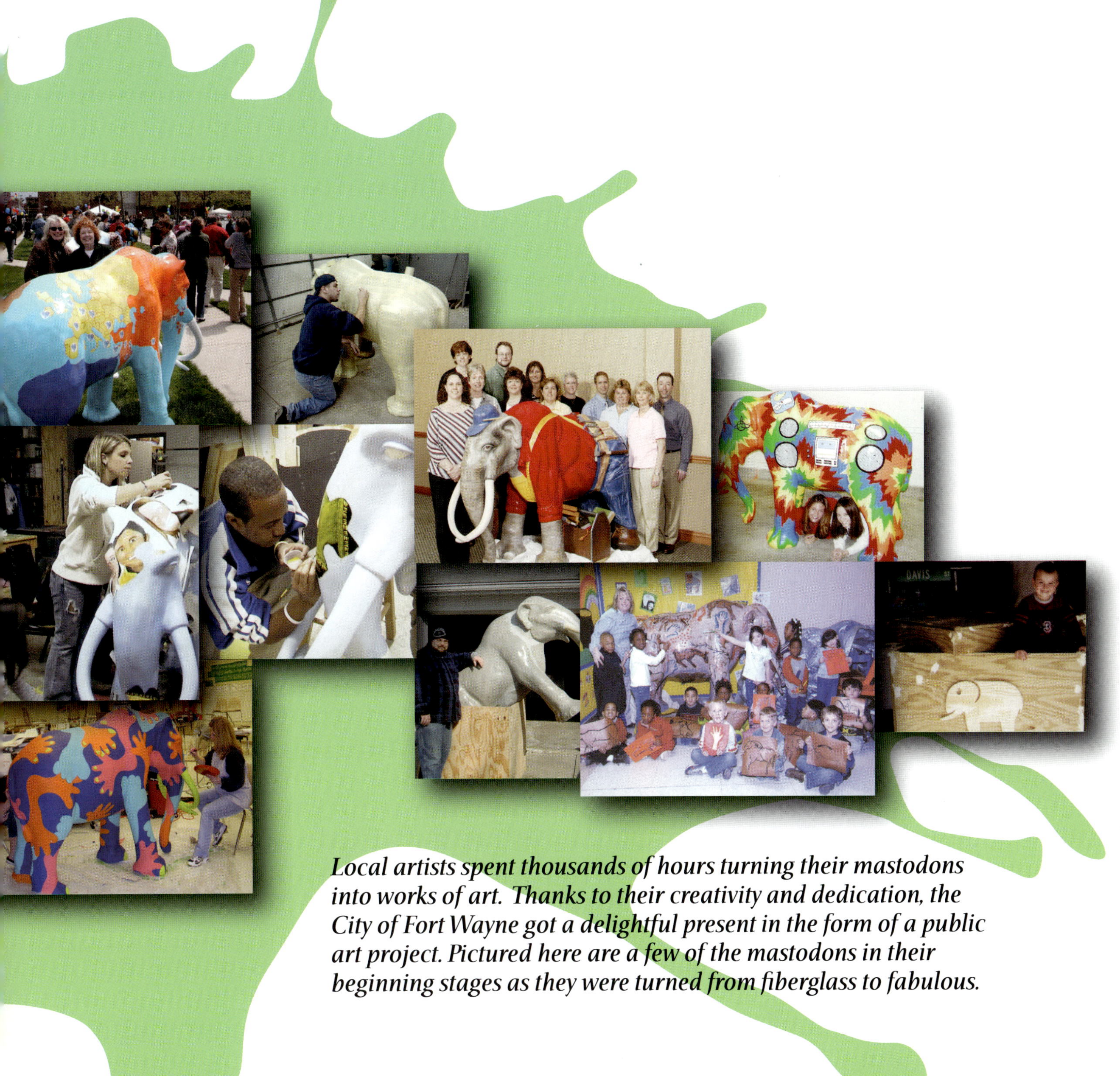

Local artists spent thousands of hours turning their mastodons into works of art. Thanks to their creativity and dedication, the City of Fort Wayne got a delightful present in the form of a public art project. Pictured here are a few of the mastodons in their beginning stages as they were turned from fiberglass to fabulous.

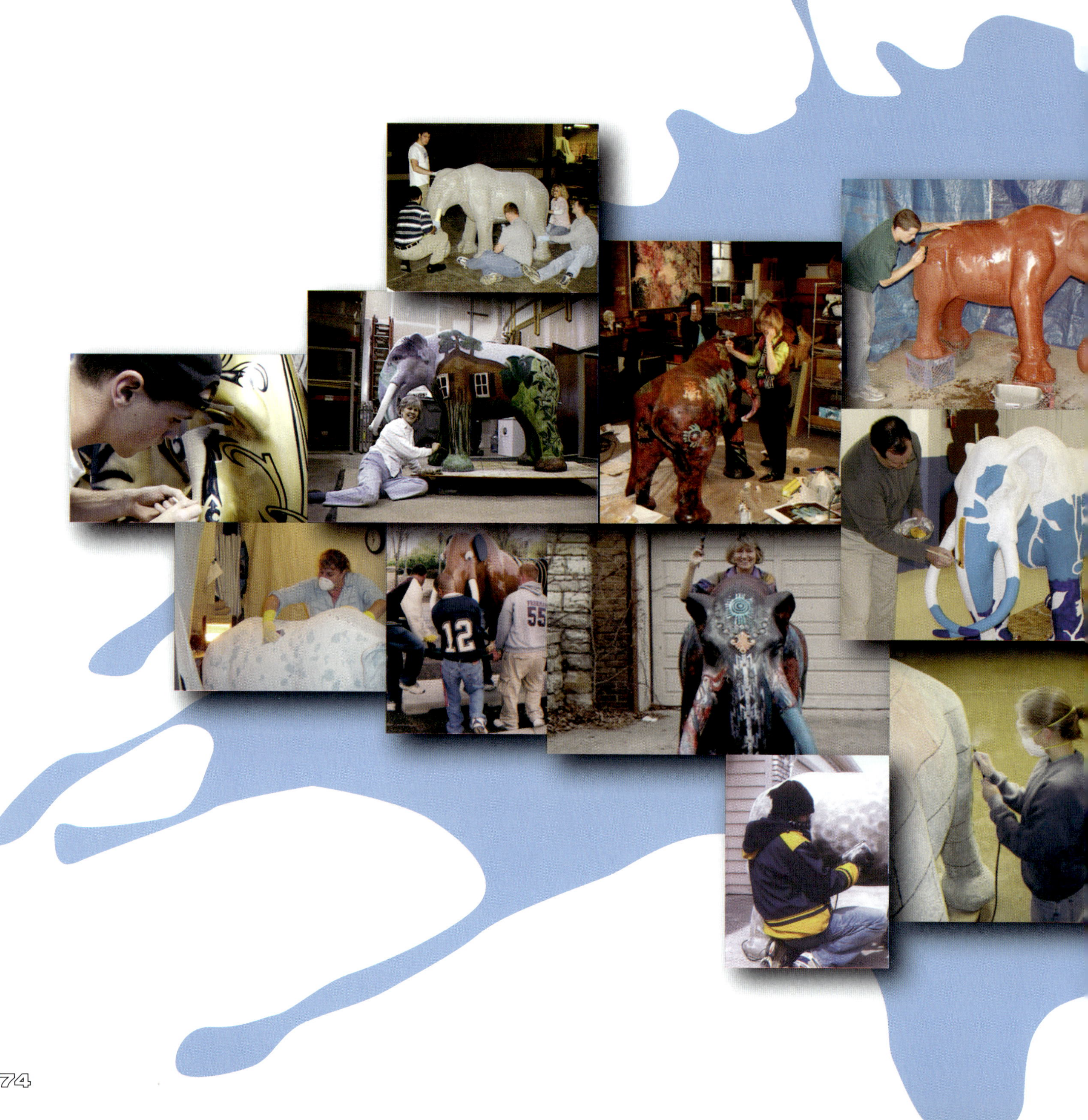

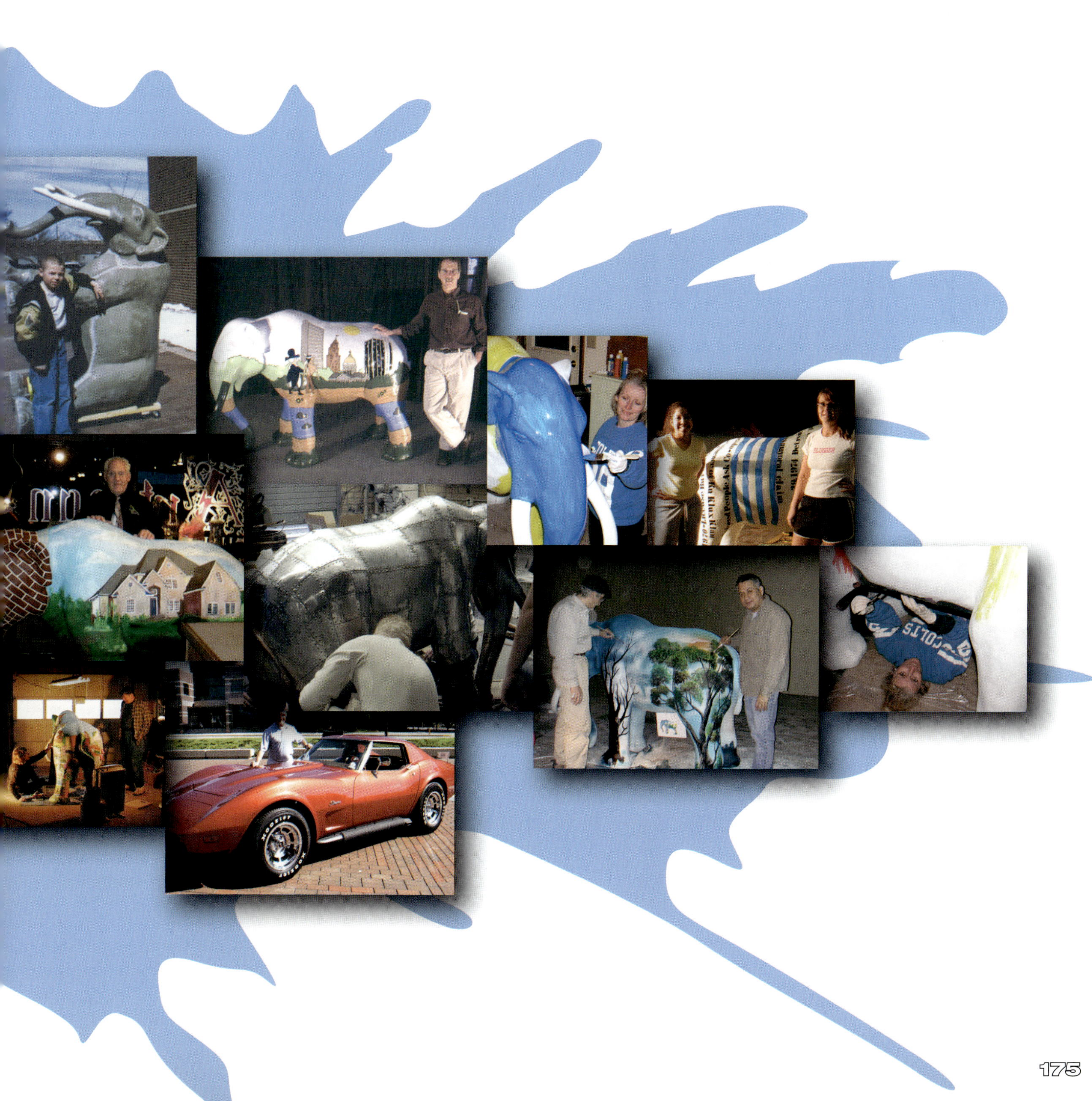

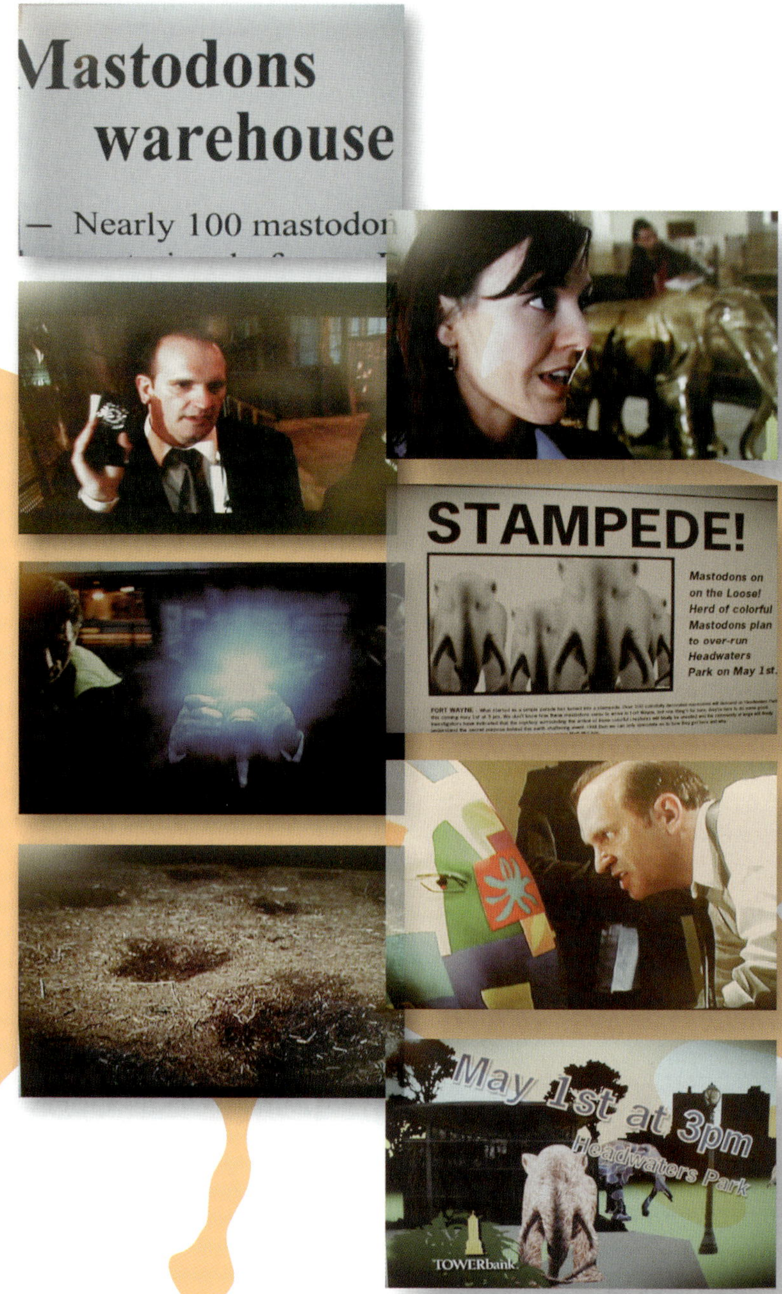

Audio Visual Integration donated its time, resources, and talent to create the mysterious public service announcements (PSA) that advertised events connected to Mastodons on Parade. The PSAs aired on local television stations and alerted the public that something big was coming.

Mastodons on Parade

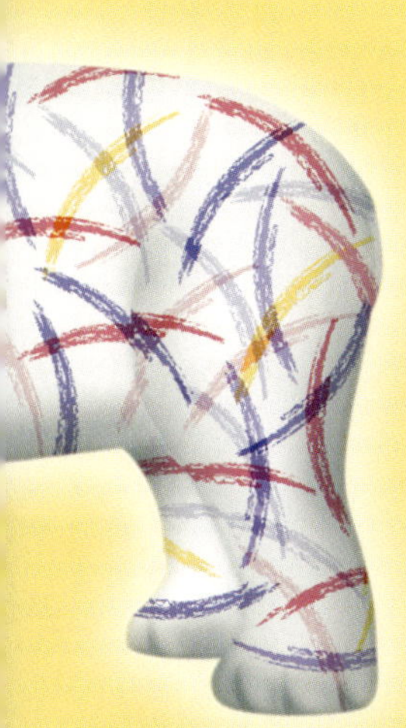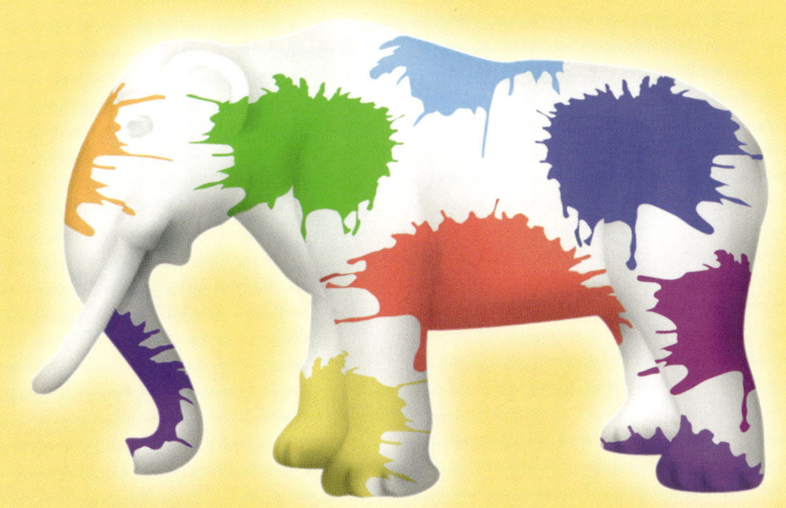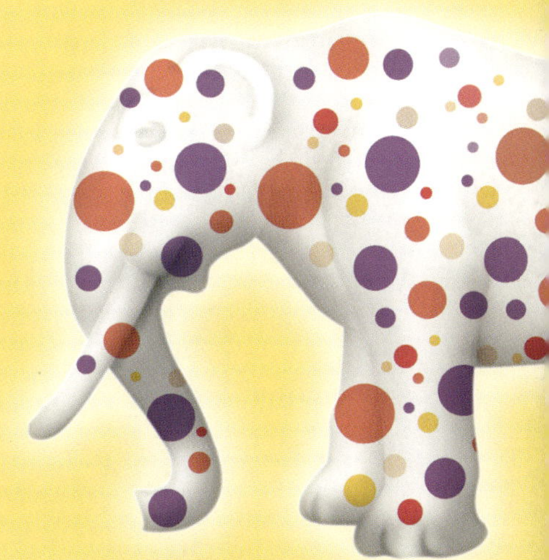

Indices

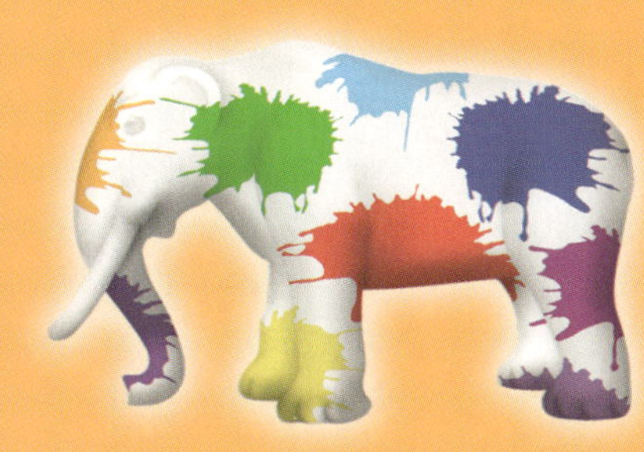

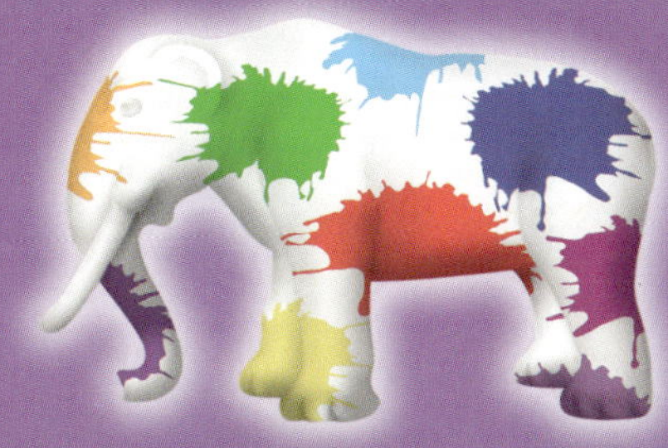

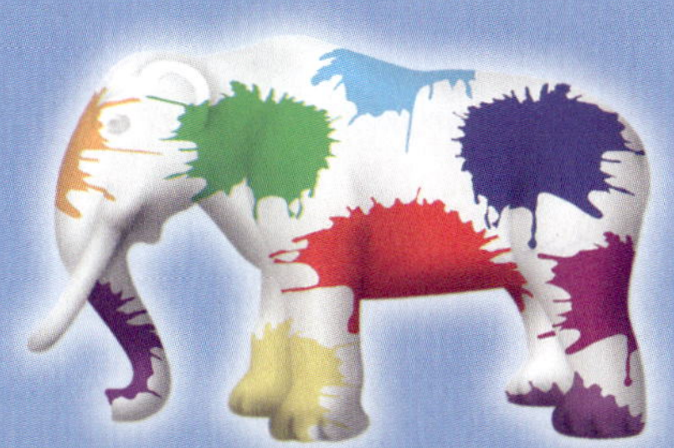

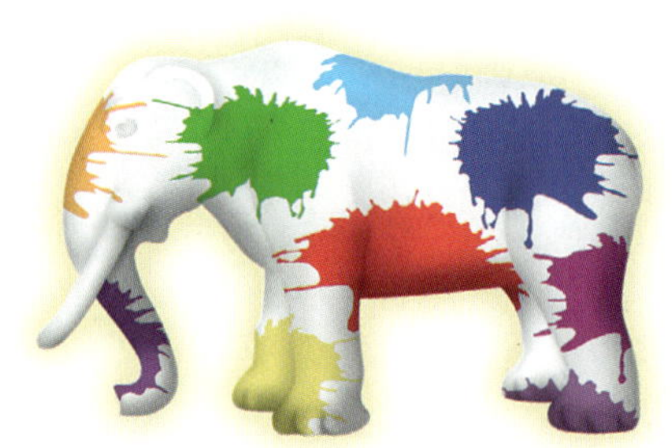

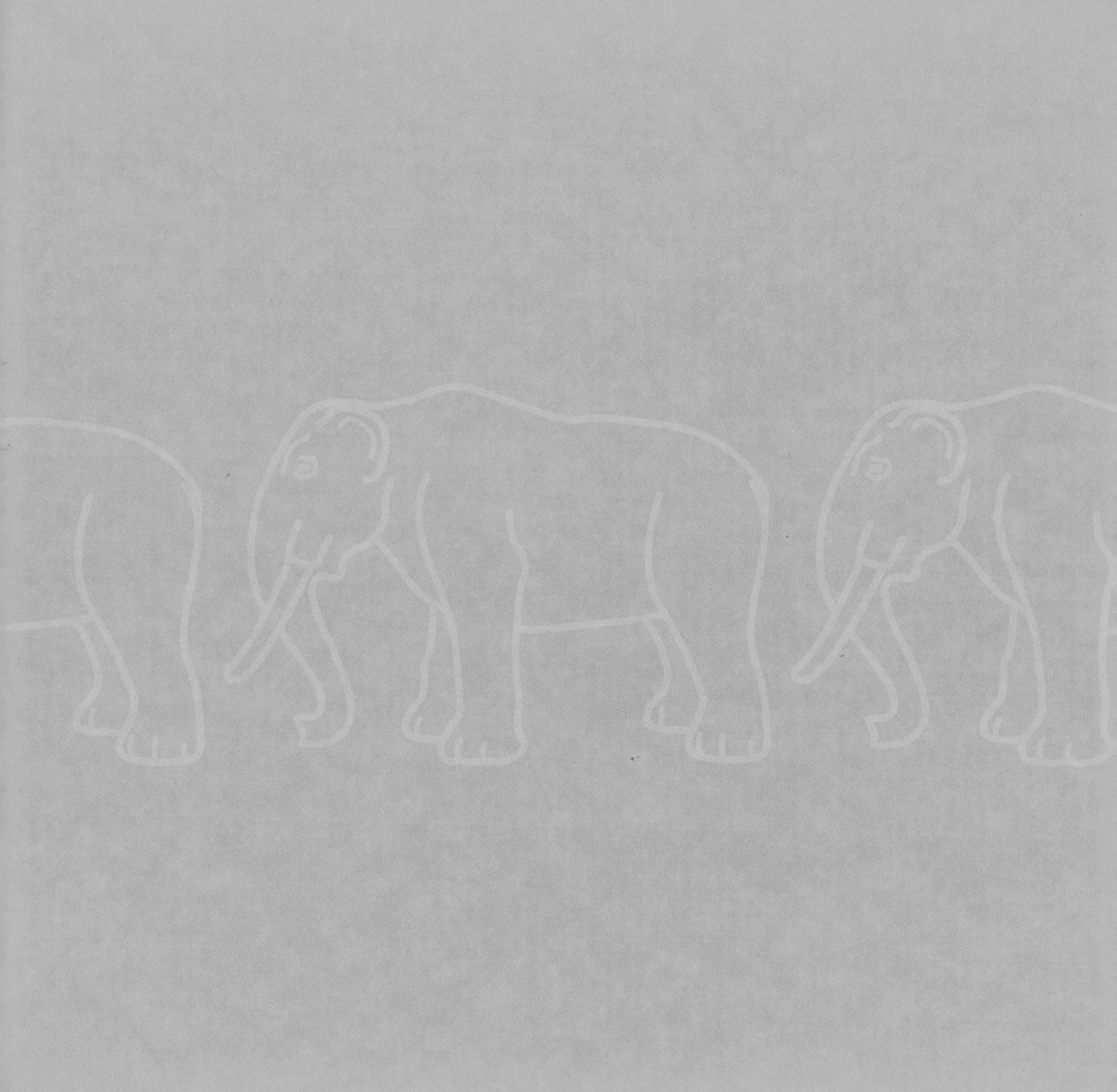